JOHN V. LINDSAY

JOHN V. LINDSAY

50TH ANNIVERSARY COMMEMORATION OF HIS ELECTION AS MAYOR OF NEW YORK CITY, NOVEMBER 2, 1965

REFLECTIONS FROM MORE THAN 260
FRIENDS AND COLLEAGUES

FOREWORD BY JAY L. KRIEGEL

International Publishers
McLean, Virginia

ISBN-13: 978-1518656415
ISBN-10: 1518656412

internationalpublishers.us

Acknowledgements:

I am grateful to Lindsay alumni Warren Wechsler and Bob Laird, who
served as volunteer editors of this volume, a daunting task, working tirelessly and skillfully; to Ambassador Gilbert Robinson who first suggested
this project and then made possible this printing; to his editor Brayton
Harris who guided our efforts wisely through impossible production deadlines; and to the generous Lindsay alumni and friends who contributed to
this 50th celebration.

--Jay L. Kriegel, Coordinator.

Cover photo by John Dominus, from *LIFE* magazine, May 24, 1968.
Courtesy Getty Images.

FOREWORD

Fifty years ago, New York City seemed in steep decline, as Mayor Robert F. Wagner contemplated running for a fourth term. In May, young Republican Congressman John V. Lindsay launched his candidacy, taking to the streets from morning until night while running powerful television commercials that emphasized his youth, energy and commitment. This unusual retail campaign was symbolized by a stark black-and-white poster with Lindsay walking in shirtsleeves and Murray Kempton's memorable quote, "He is fresh and everyone else is tired."

On November 2, 1965, Lindsay was victorious in a close three-way race. There was an immediate sense of excitement that something profound had happened, that the City was embarking on a dramatic new chapter with hope and optimism, not unlike the sense nationally with John F. Kennedy's victory in 1960. And it had, for Lindsay was committed to radical change in the policies and programs that he believed had allowed the City to stagnate and decay.

Nothing better exemplified that shift than the night in April 1968 when Dr. Martin Luther King, Jr., was killed and riots broke out in cities across the country. In Chicago, faced with widespread looting and fires, Mayor Richard J. Daley directed the police to "shoot to kill." When that news came across the wire, John Lindsay quickly issued a contrary statement: "We don't shoot children in New York City."

It was a stark contrast between the old and the new, with Daley already in office ten years, the gruff, powerful, old-line Boss, and JVL, telegenic, reform-minded, independent and principled.

As the Kerner Commission so well documented (Lindsay was the dominating Vice Chairman), the 1960s saw the combustible legacy of racial conflict and oppression, sparked by aggressive police actions, erupt in a wave of urban disorders that shook the nation like nothing in the hundred years since the Civil War Draft Riots. Lindsay stood virtually alone in empathizing with the deep discontent of the minorities and by his frequent physical presence in their depressed communities.

His courage was unquestioned. But I have never really understood what made him, coming from an elite background (St. Paul's and Yale), be so responsive to black sensibilities and hurt. As a Member of Congress (1959-65), he was one of the key Republican leaders who marshaled bi-partisan support of the two historic civil rights bills, the 1964 Public Accommodations bill and the 1965 Voting Rights Act (that was when I first met him, volunteering as a law student to serve on his staff during weeks of tense deliberations of the House Judiciary Committee).

He seemed to reflect imbedded Republican principles dating back to Lincoln, largely a theoretical and legal commitment. But that changed in the 1965 campaign when he spent every day on the streets, frequently walking in Harlem and Bed-Stuy, the South Bronx and Jamaica, for the minority community was a major Lindsay target of electoral opportunity.

He entered City Hall a few months later with unprecedented exposure to these hidden neighborhoods and their residents and a philosophy of action that said the Mayor was responsible for what happened on the streets and had to confront problems aggressively. So when racial trouble broke out in our first summer (1966), Lindsay raced to far-away East New York, met directly with the black and Italian teenage antagonists, assigned staff to stay there and invited local leaders into the Mayor's Office to meet, in clear violation of Wagner's guiding principle of keeping conflicts as far from City Hall as possible, hoping they would get diffused some other way. Once East New York happened, Lindsay kept returning to streets rarely visited by white politicians, 125th, and 138th and Fulton, unannounced and without a police entourage, just calmly walking and talking, relaxed and accessible in shirtsleeves, demonstrating that he wasn't fearful of these residents, felt comfortable with them, and had not forgotten them.

He recognized that he couldn't bring quick relief. When frustrations intensified and impatience grew, he in effect offered himself as a sign of his determination to act, and as justification for their continued patience. It struck me as an instinctive gesture, almost a religious ritual. It worked, not just because of his personal offering, but because of his forceful articulation of their plight and the policies he was advocating, beginning with the Civilian Complaint Review Board (CCRB) and police restraint.

The nation seemed to have given up on cities, which were convulsed in violence and despair, preferring the charms of greener, more pristine suburbs. Lindsay saw this in broad historic context. In his book, *The City*, he traces America's hostility to cities back to Jefferson, carried to the present through the destructive impact of multiple federal laws and programs. But Lindsay saw cities as the center of a civilization's culture and values and believed their preservation was essential to our nation's future.

As the most compelling voice for urban America, he rallied a group of young Mayors to lobby for federal attention and revenue sharing. He argued with senators about the vast amount of funds needed to meet urban needs and he challenged the nation's priorities when President Lyndon Johnson's Vietnam escalations diminished his own Great Society programs, dooming cities to further decay. Lindsay never wavered in his profound belief that national greatness could only flow from the diversity, complexity, conflict and pressure found in big cities, making him a rare urban prophet, or as Sam Roberts called him, "America's Mayor."

Today, he would be pleased to see his conviction vindicated, not just by the growth of New York to an unthinkable 9 million and the revival of long despairing neighborhoods from Harlem to the Brooklyn-Queens waterfront, but also by the rejuvenation of older cities everywhere from Pittsburgh, to

Kansas City, and now even Buffalo.

He believed that cities had to be managed professionally, so he made it a priority to recruit talent, creating his own internal headhunting firm (Talent Search), trusting his instincts over résumés and taking risks with minorities and youth (like this writer) without experience. He spurred a new breed of disciplined, professional managers with whom he felt a special bond, and who have populated so many public jobs during the 40-plus years since.

So many of the Lindsay reforms have remained, from the reorganization of a hodge-podge of 50 agencies into streamlined super-agencies and the decentralization of city services for responsive local delivery, to a massive investment in information and tracking systems that allowed the creation of the Mayor's Management Report, groundbreaking productivity programs, our advanced Project Management system, and even the incredibly simple but wildly successful process that has stimulated filmmaking. Lindsay first closed the parks to traffic, now a world-wide practice, air conditioned the subways, installed the first 911 emergency dispatch system, initiated the massive Third Water Tunnel still under construction, created the rent stabilization regime, and built new Broadway theatres and the TKTS discount ticket booth. With all of this, as with program budgeting, district service cabinets, and incentive zoning, today's modern city government dates from Lindsay

Lindsay had clarity of vision, often seeing issues in terms of moral absolutes. I always thought this came from his experience in World War II, where colleagues died and the fundamental issue was survival. So he was an early opponent of the Vietnam War (reportedly the third elected official after Senators Gruening and Morse) and unwavering on issues of racial justice. He sent a clear signal by making his first appointment a black commissioner of the Fire Department, the whitest of all city agencies (then, and sadly, still now). And despite vociferous charges of "political interference," he never wavered on the need for police restraint in the use of deadly force and the ultimate responsibility of the mayor, not the police, to set such policy (paralleling the Constitution's civilian control of the military and inserted by him in a powerful statement in the Kerner Commission Report).

He believed his role was to assault the fortresses of power and to force open the gates that had blocked those of color. It was the same instinct toward inclusion that led him later to issue the first government rules any-where accepting gays and to be an early and ardent supporter of women's rights. He battled the "special interests," the forces of exclusion and privi-lege. And believing he was right, he never feared the consequences or the risks of losing. His was a great crusade for racial justice, with the most celebrated battles being the Civilian Complaint Review Board (1966), the three horrendous teachers' strikes of 1968 and the Forest Hills scatter-site housing project of 1971. Robert Kennedy presented a telling contrast of political style and instinct when he felt compelled to support Lindsay's CCRB as liberal dogma but hated the issue as futile, a guaranteed loser and divisive to his base of minorities and blue collar whites. (It seems ironic that "Man of La Mancha" opened three weeks after Lindsay's election, with its "Impossible Dream.")

We rushed headlong into battles without gauging carefully the risks and obstacles, so we lost more than our share, though we certainly had our tri-umphs as well (most especially the 1969 re-election with the War a central deflecting theme and the great "Mistakes" commercial providing a softer, humble tone). In retrospect, we could have executed smarter and more skillfully. Lindsay tended to demonize opponents, as with his simplistic (naive perhaps) attack on the "Power Brokers" in the midst of the 1966 transit strike. But I suspect he would not regret any of those great conflicts and would willingly engage in them again. And so would most of us, for the principles still stand.

Perhaps this was why Lindsay was so fond of young people who provided energy, fresh thinking and a willingness to enter into battle at his side, where older, wiser warriors might have been restrained by doubts. He encouraged us to challenge, to test, to make mistakes. I never doubted his judgment on the most sensitive issues of public policy (like the War), or balancing complex competing interests (especially racial issues). That is a rare feeling for any of us in public service and one reason for our passionate devotion to him even today.

For someone young, still believing in that Impossible Dream--that we could make this city a better place, removing the shackles of history, opening long-sealed doors, improving lives—there could be no better boss. It is why you want to be in politics and government when you are young, fearless, tireless, filled with hope. And why we still celebrate John Lindsay and our time at his side.

This book creates a mosaic of more than 260 recollections written by those who worked with John Lindsay or encountered and observed him, with a wide range of perspectives and personal anecdotes about the passions, pressures, conflicts and joys, the setbacks and triumphs, of the Lindsay Years. It also includes a detailed chronolgy of those years, reminding us of the intensity and complexity of the forces that buffeted us and the many initiatives we launched from City Hall, as well as the external cultural, politicial, and international events that enriched and compounded those times.

-- *Jay L. Kriegel*

TABLE OF CONTENTS

THE NARRATIVES

CHRONOLOGY

THE NARRATIVES

Robert Abrams

In 1969, after I won the Democratic primary for Bronx Borough President as the reform candidate against the Bronx Democratic organization, I decided I could not in good conscience support Mario Procaccino, the Democratic nominee for Mayor, a conservative clubhouse Bronx organization pol. I bolted my party and strongly endorsed John Lindsay's reelection. I was running on the Liberal line (so was Lindsay) as well as the Democratic line.

We both won—Lindsay by 180,000 votes—and I asked him to attend my swearing in as Borough President at my alma mater Christopher Columbus High School. He agreed. Everyone in my Pelham Parkway neighborhood was excited to hear that the Mayor was coming. Their excitement turned into amazement when a Sanitation Department convoy of mechanical sweepers patrolled the area for two days before the inauguration until the streets there were cleaner than at any time in living memory. The Mayor spoke eloquently at the event to a packed, enthusiastic crowd.

In late 1969, *New York Post* sports columnist Maury Allen reported that the Yankees were thinking about leaving The Bronx because of inadequate parking and an outdated stadium with poor sight lines. After reading that, I met with Michael Burke, President of the Yankees. He confirmed what Allen wrote. I was terrified that the Bronx would lose the Yankees on my watch as Borough President. I went to City Hall and met with the newly re-elected Mayor. " John," I said, "you owe it to the people of The Bronx to spend as much as the residents of Queens got from the City when $24 million was spent on a new home for the Mets." The Mayor agreed to put $24 million in the budget for a refurbished Yankee Stadium with improved parking. We nipped that problem in the bud. The Yankees continued to call The Bronx home and went on to win many more championships.

I later learned that the Mayor was not an avid baseball fan. When we attended a Yankee opening day together, I was distracted while talking to someone else, then leaned over to him and asked what the count was. "Two and three," he responded firmly.

Mayor Lindsay and Parks Commissioner Tom Hoving took the brilliant, provocative step of closing Central Park to automobiles to provide safe, fume-free space for bike riding. They inspired me to do something like that for The Bronx. I convinced Borough Police Commander Tony Bouza, to close the Grand Concourse on Sundays from 1pm-5pm. To inaugurate the program, the press announced, the Mayor and I would ride up the Concourse on bikes from 161st Street to Poe Park.

My office received a threat that our heads would be blown off by a sniper as we crossed Burnside Avenue. The Police Department wanted to cancel the event but I prevailed upon them to let it go forward, minimizing the threat as idle or a prank. They allowed the event to take place, but under heavy security. I confess that as we traversed Burnside and the Concourse I was nervously looking around at all sides. Nothing untoward happened.

It was always exciting being with John Lindsay. ∎

Robert Abrams *served in the New York State Assembly, as Bronx Borough President, and, from 1979, as New York State Attorney General. He is a Partner in the law firm of Stroock & Stroock & Lavan.*

Stan Altman

In 1970, faculty from SUNY Stony Brook began working with the Sanitation Department on the "Chart Day Problem," the assignment system for sanitation workers.

In early December, I was asked to accompany EPA Administrator Jerry Kretchmer and Sanitation Commissioner Herb Elish to a meeting with the Sanitationmen's Union to present our work. En route, Kretchmer warned that he might have to disavow Stony Brook's ideas if the union voiced major objections.

Union head John DeLury and his cunning financial advisor Jack Bigel did raise objections to our proposals. Kretchmer kept his word and "threw" us under the bus, offering to get rid of the Stony Brook group. Bigel then screamed that Kretchmer should be ashamed of his performance, given the outstanding work that Stony Brook was doing. Turning to me, the financial advisor said, "If you want to be useful, analyze the union's own proposal for a five-day workweek."

With Kretchmer and Elish's consent, we decided that the union's recommended five-day workweek was reasonable, on condition that they accepted differential pay among its members based on their assignments. Months later, the union withdrew this proposal because differential pay was unacceptable to its members. Unexpectedly, they agreed instead to work rule changes somewhat similar to those we had originally proposed.

—

Herb Elish lent me his car and driver to conduct field interviews with district garage personnel. "How long are we going to be out," the driver asked me. "I need to be back by 11:30 to cash my paycheck, but it's your call," he said. I decided to work fast and get back by 11:30 so he could cash his paycheck.

A year later I was staffing a Department meeting to discuss implementation of a new work schedule for household refuse collection, and thought
I recognized that same driver, who served as a clerk in one of the district
garages. But he informed me that he was the twin brother of the Commissioner's driver, but he knew about the morning his brother and I spent
together. He quietly asked me if I wanted to see the data and reports he
prepared for the Commissioner's office - - or the real data?

—

Commissioner Elish wanted to increase accountability for street cleaning by adopting a rating system similar to the one the Urban Institute had
developed for the District of Columbia. I offered to help with the new
system, but Elish wanted to do it internally with his agency's personnel. He devised a test involving District Superintendents. He distributed
photos showing different levels of street cleanliness as a basis for grading
performance. He then took his team out into the field to rate each street's
cleanliness using these pictures as his yardstick.

But every street they visited was perfectly clean. "How is this possible?"
Elish asked. "We had them cleaned this morning before we started because
we know that you want to see clean streets," they replied candidly. That
convinced Elish that the ratings had to be conducted by non-Department
personnel. So Project Scorecard was created and has operated independent
of the Department since 1974.■

*Stan Altman was an Associate Professor and deputy to the President at
at SUNY Stony Brook and an Associate Provost for SUNY. He served as
interim President of Baruch College (2009-10) and is now a Professor in
Baruch's School of Public Affairs.*

Michael Armstrong

I was not a fan of John Lindsay's. Although we'd never met, my opinion of him was distinctly unfavorable.

He had been elected as a charismatic John Kennedy-like figure who would lead New York City out of the doldrums where, according to Lindsay, it was mired under the leadership of his predecessor Bob Wagner. Wagner was as short and colorless as Lindsay was tall and magnificent.

A devastating citywide transit strike that had been brewing for quite some time greeted Lindsay on his first day in office. He proved no match for his adversary, Transit Workers Union boss Michael Quill, an old Irishman with a heavy brogue. Quill bested Lindsay; the contract he negotiated was more favorable to his rank-and-file than meeting their original demands would have been. The new Mayor's performance was not impressive.

In my opinion, everything went downhill from there. Lindsay probably wasn't a worse Mayor than anyone else would have been in that impossible job during an impossible time. But he appeared to take himself so seriously, and seemed so swept away by grandiose visions that people like me tended to judge him by what he promised instead of by what was possible. I also thought of him as being too earnest, too self-righteous and, most of all, humorless.

Unaware of my prejudice against Lindsay, Whitman Knapp, who had agreed to chair a commission investigating police corruption (I would be its chief counsel), made an appointment for me to meet the Mayor. Knapp and I arrived at Lindsay's office where two of his top aides, Jay Kriegel and Dick Aurelio, joined us. The Mayor was at a City Council meeting. Kriegel was the "enfant terrible" of the Lindsay Administration. Now thirty-one years old, he had joined Lindsay soon after graduating from Harvard Law School and was Counsel to the Mayor. He had a reputation for being as brilliant as he was abrasive. Thin, bird-like, nervous, constantly moving, his eyes darting about behind large glasses, he thought as fast as, and certainly talked faster than just about anyone I had ever met. Aurelio was a large, shrewd, friendly man with a moustache and a reputation for being a deft politician.

Waiting for Lindsay, our conversation was cordial, if guarded. Finally, the Mayor arrived, fresh from a pitched battle with the Council in which he had been double-crossed. Flopping down on the couch, Lindsay heaved a great sigh. Instead of uttering some ponderous platitude about good government, he exclaimed, "We have got to get back to boss rule in this city. Democracy is no way to run a town like this." He proceeded to lead us in a relaxed discussion of the commission's goals and how we planned to achieve them.

Lindsay, I resentfully realized, was a good guy. He had a sense of humor after all. The cardboard figure of him in my mind became three-dimensional. I was acutely disappointed. It is maddening to have one's prejudice against a public figure undermined by meeting him. ■

Michael Armstrong *has been an Assistant United States Attorney and District Attorney of Queens County. He is a partner in the law firm of McLaughin & Stern. This recollection is a condensed exerpt from* They Wished They Were Honest *(2012) by Mr. Armstrong.*

George Artz

John Lindsay and Ed Koch were both Mayors of New York, but that is where the similarities end and the hostilities begin.

Lindsay was patrician WASP, suave, and handsome. Koch was a street fighter, outspoken, sometimes bombastic, and a Polish Jew. Lindsay wrote himself into city lore by walking the streets of Harlem right after the assassination of Martin Luther King. Koch wrote himself into city lore by cheering people on as they crossed the Brooklyn Bridge during the transit strike.

The two were rising stars in their respective parties, and their paths crossed frequently. Their relationship would forever be defined by the partisan events following Koch's decision to break with the Democratic Party in 1965 to support the Republican mayoral candidate, John Lindsay.

Koch's own club, the Village Independent Democrats (VID), voted to stay neutral in the 1965 race. Koch and other VID members were leaning toward Lindsay over clubhouse pol, Abe Beame, the Democratic candidate. The weekend before the election Lindsay's campaign manager, Bob Price, put out a feeler to see if Koch would go with Lindsay.

It was a very close race with polls differing on who would win. Koch decided he would back Lindsay and announce his endorsement at a press conference the next morning. Not knowing how other Democrats would react, Koch reached out to his co-Village district leader, Carol Greitzer, and to Marty Berger, the President of VID. Both Greitzer and Berger decided to join him. At the time, it was the biggest press conference Koch had ever had, and his law office was swarming with media. The very next day the *Daily News* ran the headline "LBJ and Humphrey Push Beame; Reform Dem Koch Backs Lindsay."

Lindsay won the election and Koch believed he played a key role in the victory. It was a move that earned Koch the censure of famed Harlem powerbroker and feared Tammany Leader, J. Raymond Jones. Indeed, Jones held a censure "trial" for Koch and Greitzer in an effort to prevent Democratic District Leaders from ever crossing party lines again - now known as the Koch Greitzer rule.

Koch soon found himself running for the City Council against the GOP candidate Woody Kingman. He never reckoned with the notion and impact of party loyalty. With the popular Governor Nelson Rockefeller at the top of the ballot, Koch feared for the worst, but as soon as the overwhelmingly Democratic Chelsea districts started coming in, it was clear that he would win handily. Lindsay did not play a role.

In the Council, Koch was the same maverick as he was soon to be widely known for as Mayor. While in the Council, he received a phone call from top Lindsay aide Tom Hoving, the Parks Commissioner, who said, "Listen Ed, the Mayor is very upset that you're sniping at him and you're attacking this and attacking that and he wants you to stop it." Koch, furious, said to Hoving, "I'm not the Mayor's man on the City Council, I am my own man on the Council, and I'll vote the way I want to vote." Still the *coup de gras* for Koch was yet to come.

In 1968, Koch ran for Congress against Republican stalwart Whitney North Seymour, Jr. (who Koch referred to as the man with three last names) thinking he would have Lindsay's support in light of Koch's past help. Koch was wrong again. In a radio interview Seymour announced he had Mayor Lindsay's support, and Koch believed at that moment he lost the race for the Silk Stocking District.

Koch immediately reached out to Lindsay's Deputy Mayor Bob Sweet for a meeting with Mayor Lindsay. The meeting did not take place for months because of the teachers' strike that took place in the fall of that year. At the meeting, for which Lindsay left Koch waiting outside his office for an hour, Koch said to the Mayor that though he did not expect the Mayor to endorse him, he certainly did not expect the Mayor to endorse his competitor, "in view of what I did for you. Maybe you have forgotten about it." Koch then threw down a copy of his campaign literature which featured the *Daily News* headline about Koch backing Lindsay and said, "Mr. Mayor, you're looking at the guy that is going to win!" and stormed out.

Koch did win, and Lindsay referred to Koch's victory as, "a catastrophe for the City." Not to be outdone, Mary Lindsay was quoted in the Sunday *Times* Magazine as saying, "Why is there antipathy between Koch and John? Jealousy! John is attractive and sexy; he's neither." From then on Koch attacked Lindsay unmercifully at every opportunity.

In the campaign of 1969 with Lindsay losing in the Republican primary to John Marchi, Lindsay needed the support of Democratic reformers to win. Lindsay's people reached out to VID and the other reformers in the New Democratic Coalition (or to skeptics the November Don't Count Coalition) for their support. And in a bloody, riotous vote at the Hotel Diplomat, Lindsay won the endorsement by one vote. Since Koch was no fan of the Democratic nominee, Mario Procaccino, who he viewed as a political hack, he grudgingly endorsed Lindsay.

Still, Koch did not hold back on Lindsay, and in 1972 when Lindsay was running for President, now as a Democrat, Koch was asked why Lindsay seemed to be so popular in Arizona and Oregon, but not in New York City. Koch said, "Well, to know him is not to love him." Lindsay was furious.

Even as a candidate for Mayor in 1977 Koch ran under the slogan, "After 8 years of charisma and 4 years of the clubhouse, why not try competence," in a clear swipe at both Lindsay's and Beame's respective tenures. The catchy slogan was created by David Garth who also guided Lindsay's campaigns. But that didn't matter to Koch.

Even after he won, Koch never forgot Lindsay's snub and took every opportunity to cast aspersions on Lindsay, his fiscal stewardship of the City, his school decentralization plans, and his abandonment of the middle class.

After two years of Mayor Koch's non-stop criticism of the Lindsay Administration, Lindsay aides reached out to Koch Deputy Mayor Nat Leventhal. Leventhal was formerly Lindsay's Chief of Staff and he agreed to intercede with Koch. Leventhal's intervention, and Lindsay's declining health at the time led Koch to stop the onslaught and call a truce—though Koch could not help jabbing Lindsay every once in a while.

The moral of all this, to paraphrase Tip O'Neill, is that all politics is personal. ■

George Artz is President of George Artz Communications, a public, community and government relations firm. He has been Executive Director of WNYW Fox-5's News Division, Press Secretary to Mayor Edward Koch and the New York Post's City Hall Bureau Chief.

Charles Atkins

Some of us in the Health Services Administration had been invited to a private showing of the film "Catch-22." Before the lights went down, I was standing with Jeff Weiss and a half dozen other colleagues when I noticed the Mayor talking with a small group nearby. Then the Mayor walked over to us. "Jeff," he said, "why don't you introduce me to your friends." After he chatted with us for a few minutes, JVL went off to join some other people. "Jeff, I'm very impressed," I told my colleague. "I didn't know you knew the Mayor." He replied, "I've never met him before." Whether an alert staffer adroitly whispered Jeff's name to the Mayor or JVL skillfully caught the name of someone in our group while conversing with others, his social grace was pure class.■

Charles Atkins' career includes working for Citibank, Harvard University, Arthur D. Little, Boston Mayor Kevin White and Massachusetts Gov. Michael Dukakis. He now has his own business on St. John in the U.S. Virgin Islands.

Ken Auletta

Howard Samuels was a Democrat, but, as was true of John Lindsay and the Republican Party, the Democratic Party was not his church. When Democrats nominated a conservative non-entity, Mario Procaccino, as their candidate for Mayor in 1969, Howard was outraged. Although he planned to run for Governor in 1970 as a Democrat, and some advisors cautioned him not to do it, he crossed party lines and became the first prominent Democrat to endorse John Lindsay for re-election. He became the Chairman of Democrats for Lindsay.

Naturally, the established Democratic Party did not forget. They opposed Howard when he ran for Governor in 1970, and he narrowly lost.

Soon after, the state legislature, with scant forethought, passed a bill allowing the city to establish the nation's first public off track betting corporation, computing on the back of an envelope the riches that would be earmarked for education. The legislature did do one thing right, though: Rather than obliging him to create OTB as a mayoral agency that might get bogged down in bureaucracy, they heeded John Lindsay's demand for freedom to establish OTB as a public corporation.

His first step was to recruit a businessman to serve as the corporation's Chairman and CEO. That businessman was Howard Samuels. Lindsay honored his pledge to let Howard run OTB like a business.

Howard did something other wealthy men like Mayor Bloomberg have done: He insisted on working for $1 a year. With Lindsay's backing, and with the wise counsel of Deputy Mayor Richard Aurelio, who served on the OTB board, Howard did extraordinary things.

• He set up a public bidding system for a computerized betting system and within two years they automated nearly one million daily transactions.

- He opened 140 OTB parlors within a couple of years.

- He recruited business executives to help run the corporation.

- By the end of year one, OTB produced $17 million in profits. In year two, $42 million. By year three, $60 million.

- He maneuvered to keep unions with organized crime ties from representing OTB workers.

- And, working with Herb Sturz of the Vera Institute, he established four OTB offices operated by former drug addicts, ex-prisoners, and others seeking to forge a second life.

Were there shortcomings and mistakes? Sure. But when Howard left OTB in 1973 to run for Governor the following year, OTB was considered one of the Lindsay Administration's luminous successes.

No one anticipated OTB would, three decades later, be deemed a failure. Blame it on politics, on the legislature, on frightened, reactionary racing interests.

But don't blame it on John Lindsay.■

Ken Auletta is the author of ten books and frequently writes on media matters for The New Yorker. *He was Executive Director of the Off Track Betting Corporation.*

Richard Aurelio

John Lindsay began to think about switching parties following his 1969 re-election after having been repudiated in the Republican primary and forced to run as a Liberal Party and independent candidate. Some friends and advisors argued that if he had any national ambitions, the Democratic Party was his more natural home. The primary defeat offered the perfect rationale for making the change. In 1970, the Mayor endorsed Democrat-Liberal Arthur Goldberg for governor in his race against incumbent Nelson Rockefeller. Goldberg had endorsed Lindsay's re-election months before while Rockefeller had deserted the Mayor. No one was surprised. American politics was realigning. Lyndon Johnson's Great Society and civil rights breakthroughs drove many Southern Democrats to vote Republican. The Mayor, increasingly anguished by mounting Vietnam casualties, the slaughter of civilians at My Lai and federal indifference to urban dilemmas, finally decided that his Republican Party had abandoned its core principles making him unwelcome there. His change of party in August, 1971 drew massive press coverage.

Three months later Mayor Lindsay announced at a somewhat jubilant news conference that I would be leaving City Hall in December to explore "the national political situation to assist in determining what role I can play in 1972." The *Daily News* trumpeted the story with a front-page headline: LINDSAY TOSSES AURELIO IN RING.

The Mayor recognized that he was a very long shot whose candidacy would stir resentment within the Democratic Party for a newcomer with such lofty ambitions. But he pointedly noted that very few people have a chance to run for president, and the opportunity to bring urban issues to the forefront of the campaign debate, along with his consistent anti-Vietnam War message and a plea for re-ordering national priorities, was very hard to pass up. He also looked forward to the venture as a diversion from what he called "the pressure cooker of City Hall" where he was hamstrung by budget constraints and disastrous federal policies.

Returning from a month of travel, I gave him the expected feedback from Democratic leaders—welcoming and polite but wary and highly skeptical. He wasn't deterred. Our campaign team made a plan and he approved a formal announcement in Miami for December. The Mayor called a cabinet meeting to break the news and have me discuss his strategy. I described his decision to run as daring and audacious, worthy of the cabinet's enthusiastic support because of JVL's willingness to suffer the brickbats he'd draw for pushing his views on Vietnam and the urban crisis. Following the meeting, media guru David Garth, clearly uncomfortable with the decision, asked me if the Mayor knew how impossible a situation he faced. I brought him into the Mayor's office. After reiterating that he was under no illusions about the road ahead and his determination to spotlight urban issues and our maddeningly lopsided national agenda, John Lindsay said something I've never forgotten. "Bad things happen when good people do nothing, and running was better than doing nothing."

Was he invoking Edmund Burke? I don't really know, but that's why he ran for President.■

*First Deputy Mayor in the second Lindsay Administration and campaign manager of the Mayor's re-election campaign, **Richard Aurelio** was also President of Time Warner Cable's New York City Cable Group where he founded NY1, the cable station that provides 24-hour news coverage of the five boroughs. In addition, he was Senator Jacob K. Javits' chief of staff, an editor of* Newsday, *a public relations executive and restaurateur.*

David Axelrod

I'm pretty sure I met John Lindsay before he was running—and before I was even walking. He lived briefly in the building that was my first home, 622 E. 20th St., in Stuyvesant Town. Legend has it that women, and maybe some men, timed their exits in the morning to share an elevator with the dashing young lawyer.

My attraction came years later, when I was ten. Already imbued with the spirit of John F. Kennedy, I saw politics as big and noble, a way to steer history's course. Democrats in New York City had slated a hack for Mayor in 1965, so I walked over to the Liberal Party outpost in the neighborhood and volunteered for Lindsay, now our local Congressman. Though a Republican, he was young, challenging, and idealistic. He inspired me the way JFK had. So I was a ten-year-old foot soldier in Lindsay's army for change.■

*Political consultant and journalist **David Axelrod** was a senior adviser to President Barack Obama. He is Director of the Institute of Politics at the University of Chicago.*

Carter Bales

I first met John Lindsay when, as a young McKinsey Associate, I was advising Tim Costello, then the City Administrator, on Local Law 14: the recently-enacted municipal law governing garbage disposal in NYC apartment buildings. I had developed an "Issue Map" on the implementation choices facing the City, which I subsequently presented to the Mayor's Policy Planning Council in a meeting at Gracie Mansion, resulting in a Mayoral decision on how to implement the law. In the process, I also met Fred Hayes, Bob Sweet and Don Elliott, in addition to Peter Goldmark, Jay Kriegel and several other young stars of the Lindsay Administration.

I subsequently accepted an offer from Fred Hayes to join the Bureau of the Budget as Assistant Budget Director (Acting) with responsibility for Program Budget Systems, an amazing opportunity for a 27-year old. There I was privileged to work with Fred, Peter, Dave Grossman, the Bureau program planning staff, various Assistants to the Mayor, and, of course, the Mayor himself.

One of the qualities that struck me about JVL at the time I met him and many times thereafter was his curiosity and genuine interest in grasping the complexity of the many issues facing the City. John wanted to understand the policy choices, their economic and budgetary considerations, the impact of possible policies on various citizen groups, and the feasibility of actually making change happen. He made himself available for discussions on the policy choices. And he often spoke of "blowing through a straw" as an image in expecting a favorable outcome from a new policy or program: you blow and blow and just maybe something good may happen at the other end of the straw.

But it was JVL's enthusiasm for the job and his City and the relish he brought to everything he did that most sticks in my memory. He loved the contest and brought great energy and spirit to it every day. He was not afraid to show his often "boyish" enthusiasm. One day a group of us were lunching with some visiting dignitaries at Gracie Mansion when John quipped, "Oh great, we're having cheese yummies for lunch." No one else knew what a cheese yummy was, but that did not dampen John's enthusiasm.

I loved JVL's caring and loyalty for his team, feeling amply returned by the broader Lindsay staff, a "family" of all ages on a fascinating journey toward making a more civilized, more inclusive and better functioning city. This loyalty allowed John to sometimes take strong positions on change that he wanted to see happen, telling his senior managers to simply "get it done." While John was clearly a man of courage and commitment, the close relationship he had with his team gave him additional moral authority to move things along in the right direction.

Overall, I remember John Lindsay's genuine good heartedness and largeness of spirit. He really cared about public service, his City, his team and more generally people in need. John was not a politician—he was a true public servant. He was a true spirit for good. I have known none better.∎

Carter Bales is an investor, asset manager, environmentalist, conservationist, philanthropist and public servant. He is co-founder, Chairman and Managing Partner of NewWorld Capital Group. A former Principal of McKinsey & Company, he is an Emeritus Director and Senior Advisor to the management consulting firm,

William Bardel

The Office of Midtown Planning proposed closing Madison Avenue to vehicles from about 42nd Street to 59th Street. The Traffic Department's engineers thought it was a lunatic idea. The Mayor's Office of Midtown Planning and Development had no traffic engineers, but engaged consultant Sandy Van Ginkel, a Dutch expert in this field from Canada, to advise OMPD's architects and land use planners. Our proposal's audacity and forward-looking environmental implications appealed to the Mayor, who listened closely to his "young urbanists."

Lindsay met with Jaque Robertson, the head of our office, the Traffic Commissioner, me and some other aides to review the proposal. He was particularly receptive to OMPD's request that the avenue be repaved to make it more agreeable to pedestrians. The Ttraffic Commissioner said it would be a waste of money to repave Madison Avenue, which, he pointed out, wasn't one of the worst surfaces in Manhattan. The Mayor went ballistic. "No it's not one of the worst streets in NY," he said firmly, "but it would be the worst street in Chicago, Philadelphia, or any other city in the country!"

The Mayor then dismissed the idea that the ban would immobilize traffic throughout Manhattan. He also refused to reject testing the so-called GinkelVans to carry modest numbers of people along the avenue, even though they had yet to be built, let alone tested. He doubted, as well, that commercial deliveries would be totally disrupted by a single street closing.

Given an opportunity to try something dramatic to deal with pollution and congestion in midtown, the Mayor was ready to take significant political risks. It was uncertain that this approach would work in the Manhattan grid, but the closing would certainly be a highly visible initiative.

Lindsay lobbied very hard for the proposal at the Board of Estimate, where he appeared to have the votes. Late in the day, however, Manhattan

Borough President Percy Sutton, in a last-minute reversal, decided not to support the closing, handing the Mayor a narrow defeat.

The episode was an interesting forerunner to the current debates over Times Square.■

William Bardel has been an investment banker at Lehman Brothers and an administrator at The Lawrenceville School.

Mimi Barker

T he first time I heard the word "charisma" was when my mother said it: "Oh, that John Lindsay. He has so much charisma." And my father probably followed up with something like, "Yeah, well he better have more than that if he's gonna stand up to Mike Quill."

My parents worked for a local newspaper in Mt. Kisco, New York, where we lived. A man named Carll Tucker, a classmate of the Mayor's at Yale, owned the paper.

Carll's take on JVL was similar to my mother's: John Lindsay was the rising star of the Republican Party, sure to become president one day.

I was smitten. I knew right then that I wanted to work for the Mayor who had been on the cover of *Time* Magazine, the Mayor who seemed a star come to earth, a progressive, impressive and amazingly handsome politician.

The dream stuck, and I headed for New York City in 1968, fresh out of Skidmore College and armed with a BA in American Studies. I needed a job—any job—and took an entry-level position in publishing while keeping an eye out for city government opportunities. Luck, coincidence, and the social swirl (a date who worked for the city) led me to an administrative assistant position with the Parks, Recreation and Cultural Affairs Administration (PRCAA)—one of the "super agencies" the Lindsay Administration had created in an effort to re-configure what had been a sprawling, chaotic and expensive governmental structure.

The PRCAA was headed by the impeccable Commissioner August Heckscher, affectionately known as Augie, and well known for the bow ties he always wore. Augie, like the Mayor, believed that the "parks belong to the people." Vest Pocket parks sprung up in all five boroughs, and the major parks were closed to cars on weekends for the first time. I first saw John Lindsay in person (just as tall, handsome, funny, and warm as I expected) when he visited our office to thank us for our work on some adventurous happening in Central Park. It may have been for the birthday party for the Broadway hit "Hair".

From Parks I moved to the office of Dick Aurelio, the First Deputy Mayor, just down the hall from His Honor. It was a thrilling time. The best and the brightest of the JVL Administration—invariably charming, brilliant and dedicated—came to Dick's office regularly.

My childhood dream of "graduating from college and going to work for the government" had come true. The Lindsay hallmark—that government is to serve the people—is an ideal that has served me well throughout my career. I went from City Hall to the Mayor's ill-fated presidential campaign, then to work as press secretary for Congresswoman Patricia Schroeder, and later to the Planned Parenthood Federation of America.

I eventually gave up on politics and political fights, and went to work in the private sector. But I'll always remember my stint in the Lindsay Administration as the first—and perhaps last—time I really loved my job.■

Mimi Barker was press secretary to Rep. Patricia Schroeder (1972-75) and then director of communications and marketing for Standard & Poor's.

Ben Barnes

Back when I was Lieutenant Governor of Texas, I traveled to New York to visit Mayor John Lindsay. Everyone loved him and thought he should run for President. He was the new Boy Wonder. As we walked down the street, several people ran up to John to tell him how great he was and ask for his autograph. He loved every minute of it. All of a sudden, three young women came running down the street screaming excitedly, but they weren't shouting, "John Lindsay, John Lindsay." They were shouting, "Ben Barnes, Ben Barnes." John looked at me in utter dismay and disbelief.■

Ben Barnes was the youngest Speaker of the House in Texas history and served as representative of the United States to the United Nations and other international organizations in Geneva, Switzerland. He has also been a real estate executive and lobbyist.

Mike Barnicle

E arly in the afternoon of a beautiful and quite warm week day in April 1971, I was sitting on a bench in City Hall Park with a sandwich in one hand and the New York Daily News sports page in the other. I was 28 years old and had been a speechwriter for John V. Lindsay, then the Mayor of New York City, for about two months and I was miserable.

My unhappiness had nothing to do with the Mayor, the city, the still fledgling plan for Lindsay to run for president as a Democrat, his staff, his travel schedule or anything else revolving around this guy who already had many people talking about him as a candidate who could calm and lead a nation in turmoil. My deal was all personal: it was about me missing my very young children who would not be moving to New York, and living with the weight of daily regret for not being there to help raise them.

So there I am, trying to lose myself in the distraction of reading box scores when two familiar faces come strolling through the park: a New York City police detective who was the head of the Mayor's security detail, Pat Vecchio, and John Lindsay. When Lindsay spotted me he stopped, not out of familiarity but out of politeness I think. He barely knew me. I'd been with him on a couple trips he took for speeches but other than that I'm sure I was just one more vaguely familiar face he saw each day around City Hall.

Maybe he was bored. Maybe he didn't want to go back to the office just yet. Maybe it was the sunshine and the splendid early afternoon that momentarily lured him. Who knows? But he sat down alongside me on the bench and asked what I was doing and how I was doing?

I decided to give him a brief synopsis of my problem. I tried to be brief and to the point. After all, he—like any mayor of New York—always has the spectacle of tragedy at the door, always lives hourly with the prospect of urban trauma erupting over a shooting, a cop getting killed, a civilian being shot by police, a sanitation workers' strike, the schools, the subways, the bureaucracy, the homeless, the fiscal nightmare of simply keeping the lights on in the world's most important city.

Lindsay was an eye contact guy. He looked directly at me as I told him a bit about my life then. He didn't interrupt. He simply sat and listened as Vecchio stood by the park bench, arms folded, staring at the two of us as I finished talking.

"You know what?" John Lindsay said to me.

"What?" I asked.

"You've got to go home," he told me. "Your kids are far more important than anything I'm doing or might do."

So I did. And I never forgot the time he took, less than ten minutes, on that long gone spring day to listen and give me some advice that I have never, not once, regretted taking.■

Mike Barnicle, a veteran print and broadcast journalist, has been a columnist for the New York Daily News, *the* Boston Globe *and the* Boston Herald.

Jonathan Barnett

It was 1967. Don Elliott, the Planning Commissioner, had come down from his office to the Urban Design Group space on the floor below. "I have a problem for you guys," he said, "and you have a meeting with the Mayor at 10:00 a.m. the day after tomorrow to advise him on what to do about it."

Powerful real-estate interests had proposed rezoning a six-block area on the Upper East Side. The blocks were zoned for apartment buildings on the avenue frontages, and town houses or smaller buildings on the side streets in between. The developers had a simple proposal: Be consistent. Make the entire blocks apartment-house zoning, or, in zoning-speak, change the mid-blocks from R6 to R10.

We knew that, if adopted, this seemingly simple technical change would be a precedent that could be applied all over the city, where most avenues had a higher zoning than the side streets.

In our tiny Urban Design Group meeting room, Jaque Robertson, Richard Weinstein and I devised a strategy.

We would present three visions of the area to the Mayor—the way it looked now, the way it would look if all the development permitted by the current zoning occurred, and what it would be like if the proposed zoning change was enacted and all the newly permitted towers were built.

Today, we can illustrate the alternatives in 3–D on a computer, but back then such simulations had to be made with photographs that were turned into collages by hand. The police department agreed to let our contracted photographer, Jerry Spearman, take pictures of the Upper East Side area under consideration from helicopters.

On the morning we were to meet with the Mayor, I went up to Jerry

Spearman's studio in Washington Heights where he and two of our junior staff had spent much of the night cutting and pasting bits of photographs for the illustrations that accompanied the scenarios. Jerry had rephotographed the results. The three photos, still a little damp from the darkroom chemicals, were mounted on cardboard and I took them down to City Hall.

Jaque, Richard, and I sat on the long couch in the Mayor's office, while he pulled up an armchair, the position of power. I took the three photos and arranged them on the table facing the Mayor.

Lindsay looked at the photos and said: "OK, I see what you are telling me. We won't do it."

There had been no need for our carefully prepared presentation. The whole meeting took less than five minutes.

John Lindsay's understanding of planning and design, and his willingness to give political cover to Donald Elliott and his team, made possible many initiatives that gave us the New York we know today. The rezoning of SoHo, then a derelict industrial area; Midtown Manhattan's special zoning districts, the height limits in Brooklyn Heights that fortify the neighborhood's landmark designation, redevelopment plans now realized for downtown Brooklyn and downtown Jamaica, housing developments that reinforce rather than consume communities, and a planning process that incorporates the participation of local residents were all innovations and part of John Lindsay's legacy.■

Jonathan Barnett is an emeritus professor of city and regional planning and the former director of the urban design program at the University of Pennsylvania.

Cornelius "Neil" Behan

I was a Captain in the NYC Police Department when John Lindsay was elected Mayor. His new Police Commissioner Howard Leary, a generally remote loner, had big plans to modernize the department. Soon after, he asked me to become head of the Planning Division and to aggressively propose reforms, which I happily accept.

Leary prodded for greater innovations, and skillfully pushed them forward over considerable bureaucratic resistance.

Lindsay and his young staff were deeply involved. At first, Lindsay's whiz kids seemed to frenetically race from one issue to another and felt like pains in the ass. But it soon became clear that they were serious minded and effective in managing change, and the Mayor enthusiastically provided us with resources and the talent of his Budget Bureau staff.

One key tool the Mayor provided was the Rand Institute, which he and Budget Director Fred Hayes had attracted to New York. RAND gave the NYPD an unprecedented analytical capacity. One of Rand's most significant projects was an extensive study of the work of the hide-bound Detective Bureau, which hadn't changed its methods in decades.

The resulting reform effort caused a storm within the ranks—Leary stood firm, but the reaction showed how contentious big changes could be.

Sometimes these issues became personal. I had developed a plan to convert an old section of the communications complex into a modern Command and Control Center. But the department's head of administration was dead set against this intrusion. My break came when he had an extended leave for a family illness and we moved rapidly to rip up the floor. Now there was no going back and we built a modern command facility as the future base of operations for any kind of crisis or disorder. It has been well used and appreciated ever since.

The Command Center, made possible by the Mayor's extensive financial backing, enabled us to transform the department's infrastructure. Most important, perhaps, was the new, state-of-the-art 911 Communications Center. As the Mayor promised in his campaign, every officer on patrol would have a miniature walkie-talkie.

With Rand's analysis of staffing levels measured against need, it became clear that the Department's historic three shifts were too rigid and did not reflect the hours of highest crime. We worked on the problem with the Mayor's staff and went to Albany in 1969 to lobby for a Fourth Platoon, a reform the City had been seeking since 1908 and which the police unions always blocked.

But this time, the Mayor made it a major issue and succeeded. Police could now be assigned to a fourth platoon during the high crime hours of 6 pm to 2 am, dramatically and efficiently increasing coverage as needed.

I admired Mayor Lindsay and considered him a friend of both mine and the Department.■

Cornelius J. Behan *served for 41 years in the New York City Police Department, retiring in 1977 to become Chief of the Baltimore County Police, where he served for 17 years. He then represented the Major Cities Chiefs of Police in Washington for 10 years.*

Carol Bellamy

I left a law firm to work in the Lindsay Administration's mental health agency in its second term under Gordon Chase, who oversaw all health services. Gordon had attracted a talented team with unusually strong management skills and achievements. But having previously worked in the White House on foreign policy, he had no public health credentials. His appointment was extremely controversial with the profession's establishment. The Mayor, however, had become frustrated with the caution of healthcare veterans he recruited earlier for their reluctance to challenge long-standing practices. He wanted to bring in outsiders who would not be intimidated and examine those practices with fresh eyes, people capable of questioning old assumptions and forcing innovation. Unfazed by the opposition, Mayor Lindsay gave Gordon his full backing.

Together, Gordon and the Mayor focused on under-attended areas of need, like lead poisoning, methadone maintenance and prison health.

One of their major projects was the creation of an independent corporation to take over the ownership and operation of the City's vast municipal hospital system, an effort led by Gordon's deputy and general counsel Gerry Frug. The corporation was a pace-setting attempt to eliminate the bureaucratic red-tape and legal constraints on hiring and contracting imposed on city agencies, to increase federal reimbursements and enhance hospital financing capabilities.

Another of Gordon's most significant initiatives was taking over the prison health system, which had been run by the Department of Corrections with limited staff, scant resources, little professional healthcare or administrative talent and no independence. Gordon contracted with Montefiore, linking a major hospital to the prison system for the first time, to provide better, faster and more comprehensive care. Treating prisoners, especially those with serious conditions—both physical and mental—was a complicated challenge that had long gone insufficiently addressed. Prisoners did not have much public sympathy or support, making this one of the most difficult programs mounted by Gordon and our team. But we set a new, much higher standard for care, a source of great pride for the agency.

In mental health, where I was based, Barbara Blum was a quiet leader of enormous knowledge and insight. Barbara and her deputy Bob Horner set out to monitor and measure the quality of services provided by private contractors, an early attempt at devising metrics to provide some accountability for performance.

Those years were the start of my career in public service, soon followed by election to the State Senate and then City Council President. The Lindsay Administration set a standard for energetic government that attracted enormously dedicated and fearless talent. Their accomplishments were significant and many went on to serve and contribute elsewhere in public life.■

Carol Bellamy has served as Director of the Peace Corps under President Clinton, and as Executive Director of the United Nations Children's Fund (UNICEF). She has been President and Chief Executive Officer of World Learning and a Fellow of the Kennedy School of Government's Institute of Politics at Harvard University.

Barry Benape

When John Lindsay was elected I looked forward to New York City turning a corner and recovering from an image of a crime-ridden city that aspiring white people were leaving for the hinterlands as fast as their autos and mortgages could carry them. Mayor Lindsay took effective measures to reverse what was then referred to as "white flight" and became our leading spokesman for the intrinsic values that this gracious metropolis embodied in its rich urban fabric, its extraordinary parks, museums, theaters and waterfront and above all, its people. He had faith in the dedication, good will and optimism of its citizens.

He rolled up his sleeves and walked the streets of Harlem and spoke with people on the sidewalks, listening to their grievances and suggestions. He worked hard to obtain federal and state money to build needed housing, not only new buildings, but to retrofit the existing housing stock, reinforcing the best of what local communities had to offer—rows of handsome humanly-scaled brownstones on tree-lined sidewalks. Similarly he addressed the economic needs of central area businesses.

One of his exciting initiatives was to close Madison Avenue on occasion, which displaced the roar of traffic with thousands of quiet footfalls of walkers who, for the first time, could appreciate the beauty of the city under the cloud-studded blue skies overhead rather than the grey plumes of auto exhausts in our faces. I looked north from Murray Hill over the brown fuzzy sea of heads now laid bare because President John Kennedy changed America's dress code, giving us the informality of the new age.

John Lindsay appointed Tom Hoving as his Parks Commissioner to realize the great potential of parks to bring enjoyment. "Hoving Happenings" became the norm for Central Park where residents could walk in and enjoy each other's company without the fear of crime. Parks became places to have fun and enjoy natural surroundings. In 1966, Manhattan and

Brooklyn residents formed Transportation Alternatives whose advocacy led the way to ridding the Central Park and Prospect Drives of noisy, polluting and unsafe auto traffic so that walker and bicyclist could once more enjoy these great 19th century parks designed by Calvert Vaux and Frederick Law Olmsted. The Mayor and Commissioner Hoving supported and extended these closings.

Later on, Commissioner Hoving asked me to prepare alternative plans for a Staten Island expressway which Robert Moses had designed for the pleasure and speed of motorists, but would impose a barrier to waterfront access for park users. When we moved the road inland the park could present a natural storm-resistant face to the sea.

John Lindsay embodied an "espirit de ville" which recognized the essential values of urban living, the true historic beauty of our architecture and streets. He brought out the best in the citizens of New York, reinforcing their best instincts and realizing their talents. He was dedicated to the welfare of the city, not only during his tenure as Mayor, but previously as a congressman. He was a true proponent of healthy urbanism.■

*Urban planner **Barry Benape**, founder of the Greenmarket movement in New York City, which he led for decades, is now a writer and community activist. He is the father of former Parks Commissioner Adrian Benape.*

Samuel "Sandy" Berger

John Lindsay, a Republican for most of his political career, confronted a crowded field for the 1972 Democratic Presidential nomination that included such imposing party veterans as Edmund Muskie, George McGovern, Henry Jackson, George Wallace, Hubert Humphrey, Eugene McCarthy and Wilbur Mills. The federal government's role in the life of cities was a significant issue, but the divisive Vietnam War dominated the debate.

Lindsay's brain trust saw a path to the nomination for him. JVL's credentials included his fierce opposition to the War and his unique standing as a national spokesman for urban America. Lindsay also had charisma and a respected record for government innovation at City Hall. His advisers hoped that Lindsay could make a mark in the early primaries and break out as the leader in Florida, where many transplanted New Yorkers voted.

Bob Shrum, Lindsay's speechwriter, was leaving to work for Senator Muskie's campaign. To ease his exit, Bob recommended me to Jay Kriegel as a replacement. I'd never met the Mayor. My only experience writing speeches had been drafting Senator Harold Hughes' announcement that his quixotic bid for the presidency was over. At the urging of my close friend Eli Segal, a rising Democratic political operative, I'd surrendered a federal judicial clerkship to work for the admirable Iowa senator and was now available for employment.

After being hired, I sat in a small office next to Jay's grinding out speeches. Before long, I found myself travelling on the Lindsay campaign plane with Dick Aurelio, the field commander, Dave Garth, the strategist, and Gordon Davis, the other speechwriter. Sid Davidoff operated the campaign's machinery and made things happen.

On a trip to Florida, I was looking for a subject to write about for a rally in Tampa. Our advance man there provided us with a memorandum that began; "The shrimp are dying in Scambia Bay." I thought that would be a great title for a book on the mindless hysteria of political campaigns. Lindsay campaigned tirelessly there but George Wallace carried the essentially rural, conservative state with 47% of the vote in a seven-person race. John Lindsay finished a distant fifth. Dade County, where former New Yorkers settled in greatest numbers, was atypical of Florida, a major miscalculation by Lindsay's political handlers. When the Mayor lost the Wisconsin contest, I drafted his concession speech, my second such address of the cycle. What I recall most vividly of that primary was bowling with Dick Aurelio, long, enjoyable dinners and lots of laughter.

After returning to New York for a few weeks, I migrated to Senator McGovern's campaign. That November I helped draft yet a third concession speech on Election Night, a record for a speechwriter in an American presidential campaign that continues to stand unchallenged.

Mayor Lindsay was an articulate, often eloquent and always passionate campaigner for the causes that mattered to him—race, cities, the War, fresh ideas about using government creatively to solve people's problems. This unsuccessful political journey was a brief, but noble chapter in his public life.■

Samuel "Sandy" Berger's federal service included serving as Deputy Director of Planning at the Department of State during the Carter Administration and as Assistant to the President for National Security Affairs during the Clinton Administration. He was also a partner in the law firm of Hogan & Hartson and is co-chairman, along with former Secretary of State Madeline Albright, of Albright-Stonebridge, an international advisory group.

Laura Blackburne

My first assignment in the Lindsay Administration was working with Carl Irish on the Mayor's Education Task Force. We were the "trouble shooters" in the schools and neighborhoods during the turbulent Ocean Hill Brownsville experiment.

I became an Assistant to the Mayor in his second term. My area was Health and Hospitals. The Mayor visited the City hospitals regularly and I often accompanied him. My most memorable visit was to a facility on Staten Island. The Mayor and I travelled there by helicopter. Knowing that I had never been on one before, he instructed the pilot to make some "dramatic" dips and turns that, of course, terrified me. He had a few good laughs as I screamed and turned pale, or as pale as I could. That amused him even more.

I remember most vividly his concerns about the hospitalized children. One young patient in a wheel chair, no more than five or six years old, asked him why he decided to be a Mayor and not a doctor, or at least an ambulance driver. The Mayor smiled and said he could not drive well or fast enough to be an ambulance driver.

For all the difficult issues and turmoil we faced those years he always remained positive and upbeat, both in the public eye and inside City Hall. He made our staff feel like we were an important part of his "family," not just people who worked for him.

Those were often hard times for the city in so many ways but Mayor Lindsay was optimistic that we could do better for all New Yorkers, not just the privileged few.■

*Having retired as a NY State Supreme Court Judge, **Laura Blackburne** serves as Chairman and Publisher of 106-year-old Crisis Magazine, the official publication of the NAACP, and hosts a weekly radio talk show.*

Robert Blum

In 1965 I was one of three borough coordinators for the Lindsay mayoral campaign in Brooklyn. After his election, in addition to my government duties, I informally patrolled Brooklyn issues for the Mayor for the next few years.

One Saturday afternoon in 1966, JVL called me at my office. "Bay Ridge has more residents of Norwegian descent than any city in the United States," he said. "So?" I replied. "The King of Norway is coming here in a few weeks," he advised, "and I want to hold a party for him in Brooklyn, not in the usual Manhattan places. I want to do it at the Brooklyn Museum and invite Brooklynites…from Bay Ridge, of course, but from all over the borough as well. And I want the invitees to be people who count for something meaningful there."

And so we did. It was a grand party with perhaps one hundred people on hand at the Mayor's personal invitation. Everyone had a grand time, especially Mayor Lindsay and the King of Norway.

—

Eventually, I became involved in creating the Department of Consumer Affairs, an idea that originated not with JVL, but in a proposal from my law school classmate, then Queens Councilman Edward Sadowsky. The Administration adopted the idea enthusiastically.

My late wife Barbara (then Assistant Administrator of Special Services for Children) suggested former Miss America and television personality Bess Myerson as a possible commissioner for the new agency. Bob Sweet and the Mayor thought she would be a fine appointment, but JVL wondered if Bess would serve. She had never held a government post before.

Although the Mayor hadn't met Bess he did know her husband Arnold

Grant, a prominent lawyer. He phoned Grant to ask if he thought Bess would be interested in joining the Administration. Grant recoiled and said he hoped she would not. John pleaded, "But Arnold, you wouldn't be losing a wife. You'd be gaining a city!" Grant countered, "But John, my wife is in a hell of a lot better shape than your city."

Bess did accept the Mayor's invitation and her tenure was a great success.■

Robert Blum headed the litigation practice at Bangser Klein Rocca & Blum before becoming a Bureau Chief in the NYS Attorney General's Office. He has sat on the State's Office of Court Administration's Advisory Committee on Civil Practice since 1984.

Michael Blumenfeld

Here are my three favorite memories of those years: JVL swore me in as Deputy Health Services Administrator in the spring of 1970. My wife Cathy stood very close at his side. After I took the oath, she whispered in my ear, not "Congratulations, dear" or anything like it, but, "Y'know, he's like steel from the waist up."

—

On my first day at HSA, I was making the rounds to introduce myself. An Assistant Commissioner asked what I planned to do about smoking. He was wondering, of course, what sort of new anti-smoking program I might have in mind. Much to his surprise, I replied, "I plan to give it up as soon as I lose 15 pounds."

—

Barry Gottehrer assigned me to serve on the board of a Brooklyn comunity action agency. At one of his meetings, a citizen suddenly began waving a pistol around to show how strongly he felt about an issue we were discussing. I exited to safety out of a bathroom window rather than wait to see what he might do next.■

Michael Blumenfeld was Deputy Health Services Administrator for Public Affairs and Education where he oversaw city government's implementation of New York State's newly liberalized abortion law. He subsequently held administrative posts at Harvard and New York Universities and managerial posts in the public utility and health insurance industries. As Assistant Secretary of the Army (Civil Works) in the Carter Administration, he was involved in matters concerning the Panama Canal, running that facility from the time the treaties took effect until its turnover to Panama in 1999. He is retired and lives in Lawrence, Kansas.

Lois Bernstein Bohm

I served in the Department of Consumer Affairs' Office of Public Information when Bess Myerson Grant was commissioner of this newly formed agency. No other major American city had created such a unit. As the first Earth Day approached, we had no money in our budget for this massive event aimed at raising public awareness of environmental concerns. Naomi Feigelson, leader of our five-member staff, found a way around that obstacle. "Let's just do the posters ourselves and make the best display we can." We bought oak tag and magic markers and got to work. We loved doing our part to make this far-sighted project a success. Earth Day made a deep impression on New York City and the nation, as we expected. We were so proud to be members of the Lindsay Administration and seize the opportunity for educating the public that this unique occasion provided.

Another memory: Once I splurged on a cab to Gracie Mansion, but absent-mindedly left my wallet in it. As I walked into the front hallway I realized what I had done. I found Joan Gregory in the kitchen and, in a panic, told her that I remembered the driver's name but not the hack number, although it being a Yellow cab would narrow my search. Joan announced, sarcastically, "Lois, all cabs are now yellow. JVL just changed the code and made them so."■

*In addition to her work in the Department of Consumer Affairs and Health Services Administration Offices of Public Information, **Lois Bernstein Bohm** was also an aide to Assistant to the Mayor Tony Smith, who dealt with the uniformed services. She was an aide in Hugh Carey's first successful campaign for Governor of New York State, and then had careers in public relations and in the moving and storage industry.*

Leon Botstein

I did not know John Lindsay when he was Mayor, but he was immensely helpful to me at Bard College years later, opening doors and showing a kind and avuncular empathy for our efforts to build the institution. The Mayor's generosity of spirit, especially to young ambitious people, was always exceptional.

My unforgettable encounter with John Lindsay while a member of the first class of the Sloan Foundation's Urban Fellows in 1969 epitomized the Mayor's grace and uncanny intuition of how to react to an awkward circumstance.

The Mayor gave an intimate dinner at a midtown hotel for the few Urban Fellows working in his office. I was 22 and had very little experience drinking alcohol. A colleague ordered a drink with the odd name Rob Roy. In imitation of her obviously sophisticated tastes, I ordered one. It seemed harmless and was very tasty.

By the time dinner was served, though, I was having difficulty walking. I don't remember how many Rob Roys I had consumed, but still managed to sit down. When that tipsy, one can delude oneself that nobody notices. Much to my horror, every fellow had to get up and give a talk about what he or she was doing in city government. As the only graduate student, I was asked to speak first. I got up, clutched the table, and thought that I was exceptionally successful at hiding my state. After all, this was my introduction to the Mayor and I was intent on making a good impression. When I was done, I realized it would be best for me to exit the scene before anything terrible occurred.

I turned around gingerly and made my way through what I thought was a very narrow doorway, through the bar, and yet another very narrow doorway to the hallway where the bathrooms were. As I later discovered, both those doors were massive double-sided sliding door apertures. I thought

I had inconspicuously and discreetly left the scene, feeling triumphantly that I had fooled everyone and managed to walk in a straight line through these two truly narrow doors to the restrooms. What I did not realize is that everyone, including the Mayor, watched this spectacular exit in silence until I vanished from sight.

The next thing I remember was that I was lying on the floor of the bathroom looking up. Standing over me was the Mayor. As I opened my eyes in a somewhat less compromised mental state, he said in a very kind voice, "I just wanted to make sure before I left that you are okay and that you'll be able to get home safely." He had come to see how I was doing. I did not have the strength to get up. I was mortified: this was my introduction to the Mayor of the City of New York and would most likely be the most memorable impression I would make on him.

I will never forget his gracious, non-judgmental, forgiving and bemused presence. How many individuals of power and fame retain a capacity for the simple human gesture that carries no shred of self-interest?■

Leon Botstein has been President of Bard College for forty years and Musical Director and Principal Conductor of the American Symphony Orchestra.

Anthony Bouza

Napoleon Bonaparte was asked which soldiers make the best generals. "Lucky ones" he answered.

John V. Lindsay was probably New York's unluckiest Mayor. In his first moment in office Michael J. Quill threw him a devastating transit strike. During his 1972 presidential campaign an airplane trailer reading "Lindsay spells Tsuris (trouble)" appeared over Miami beaches, where New York's Jews vacationed. But he got lucky enough to win two mayoral elections with just over 40% of the vote because he drew hapless Democratic and strong Republican rivals.

I was a centrally positioned fly on the wall as an NYPD Captain and the key Chief's aide. I swelled with the years, ending as the Bronx Borough Commander.

When asked to write an essay on those years, I thought it the biggest compliment I've ever been paid.

Lindsay was a patrician, yet terminally decent, honest, and caring. The times, though, were hard.

Lindsay embraced gay rights. He directed us to stop arresting gays long before the Stonewall uprising, which can best be understood as the response of an incompetent police commander skillfully exploited by gay leaders.

Lindsay employed the century's worst police commissioner, Howard R. Leary, formerly of Philadelphia. Then he hired the man who I believe to be the finest police executive the U.S. has ever seen—Patrick V. Murphy. He lasted only 30 months, but what months they were!

Murphy was an unbelievably brave reformer who took on issues all of us had long accepted as hopeless—including the Serpico mess. He became my model although I could only aspire to his attainments.

Lindsay championed civil rights, adopted the Black cause and insisted that the NYPD respond to its grievances substantively.

He created a review board—chaired by Franklin Thomas—to examine the cases of minority applicants rejected by the department.

Mostly black and Hispanic, those rejectees often presented less than perfect military records (despite Honorable Discharges). Some had fathered children out of wedlock (despite assuming full responsibility for the child). Others had committed minor traffic violations or experienced job problems of a not very serious nature.

One candidate was flunked because he'd worn a slave bracelet to an interview. I asked what this meant. The investigator said it signified sodomy—a crime. "Oh, and do we ask heterosexuals about the inventive things they practice in their conjugal beds?" "Well, no," was the reluctant response. The slave was hired. And we had no closeted gays in the ranks, right?

Lindsay was driven by that simplest of all formulas in public life—do the right thing!

The late sixties and the early seventies were a fraught period. Nineteen sixty-eight was a seminal year—Robert Kennedy and Martin Luther King, Jr. assassinated, urban riots, the Columbia University bust (a huge police mistake). The nation reeled. Lindsay and his cohort of brilliant aides soldiered on.

Lindsay presided over all of it with grace, style, elegance and unwavering faith in racial, social and economic justice. His was a Kennedy-esque approach without the womanizing or Hollywood bling. The man had character.

It was a unique privilege to have served as a spear-carrier in the Lindsay opera.■

Anthony Bouza served as Bronx Borough Commander in the NYPD, and then as Chief of Police of Minneapolis for nine years (1980-89).

Gale Brewer

In 1972 I was a part-time student at Columbia University's School of General Studies, and one of my political science classmates was the brilliant, beautiful Micho Fernandez, who gave me my first big break. Micho worked at the Parks Department and told me about a job opening there. Next thing I knew, I was a Publicity Assistant in the press office.

Each morning I bicycled to the Arsenal, the agency's headquarters. August Heckscher was Commissioner and Ted Mastroianni his Deputy. Patrick Dunn was my boss. The staff—a mix of long-term city employees and newcomers who had been hired because they worked on Lindsay's unsuccessful presidential campaign—was uniformly pleasant. Even then, I could tell the difference!

My main business was press releases, but we also set up the first telephone number that people could call to find out about free park events. One day I accompanied Commissioner Heckscher—sporting his trademark bow tie —to roll out the new Parks and Recreation "leaf" logo.

On Monday mornings I represented Parks at the Mayor's all-agency meeting in the Blue Room on gang activity. It was run by Carl Irish of the Youth Services Agency. He was charismatic and street-smart in a Brooklyn sort of way, knew all the agencies and criminal justice. He made a lasting impression on me about the kind of smarts it takes to run the city.

I loved my time at Parks. These days I'm often at meetings in the same rooms and offices where I worked in 1972. I still think of Micho and the whole Lindsay crowd, and of all I owe them for opening the door.■

Gale Brewer is Manhattan Borough President. She served as a member of the City Council for 12 years.

Stanley Brezenoff

It's late 1966 and I'm unemployed because of my civil rights arrest record as a Brooklyn CORE activist and my work on the school boycotts as operations leader for the Reverend Milton Galamison. I couldn't possibly hope to get a decent job. Even the Police Department's Hack Bureau told me not to bother applying for a taxi driver license.

Enter the Lindsay Administration and its creative approach to engaging the Great Society's War on Poverty. The Mayor recruited Mike Sviridoff to reorganize and re-energize social and community development programs and services. Together, they created the Human Resources Administration, a super agency to oversee and coordinate these efforts.

The Community Development Agency was established to take on the direct federal OEO community organizing and empowerment responsibility. George Nicolau, a colleague of Sargent Shriver's, was its leader. George, in turn, tapped Frank Espada, a well known and accomplished leader of the Puerto Rican community, to head the critical organizing effort in neighborhood development corporations and health centers. Frank had founded and led East New York Action. Having come from East New York myself I had been part of several Brooklyn CORE's collaborative efforts with Frank's organization.

Frank offered me a job on one of his teams of organizers and representatives. Although Commissioner Nicolau agreed, the city's Personnel Department couldn't authorize the hire because of my arrest record. Espada and Nicolau were furious and vowed to fight and overturn the agency's decision.

They assigned the redoubtable and resourceful Siobhan Oppenheimer, Nicolau's special assistant, to the task. She besieged Personnel to no avail and then approached City Hall. Siobhan found lots of sympathy for me there but said no one seemed willing or able to override Personnel and get me hired. Undaunted, she seized the challenge and figured out a way to approach the Mayor directly. John Lindsay's response, as she reported it, was "Nonsense... exactly the kind of individual we need and want in the anti-poverty program."

This is not an epic tale, but a true one that illustrates the idealism that always characterized JVL. ∎

*Mayor Bill deBlasio appointed **Stanley Brezenoff** Chairman of the New York City Board of Corrections. He was Chief Operating Officer of Continuum Health Partners and has served as Executive Director of the Port Authority of New York and New Jersey and First Deputy Mayor under Mayor Ed Koch.*

Steven Brill

I was known around City Hall as "Jay's Jay." Although I didn't know it at the time, it was not meant as a compliment. Other than Tom Morgan referring to me as "a miniature poodle yapping at my heels" when I had the temerity to argue when he dared to edit my attempts at drafting speeches for JVL, I thought I was a nice, if ambitious, deferential kid.

In fact, I remember telling my then-fiancé, now wife, Cynthia, about the great relationship I had established with a young, tough but polite detective who had been assigned to work with me on a project I had dreamed up called the "Merchant's Protection Program." I had really developed a great camaraderie with him, I told her.

The idea for the merchants' program had grown out of the plight of my father, who owned a small liquor store on Chambers Street near City Hall. He had been held up at gunpoint several times, and—in part because I had worked behind the counter as a teen—I had a real sense of his terror and his helplessness. So I had suggested that the City do a pilot program of supplying silent hold-up alarms to small retailers. The Mayor and Jay liked the idea and before long we were planning installations along Tremont Avenue, Astoria Boulevard, and Chambers Street, among other places.

Along with a kid from McKinsey, this young police detective and I ran the project. Again, I was sure that the detective liked me—that my people skills were as awesome as my vision for wiping out retail stick-ups.

So imagine my surprise years later when I was running Court TV and came down to the studio to thank Ray Kelly for appearing as a guest. After he finished and we walked off the set, Ray turned to me and said, "You don't remember me, do you?"

I looked at him blankly.

"You're the reason I went to law school," he continued.

Huh?

Kelly went on to explain that he was the detective who had had the bad luck to be assigned to me for the hold-up alarms program. And, as he put it, "I'd come home every night and tell my wife that I was taking orders from this arrogant asshole who somehow was going to Yale Law School while working for the Mayor, and who didn't know a damn thing, but was ordering me around. I couldn't stand it."

"So my wife said," Kelly continued, "'Well, you should go to law school, too, so you don't have to put up with that.' You actually played a big role at some point in making me ambitious," Kelly added.

Nice to know I had such a positive impact on the City. ■

Steven Brill, a lawyer, journalist and entrepreneur, was co-founder of The American Lawyer, creator of Court TV (now TruTV) and publisher of Brill's Content. He has written books on such subjects as public education, healthcare spending and America's response to the 9/11 terrorist attacks.

Richard Brown

I was the City's Albany legislative representative during the early 1970s. *The New York Times'* early edition almost always included a story about something going on in the state capitol. Each evening, after the paper hit the newsstands, Jay Kriegel and I discussed how we could get the Lindsay Administration's point of view on the matter into the following morning's *Times*.

Before leaving for a vacation, Jay instructed the Mayor to call me in Albany each night and "read Dick Brown the *Times*." JVL took him literally. John Lindsay got as far as the Sports section, having read most of the newspaper to me over the telephone as I struggled to stay awake. Finally, I had to tell the Mayor that I had heard enough.■

After serving as the city's Albany Legislative Representative, **Richard Brown** *was a Judge and Supervising Judge of the Brooklyn Criminal Court, a Justice of the Supreme Court in Queens, Counsel to Governor Hugh Carey and an Associate Justice in the Appellate Division's Second Department. He has been District Attorney of Queens County since 1991.*

Christopher Buckley

My good friend Jay Kriegel, being a good liberal and as such, a champion of diversity, asked me to contribute a few lines to this omnium-gatherum of tributes to his former boss and patron, John V. Lindsay.

I do so happily, though alas I don't have much to offer, other than my memories of the 1965 New York City mayoral campaign, to which my father, William F. Buckley, Jr. contributed a heaping helping of *panache, elan* and *je ne sais quoi*, as we of the Mandarin conservative persuasion say.

This November marks the—good heavens—50th anniversary of that contest. To mark the occasion, my father's book, *The Unmaking of a Mayor*, is being reissued, with a foreward by WFB's campaign manager, Neal Freeman, and an afterword by Joe Scarborough.

"Unmaking" is one of WFB's most durable books. Joe Klein, *Time's* political correspondent and the (no longer anonymous) author of the excellent novel, *Primary Colors*, once told WFB that he thought it one of the best books ever written on American politics. That's high praise from a real pro (and no conservative). Over the years, I've heard a lot of smart politicos from across the spectrum say the same thing.

My father said many smart and memorable things over the course of his career, but "Demand a recount" surely remains his most famous. The occasion was the press conference announcing his candidacy when he was asked what he would do in the unlikely, indeed inconceivable, event that he won. For his answer, see above.

He said something else during the campaign that remains one of his most durable utterances. In "Unmaking," he slightly altered the original version: "I would rather be governed by the first 2,000 names in the Long

Island City phone book than by the faculty of Harvard." In the book, he changed that to "the Boston phone book." I wonder if he did that to pique his friend John Kenneth Galbraith. I like to think he did.

They are all gone, now, the combatants of that lively contest of 1965. How good it is that Jay has brought his man back into the ring. Those were fun times, and worth the celebrating.■

Christopher Buckley *is a novelist, essayist, humorist, critic and magazine editor. He has also been a merchant seaman and a White House speech-writer during President George H. W. Bush's administration. He wrote* Losing Mum and Pup: A Memoir *(2009) about his late parents and his next novel* The Rebel Master *will be published in December 2015.*

Bob Carroll

Icame to the Lindsay Administration in 1968 from Florida where I had served as the first Director of Minority Relations for the Florida Democratic Executive Committee. Jeff Greenfield and David Garth recruited me. I eventually became Deputy Commissioner of the Department of Social Services.

At that time New York's welfare caseload was skyrocketing, eventually hitting one million recipients. Media attention was intense. The *Daily News* wanted to run a contest honoring the one millionth "client" who came onto the welfare rolls.

Broadcast reporters would start placing early morning calls to Mayor Lindsay at City Hall and Gracie Mansion around 4:30 a.m., hoping to get a quote for their "Drive Time" segments.

Dick Aurelio called and said, "Bob, the Mayor is upset. We have to do something about these early morning calls. You know the issues better than most of us. You have to handle these calls." My wife and I took those calls for about six months until the press seemed to tire of daily welfare stories. John was delighted. But those reporters kept my telephone numbers handy and began to call about other issues. I wound up being a press source for years, even while serving as a vice president at CCNY and working in Congress.

Several of us took leaves of absence from the government to help John in his 1972 Presidential bid. Sid Davidoff was the Florida coordinator and I was his deputy. Campaigning in that state was difficult. In New York City, you often campaigned vertically in high-rise buildings. In Florida, which seemed about a thousand miles long and relatively flat from the Keys to the Pan Handle, you campaigned horizontally. Driving long distances was very time consuming and we campaigned mostly on weekends because John was a full-time Mayor during the week.

John earned devoted support when he walked the streets of minority communities like Harlem and Bed-Stuyvesant during periods of unrest. It was great political theatre. I suggested that he visit Florida's Black churches on Sunday mornings before he headed back to the city. He was well-known in those communities and favorably regarded.

Black ministers and leaders I approached with the idea were very receptive. According to the format, John would make a brief speech, then request a spiritual from the choir and leave. Gordon Davis and I taught John two spirituals ("Amazing Grace" and "Precious Lord"). The churchgoers were usually surprised at John's knowledgeable suggestions and expressed their approval by murmuring and patting their feet. They did not expect this tall, good-looking, white guy from New York to know these songs.

At first, John was not comfortable sitting in the pulpit. Gordon Davis and I coached him on the ritualistic requirements of clapping his hands and positioning his feet. When seated, you cross your legs and clap your hands. Your toes are pointed upward. When your hands come together, your toes are pointed downward. The audience in the pews easily detects any awkwardness. In the end John enjoyed the activity and his movements were "*a la* James Brown." The crowd was delighted.

We always left the churches to vigorous applause and foot stomping. John was always upbeat.■

Bob Carroll *served in New York's municipal government, as Vice President for Communications and Public Affairs at the City College of New York and on Capitol Hill.*

Maurice "Mickey" Carroll

I remember what a delight Mayor Lindsay was at the Inner Circle shows. I entered the organization—an association of New York City journalists that holds an annual dinner benefit to support worthy causes—without any idea of what it was. That's how things happened in Room 9, where the City Hall press corps is billeted. The traditionalist reporters of the day, every bit as hide-bound as the "power brokers" JVL ousted, didn't want to abandon the stage to the Mayor. Wagner, as I understand, would stand amid the reporters and give a talk following the journalists' show, a satire of what was going on in municipal government that year.

Harold Harris, the Inner Circle's president, had to convene a pre-show meeting and take a vote to decide whether to let Mayor Lindsay go on alone. They did, of course, and, wearing a top hat and sporting a cane (both now on display in a case in Room 9), he brought the house down.

—

One of the Mayor's customs was to host a Christmas party for (all male) Room 9. After one of these parties, held upstairs in Sardi's, he led a very tipsy crowd out onto 43rd Street in the dark of night. Hand out-stretched, he accosted a couple of tourists and announced, "Hi, I'm the Mayor." Fearing a mugging, they recoiled.

The crowd, including Lindsay, went to some Greek saloon where they danced, handkerchiefs stuck in belts, the whole shebang, or so I'm told. Prudently, I'd gone home to New Jersey. Someone telephoned the Associated Press and said, "Mayor Lindsay is here dancing with a bunch of drunken businessmen." Jimmy Ryan was on the AP desk. "We'll get right on it," he said. But we protected our own, including our friend the Mayor. At that point, the big story stopped.

—

When Mrs. Lindsay was asked at a lunch why the Mayor had endorsed Spiro Agnew for vice president, she said, "Politics make strange bedfellows."

And what, I asked Tom Morgan, the press secretary, did the Mayor say?

"Bedfellows make strange politics," Tom replied and, in my best wise-guy mode, I said, "Oh, Mayor Lindsay said through a spokesman…"

"No," said Tom. "Give the guy credit. I didn't make this up. He said it himself."

—

An addendum about the pleasures of working for *Times* editors: When I used that anecdote in an end-of-his-term story, some helpful editor used it, but, in the interest of saving space, I guess, chopped out the last line.∎

Maurice "Mickey" Carroll is Assistant Director of the Quinnipiac University Poll. During a 40-year career, he has been a political writer and columnist for several newspapers, including The New York Times, *News-day,* The New York Post, *the* Passaic Herald-News *and the* Newark Star-Ledger.

Naomi Feigelson Chase

I ran the Lindsay mayoral campaign's Negative Research Office for Barry Gottehrer.

Following the election, I was appointed Director of Public Information for the Department of Consumer Affairs. Bess Myerson, our commissioner, posted many accomplishments and led the Lindsay Administration's introduction of unit pricing in stores, a practice that spread from NYC to the rest of the country. I recall sitting with Bess in her office on a weekend when she had six-packs of Coca-Cola with bottles of all available sizes on her desk and elsewhere. She called her deputy Henry Stern at home and had him give her the unit pricing of every type.

I next served as Director of Public Information for the Health Services Administration, whose jurisdiction included the Department of Health, the Health and Hospitals Corporation and the Addiction Services Agency. Gordon Chase was the Administrator.

When I arrived at HSA to take the job, Mike Blumenteld, my predecessor, warned me that the minute Gordon finished a project, he'd pull out his lined yellow pad and say, "What's next?" Gordon was so completely absorbed in his work that his secretary would sometimes have to cut loose threads off his suit as he was leaving his office for a meeting.

Gordon Chase's successful management of the Lindsay Administration's abortion program provided major evidence for the US Supreme Court's decision in Roe v. Wade. Under his leadership, New York City's programs in such areas as tuberculosis prevention and treatment, lead paint poisoning, children's health, mental health, and methadone maintenance made the Lindsay Administration a national pacesetter in delivering public health services

I eventually married Gordon and we moved to the Boston area where

I worked for Massachusetts Governor Frank Sargent. Gordon taught at Harvard's Law School, its School of Public Health and its Kennedy School of Government, as well as at Brandeis University. His book, *How to Manage in the Public Sector,* is based largely on his work for John Lindsay.

After Gordon died I worked for the Kennedy School and the Massachusetts Institute of Technology.∎

Naomi Feigelson Chase later became Marketing Director for the Metropolitan Transit Authority and ran her own public relations and marketing agency. She is also the author of several books.

June Jackson Christmas

One of the running routines that Mayor Lindsay would go through when we met outside a formal setting was to introduce me to whoever was there as "Dr. June Jackson Christmas, who is my psychiatrist." The other person would hesitate, wondering if he were serious or speaking in jest. He would follow this with, "She is in charge of my mental health and yours, too." Then he would explain that the mental health of all New Yorkers ought to be as important as their physical health. This was my cue to chime in with whatever issue was our priority at the time.

Mayor Lindsay had appointed me Commissioner after I served for six months as Deputy Commissioner in the Department of Mental Health and Retardation. When we met, he told me that he really didn't understand what the Department did, since New York State was responsible for all the people still being discharged from the large hospitals where they had been warehoused, many for years. He had been told that the program we had started in Harlem had psychiatric rehabilitation as its goal and used the community as its laboratory. He believed it was necessary to get the sense of what people think by listening to them and he encouraged this approach in his commissioners. He added that I must have heard a lot and asked that I keep giving him a broader and deeper sense of our programs and how they related to psychiatry, because it was hard for people to conceive of mental illness.

These were what would be the last years of his administration. It was a time before the fiscal crisis when we able to expand mental health services through contracts with non-profit agencies and the Health and Hospitals Corporation. We were able to set up programs for children and youth, the elderly, retarded people, and neighborhoods with few outpatient services. So when I received a call from Mayor Lindsay asking me to appear on a TV program with him on New Year's Eve, I decided to arm myself with a briefing book that would inform him and the viewing public while we waited for the ball to drop. But I didn't need it, for John Lindsay proved an able student, leading the discussion to the appropriate topics of dealing with holiday depression and alcohol abuse; poverty in a world of affluence; and education and discouraged youth—in short, to areas of mental health concern.

John Lindsay was a gentleman who could be not "gentle" when something aroused his ire, though I never experienced that. Another cherished memory is of his call to me when I was in the hospital recuperating from an appendectomy. After being cheered up by him (and trying not to laugh), I hung up as I heard a knock at the door. There he was with the biggest bunch of assorted spring flowers I had ever seen. He said he wanted to make sure that I was in the mood for a visitor before he actually came! He was pleased that he had surprised me (and the whole floor). That was one time where we did not talk business, just life. I am so very glad he gave me the opportunity to enter public service and to serve with him.■

June Jackson Christmas, *MD, was Commissioner of New York City's Department of Mental Health, Mental Retardation and Alcoholism Services from 1972 to 1980, for three Mayors. She is Medical Professor Emeritus of Behavioral Science at the City University (CUNY) and in the practice of psychiatry.*

Gail Clott

During JVL's second Administration I was assistant to Deputy Mayor Ed Morrison. Ed represented the Mayor at the Board of Estimate, the governing panel that consisted of the three citywide elected officials and the five borough presidents. (The board, which the Supreme Court struck down for violating the one person, one vote rule—Staten Island had as much voting power as Brooklyn—was eliminated in the 1989 City Charter revision, with its powers re-apportioned between the Mayor and the City Council.)

Prior to the adoption of "sunshine" laws that required such bodies to meet publicly in the interest of transparency, so-called executive sessions of the Board of Estimate were held behind closed doors on the afternoon prior to its public meetings. More often than not, major decisions were made during these sessions and merely formalized the following day with the public and press looking on. JVL rarely attended executive sessions, although the other elected officials usually did.

Inevitably, though, some controversial item of great importance would demand the Mayor's presence. On those occasions, Ed and I knew that only JVL could persuade the other board members to vote his way. When the item came up, we signaled the Mayor's secretary to have JVL come up to the chamber. When he entered, the room became eerily quiet. All eyes turned toward him. His smile, charm and stature were mesmerizing. The Mayor almost always convinced the other board members to go along with him.

When I was a young woman, John Lindsay was my hero. I wish he were here today.■

Gail Clott was in private law practice, served as Assistant Commissioner for Policy and Planning in the city's Department of Homeless Services (1999-2002) and is now a Manhattan Civil Court mediator.

David Condliffe

In the late 60s, I was a research assistant to Professor Suzanne Farkas. She was an expert on the role major city mayors played in urban lobbying. As *The New York Times* editorial board once noted, John Lindsay had become "the nation's leading exponent of increased federal and state aid for the cities." It is not an exaggeration to say Lindsay had become a hero to those of us interested in the future of America's cities.

Part of my job included attending meetings of the United States Conference of Mayors to assist Professor Farkas interviewing mayors. While in the men's room at one such meeting, John Lindsay suddenly appeared at the urinal next to mine. Impetuously, I extended my hand to introduce myself. Lindsay laughed and shook my hand.

Years later when Ed Hamilton hired me as assistant to the deputy mayor, John reminded me that I had previously met him in a men's room in Philadelphia.■

David Condliffe was Director of the Mayor's Office of Drug Abuse Policy in the Dinkins Administration and has worked for the Drug Policy Foundation, the Rutgers School of Law-Newark and the Osborne Association. He is now in private law practice.

Alexander Cooper

In 1967, a delegation of Japanese businessmen, invited to New York by Mayor Lindsay in hopes of luring them into making a commitment to the city, arrived at LaGuardia late one summer morning.

A driver with instructions to take them to City Hall for a brief visit with the Mayor, met the Japanese businessmen and escorted them to a limousine. Going south on the FDR Drive, the car suffered a flat tire and the driver pulled off the road onto a grassy patch near 116th Street. Since AAA help was a half hour away, the driver enterprisingly suggested that the four visitors take a quick tour of East Harlem while the car was being fixed.

After a half-hour walk on 116th Street, the group returned to the car to find all four of its tires stolen and the remaining portion of it resting comfortably on wooden blocks.

The AAA arrived eventually, but when the repair was finally complete, the visitors decided to pass on their meeting with the Mayor and insisted on returning to the airport to escape New York as quickly as possible.

When the Mayor heard of all this, he broke into a stream of laughter that ebbed and flowed throughout the day. The tire thieves were never pursued.■

*Architect and urban designer **Alexander Cooper** is a Partner in Cooper, Robertson & Partners. He was Director of the Lindsay Administration's Urban Design Group and a member of the City Planning Commission. He has written design guidelines for such projects as Battery Park City, the Hudson River Esplanade and Zuccotti Park.*

Walter J.M. Curley

In the summer of 1971, John and Mary Lindsay visited our family in Ireland. The younger Curleys were as proud as their parents to have the Mayor of New York City, my classmate at Yale, and his wife as houseguests.

After a stag lunch I gave for John at Dublin's Kildare Street Club attended by the newly appointed U.S. Ambassador to Ireland, we visited the Irish President Erskine Childers. Deeply intellectual and physically courageous, Childers, a Protestant, had been a fierce anti-British activist in his country's struggle for independence. John replied skillfully to Childers' questions about New York's challenges, then asked the president what he considered to be Ireland's biggest problem. "The round," said Childers, referring to Irishmen's longstanding custom of never leaving the pub until everyone had brought a round for all on hand.

A year later, just weeks after his family, other old friends, my wife Tatsie and I had celebrated John's 50th birthday at Gracie Mansion, he invited me to his office at City Hall and asked me to serve as Commissioner of Public Events for the remaining sixteen months of his mayoralty. I insisted on serving as an unpaid volunteer, but JVL paid me a dollar a year instead to avoid any legal and administrative complications. My employer Jock Whitney supported my decision to join the Administration on condition that I return to my desk at J.H. Whitney Company after Lindsay left office. Jock, a Republican like me, had been a longtime Lindsay supporter, but soured on JVL politically when the Mayor became a Democrat. Nevertheless, he was fond of John personally.

With just a few months left to his last term, John suggested that we come up with a splendid ceremonial event that would put the City's best foot forward and help cap his tenure—an occasion that would give New York a chance to "strut its stuff," he said, with municipal government's version of a state dinner.

An opportunity arose when the State Department advised us that Pakistan's Prime Minister Zulfigar Ali Bhutto would be passing through New York to make a courtesy call at the United Nations. I proposed that we host Bhutto and his party at the Waldorf-Astoria, but John trumped me with a far better idea. He was committed to holding such formal receptions at the city's distinguished cultural institutions and chose the Metropolitan Museum's Medieval Court for this particular enchanted evening.

The night was a heady mixture of glamour and fun. The Mayor and the Prime Minister each spoke eloquently, but concisely. Bhutto, his wife and his daughter Benazir were elegantly turned out, the ladies shimmering in their amber saris. Who could foresee that both father and daughter (eventually a two-term Pakistani Prime Minister as well) would be tragically assassinated? The Medieval Court glowed with candlelight. An orchestra played in the gallery above.

Tatsie and I were home in just five minutes, living only a few blocks away, but it would take us forever to forget that event.

John, a hero to me, left City Hall after eight turbulent years there. He returned to Webster & Sheffield and I to J.H.Whitney.■

Walter J.M. Curley, a partner in J.H.Whitney & Company, served as Ambassador to Ireland under President Gerald Ford and as Ambassador to France under President George H.W. Bush. He has also been a trustee of the New York Public Library and Barnard College as well as a director of the Irish Georgian Society.

Sid Davidoff

On April 4, 1968, at about 7:15 p.m., my phone rang. It was Oppy, John Lindsay's night secretary, the keeper of everyone's whereabouts—and that included anyone the Mayor might want to get hold of.

"Boss, the big, big Boss wants you to call him at the Mansion, a.s.a.p.," he rasped.

I called the Mayor immediately. He asked if I'd seen the news. I hadn't. Martin Luther King, Jr. had been assassinated, he told me. Within minutes, I was on the phone with another mayoral assistant, my unofficial partner Barry Gottehrer, and the two of us agreed to meet at the Shalimar Bar in Harlem.

The Shalimar was Allah's hangout—not THAT Allah, but the one who headed the Five Percenters, mostly ex-cons who followed his preachings. They were our major local contacts in every black neighborhood. When we arrived at the bar, the streets were boiling with people who were angry, sad and frustrated. A mob was forming. Reports from the city's other black communities told the same story. We checked in with the Mayor.

"I'm coming to Harlem," he said. "Where do you want me to meet you?" Impossible, we told him. There was no telling what the crowd would do. We might face a rolling riot.

"There is no way to protect you, Mr. Mayor," we warned.

"Where do you want me to meet you," he answered.

We knew there was no way to stop him "Can you give us an hour," we asked?

"I can give you 45 minutes," he said.

Allah sent as many Five Percenters into the streets as possible. I called Bumpy Johnson (played by Denzel Washington in the film "American Gangster") who headed the Harlem "syndicate." He agreed to send his daughter and his "lieutenants" to meet us. (Bumpy never appeared in public himself, but had ways of making his presence felt.) Barry, seeking additional support, called Charlie Kenyatta, a sidewalk orator with a large following who carried a Bible on a spear and wore a machete on his waistband.

Finally, Mayor Lindsay arrived in an unmarked sedan with just Detective Sergeant Pat Vecchio and his driver, his entire security team. At the same moment, Percy Sutton, Borough President of Manhattan who represented Harlem's political leadership, showed up. Everyone seemed to know the Mayor and the borough president were on hand—except the press and the police. The last things we wanted were uniforms and camera lights.

Barry and I stepped to the back of the crowd and let the Mayor be surrounded by "our guys"—the gangsters, numbers runners and others whose voices counted in a special way around there. Word of all this spread quickly, even to the outer boroughs. The whole town knew that Mayor Lindsay was in Harlem, sharing its grief and mourning the death of one of the greatest American leaders of our time with its people.

The Mayor's decision to come was the right one. As we saw the flames of Newark in the distance and other major cities around the country burned, New York City under Mayor Lindsay stood strong and proud.

—

The Vietnam War and its daily damage to America's cities became a major issue of John Lindsay's 1969 re-election campaign, especially since both our opponents, Democrat Abe Beame and Republican John Marchi, supported the War.

Bella Abzug, a colorful, brash lawyer, always in an enormous wide-brimmed hat, offered to help mobilize support, particularly among women. (She was a founder of Women's Strike for Peace). Abzug demonstrated her ability to deliver by producing thousands at a dramatic candle-light rally at Flushing Town Hall, which the Mayor keynoted with a powerful attack on the War.

All good. Then one day, Bella stormed into Lindsay Campaign Headquarters in the old De Pinna Department Store on Fifth Avenue, wanting (demanding) that the campaign pay for a full-page anti-War ad in *The Times*. After Campaign Manager Dick Aurelio turned her down, she threw a tantrum in his office. So I decided to do it. It was important for Bella and therefore it was important for us.

I called my friend Vince Albano head of Century Bank and Republican County Chairman for Manhattan, who agreed to give me a personal loan, with my personal guarantee (not worth much back then). The caveat? I was sworn not tell his conservative boss the purpose of the loan. So Bella got her full-page ad attacking the War (and the Republican President), while supporting John Lindsay's re-election, which was effectively financed by the Republican County Chairman.

Bella remained a vociferous, energetic, temperamental presence in the campaign. And later went on to serve two terms in Congress, a celebrated figure with her massive hats and fearless voice.■

Sid Davidoff is a founder and senior partner at the firm of Davidoff Hutcher & Citron and was a proud member of the Nixon Enemies List.

Joan Davidson

On a bright day in 1970, on Manhattan's far West Side in Greenwich Village, with the Hudson River shining behind him, handsome Mayor Lindsay presided over the splendid opening of Westbeth, the world's biggest and our country's first live/work place for artists of all disciplines. (Westbeth's name comes from being placed at West and Bethune Streets).

Westbeth, the creature of the National Endowment on the Arts under Roger Stevens' leadership in partnership with our family foundation, the J.M. Kaplan Fund, under the leadership of my father, Jack Kaplan, broke exciting new ground—for the lives of working artists, housing in the United States, the repurposing of historic structures, and for the revitalization of downtown New York. The development converted a 68 year-old industrial complex of five buildings, long Bell Labs' cutting-edge research center, to 383 live/work studio apartments, along with performance and rehearsal spaces, communal and individual artist studios and rooms for non-profit cultural institutions—all at relatively modest rents.

As the first major project by young architect Richard Meier, Westbeth faced difficult legal challenges, in particular the need to overcome a long-time City prohibition on residential units in an area zoned for industrial or commercial use. But the Lindsay Administration responded enthusiastically, and the City Planning Commission approved a new zoning provision in 1968, a precursor of the regulations that later made it possible for artists to live in SoHo's lofts and other former industrial areas. It was the Lindsay Administration's creative interpretation of restrictive building code provisions that allowed these essential conversions to proceed.

John Lindsay and his key staffers played a crucial role in bringing this complicated project to fruition—helping it over hurdles, providing essential assistance when it was most needed, and demonstrating once again their imagination and grand vision for the city.

Let's hope that future administrations will care as much!■

Joan K. Davidson is president emeritus of the J.M. Kaplan Fund and founding president of Westbeth. She chaired the New York State Council on the Arts and was Commissioner of the New York State Department of Parks, Recreation and Historic Preservation.

Evan Davis

I became a full-time part of the Lindsay Administration in 1971 after finishing my clerkship with Supreme Court Associate Justice Potter Stewart. Gene Keilin and I had sort of a Gene and Evan's Excellent Adventure life after we both started at the Bureau of the Budget in August of that year. We were having trouble getting phones for the reclaimed office space we were given so we wired phones that we purchased into our fax line. We interviewed 150 candidates to be our shared assistant and selected Joanne Witty. We did that job so well that Gene and Joanne later married. We crashed the high level gathering at the Mayor's office the night the budget was adopted in June 1972. I was surprised by the civility of the festivities.

I worked with Ken Hartman to draft legislation to finance the construction of the Second Avenue Subway based on a fractional purchase methodology developed by John Mitchell, with whom I consulted. He had used this methodology to finance MTA's purchase of a new fleet of subway cars which would then be purchased car by car by the Transit Authority. Our legislation was passed but repealed when denounced by Mayor Beame during the fiscal crisis as resulting in the payment of interest on interest. As my daughters would say, "Duh!"

Back to the Excellent Adventures, Gene and I attended a NIMLO conference to extol the policy logic of federal revenue sharing which, the conference having taken place in Hawaii, earned me a threatened *Daily News* story that Tom Morgan somehow managed to kill.

In May of 1972 Gene and I were tasked by Jim Cavanagh to go to Albany to work with Dick Brown to enact a mechanism to fund on a medium-term basis, short-term debt that was being rolled-over annually. The mechanism, the First Instance Reserve Corporation, was enacted and later morphed into the Municipal Assistance Corporation. (In 1989 when I was Counsel to Governor Mario Cuomo we used a similar mechanism to bond out the State's annual short-term borrowing that for many years had been used to fund the State's accumulated deficit.). Gene and I would say half in jest, "If you can't fund it, FIRC it."

In the fall of 1972 Norman Redlich appointed me to head the Consumer Protection Division in the Law Department. Most notable was the case of New York City v. Nixon to challenge the President's impounding of billions of dollars of water pollution money. The statutory construction issue turned on the meaning of the word "all" in the context in which Congress had used it. It was a "What part of the word 'no' don't you understand?" kind of argument. We won at every level, including the U. S. Supreme Court.

I am very grateful to John Lindsay for being such a strong magnet for young "we can do it" people and for allowing me to engage in such Excellent Adventures.■

Evan Davis is Senior Counsel to the firm of Cleary Gottlieb, specializing in litigation and international dispute resolution. He served as Counsel to Governor Mario Cuomo (1985-91).

Gordon Davis

On January 1, 1973, Mayor John Lindsay appointed me to an eight-year term on the then seven-member New York City Planning Commission. What possessed the Mayor to appoint a City Hall staffer and mayoral speechwriter to a plum position that had an eight-year term, public status and a nice monetary stipend was somewhat mystifying. (Disloyalty prompted the Mayor to not re-appoint the incumbent Ivan Michaels, the first black member of the commission and Basil Paterson's law partner, but why me in his place?) For sure, mine was not an appointment that got the Mayor a lot of kudos. The January 6, 1973 full front-page *Amsterdam News* headline screamed" "BLACKS RIP LINDSAY ON DAVIS APPOINTMENT" and the related news article quoted an important Harlem civic leader describing me as "a proven non-entity." I was young and unfazed. The Mayor offered this sage advice: "You have eight years to prove them wrong—[pause]—I am sure you will."

Almost five years later to the day, in late December 1977, I found myself being interviewed by Mayor-elect Ed Koch in the basement of 345 Park Avenue. Twenty minutes into the interview, he asked me to be New York City's Parks Commissioner. "Surprise" doesn't begin to describe my reaction to being interviewed, much less offered the job of Parks Commissioner by a newly elected Mayor I had never met, had voted against three times in a row (the primary, the runoff and the general election) and who, as far as I could tell, I did not like much at all. (I grew to admire greatly and enjoy immensely my friend Ed Koch. And I honored his courageous decision to endorse Barack Obama for President in 2008.) During the interview the Mayor-elect mentioned my service on the Planning Commission ("…one of Jack Newfield's 1977 *Village Voice* 'good guys,'" noted Koch) and indicated that I had been highly recommended by Tony Olivieri. Ah ha! Now I understood why I was in the room. Antonio Olivieri, a very close friend, former state assemblyman and soon to be councilman-at-large, was very close to Ed Koch, had campaigned for him from the beginning (for which I used to ridicule him—"He doesn't have a chance," said I throughout 1976 and 1977) and had, unbeknownst to me, recommended me first for City Planning Chair (Bobby Wagner had the position sewed up) and then Parks Commissioner.

After the Mayor-elect offered me the job, I asked him for a day or two to think about it. He said o.k. I then called JVL to ask his blessing. Koch and JVL had a long-standing dislike for one another and after the 1977 election they were exchanging hostile words in the press on an almost daily basis, a grudge for which Koch had good cause. When I told him I wanted his approval before I accepted the position, this is what John Lindsay said to me after a long pause: "Some things are more important than politics. This is one of them. Take the job." I loved John Lindsay. I owe him more than I can ever recount. He was my Mayor and always will be.■

Gordon Davis, a partner in the law firm of Venable LLP, has served as a member of the City Planning Commission, was Commissioner of the New York City Department of Parks and Recreation, co-founder of the Central Park and Prospect Park Conservancies, President of Lincoln Center for the Performing Arts and Founding Director of Jazz at Lincoln Center, among other civic and government posts.

Perry Davis

I was a senior at Yeshiva College majoring in political science when John Lindsay ran for re-election in 1969.

As an Orthodox Jew in Queens, I often debated with friends and neighbors who cited school decentralization, the Forest Hills mixed-income housing program and even the infamous snowstorm as evidence of the Mayor's antipathy to middle class white and, particularly, Jewish interests.

But I admired the Mayor's concern for those in greatest need and his masterful work on the Kerner Commission report. I volunteered for his campaign, where I met his aide Marvin Schick.

During the campaign, without official approval, I invited the Mayor to address Yeshiva's student body. The Mayor charmed a hesitant audience of students and faculty, playing "Daniel in the Lion's Den" to the hilt.

A Woodrow Wilson and a New York State Fellowship enabled me to pursue a political science Ph.D. at Columbia. Professor Wallace Sayre, my advisor and dean of New York City scholars, helped me obtain a Ford Foundation grant for a City Hall internship, where Marvin hired me for the summer. He made sure I attended staff meetings and had meaningful work. Eventually, I wrote my doctoral dissertation on the Lindsay City Hall Staff System as a model of public sector executive office coordination and control.

The world was horrified by the massacre of Israeli athletes by terrorists during the 1972 Munich Summer Olympics. Marvin wrote the Mayor's speech commemorating the tragedy and I drafted remarks for Jack Weiler, the lay leader of the New York Jewish community.

Marvin stepped down as the Mayor's administrative assistant in 1973, and, at his recommendation, I replaced him. My duties included serving as City

Hall's point person with the Jewish community, as well liaison with the Mayor's Offices for the Aging and Veterans Affairs.

On my second day, John told the staff, and then the public that he would not seek a third term. But the remaining eleven months were memorable.

The worldwide crusade to free millions of Soviet Jews from anti-Semitic repression was spearheaded by the New York Conference on Soviet Jewry. Every spring the Conference ran Solidarity Sunday, a march down Fifth Avenue to Hammarskjold Plaza in front of the U.N. As the Mayor's liaison with the involved city agencies to make sure that potential disruptions by the militant Jewish Defense League were averted and other logistical needs were met, I worked closely with the head of the Conference—Malcolm Hoenlein and his deputy Margy-Ruth Greenbaum. She and I had attended Columbia in overlapping years but never met. Our first date followed the rally supporting Soviet Jewry. A week later, we decided to get married. As wedding gifts, the Mayor promoted me to Assistant, raised my salary and hosted us at Gracie Mansion shortly after our engagement. ■

Perry Davis, *a mayoral assistant, served as Executive Assistant to the President of the New York City Board of Education, the Chancellor's special assistant on civil rights matters and the New York City Partnership's Vice President for Economic Development. He is a fund-raising consultant.*

Sean Deveney

Joe meets John, January 1969. It was 8 a.m. on January 22 when, outside City Hall, a crowd began to gather—about 90 percent (by one estimate) truant teenagers, and most of them female. By noon, the crowd would grow to about 6,000, when the door of City Hall opened and Lindsay came out, striding to a podium. He was met with, one reporter wrote, "solid booing, as though the Mayor was a Baltimore Colt." Just behind Lindsay, Joe Namath, in a gray plaid double-breasted suit, with a broadsword tie and silver-buckled shoes, stepped forth and the booing was replaced by high-pitched cheers. While Lindsay addressed the crowd, lauding, "our conquering team," a chant of, "Namath for Mayor!" went up, and Lindsay was drowned out. Namath stood up, motioning to hush the hyperventilating young ladies, and allow Lindsay to finish. Lindsay presented the Jets with cufflinks and tie clasps engraved with the city seal, and the team presented Lindsay with a LeRoy Neiman painting of Namath in action. Addressing the crowd, Namath said, "We're the new faces for the new generation."

After the Jets ceremony, Namath bounced around the city making appearances. Reporter Joseph Durso wrote of Namath's day: "It was like a combined appearance by Frank Sinatra, the Beatles and Tiny Tim."

—

The Mets "endorsement," October 1969, After the Mets clinched their spot in the playoffs, weeks before the 1969 election, Jimmy Breslin was seated alongside John Lindsay on October 6, for Game 3 against the Atlanta Braves, in a box next to the Mets dugout. The Mets had already won the first two games of the series.

When the Mets won Game 3, Lindsay and his aides went to the Mets locker room to join the celebration. What happened next is the subject of different interpretations, but whatever the provenance, the result was a photo that ran all over the city: embattled John Lindsay, standing next to outfielder Rod Gaspar as he empties a bottle of champagne, while Jerry Grote stands behind the Mayor, swirling the foam into his hair as other Mets look on.

Gaspar said, "I said to Tom [Seaver], let's get him. I always liked him, he seems like a good man, and it's just something we decided to do on the spur of the moment." Manager Hodges reportedly refused to endorse Lindsay. But when pitcher Jerry Koosman poured champagne on the Mayor's classic head during a stagey televised locker-room party, he was also bestowing what was construed by the fans as an endorsement from the whole team.

—

Knicks "draftees," 1970. John Lindsay made good on the arrangement he'd worked out with forward Dave DeBusschere, who had told him seven months earlier at the Mayor's party for the World Series champion Mets that the Knicks would be back, expecting their own party in May.

Now it was noon on May 15, 1970, and the Knicks had just completed their stunning defeat of the Lakers in the NBA Finals, hobbled big man Willis Reed carrying the team past Wilt Chamberlain and L.A. That completed what would go down as one of the greatest years a city has ever had in sports, adding their own victory to the Jets' upset over the Colts and the Mets' run through the Braves and Orioles in baseball's playoffs. The Knicks and 100 or so dignitaries from sports, entertainment and politics gathered on the lawn of Gracie Mansion, with Reed limping the grounds in his suit, downing a hot dog, while the Smith Street Dixieland Jazz band played. Lindsay prepared to congratulate the Knicks on their first title, but he wanted to, rather somberly, wish good luck to three players who would no longer be with the Knicks: John Warren, Don May and Bill

Hosket. "Unfortunately," Lindsay said, "three members of the team have been drafted by Uncle Sam."

The Mayor had misunderstood, however. The players were not drafted to fight in Vietnam. They had been chosen in the NBA's expansion draft. Hosket and May would leave the Knicks to play for the Buffalo Braves, and Warren was going to the Cavaliers. "I was drafted by Uncle Cleveland," Warren objected, "not Uncle Sam."■

Sean Deveney *is a writer for* The Sporting News *and author of the book from which these anecdotes were adapted:* Fun CIty: John Lindsay, Joe Namath, and How Sports Saved New York in the 1960s, *published in October 2015.*

David Dinkins

When the charismatic J. Raymond "Ray" Jones, known as the Harlem Fox, decided to step down as district leader in 1967, he selected yours truly to be his successor. Ray had amassed great influence, having founded the Carver Democratic Club, where my career began, during the 1920s. He also served as a City Councilman and was the first Black Democratic Party County Leader in the nation. I stepped into the role pretty smoothly at the time. But when the term I filled out came to an end and the people went to the polls to vote for their next full-term leader, my opponent stole the election right out from under us. Not knowing much about the process at the time, I failed to put election-site watchers in place and lost an election I'd been favored to win.

By the time the next election for district leader came around, however, I'd learned my lessons well. We had poll watchers on duty and re-captured the office. As a new district leader elected in my own right, one of my first acts was to endorse John Lindsay for re-election as Mayor on the Liberal Party line. At one point, he wanted to name me as his Deputy Commissioner of Human Resources. Unfortunately, the time was wrong for me and I had to turn Mayor Lindsay down in order to continue my law practice. But our friendship had long been sealed and I have always carried great fondness and respect for John Lindsay. I called him "Big John" and we remained friends until he died.■

David Dinkins, the 106th Mayor of the City of New York and the first African American elected to the highest citywide post, also served in the New York State Assembly. In addition, he was President of the Board of Elections, City Clerk and Manhattan Borough President. Mayor Dinkins is Professor in the Practice of Public Affairs at Columbia University's School of International and Public Affairs.

Bob Dole

I went to Congress in 1961, two years after John Lindsay. He was already a standout in the Republican caucus. We shared the profound experience of serving in World War II, and we later worked together on some of the most significant legislation of our time, including the Civil Rights Act of 1964, the Voting Rights Act of 1965, and the 1965 Immigration Act.

By 1968, when I ran for the U.S. Senate, John was already a major media presence as Mayor of New York—tall, handsome, telegenic, and famous for walking the streets to maintain calm while other cities were erupting in racial conflict.

He graciously agreed to travel to Kansas to campaign for me and for my friend, Rick Harmon, the great Kansas State All-American basketball star, who was then running for Governor. There was great interest in hearing this new political voice from the East, and the turnout was terrific at a Mission Hills luncheon. John didn't disappoint, and we raised what then seemed like an impressive $12,000.

While our political paths later diverged as John switched parties, he remained a compelling figure and a friend. Years later, in a speech in New York, I said that while I had never met the perfect political candidate, John Lindsay was probably the closest.■

Bob Dole represented Kansas in the United States Senate for 27 years, serving a period as its Majority Leader. He was the Republican candidate for Vice President in 1976 and his party's candidate for President in 1996. A decorated hero of World War II, he was awarded two Purple Hearts and a Bronze Star with a combat V.

Robert Douglass

The rivalry between Governor Nelson Rockefeller and Mayor John Lindsay took many forms. At one of our senior staff meetings during the early years of the Lindsay mayoralty, when an embattled New York faced financial and racial pressures, the Governor threw out the idea that the State should build a modern metropolis within the city limits to show the Mayor's people how great architecture could transform a community and leave a powerful legacy.

"But Governor," I said, "the State doesn't own enough land and this would violate the principle of home rule."

"There must be some way we can show the city what can be done," he replied quickly.

Then Bill Ronan, the Governor's top aide and powerful Secretary, suddenly mused, "Well, the State does own everything out to the middle of the Hudson River."

"That's it," shot the Governor with excitement. "We'll find a way to use that to make a point."

And so the Battery Park City project was born out of this Lindsay/ Rockefeller competition. And the Governor did indeed make his point.

Robert Douglass *was Counsel and then Secretary to Governor Nelson Rockefeller and, subsequently, a lawyer at Milbank Tweed and the Chair of the Downtown Alliance.*

Christopher Drew

After graduating from college in 1968, I took a summer job as a teacher with The Real Great Society, a community organization, in their University of the Streets program. Classes for neighborhood youth were held in the City-owned Christadora House near Tompkins Square Park.

I was assigned to create a course for drug offenders and directed to a local outpost of the City's Addiction Services Agency for information, brochures, and other available teaching aids. My contact there suggested instead that I attend the agency's upcoming meeting of ASA staff, former and current addicts, relatives of drug users and community activists.

Encounter groups were collective efforts at increasing addicts' self-knowledge, emotional openness and authenticity through direct confrontation with others, self-disclosure and emotional expression. The meeting would be my first exposure to the agency's encounter group methods for treating and preventing drug addiction.

That night, I watched one group member jump out of her seat and scream at another because of something he'd said. Something similar involving other members occurred a few more times. This behavior became less shocking to me as the evening went on. Parents, teachers, coaches, friends had yelled at me, but never with such intensity. It was like witnessing a terrible accident up close. I left the meeting shaken, but exhilarated. I wondered how a City agency could countenance such conduct but looked forward to the next week's AWARE meeting.

In preparation, I decided to offer up some piece of self-disclosure. I assumed I'd be criticized by some and planned to express regret for my actions and appreciation for the opportunity to share and learn.

The same participants and a few new ones showed up at the following meeting. Partway into the evening, I stood up and told of giving a panhandler a couple of dollars earlier that day, adding that the panhandler had been an attractive young woman in hippie garb of the time. Perhaps, I said, that made me forget valid reasons for not giving panhandlers money. Then, the roof fell in on me. Two or three people started screaming at me, and not about money and panhandlers. "What do you think you're doing wasting our time with this story," they yelled. "You're a cheap fraud."

I seized up, then made the situation worse for myself by admitting that I was wrong to talk about the episode before I'd come to understand it myself. When someone asked if I was scared by the group's reaction, I answered that I was not scared but was experiencing free-floating anxiety. I think some group members believed I was deliberately provoking them with my responses.

Just as the group had decided I was up to no good, they finally concluded that no more good could come from pursuing this line of attack with me. After a time, the group meeting broke up and I departed.

I passed the next week in a daze, unable to explain what had happened.■

Christopher Drew served with the Environmental Protection Administration, Addiction Services Agency and Urban Action Task Force on Manhattan's Lower East Side. In the years since he has been an organization development practitioner for corporations, public agencies and non-profits in the U.S. and Europe.

Kathleen Modry Drew

In 1968 Assistant to the Mayor Michael Dontzin hired me to answer letters complaining about city services addressed to JVL. Mike also asked me to help him with the Urban Action Task Force he led in the Bronx's Fordham/East Tremont section. Jay Kriegel's office was next to ours. When Jay dropped by, he stirred us with a sense of urgency and how important it was to serve the Mayor. Jay moved quickly, always looking straight ahead.

Phone calls to and from the Bronx dominated my work life. I was always asking Mike how to get the Department of Sanitation to pick up trash on a street that they had missed, or when we could meet with merchants on Arthur Avenue or with frustrated, unemployed kids at youth centers. Many letters from aggrieved New Yorkers awaited answers.

When Mike left City Hall to work on Mayor Lindsay's re-election campaign, I moved to Lance Liebman's office where Urban Action Task Force staffers were concentrated. I sat next to Eloise Hirsch. We were ten purposeful young women assigned to Task Force neighborhoods and following up on issues raised by residents.

Lance had me coordinate the Mayor's Playstreet Program. Eloise, the previous year's coordinator and a generous, experienced colleague, explained that neighborhood groups wanting a safe place for their kids to play in the summer would call to request a "Playstreet Permit." The permit would stipulate the hours when the street would be closed to traffic, giving the kids a more protected play environment. I was to take calls from applicants and see that the appropriate forms were completed and filed.

One day, Eloise interrupted my telephone conversation with an applicant named Sonny Carson and told me to pushed the "hold" button. "For Sonny, you should fill out the form in person," she said. I had learned that great care was taken with important community leaders and Sonny was one of them.

I met Sonny at an uptown law firm. He was about ten years older than I, modest, self-confident and magnetic. Like many African American community leaders at the time, Sonny wore an Afro and dashiki. His manner, however, distinguished him more than his appearance in this all-white office.

After he completed the application Sonny offered me a ride home on his way back to Brooklyn.

He was easy to be with. We took pleasure in discovering that our mothers had the same birthday. He spoke of his mother with great affection. Just one year out of college, I loved inviting people for dinner and it seemed natural to ask Sonny to join my boyfriend Chris Drew me and for a meal. He accepted.

Sonny and Chris discussed their contrasting views on drug treatment while I prepared chicken with avocadoes. Having used drugs for years, Sonny disputed Chris's new-found convictions about "confronting one's own reality and taking personal responsibility" acquired from his job with the Addiction Services Agency.

Sonny was a gracious guest. The next morning I told Eloise about an unlikely encounter of New Yorkers from different worlds and lives that had brushed against each other, however briefly.■

Kathleen Modry Drew was an Assistant to Mayoral Counsel Michael Dontzin and a staff member of the Urban Action Task Force. She now teaches 5th and 6th grades in Cambridge, Mass., and has renovated and sold abandoned homes in Boston through a non-profit.

Ted Dreyfus

I was a latecomer to City Hall, having been overseas during the first Lindsay Administration. After two years in the Budget Bureau I became an Assistant to the Mayor. By then, the Administration's big personalities, roles and war stores were well established. I was quite intimidated. As the Lindsay years wound down, staffers were leaving for the agencies or life beyond the government. Over time, I picked up liaison responsibilities with more agencies, including Transportation. I hustled to catch up or catch on.

Learning came in odd ways and at strange times. I was leaving work one night at around 10 p.m., wiped out, but feeling guilty because the Mayor, Ed Hamilton, Jay Kriegel and Steve Isenberg were still huddled in a meeting. I ran into Jay's secretary going down the steps of City Hall and said I couldn't believe the long hours everyone worked. "That's why they make such bad decisions," she replied.

—

I often hesitated to speak my mind. On a hot Saturday afternoon, I was wiped out again, this time after running the full circuit of Central Park. I was leaning over and panting when the Mayor came by riding a bike. He stopped and invited me to join him as he pedaled up the East Side. I obediently jogged beside him, afraid to let on that I was probably dying as he smiled at walkers and runners while chatting with me over his shoulder.

—

Sometimes, I was a sucker. One morning, Steve said the Mayor was taking a police helicopter to inspect traffic and wanted me to go along. I was surprised that no one else got the honor. The Mayor, the police pilot and I climbed aboard the helicopter near the Brooklyn Bridge. The Mayor sat beside the police pilot with me behind. We were no more than five feet off the pier when the pilot turned to the Mayor and said, "OK, it's all yours." The Mayor grabbed the stick and we zoomed practically straight up. He ducked the 'copter forward, charging toward the tall buildings of Wall Street. As we scraped by the Twin Towers and headed up over

Broadway, my panic subsided enough for me to realize why the City Hall staff had bestowed this honor on me.

—

On a hot summer noon, I arrived at City Hall via subway from Queens, drenched in sweat. Steve said the Mayor wanted to see me. I walked into the Mayor's office while he was writing something. He started talking without looking up. When he finally saw me dripping, he went pale, asked how I felt, then ushered me out to go see a doctor immediately. I was diagnosed with hypoglycemia and told to cut out all sugars. How observant, kind and attentive the Mayor had been. Steve informed me that the week before, a visitor had a heart attack while alone with the Mayor in his office.

—

In December, 1973, I met Acting Highways Commissioner Manny Carballo at 12th Street on the West Side Highway. He was looking down into the space left by a vast section of concrete that had fallen out of the road. The beginning of the end.■

Ted Dreyfus, a project director and investment manager, has been a banker and Managing Director for Forestry and Development at the Clinton Climate Initiative of the Clinton Foundation.

June Margolin Eisland

I was Community Liaison in the Northwest Bronx (Riverdale) Office of the Mayor's Urban Action Task Force. We frequently met on Saturdays in the Blue Room at City Hall.

One Saturday, unable to get a baby sitter, I brought my four-year-old son Bruce to the task force meeting. At one point, he started to run around. The Mayor came over, picked Bruce up and swung him around. "Would you like to come to my office," the Mayor asked Bruce, adding, "You can sit in my chair." Bruce responded, "No thanks, I already sat in Ed Hamilton's chair."■

June Eisland *was Chair of the Bronx's Community Board 8. She was elected to the City Council in 1979 and served as Chair of its Transportation and Land Use committees. She has a consulting business.*

Bruce Eissner

The Black Panthers and Young Lords had taken over Lincoln Hospital in the Bronx, and they were pretty militant. I was working with McKinsey to help the Mayor set up the Health and Hospitals Corporation, a new governing scheme based on public benefit corporations for the City's hospitals, Ubtil then, each had been run under contracts with various teaching hospitals and medical schools over which the city had little oversight.

The Mayor wanted to know what was really going on with the takeover at Lincoln. Aside from the drama, were there legitimate issues? So I went up there, scared out of my wits, only to find that the occupiers were receptive and had a compelling case. They provided the evidence, which I was able to corroborate and then report. The resolution of the crisis provided even more urgency and justification for Lindsay's forward-looking reorganization of the city's hospital system, which turned it into one of the finest in the country. Lindsay's ability and desire to seek and weigh carefully the evidence in midst of so much clamor was inspiring - not just leadership, but real vision under fire.■

Bruce Eissner *was the first physician ever hired by McKinsey. He later went into medical practice in Massachusetts.*

Ronnie Eldridge

Having helped to gather liberal Democratic support for John Lindsay in the 1969 general election after he'd lost the Republican primary, I met the Mayor for the first time the night he won a second term at City Hall when he mentioned my name in his victory speech. Soon after, he invited me to join his new Administration. I told him I didn't want to be an au pair. Although I'd been active in reform West Side politics as a district leader and ally of Robert Kennedy, this would be my first paid position in government. Having been a stay-at-home mother of three, but encouraged by my late husband Larry Eldridge to follow my star, I asked to be a Special Assistant to the Mayor and reticently requested a salary of $25,000. JVL agreed and I moved into a basement office in City Hall to work for a Mayor whose convictions drove his programs to improve the lives of so many.

I learned that it takes perseverance and time to make or change policies. With great effort, the Lindsay Administration created the path-finding Bureau of Lead Poisoning in response to community action by the Young Lords and pressure from activist physicians. But it took a caring government with a conscience and an eager, talented official like Health Services Administrator Gordon Chase to make it happen.

The Mayor's executive order prohibiting discrimination because of sexual preference took longer to accomplish. Mark Ruben, a public school teacher, father and gay activist, came to see me after the Stonewall episode to complain of police harassment. He told me about a trio of men walking abreast and being asked for permits, and raids on bathhouses—a world I knew nothing of. The next day, an adorable young man arrived at my office and announced, "Hi, I'm Pete, Mark's lover." He represented the Gay Activist Alliance, a new, militant, confrontational all-male group. Excluding lesbians reflected their own problems with equality. I recall a slur following a planning session for the first Gay Pride march that occurred a year after Stonewall. "That was a fruitful meeting," someone quipped. Years later, after the AIDS crisis and its relentless memorials, a raft of court decisions and much more enlightenment, such a bigoted pun would rightly be taken as disrespectable and despicable. Not too long ago, I spoke at Mark's funeral.

As the only openly Democratic political operative in City Hall, the Mayor used me as a bridge toward his future party with occasionally comic results. One day, he said that Sargent Shriver, RFK's brother-in-law, former ambassador and head of the Peace Corps had called and passed on a "Hello." I replied that I'd never met Shriver. A few weeks later, JVL asked me to thank the ambassador for inviting him to a Knicks game and explain that he had a prior commitment. I agreed to, but repeated that I didn't know Shriver. At a luncheon, JVL told the ambassador, "Here comes an old friend, Ronnie Eldridge." Shriver embraced me. A few weeks later, Noel Klores, the city's representative in Washington, D.C., said he'd run into Sargent Shriver there. "Who is Ronnie Eldridge?" Shriver asked.■

Ronnie Eldridge *is host of the weekly CUNY television program "Eldridge & Co." She was the only female member of Governor Mario Cuomo's cabinet, serving as Director of the Division for Women, and represented a West Side Manhattan district as an elected member of New York's City Council.*

Herb Elish

I joined the Administration early in the second term, so I missed the growing pains and events of the first four years, including those involving the Sanitation Department—snow removal in Queens and garbage collection problems.

When I became Sanitation Commissioner in 1971 memories of the Queens snowstorm still remained painful for the Administration. While progress had been made in collecting the garbage under Jerry Kretchmer, improvement in Sanitation performance was essential and a top mayoral priority. As a result I saw and heard from the Mayor more often than most commissioners. The necessary sharp changes in the department's management systems and culture were controversial and difficult to achieve. Through it all, though, the Mayor was interested in the details of our efforts, fully supportive, and generous with praise for progress. At the same time, he was impatient to make sanitation services an example of the management reforms he was fostering throughout the government, and I felt that impatience often.

An event early in my tenure told me a lot about the Mayor and the job that lay ahead of us. Late one afternoon I got a call from City Hall telling me to come over at five o'clock to accompany him on a neighborhood tour. During his first term, these unannounced, impromptu visits to various parts of the city had become a mark of how he ran the city but I had never been along on one.

We were on our way to Bedford-Stuyvesant, he told me, because the garbage had not been picked up there for several days (Department reports to the contrary) and the community was very angry. During our ride out, I wondered whether we, or more particularly I, needed more than the minimal security on hand.

A large crowd was waiting when we arrived. As John got out of the car, I recognized that these people were not there to express anger, but to greet him affectionately as someone they believed would solve their problems. I can still see his tall, patrician figure walking through the crowds, greeting people, and receiving their warmth in return. It was quite extraordinary. The mood changed when he introduced me as the new Sanitation Commissioner and told them I was there to listen and solve their problems. Then he walked away and left me with the crowd and the issues involved in serving their community. My greeting wasn't nearly as friendly. The crowd was polite, but I detected some undertones of anger and suspicion. That sort of reception was a new experience for me.

Later, when I had a chance to digest what had happened, I realized that one of his purposes that day was to teach me the importance of listening closely to the people we were serving, and that the improvements he expected were important to people's lives. Satisfying New Yorkers would be the most important measure of our success.■

Herb Elish is Chief Executive Officer of The College Board. He was Chairman and Chief Executive Office of the Weirton Steel Company and Director of the Carnegie Library of Pittsburgh.

Donald Elliott

D uring John Lindsay's first campaign for Mayor, a group of young architects who believed urban design would solve New York's problems organized to support JVL by preparing a plan with the local community for Coney Island. They presented it to the candidate to demonstrate how planning in collaboration with the affected neighborhood could work in a Lindsay Administration. The architects urged him to discuss this example in the campaign. The pros in the campaign thought it wouldn't work. JVL went with the architects, though, and the presentation was a great success in Coney Island.

—

Early in his first Administration, the Mayor was visited by the top man in the Transit Authority with a proposal to buy new cars for the subway. When JVL asked whether they would be air conditioned, he was told that the issue had been carefully studied, but the size of the cars made it impossible. The Mayor's response was unequivocal: No air conditioning, no new cars. As a result, New York got its first air-conditioned subway cars, and all new subway cars have been air-conditioned since then.

—

A proposal to build new high schools drawing from a broad enough area to assure a diverse student body drew intense controversy. A suggested location for one such school was in a contemplated educational park in the East New York area of Brooklyn. The alternate possible use of the site was as an industrial park. The issue was a complex one and the Mayor finally decided to support the industrial park. Some disappointed advocates for the educational park decided to picket at the site when the Mayor visited. The protesting teenagers were so amazed that the Mayor, accompanied by minimal security, came to their community that they picked JVL up on their shoulders and carried him aloft like a hero.

—

The first section of the Third Water Tunnel augmenting the other two that supply NYC's water opened in 2013. Mayor Lindsay had approved the project more than 40 years earlier, even though there was no conclusive evidence that the first two tunnels were in danger of failing. JVL was given significant advice on whether or not to build another and decided in favor of construction. The project was supposed to take a decade. He reasoned, in part, that he did not want to be the Mayor responsible for NYC running out of water.

—

The borough presidents opposed JVL's program to build low-income housing with federal money in middle class areas, but they recognized the need for these units. So they agreed to each oppose such projects in their own boroughs, but to vote for them elsewhere in the City, assuring that all were approved.

—

JVL proposed a special district to encourage the construction of legitimate theaters in midtown Manhattan. None had been built in decades. Theater owners were against creating the district. But Richard Weinstein recruited every stage star in town to appear at the Board of Estimate to support the proposal. It sailed through and, as a result, four new legitimate theaters were built.■

Donald Elliott was Chairman of the City Planning Commission for six of John Lindsay's eight years as Mayor. He has been Counsel to the Trust for Cultural Resources of the City of New York, served on the board of WNET-13 and the Metropolitan Transportation Authority, and was Chairman of the New York City Urban Coalition and Long Island University. A recipient of the Municipal Art Society's Medal of Honor, he is of Counsel to the law firm of Bryant Rabbino LLP.

Robert Esnard

I was practicing architecture with a small firm in the Bronx and working on a study of the South Bronx. The area had many problems. The threatened closing of St. Mary's Hospital and a decision to locate a new community college in Queens rather than the Bronx (as we had hoped) were likely to create further strains. A *New York Times* article on my work resulted in a federal planning grant, and I was invited to appear before a hearing chaired by Don Elliott, Mayor Lindsay's new Chairman of the City Planning Commission

To my surprise, Elliott offered me a job of leading the Planning Department's first local office, which was situated in the Bronx. These offices represented a radical departure from the City's long-standing policy of keeping planning operations centralized in downtown Manhattan. This Lindsay Administration outreach to neighborhoods like the South Bronx persuaded me to change careers and enter government. As the new head of Bronx planning, I jumped into a number of serious issues, including the debate over whether to demolish the Third Avenue El. The structure was in terrible disrepair, with pieces of metal falling off its columns.

Bronx Borough President Bob Abrams initially opposed demolition, but I showed him ways to remove the El and estimated the possible effects. He eventually decided to support taking down the El, which opened shadowed sections of the Mid-Bronx to the sky for the first time in generations, sparked new development, and led to the Borough President's making me his Deputy.

I continued to serve in government in various planning positions, culminating in my appointment as Deputy Mayor by Ed Koch.

One day, I attended a city-sponsored meeting of architects and planners to discuss housing issues. Former Mayor Lindsay was also on hand. We barely had any direct contact when I had served in his government, so I was delighted to introduce myself to Lindsay, shake his hand and thank him for making it possible for me to follow my unusual route from South Bronx architect to Deputy Mayor.■

Robert Esnard *was the first director of the Bronx Borough Planning Office and is now President of the Donald Zucker Organization.*

Charles Evers

In 1969, I was elected Mayor of Fayette, Mississippi's first black mayor since Reconstruction. Fayette had a majority black population among its 2,000 residents, but we were not allowed to vote until passage of the 1965 Voting Rights Act transformed the politics of the Deep South.

My election was not well received by the white community and the entire police force walked out and resigned the day I took office. So we had no police or fire protection, or even a garbage truck.

I didn't know much about running a city, even a very small one, but John Lindsay reached out to me and offered help. First, he found a way to send us an old city garbage truck, which someone on his staff drove to Mississippi. Its arrival caused great excitement. (I never knew how he was able to give us the truck). He also sent an experienced black NYPD officer who stayed for a year and helped rebuild the Fayette Police. John Lindsay was incredibly thoughtful and generous. We stayed in touch, talking occasionally. I never understood why he was so kind, but he seemed to care a great deal.

In 1971, I decided to run for Governor. Because the State Democratic Party still wouldn't allow blacks to participate, I got permission from Democratic National Chairman Larry O'Brien to run as an independent. Nonetheless, most lnational eaders of the Democratic Party were afraid of offending Southern Democrats and declined to support my candidacy, including presidential candidates Edmund Muskie and Henry (Scoop) Jackson, as well as Teddy Kennedy, who did, however, host a fundraiser in Boston (I had campaigned extensively for his brother Bobby, my hero, in 1968). Among those running for President, only John Lindsay came to Mississippi to campaign for me. He visited my campaign headquarters in Jackson, which gave everyone a great boost, and then delivered a speech at a church in Laurel. When I introduced John as "the nation's second best Mayor," it got a big laugh and a lot of press. There had been some threats against the church that day. The congregation and the minister were very fearful. But John never wavered. He was determined and courageous and gave a very emotional talk.

I was deeply grateful and reciprocated by endorsing Lindsay for President. I campaigned for him in Florida in 1972, visiting the state capital in Tallahassee and two universities, Florida State and Florida A&M. I also toured the docks at Jacksonville with him and endorsed him in a television commercial.

Lindsay remained a good friend, always available, interested, and helpful. I visited him in New York in 1973 when we went for a walk together in Harlem. It was remarkable how relaxed and comfortable he was among crowds in the black community, and how welcoming people were. He obviously had been there often.

Lindsay had a unique feeling toward the black community and people in need, whether in Harlem or Laurel, Mississippi. During those years of incredible racial tension and conflict, he set an example and was a beacon for all of us--regardless of color--of how our nation should be.∎

In addition to serving as the first black mayor of a Mississippi city since Reconstruction, civil rights leader **Charles Evers** *ran for Mississippi governor in 1971 and senator in 1978 and has been active in radio as a disc jockey and station general manager.*

Lew Feldstein

Helicoptering along the East River from a morning meeting at Gracie Mansion to City Hall with the Mayor in the summer of 1967, the police officer calls our attention to something hanging from the Williamsburg Bridge's north face. As we approach, we see it is a huge sign that reads "ALICE'S RESTAURANT." Each letter is emblazoned on a full bed sheet. The whole contraption is attached to 2-by-4s and hangs from thick chains.

The Mayor, very pissed, growls, "Damn hippies. Encourage them to start new businesses, to move here and they go and advertise their new restaurant by hanging a damn sign on a city bridge!"

John Lindsay had never heard of the song "Alice's Restaurant" or its composer, 20-year-old Arlo Guthrie, who also recorded the 20-minute piece. In fact, just about nobody had heard of the song or its composer at that point, unless you listened to a weird disc jockey named Bob Fass on WBAI, an obscure politically leftward-leaning FM radio station. Fass began playing "Alice's Restaurant" every night at around three or four in the morning. I was a listener.

When we arrived at the Wall Street landing pad, I asked the Mayor if I could have the sign when it was taken down. I gave my business card to the ranking police officer on the scene. Two hours late five cops lugged the whole pile into my City Hall office.

That evening I stripped off the two-by-fours and the chains and boxed all the sheets to send them to my brother, who was serving in Vietnam. How perfect, given the song's anti-war sentiments. But since my brother was often in the field for weeks, I sent it to a mutual friend with a secure address—former colleague Sid Gardner who had recently arrived at the US Embassy in Saigon to serve as Ambassador Ellsworth Bunker's speechwriter.

This story ends abruptly. The package never arrived and I was unable to trace it through the post office.■

Lew Feldstein *is co-chair of the Saguro Seminar, which promotes civic engagement. He was President of the New Hampshire Charitable Foundation, served as a civil rights worker in Mississippi and was wine steward and personal assistant to John Wayne on the actor's yacht.*

Rosalind Fink

I began my stint in the Mayor's Ofice as a summer intern in 1968, working for Jay Kriegel in the basement of City Hall. I returned the following year, taking a semester off before returning to law school.

Our corner of City Hall's basement felt like the center of the universe, constantly buzzing with Lance (Liebman)'s Ladies. There were frequent visits from Jeff Greenfield, Peter Goldmark, Sid Davidoff, Barry Gottehrer, Jeffrey Katzenberg (who knew!) and, occasionally, Bella Abzug. Kriegel's secretary Ann Manwaring presided.

The Intern program began with a reception at Gracie Mansion. Being ignorant of New York social conventions, I arrived at the time on the invitation—5 p.m. To my profound embarrassment, NO ONE was there, except John and Mary Lindsay. They were gracious beyond words. Mary even gave me a tour of the Mansion. I can't recall what the Mayor said to me. All I remember was staring up at him, open mouthed and wide eyed. He was far handsomer—and much taller—than I had anticipated.

That afternoon taught me a lesson I've never forgotten. Over the following forty-plus years, I have never arrived at a cocktail party in New York on time.■

Rosalind Fink *served in the New York State Attorney General's office, headed Columbia University's Office of Equal Opportunity and Affirmative Action and practices employment and higher education law at Brill & Meisel.*

John Fiorillo

During my tenure as Chief of Staff of the Health Services Administration, we learned that the Little Sisters of the Poor were planning to close a hospital they ran in the South Bronx. Small as it was, this facility was essential to that neighborhood's health care. Cardinal Spellman had asked the sisters to keep the hospital operating until the new Lincoln Hospital opened. The Sisters refused the Cardinal's request because they no longer had the money to support the facility and told him they would move back to their order's headquarters in Milwaukee within a few weeks. The Cardinal then appealed to Mayor Lindsay for help.

An emergency meeting was held in the office of HSA Administrator Dr. Howard Brown. In addition to the Mayor and Dr. Brown, the deputy commissioner and Monsignor Cassidy, representing the Cardinal, the head of the city's Health Planning Agency and I were present. The Monsignor reported that the Cardinal was willing to give the Sisters his personal stamp collection—valued at the time at over one millions dollars—if they would keep the hospital open. After much discussion, I was instructed to go to the Bronx to reason with the Mother Superior, tell her of the Cardinal's offer and plead with her to keep the hospital open a while longer. So up to the Bronx I went.

The Mother Superior met me at the convent door and rather reluctantly let me in. I made my pitch and told her of the Cardinal's offer. She was unimpressed and, in plain language, told me what the Cardinal could do with his stamp collection. Then she threw me out.

I returned to the same office where the same group had convened to hear my report. When they heard the bad news, the Mayor leaned back and said, "Many things have happened to me in my career, but this is the first time I've ever been screwed by a nun." At which, the group dissolved in laughter.■

John Fiorillo was Associate VP for Health Sciences at Columbia University and held posts in other health-related institutions. He is a playwright.

Joy Manhoff Flink

John Lindsay had numerous friends in theater and entertainment and heard many complaints about the cumbersome municipal approval process for film shoots and New Yorkers' resentment at having to go to Hollywood to work in movies.

During his 1965 mayoral campaign, Lindsay pledged to streamline the approvals process. After his election, he told his Assistant Barry Gottehrer to come up with a plan. Barry learned that filmmakers here needed a separate permit from the local police precinct for each day's shoot at each location. Furthermore, that permit had to be issued the day before filming. Even a shoot lasting just a few days could require dozens of permits from several precincts; a theatrical feature might need hundreds. The precinct also had to assign officers to the filming site. Different officers would be assigned when the location changed. Cash payments to the police had become an accepted part of a film's daily budget.

Some city agencies wouldn't give their approval without reviewing the script (often refusing if they thought it critical of New York or their work). A full-time city electrician was assigned every day (and paid by the movie), even though such work was almost never needed.

In May 1966, during his fifth month as Mayor, Lindsay issued Executive Order No 10, which put Barry's bold plan in place:

• A single permit issued by City Hall would cover all locations and all days of filming—a breathtaking reform in its simplicity—with all city agencies directed to cooperate without any script review (the permits were administered by the incredibly talented Mary Imperato);

• A single police unit would be assigned to provide security support for the entire filming, eliminating the accepted practice of paying graft to each precinct; and

- A senior mayoral aide (Gottehrer) would oversee the process.

Barry hired me to work full-time with the industry after David Garth introduced us. My job was to persuade producers and directors to film in New York. The results were immediate and dramatic. We went from 11 films partially shot in the city the year before, to more than 25, with a growing number shot in their entirety.

One of my first challenges was obtaining a fireboat in response to a call from the team making "Funny Girl." I had several lengthy conversations with Fire Commissioner Robert Lowery and we all know the result—that spectacular scene of Barbra Streisand singing "Don't Rain on My Parade" from the bow of a fireboat, surrounded by water jets at full blast.

But there was another more complex problem to making movies in New York—dealing with the film unions' onerous and expensive work rules. While Barry found allies in Steve D'Inzillo of the Projectionists, Ken Fundus (IATSE) and Tom O'Donnell (Teamsters), a comprehensive plan to deal with this issue proved elusive.

So Barry proposed that new, less-costly rules apply each time a full (theatrical) film was shot here. Since such productions had not ocurred previously, all jobs created under this new format would be new ones. I now had the added assignment of negotiating with both the filmmakers and the unions on each film. Every deal over rules and rates was specific to the individual production. This approach succeeded in significantly lowering the cost of shooting in New York, entailed a time-consuming film-by-film process. There were an awful lot of meetings at Downey's and other pubs favored by the union leaders. I was grateful to have a good liver.

Each film also required extensive negotiations with the involved city agencies. With the Mayor's unwavering advocacy and pressure, we found increasing support, even enthusiasm from government bureaucrats and a growing cadre of experienced officials who took pride in the process. Norman Lear's experience with "The Night They Raided Minsky's" was exemplary. He was quoted saying that he had never had more cooperation from any city in the world.

New York became the backdrop for a vast array of great (and not so great) films, from the classic "Midnight Cowboy" to a long body of work by the great Sidney Lumet ("Network," "Dog Day Afternoon," "Serpico") and, of course, to films of New York's quintessential Woody Allen.

The Mayor loved to visit the set of each major film, and joked comfortably with the cast. No actor was here more often than Jack Lemmon. He and Lindsay always had a great time deadpanning together.

Overall, 366 feature films were shot in New York over Lindsay's two terms, as well as 85 percent of the nation's television commercials, a major New York industry which we also supported. This activity had a tremendous impact on the city's economy, generating vast numbers of jobs (many well-paid, skilled blue collar technical trades) and tax revenue.

New York enjoyed, as well, wonderful marketing globally from scenes like Barbra Streisand singing in the harbor and so many other great stars in vivid locations, all resulting from the modern technology that enabled directors to liberate filmmaking from expensive sound stages and take it to the streets.

All that continues today. Next year marks the 50th anniversary of Barry and John Lindsay's transformative Executive Order that remade filmmaking in New York and transformed the city into the world's model for the industry.

Lindsay's 1966 Executive Order may rank as one of the most economically productive documents ever issued by a city government, generating billions in wages and taxes at virtually no cost.■

Joy Manhoff Flink was the first Director of the Mayor's Office of Film, Theater and Broadcasting.

Susan Fisher *and* Judith Friess Katten

W hat could possibly have equaled being young, idealistic—and working in City Hall's Room One during the Lindsay years? A world of constant chaos and commitment, of ever-changing agendas and even more fluid assignments, where life varied with the day's headlines.

Perhaps that is the explanation—it is the only one either of us can come up with—for how it came to pass that we found ourselves traveling out to Riker's Island to attend the premiere of an all-female-inmate-production of "Sweet Charity," a theatrical work supported by and underwritten by some arts-in-prison grant that was initiated by the Mayor.

After entry through the several metal doors that clanged shut behind us and being greeted by the warden, we sat as inconspicuously as possible in an auditorium filled to capacity with women prison inmates. We were so heartened to experience first-hand the impact of this JVL program, up to the moment, that is, when the warden, from the stage, insisted on introducing us to the prison population. As "representatives of the Mayor," no less, leaving us no choice but to stand up and face the hooting that predictably followed.

There were certainly countless moments from our Lindsay years when we felt privileged to partake, but none came close in intensity to our red-faced bow on behalf of the Mayor at the women's house of detention.■

Susan Fisher worked in Nairobi, Kenya, for the Ford Foundation, for the Citizens Committee for NYC, the Population Resource Council and the Museum of Television and Radio. Judith Katten was Counsel to the Motion Picture Association of America for several years before returning to New York to practice employment discrimination law.

John Forrer

I was one of several advisers JVL invited to Gracie Mansion one day to discuss a controversial issue. Neither of the preferable alternatives would please the affected groups. Moreover, the option we agreed was in the city's best interest would draw the most opposition. After listening to us analyze our choices for the better part of an hour, the Mayor cut off the discussion. If he was going to be in trouble politically anyway, John said, he'd rather it be for doing the right thing. Everyone left the Mansion after that meeting feeling proud to be part of the Lindsay Administration.■

John Forrer was Assistant Director for Program Planning in the Budget Bureau and Assistant Administrator for Management in the Human Resources Administration. He ran a Carter Administration task force, was a real estate developer and led a company that built the largest solid waste composting plant in America.

Joseph L. Forstadt

I succeeded Joel Tyler as License Commissioner in February of 1968. Our agency's portfolio included licensing horse-drawn carriages and setting their rates, which were based on a trip's duration, regardless of how many passengers were aboard.

As prom season rolled around, we were concerned that some carriage drivers might gouge graduates celebrating their milestone with an evening ride through Central Park. One early June night, a team of inspectors and I paid a surprise visit to the park. The drivers were all demanding prices far in excess of the permissible rate. We ticketed the offenders, directing them to attend a hearing at the department where we would decide whether a fine, suspension or license revocation was in order. We also informed stable owners that we would be conducting undercover sweeps throughout the month and warned them that violators would be penalized.

A press release reporting on the results of our "sting" operation mentioned that we might require the installation of meters in horse-drawn carriages to alert passengers to their fares and deter gouging.

A few hours after the release was issued, my secretary came rushing into my office to tell me that the Mayor was calling. JVL was already on the line when I picked up the receiver. "Joe," he said, "won't meters ruin the romance of the carriage ride? Do something else!" That was a question followed by an order.

I conferred regularly with mayoral assistants assigned to oversee the License Department, but that was the only time Mayor Lindsay called me directly on an agency matter.

(Mayor Lindsay merged the License Department and the Department of Public Markets into a new Department of Consumer Affairs the following year and appointed Bess Myerson as its first commissioner.)■

Joseph L. Forstadt, *Acting Commissioner of the Departments of Licenses and Consumer Affairs as well as Assistant Administrator of the Economic Development Administration in the first Lindsay Administration, is of counsel to the law firm of Stroock & Stroock & Lavan where he has practiced for 40 years specializing in real estate and tort matters.*

Andrew C. Freedman

My overriding memory is that the Lindsay Administration was one in which, if one excelled, there was ample opportunity to move ahead. There were no limitations imposed by a lack of political connections. I know because I had none; it was a meritocracy.

Among the cases I handled for the Law Department were a number of successful defenses of the Department of Consumer Affairs, headed by Bess Myerson. One day she called and invited me to meet with her in order to thank me for my work on her Department's behalf. In the course of the meeting, she offered me the post of Assistant Counsel, which involved a pay raise. That, plus her charisma, convinced me to join the Department and within six months, the Department's Counsel left and I was promoted, serving in that capacity from 1971-1974. At the Department I had many clever and capable colleagues, including Henry Stern, First Deputy Commissioner, who later was elected to the City Council, and Bruce Ratner, Consumer Advocate, who has become a leading real estate entrepreneur in New York City.

At the close of the Lindsay Administration and without any political connections, I consulted with Norman. Redlich, who introduced me to a small law firm, Reavis & McGrath, where I have spent my legal career. At the firm was Jim Nespole, former Litigation Assistant Corporation Counsel was at the firm. Although we are now both retired senior partners and the firm, now called Norton Rose Fulbright LLP, has almost 4,000 lawyers in 55 offices, we have continued to work together and enjoy time together spent, in part, reminiscing about life in the Administration of John Lindsay.■

Andrew C. Freedman is of counsel to Norton Rose Fulbright.

Elaine French

Young and naive, but determined to save whatever part of the world I could, I jumped at the chance to join the New York City mayoral campaign of the Kennnedyesque John Lindsay as paid staff in the fall of 1969. I'd graduated from Wellesley three years before and shortly afterwards had married my longtime Harvard boyfriend. An ROTC student-become-pilot in the USMC, he had left for Vietnam in July.

The energy in the campaign headquarters was electric. Young dedicated workers fueled by equal parts ideology and hormones ran around feeling important and maybe helping Lindsay win a second term as Mayor. The prospects were uncertain; Lindsay had lost the Republican primary to John Marchi and was now running on the Liberal party ticket and an Independent line.

I was assigned to work with one of Lindsay's Democratic coalition members, Bella Abzug, whose charisma and leadership brought strong labor backing to his campaign. Perhaps more critically, Bella represented the newly energized women's movement, which looked forward hopefully to the passage of the Equal Rights Amendment. Women flocked to Lindsay's campaign, perhaps not because of his politics alone.

Lindsay was magnetic. Whenever he would turn up at headquarters, which was not often, the news of his presence would whip through the place like the wind. We'd climb up on tables, in miniskirts no less, to catch a glimpse. Getting a handshake was a gift from the gods, or in this case, God.

Most of the worker bees were about my age and it was no secret that flirtations, dalliances, and more took place among the campaigners, including more senior staff. I fended off many advances, but cannot tell a lie; I appreciated being appreciated in my husband's absence.

More problematic for me were my conflicted feelings about the Vietnam

War. Bella and other strong women in the city had formed the Women's Strike for Peace, one of the early anti-war groups. I had been hoping fervently during the three years my husband had been in aviation training that the conflict would be over before he was called to go over there. It wasn't. By 1969 I was ready to admit that I thought the effort was a mistake and joined my mother marching through the city's streets to protest the war.

But the anti-war movement's lack of sympathy for and understanding of the inescapability of military service for some of my generation made me increasingly uncomfortable in New York.

After Lindsay's reelection, I was assigned to a basement office in City Hall to work out the details of his nascent plan for a city day care program. Despite a deep commitment to that prospect as a liberating tool for women, I left New York to return to Southern California where I found greater comfort in the company of fellow Marines' wives.■

Elaine French *has evaluated education policy and developed programs in the fields of early education (including Head Start), compensatory education, day care, and juvenile court schools. She teaches art and is a trustee of The Nature Conservancy of Washington State.*

Marilyn Friedman

I have many memories of my years in the Lindsay administration, first as an attorney at the Law Department and then as Deputy General Counsel for Development at the Housing and Development Administration. Two initiatives in particular are noteworthy.

The first was a complex transaction with the Public Theater led by Joseph Papp, which was in serious financial condition. So the city purchased the theater, then leased it back to Papp for 99 years for $1/year. The deal closed in 1971, and as owner of the building, the city could now pay for capital improvements and finance the extensive renovations the building required. While negotiations had begun well before I arrived at the Law Department, it was probably the most fun closing I have ever attended. After the lease documents were signed, Joe Papp and the City's closer, Meyer Slifkin, began singing Yiddish songs. Every time I go to the Delacorte or the Public Theater itself, I take pride in having helped to establish this great civic and cultural institution.

The second initiative was the South Street Seaport, on which I worked with Edgar Lampert and Don Elliot. This was a groundbreaking deal, both literally and figuratively. The principle of transferring air rights was oncept of transferability of development rights applied in this transaction, which saved the Seaport and made possible the restoration of Schermerhorn Row. It involved long negotiations with the artists living in Schermerhorn Row at the time, an arduous but ultimately successful process which, like the Public Theater deal, protected and preserved an important piece of New York history.

I will be forever grateful for the opportunity to work with the brilliant and dedicated folks in the Lindsay administration.∎

Marilyn Friedman was Counsel to the Municipal Assistance Corporation during the fiscal crisis, then taught and practiced law, and became a design historian and author.

Floss Frucher

I came to New York in the fall of 1964 for two reasons: because three college friends had found an apartment in a brownstone on 74th Street between Central Park West and Columbus Avenue for $125/month and offered me a bed…and to try to work for John Lindsay. I had seen him in Washington just after I'd graduated from Stanford in June of 1963 and gone straight there with some fellow Stanfordites to try to help further JFK's initiatives. All through that memorable, tragic summer and fall spanning Martin Luther King's speech before the great assembly gathered before the Lincoln Memorial and President Kennedy's assassination, I had followed Lindsay's work and began to think of him as the emerging architect of enlightened public policy in our country.

The day after landing in New York a year later, I made an appointment to meet him. He had just been re-elected to Congress. I carefully structured what I would say in our meeting and arrived exactly on time at his office in the Armed Forces building on 44th Street. It was high noon when I was ushered into his "inner sanctum." There he sat, a long-legged Adonis-like creature with his feet crossed on top of his desk and a skylight beaming sunshine straight down on his blond head.

We had a wide-ranging conversation about several topics: my background and why I had come to New York, some elements of his own life, and the general state of the city, state and nation. After twenty or so minutes of this, I gathered all my courage and told him flat-out that the reason I thought he would benefit from having me on his staff (my firmly believing that he was a future Presidential contender) was that I could bring "a healthy Western perspective to the jaded East" in the work I would do for him. He laughed heartily and indulgently, said he would love my help and then steered me outside his office to Connie Eristoff who announced that I was 46th in line for a paying job.

Soon after, agreeing to volunteer for him, but also needing to survive,

I found a job with the Wagner Administration in one of LBJ's Great Society programs. But when Lindsay announced his first mayoral campaign the following spring, I answered the call and left my job to run a campaign storefront for him in the northern Bronx for six months. (To this day, it was the most fun I've ever had—working!) After Lindsay became Mayor I joined his Administration, participating on a task force studying the poverty program in its ten designated areas of the city. The task force was guided by Bill Haddad and managed directly by Sandy Frucher, who subsequently became my husband. I worked for three more years with Sid Gardner and Lew Feldstein, always within the ubiquitous oversight of one Mr. Kriegel! Never was there a better time to be in public service.

During those years, I had glancing contact with John Lindsay, but nothing ever approached the extended moment of our first meeting. It was a jewel I've treasured ever since.■

Floss Frucher, Adjunct Professor of Public Affairs at Baruch College, has held executive posts in many public and non-profit organizations concerned with policy in such areas as corrections, aging advocacy and healthcare.

Gerald Frug

What most struck me about Mayor Lindsay at the time I worked for him – the entire second term – was his remarkable ability to find and recruit talented people to the city government. More than that: once the people he hired began to do their work, he inspired them to be creative, he trusted their decisions, and he backed them up when others threw up roadblocks.

I would like to offer one example of what I'm describing: Gordon Chase, whom the Mayor named as the Administrator of the Health Services Administration, where I worked. The Health Services Administration was one of Lindsay's super-agencies, designed to bring related city departments together under one institutional umbrella. In this case, the departments were the Health, Mental Health, Addiction Services, and the Office of the Chief Medical Examiner (the morgue). The Administrator was also Chairman of the Board of the New York City Health and Hospitals Corporation, a semi-independent authority that ran the (then) 18 municipal hospitals. The combination of all these health-related city agencies was itself quite a giant enterprise—more than 40,000 people worked for HSA.

Gordon Chase was an unlikely—and controversial—choice to run the Health Services Administration. He was not a doctor—not even a health services professional of any kind. Many people asked: how could such an appointment be justified? There was an answer to this question, one that the Mayor well understood. The job required someone who had the experience and the talent necessary to manage a government bureaucracy. Gordon Chase was such a guy. He had worked for the federal government in a variety of positions: on national security issues at the White House, at the Agency for International Development, at the US Equal Employment Opportunity Commission. He knew how to get things done in a government position. Most people don't.

But how did he do it? Gordon, like the Mayor, had a talent for finding and hiring good people. He would recruit them by making his own enthusiasm contagious. "The problems are big," he'd say, "we can really do something, we need you to help." Almost everyone he wanted to hire came. Then, once they were on the job, again like the Mayor, Gordon inspired them, he trusted their decisions, and he backed them up when others threw up roadblocks. "You can never give someone too many compliments," Gordon would say. And, it turns out, you can't. Gordon would meet regularly, tirelessly, with staff members working on improving the city's performance on a wide range of projects. Rats, lead poisoning, methadone maintenance clinics, abortion clinics, hospital contracts with medical schools, even a (fake) scandal at the Chief Medical Examiner's Office – there was much to do. Gordon questioned his staff, prodded them. But he made them feel important, he made them proud of their work, he wanted them to know he believed in them. That belief, quite genuine, helped produce the work Gordon was praising. I witnessed this hundreds of times; I went to all the meetings. (I was Gordon's Deputy.)■

Gerald Frug is Louis D. Brandeis Professor of Law at the Harvard Law School. He also served as Special Assistant to the Chairman of the United States Equal Employment Opportunity Commission. He teaches local government law and has taught a course in contracts throughout his academic career.

Sid Gardner

Through the haze of a half-century I recall a brief snafu in 1966 over accruals of federal aid in New York's "war on poverty." I was serving as Executive Secretary of the Council Against Poverty, the group overseeing the city's community action agencies. Steve Roberts of *The New York Times* (with research done by John Kifner, I believe) had uncovered some accrued funding from Washington that we hadn't spent. In such situations, some or all of the accrued money reverted to the federal government. Not a great story for us, but not the end of the world either since other funding continued to arrive in abundance.

Unfortunately, we weren't deft enough yet to point out that the vast majority of this unspent money began piling up during the Wagner Administration. So we took some hits in the newspapers for a few days, but this "crisis" blew over and other crises came and went.

Even in the early days of his Administration, JVL took such setbacks in stride. He was never happy about bad headlines, of course, but disinclined to shift blame or look for scapegoats. His attitude made me much more willing to venture out and take risks, knowing that the Mayor was a grown-up, unlike a lot of politicians then—and now.

(To this day, I remain convinced that John Kifner learned to read upside down at my desk at the Council Against Poverty.)■

Sid Gardner served in the Army in Vietnam, was Deputy Assistant Secretary of HEW, worked on the staff of the Children's Defense Fund, and served two terms on the Hartford City Council (1977-81). He has taught in seven universities and published four nonfiction books and six novels. He is now President of Children and Family Futures, a national nonprofit based in California.

Bernard Gersten

In the spring of 1984, Linda LeRoy Janklow led a small deeply committed group of Vivian Beaumont Theater Board members in the attempt to reactivate the theater which had stood unoccupied for four years. I believe it was Linda who embraced the brilliant idea of asking John Lindsay to serve as chairman of the Board. It was an idea whose time had come and *MIRABILE DICTU*, John said yes. So began the fifth attempt to create a permanent theater at Lincoln Center.

John set about his tasks with a vengeance; building the Board, raising funds to finance the first year of production and, in short order, hiring Gregory Mosher as artistic director and me as executive producer.

John very early on would say, "We need a hit" and we would patiently explain that we were a not for profit theater, not in the business of looking for hits but hoping to produce works of quality that would eventually give the theater distinction and facilitate Board-building and fundraising. John was never quite convinced that we didn't "need a hit." Of course, he was right.

In those early days all decisions about budgets and productions posed high risks. Our ambitious company struggled with fundraising and making the right artistic choices while finding its footing on the slippery slopes of New York's theater world. Potentially dire consequences lurked at every turn.

John relied on a very informed kitchen cabinet of half a dozen Board members, deeply committed and stalwart. John would hear out all the arguments regarding everything from the next production on the schedule (and how to pay for it) to the price of coffee in the lobby. From these discussions John would sense the collective feelings of the group and all pros and cons of an issue, summing it up by declaring: "Talkin's daft, doin's the thing." And so, with wisdom and instinct, the theater was assembled, dusted off, its engines started and now, 30 years later, 171 productions later, over 1 billion dollars later, LCT lives. Its stages rarely empty, its seats almost always sold out and its slogan still, "Talkin's daft, doin's the thing."■

Bernard Gersten was Executive Producer of the Lincoln Center Theater for 28 years, from its inception to his retirement in 2013. He had previously been Associate Producer at the Public Theater for 18 years.

Sigmund Ginsburg

In addition to my other responsibilities as Assistant City Administrator, I founded and served as Director of the New York Urban Fellows
program for its first three classes. The 47th class of Urban Fellows
graduated in May of 2016. Since 1970, 1,096 young men and women
have come through the program. Several of them are second-generation
graduates. Mayor Bill deBlasio was an Urban Fellow.

Mayor Lindsay and Deputy Mayor-City Administrator Tim Costello were
consistent, enthusiastic supporters of our efforts to find talented young
people from across the nation, recruit them for a tour of duty in New York's
municipal government and encourage them to consider entering public
service. The twenty "best and brightest" college students or postgraduates
selected annually as Urban Fellows were each posted to an agency where
they helped its staff perform more imaginatively and effectively on behalf
of New Yorkers. They also attended weekly seminars conducted by senior
city officials and community leaders. In addition to Mayor deBlasio, many
Fellows have gone on to distinguished careers in government. All, I'm
sure, acquired a lifelong interest in urban affairs.

I vividly recall one class of Urban Fellows that had the privilege of spending time with Mayor Lindsay at one of our seminars. After they questioned
him for about an hour on a wide range of subjects, the session was winding
down around 6:30 p.m. when one Fellow asked Mayor Lindsay how the
daily pressures he faced at City Hall affected his domestic life. After a long
pause, the Mayor said softy, "This is my second meeting this evening. I
have four more scheduled and I hope to get home in time to kiss my young
son good night and wish him a happy birthday. Since I left early this morning, I've not had a moment to be with him or speak to him." He paused
again. "Any more questions," he asked. The Fellows, understandably not
wanting to delay him, were silent. Mayor Lindsay thanked them for being
part of his government and left.■

*Sigmund Ginsburg held senior posts at the Museum of Natural History
and several colleges; and was a consultant to non-profit organizations.*

Rudolph Giuliani

When I was young, I watched the emergence of John Lindsay as an attractive candidate, a new political star, seemingly a Republican Kennedy.

When he ran for Mayor in 1965, he brought a spirit of reform to a tired city. These were most difficult times and through his personal courage and energetic style of visibility, he seemed to have a lot to do with keeping New York calm when so many other cities were in flames.

I first met John when he swore in my friend Nick Scoppetta (whom I had worked with on the Knapp Commission) as Investigation Commissioner in late 1972. I was impressed by how tall and good-looking he was in person. He had a larger than life presence that obviously enhanced his charisma. Meeting the Mayor for the first time I was struck by how pleasant he was to a 28-year old prosecutor he didn't know. He seemed to go out of his way to be welcoming and gracious (it was obviously his nature).

While I respected his performance in response to turmoil and racial unrest, I had a less favorable view of some of his policies, especially budgeting and policing. As an Assistant US Attorney, I had investigated misuse of funds in the city's Model Cities program under Lindsay, successfully prosecuting the director, assistant director and other employees. It seemed to me at the time that he must not have been keeping close watch. But twenty-odd years later, as Mayor in my own right, I saw how difficult it was to keep control over such a massive and far-flung bureaucracy and even had some of my own problems, recognizing then that every Mayor probably had such difficulties and it wasn't really a failure of personal responsibility or attention.

I always believed that Lindsay made a terrible mistake in switching parties in 1971, becoming a Democrat. Years later, when talking to Bob Dole who had served with John in the Congress, Dole remarked on how well-liked John was among House Republicans and that, despite his moderate views, there was none of the animosity felt toward Nelson Rockefeller (which largely resulted from the bad feelings left from his battle with Barry Goldwater in 1964). I have always had the theory that if John had remained a Republican in good standing he would have been a more attractive national candidate than Rockefeller and would have most likely been selected by President Gerald Ford as his Vice President in 1974, instead of Rockefeller. And while Ford then felt compelled to drop Rockefeller from the ticket for the 1976 election because of this intense hostility, Lindsay would have remained on the ticket and, had they still been defeated by Jimmy Carter, Lindsay would have been well-positioned as a future national Republican candidate.

We didn't have much contact in the years following, and it was not unexpected that as a Democrat he endorsed David Dinkins twice over me in 1989 (Dinkins won) and in a 1993 rematch, which I won.

After my election, I called and asked John to have lunch to get his ideas on being Mayor. I didn't have too many sources of first-hand experience. Dinkins was not very communicative and Koch, while very helpful, wanted it all done his way.

At lunch, Lindsay gave sound advice about the need to balance delegating authority with micro-managing, about choosing schools and police precincts to visit which needed maintenance since a Mayoral visit always was preceded by a hasty upgrade and fix-up, and the value of surprise drop-ins to Sanitation depots and other facilities to see how the city really worked, where word-of- mouth spread rapidly across the city of the Mayor's presence and interest.

Lindsay spoke clearly about why being New York Mayor was unlike any other job (certainly governor or president) since people really believe "they own you", and that they expect you to be there whenever things happen to them, and want you available to them whenever they feel they need you. "Accept it," he said. "And enjoy it." Despite all the travail, he remained positive and upbeat about the challenges and the opportunities.

In our second meeting he gave me sound advice on hiring. He liked the process I was following, but encouraged me to keep talking publicly about reform and change which would attract better people who wanted to have an impact in addition to the traditional job seekers.

And he talked about the impact on family since I would be the first Mayor since John with school-age children living in Gracie Mansion. He urged me to talk to them about the pressures and how difficult it would be.

Peter Powers, my oldest friend and First Deputy Mayor, made two Lindsay-related contributions. First, as a witness to the catastrophic 1969 snowstorm that almost ended Lindsay's career, he insisted that we drill incessantly for snow cleaning.

And he learned that the Lindsays hadn't been back to Gracie Mansion in twenty years. So on a Sunday, we hosted them and their children, who found where they had scratched their initials in an antique window pane, and then helped my daughter do the same.

A few years later, City Council Speaker Peter Vallone came into my office and said that John was quite sick but hadn't served in the city government long enough to qualify for health care. We both liked John and felt that he had served the city with distinction and deserved better. So my Budget Director suggested that we appoint John to a city post (like UN Liaison) so he would qualify for healthcare and a deserved pension, which we did with the full support of the Council.

All mayors are products of their times and Lindsay held the city together in a most troubled era which qualifies him as a good Mayor. And, what is also apparent, despite strong ideological differences, he was widely liked and respected by those across the political spectrum.■

Rudolph Giuliani *served as Associate Attorney General and United States Attorney for the Southern District under President Reagan. He was Mayor of the City of New York from 1994 to 2001. He is founder of Giuliani Partners, a security consulting company, and a partner in the law firm of Bracewell & Giuliani.*

Patsy Glazer

I associate the Lindsay years with youth, energy, excitement, commitment, possibilities, arrogance and naïveté. We believed we were on the right side of the issues (I still believe we were), and that we would be successful in our quest (which we often weren't).

I remember, in particular, a group of irate parents from Canarsie, Brooklyn who met with me in 1972 to protest students from the Tilden Houses project being zoned into their local junior high schools. Their primary concern, they said, was overcrowding. Perhaps at some level it was. But the other, unspoken issue was the prospect that these new students would "tip" the schools racially. They threatened to keep their children home from school and stage demonstrations at the junior highs. I told them they would be unsuccessful and warned that their actions could backfire. I suggested, instead, that they try to negotiate further with the Board of Education. They left the office very unhappy with "City Hall" (and having to meet with a 25-year-old, rather than with the Mayor), and determined to move forward with their plans.

They did succeed in disrupting the schools and prevailed in keeping students from the Tilden Houses out of their junior highs. But their success was only temporary. A few years later, the courts stepped in and mandated a plan similar to the one that caused the protest.

Nothing was as simple or straightforward as we believed in those days. But I do, on occasion, grow nostalgic for the lack of cynicism, and the faith in bright possibilities that the Lindsay years represented.■

Patsy Glazer was a Mayoral aide on education and women's Issues from 1971 to 1973. Subsequently an executive at JP Morgan and then Seagram, she is now a consultant.

Harrison J. Goldin

I was introduced to John Lindsay, then a congressman from the Upper East Side's Silk Stocking District, and a candidate for Mayor, in 1965, by his twin brother David, a tax partner who befriended me at Davis Polk & Wardwell, where I was a young associate. I had won a primary for a seat in the New York State Senate. With election in November a certainty in my overwhelmingly Democratic Bronx working class district, David said I should spend some time with John to get important pointers on how to interact with constituents and organize my local office.

John and I met for breakfast in the Plaza Hotel's Edwardian Room. Elegant, charismatic and gracious, John explained patiently how important it was to set up a district office with a laser-like focus on serving constituents. "Every voter's question, complaint or request," he said, "should be taken seriously and treated respectfully with the utmost concern. I'll give you an example," he went on. "A while back I received a letter. It read: 'Dear Congressman Lindsay: Although I have been a school teacher for 32 years, I have recently had to leave my job because the CIA has been persistently transmitting on my frequency. As a result, I am not only unable to work, but my sleep and quality of life have been totally upended. Please contact the CIA and ask that they stop transmitting on my frequency. I would be very grateful. Sincerely, Sayde R. Nut.'"

I was young and must have looked at John wide-eyed in disbelief. "No, no," he went on. "I sent a letter to the Director, CIA, Washington DC. 'Dear Mr. Director: I am writing on behalf of my constitutent, Sayde R. Nut, who has complained to me that the CIA is transmitting on her frequency. Because of this transmission, Ms. Nut has lost her job, is unable to sleep and has had a serious decline in her quality of life. I would appreciate your conducting an investigation into this matter, with a view to directing that the CIA stop transmitting on Ms. Nut's frequency. Sincerely, Congressman John V. Lindsay.'"

"What happened?" I asked, assuming the agency must have sent men in white coats to see both John and his constituent.

"A week later I got a reply on the letterhead, 'Director, CIA, Washington DC. Dear Congressman Lindsay: Many thanks for your letter on behalf of your constituent, Ms. Sayde R. Nut, and for forwarding her complaint that the CIA is transmitting on her frequency. I have directed a thorough investigation into the matter and am glad to report that the CIA is not transmitting on Ms. Nut's frequency. Please advise her that the transmissions are certainly originating elsewhere, perhaps from a foreign power.'"

John concluded, "Of course, I sent the complete correspondence to the constituent. She may have wanted a different result, but there was a satisfied voter."

I got the message. During my 24 years in elected public office, every communication from a constituent got the same earnest attention, no matter how outlandish. I satisfied lots of crazy people, courtesy of John Lindsay."■

*In addition to serving in the State Senate, **Harrison J. Goldin** was a member of the U.S. Department of Justice, New York City Comptroller from 1974 to 1989, and founded Goldin Associates, a financial advisory and turnaround firm.*

Ari L. Goldman

I was crushed. It seemed that all of City Hall—and certainly all of the Mayor's office—was in Florida in the weeks before the March 1972 Democratic Presidential Primary. I, right out of college, was just a clerk in the Mayor's press office, but I felt very much a part of the team. I had even worked on Lindsay's statement announcing that he was switching parties and a second statement saying that he was throwing his hat in the ring. Well, maybe I didn't write them, but I did Xerox them!

But when it came to going to Florida, I got left behind. "You're in charge," Tom Morgan said with a wink and a grin as he left for Miami. Thanks, I thought. In charge of nothing.

The morning of the Mayor's announcement in Miami, I opened up the press office, right next to the Blue Room, and went through the morning papers. It was my job to clip—with scissors—all the articles that mentioned the Mayor every day. I put together "the clips," as they were known, and ran off enough copies for all the Mayor's aides. It was a quiet day and I couldn't imagine much more happening until I had to watch the evening broadcasts on the long console with three big television screens. They were permanently tuned to the big three: WCBS, WNBC, WABC. I had a primitive remote, complete with a long wire that enabled me to toggle between the screens. My job was to write a daily report on how the Mayor was covered.

But then the phones started to ring. "Do you have a copy of the Mayor's statement?" I didn't realize that the Mayor was declaring for President that day, but I was ready. I found the statement on Tom's desk and started to read.

"Can you speak up," the voice at the other end said. "We're recording."

"Recording?" I stammered. "But I'm not the Mayor."

"Well, we couldn't send any of our reporters to Florida, so we're calling the Mayor's press office. This is the press office, right?"

"Yes," I said.

"Good. Then you are a spokesman for the Mayor."

Newly appointed, I read with passion and feeling about the mayor's disappointment with the Republican Party, about his opposition to the war in Vietnam, about his hopes for the America's cities and for the nation as a whole.

It was the first of a dozen times that day that I read the statement to reporters who called, although only one of them actually broadcast my voice. I found out later that night when I watched the three TVs. I don't remember who it was now, but one of them put up a picture of Lindsay with the voice of a 22-year-old trying to sound like a press secretary.■

Ari L. Goldman *went from the Mayor's press office to* The New York Times *where he spent 20 years covering education, transportation, state politics and religion. He then taught at the Columbia School of Journalism. He is the author of four books, including the best-selling* The Search for God at Harvard.

Sherwin Goldman

I came to work for the Lindsay campaign the day after I completed my New York State Bar Exams, depleted but excited.

I reported to Rod Perkins, a partner at Debevoise Plimpton with whom I had worked closely at the San Francisco Republican Convention (he for Governor Rockefeller, and I for Governor Scranton and Senator Hugh Scott). Rod shared an office at Lindsay headquarters with his Debevoise partner, George Lindsay, John's older brother. They told me to prepare background materials for the upcoming mayoral debates

Truth be told, I was never much interested in research, but luck was with me. I had spent a year between Yale College and Yale Law School at Balliol College, Oxford. An annual Balliol program (endowed by an American alum named William Cooledge) sent a few of the very best graduating Balliol scholars to the US for a summer. They could travel wherever they pleased and were "hosted" wherever they went by Balliol alums. Since I was a Balliol alum, the Cooledge Traveling Fellows had been given my contact information. One of them, a cherub-countenanced lad named Christopher Patten, reached me, said he was interested in politics and asked if I could show him something of the "real thing." I invited him to Lindsay headquarters. Christopher turned out to be a much better researcher than I and became an asset to the campaign.

Chris and I collaborated in compiling Briefing Books for upcoming television debates. Although John was not inclined toward detailed preparation, he had a keen sense of the debates' likely dynamics. When George and Rod introduced Chris and me to The Candidate in our first "briefing session," John made it clear that he was more interested in how Bill Buckley might address an issue than in anything Abe Beame might say. John expected no surprises from Beame, but wanted to consider Buckley's possible, but less predictable positions and arguments. He often roared with laughter at our more frivolous guesses about Buckley's tactics and how to handle them.

When Chris and I once apologized for "wasting the candidate's time," John put his big hands on our shoulders and insisted, "You're doing me more good than you can imagine!"

The day prior to the final debate, after months of looking, I finally found an apartment: a floor-through in a rent-controlled brownstone on East 55th Street. But the landlady, wearing a big Buckley for Mayor button, said "Sorry, I don't rent to Jews."

After the final debate, the candidates and their staffs were shaking hands and wishing each other good luck. Buckley, using Rod Perkins' nickname for me, asked, "Any luck, Squirt, finding an apartment?" I told him about my recent, unpleasant encounter with one of his supporters. Surprisingly, he asked for the landlady's name. On Election Day, the landlady called to inform me that I could come sign a lease for the apartment. I would live there for the next twelve years.■

Sherwin Goldman is a theatrical producer.

Peter Goldmark

I go into JVL's office to talk—again—about his frustration with "making things happen" in the city bureaucracy. "They just don't move fast enough," he grumbles.

I'm prepared for this. I offer him a deal.

"John, the city government has all these projects. Let's imagine you can see them moving. Imagine they're flowing through your corner office right here in City Hall in a transparent pipe running from this wall to the opposite one—a huge, transparent pipe with hundreds of projects inside, like buildings, changes in agency regulations, service improvements, capital investments. There they are, all moving sluggishly, undifferentiated from one another, through the transparent pipe right in front of your eyes."

I tell him that we have been working on an instrument—a staff unit—that would allow him to reach into the pipe, grab those things of greatest importance to him and make them move faster than the others. He can choose the projects he wants to focus on, track their progress, and intervene (a.k.a. kick ass) if he thinks they're not moving fast enough.

"But there's a catch," I say. He frowns. "You can only do it with five of them at a time," I tell him. "That's the deal. You can speed up five and get them done fast, but no more. If you try to do too many, then none of them will move fast."

He jumps at it. "Yes," he says.

This transparent pipe was the Project Management Unit that we set up in City Hall after having first established the Policy Planning Council which analyzed tough choices and made big policy decisions. The Project Management team, headed by Andy Kerr, scheduled the Mayor's high-priority projects and moved them forward at his direction.

Lindsay leapt at this opportunity. Some critics said he was only interested in politics and political imagery. They were dead wrong. Although not sophisticated about its finer points, John cared deeply about management and fully supported efforts to improve managerial practices. He backed good management, chose strong, gifted leaders and stood by them even when they got him in some kind of trouble. And he cared passionately about seeing things actually change on the ground, taking as much or more pleasure and pride from such measurable successes as from making the "big decisions" or issuing "big policy pronouncements." It is no coincidence that the Lindsay Administration provided so many of the talented administrators and managers that populated both the city and state governments for decades after his time in office. ∎

Peter Goldmark *served in the Lindsay Administration's Bureau of the Budget and as City Hall's Chief of Staff for the first six months of the Mayor's second term. During his 45 years in public life, Goldmark also served as Secretary of Human Services of the Commonwealth of Massachusetts and Executive Director of the Port Authority of New York & New Jersey. He was also a senior newspaper executive at the Times Mirror Company, President of the Rockefeller Foundation, Chief Operating Officer of the* International Herald Tribune *and head of the Environmental Defense Fund's Climate and Air Program. Currently, he is an independent consultant to foundations and non-profits, an occasional newspaper columnist and self-described general troublemaker.*

Michael Goldstein

W hen Tim Costello was a candidate for City Council President in 1966 and John Lindsay's running mate I got a job as his deputy campaign secretary and speechwriter.

I wrote Tim a speech calling for broad civic engagement to replace clubhouse politics. Tim told an audience at Columbia University that, "The city and its young people have become strangers. I propose an Urban Corps to bring together the city and its young people."

The speech was reasonably well received, but Costello lost his race for City Council President.

John Lindsay appointed Tim as Deputy Mayor/City Administrator, however. I learned that the new mayor enthused about the idea I suggested to Costello for his Columbia talk. Tim had me come aboard to help create the Urban Corps.

Where would we get money to employ students in the government?

The College Work-Study Program, established three years earlier as part of the Economic Opportunity Act of 1964, was then wrapped into the Higher Education Act of 1965 and remains the foundation for all of the federal student aid programs.

Colleges would receive money to fund part-time work for needy students, either in public service or at their institution. The federal government would pay 90% of the salary. Congresswoman Shirley Chisholm, a strong supporter, said the program would lead college graduates into public service careers.

Visits to local colleges taught us that the work-study money was administered by each school's financial aid office. Without exception, we were told all work-study money was being used for school-based needs. And the financial aid officers held the purse strings tight.

Tim asked the Mayor to present the idea to New York's college presidents

The Mayor and Tim told them that the Urban Corps would provide students with needed work, enhance city services, enrich the students' education and even encourage some of these undergraduates to pursue careers in public service.

The presidents loved it. They went back to their campuses and told their assistants to enroll their school in John Lindsay's new Urban Corps program. Financial aid directors were informed that a chunk of work-study money would be allocated to the school's Urban Corps participants.

Here we were in the spring of 1966, intending to launch the program in June with 1,000 participants. Not surprisingly, we were flooded with applications. Getting good intern placements in the labyrinth of city government was more challenging, but we accomplished that, too.

Ready to go. We had put together a million dollar program and it would only cost the City $100,000.

Except we didn't have $100,000....yet. But with days to go before the first students were supposed to report to work, we persuaded Tim to tell the Mayor that either the $100,000 is found somewhere in the municipal budget, or a thousand unemployed college students will camp out on the steps of City Hall. The next day, the New York City Urban Corps was declared an anti-poverty program, the $100,000 materialized and the rest is history.

Since 1966, over a hundred thousand college students have been a part of this great effort. And all because of a campaign speech.∎

Mike Goldstein, Director of the Urban Corps, headed a Ford Foundation-funded project to help launc similar programs in thirty cities. He was Associate Vice Chancellor at the University of Illinois-Chicago and now chairs the education practice at the Cooley law firm in Washington, D.C.

Diana Gordon

In 1968, I was a restless assistant in Fred Hayes's stable of bright young things at the Budget Bureau—restless because I didn't have enough to do. I was just a lawyer, not technically sophisticated about budget issues and ignorant of New York politics, bureaucratic or otherwise, having moved to town just a year before. So I was delighted when Fred asked me to write a speech for the Mayor that he would deliver to an august group at a dinner marking the RAND Corporation's 20th anniversary. New York was chosen for the event because the think tank had opened an office in the city (one that would operate for eight years) whose mission was to apply systems analysis to urban policy issues. I worked hard on the speech and was gratified when Fred liked it.

A few days later, Mayor Lindsay's office called and asked if I would like to accompany him to the Century Association where he would give the speech the following week. I was thrilled.

On the evening of the talk, the Mayor's limousine pulled up on my block. I imagined that my neighbors were all leaning out of their windows and wondering at the fickle finger of fate that was about to deliver me to the precincts of the rich and famous. As we rode uptown the Mayor complimented me on the speech. I suggested lines that I thought might draw laughs.

When we arrived at the Century, a club official with an apologetic look told us that "the young lady" would have to wait outside the dining room. John Lindsay would have none of it. "But she wrote my speech and would like to be sure I deliver it well," he protested. The official, however, was unbending. He did say, though, that if I were willing to sit in the ladies' dining room I could have a nice steak on the house. The Mayor then asked to see the President of RAND who was in the main dining room where more than a hundred guests had gathered. RAND's president emerged and was as unyielding as the club factotum. "I'm sorry," he said, "but the club's policy is not to admit women to that room, and we are the club's guests."

At this point, Lindsay took another tack. "But she's my girlfriend," he said. Although this blatantly untrue and insulting recourse offended me, I would have taken advantage of it had the gambit succeeded and enabled me to attend the dinner and hear him deliver the speech I'd written. This was 1968, after all, and I was no feminist on the ramparts. But the RAND president was not prepared to advance my cause at the cost of offending his hosts, so I yielded and agreed to be sent home in the Mayor's limousine. I did not linger for the steak. To his credit, John Lindsay sent me a two-line note telling me that the speech went well and expressing his regret that I could not be there to hear it.■

Diana Gordon, who served in the Human Resources Administration and the Budget Bureau, was President of the National Council on Crime and Delinquency and recently retired as Professor Emerita from CUNY's Graduate Center.

Betsy Gotbaum

JVL always seemed serious and preoccupied when dealing with assistants to the mayor, but he was very warm and kind to my seven-year-old daughter on those special occasions when staff members' children were on hand. He loved having her accompany us to events and always made sure she was comfortable and well-fed. I loved that side of him, but wished he had shown those qualities toward me.■

Betsy Gotbaum, Mayor Lindsay's Special Assistant for Education, was also the Executive Director of the New York City Police Foundation, appointed New York City's Parks Commissioner by Mayor David Dinkins, the first woman to hold that post; President of the New York Historical Society, and twice elected New York City Public Advocate.

Barry Gottehrer

"Your Mayor and his associates will be seen in this city. We will visit the slums and the waterfront...We shall go forth with a selfless perspective—with the knowledge that what we do here may gain us neither gratitude nor glory except in the judgment of a later age..." (from John Lindsay's inaugural address, January 1, 1966).

We were beginners, a new mayor, a handful of aides and assistants with minimal experience with government and no sense of life in our ghetto streets. Along with Jay Kriegel and Sid Davidoff, I was the third member of what the media derisively referred to as "Lindsay's Kiddie Corps." To most people, we were an odd bunch—far different from those who had surrounded mayors in the past. In New York and in a great many other cities, mayors generally preferred to know as little as possible about potential problems until the media forced them to deal with them. By keeping their distance, the theory went, they could place the blame elsewhere if the explosion ever took place. We, on the other hand, wanted to know everything that was happening in our city and, because we were young and pure, willing to work twenty-four hours a day, unalterably committed to John Lindsay and his struggle to change things and make our city livable for all people. We really believed we could change things and make our city livable.

As Mayor, Lindsay wanted to be where the action and the people and the problems were, to see first-hand whether city services were really being delivered all the time. And so, these walking tours evolved—ultimately becoming a key element in our summer strategy and the trademark of a Mayor who cared and who wasn't afraid. We learned that out in the streets, particularly the troubled streets of our ghettos, very few people had the ability to reach those most likely to rebel. And so we made contact with those who could, including making some unusual alliances and not always with people we would have otherwise chosen to deal with. This formed the genesis of what would be the first Urban Action Task Force in the country.

And as other cities continued to burn with considerable loss of life and millions of dollars of destruction, John Lindsay's city continued to hold together.

Shortly before I left City Hall, the Mayor reflected to me about the great many urban experts who had come to work for him and most of the politicians who hadn't. "They don't know what it's like out there, out there in the streets. How poor people are forced to live, without heat, without water, without hope. Where you live by your wits and your cunning. They just don't know that out there you have to think fast and think tough. That you can't tell people you need some time to study their problem. We know what it's like, Barry. We know what it's like on the streets."■

*The late **Barry Gottehrer,** Assistant to the Mayor, organized the Urban Action Task Forces that monitored and tried to redress neighborhood grievances. As a prize-winning journalist, prior to the Lindsay Administration, he reported on municipal government's shortcomings. He had a subsequent career as a public affairs consultant in Massachusetts, North Carolina and Washington, D.C. The above passage, selected and submitted by his children Andrea Kling and Kevin Gottehrer, is excerpted from his memoir* The Mayor's Man *published by Doubleday in 1975.*

Richard Gottfried

When John Lindsay was elected Mayor in 1965, I was 18 and already involved in politics. As a candidate and as Mayor he generated feelings of heightened excitement, hope and possibility about the city and its government. It's easy to say, "Those were the 60's. It was the times, not him." But remember that those years were also a time of anger, bitterness and frustration. Lindsay made a real difference.

While I supported most of Mayor Lindsay's agenda, I strongly disagreed with his views about development in Manhattan. (I couldn't have it known it then, of course, but I would have similar disagreements with every future mayor and governor.) When he ran for re-election in 1969, though, I had the good sense to appreciate that, despite our differences and my being a committed Democrat, he had been a great Mayor and earned progressives' support. New York needed him.

In the summer of 1969, after a handful of other "West Side kids" and I were elected as Democratic district leaders, we were invited to meet with Lindsay at Gracie Mansion to solidify our support. Because I had put off buying new shoes, the soles of the ones I wore had worn all the way through. I didn't have time to buy a new pair, but couldn't go meet the Mayor with my socks showing through. So I taped some index cards together, colored one side black with a marker, and put them in the bottoms of my shoes.

A few years later, some of us met with Mayor Lindsay to tell him why we opposed his planned convention center on the Hudson River at West 44th Street. (One was built many years later, but ten blocks south.) We were pretty adamant. After a while, though, he excused himself, leaving us with his staff. I thought then, and still do, that it was a delightfully confident gesture.■

Richard Gottfried is the longest serving member of the New York State Assembly. He has represented a district on Manhattan's West Side for forty years.

Lynda Gould

In 1970, Harvey Rothenberg, the Mayor's Executive Assistant, asked me if I would be interested in becoming the Mayor's Executive Secretary because Kathy St. John was leaving to get married. I told Harvey that I didn't think my secretarial skills would cut it. He replied that there was not a lot of shorthand and typing; making sure the office ran efficiently was the heart of the job.

He also reminded me of the great support staff—Irving "Oppy" Oppenheim, the night mayor who transcribed a lot of the dictation and typing in what were usually the quiet overnight hours; Myra Feldman, the corresponding secretary who wrote better JVL letters than JVL and J.J. Jackson, the receptionist and greeter who handled what could be hundreds of phone calls per day and kept track of the many visitors.

I was currently Mary Lindsay's City Hall liaison, press secretary and community affairs assistant, a known quantity. When I told Harvey I was interested, he said that the Mayor would want to be sure we both had the same expectations about the job.

That interview has stayed with me for 45 years. The Mayor informed me was that I would have to work on the Fourth of July. Moreover, his personal staff had to be at Gracie Mansion when he greeted, thanked and tried to console the families of police and fire officers who had been killed in the line of duty the previous year. I was more than willing to agree, knowing from colleagues how strongly the Mayor felt about that. We also discussed office personalities, staffing and his high-pressure routines. Finally, the Mayor said that "schmoozing" was an important part of the job. He chuckled, seemingly pleased to get out an incongruous word for this very proper WASP. I assured him that I was quite capable of "schmoozing".

I got the job, which turned out to be a wonderful experience for someone who hadn't yet turned 30. Sitting in the office next to the Mayor and seeing the *New York Times* on my desk in the morning alongside paperwork on matters that would become the basis of future front-page stories was heady stuff. I recall juggling telephone calls, watching visiting dignitaries as they passed by, and reaching out to the Mayor in his car during urgent situations. (His code name on the car radio was "Winston.") There was the cast of characters who killed time at my desk while waiting to see the Mayor, tapping their feet, puffing nervously on their cigarettes. I see them today, many of them in important positions in the worlds of business and government and remember them as they were way back then.

John Lindsay could not have been a more considerate boss. He was always concerned about his staff, attentive to whether we were happy, overworked —or not. I never wanted to take a vacation and mostly didn't ... because it was all too good. ∎

Lynda Gould *was Executive Secretary to the Mayor, Assistant to Deputy Mayor Robert Sweet and Press Secretary/Community Liaison to Mary Lindsay. She has had a 40-year career in not-for-profit management and development.*

Jeff Greenfield

I f you were with John Lindsay for any part of his eight years in City Hall, there weren't a whole lot of "light" moments. From his first minutes in office—a citywide transit strike—through near-riots, strikes by just about every public employee union, angry clashes with neighborhoods threatened by crime, endless tensions among the city's warring tribes, "playfulness" is not the word that comes to mind.

There was, however, one small instance that showed me that John Lindsay could still call on a puckish sense of humor to ease a tense moment.

It happened just before a Mayoral debate in 1969. Lindsay was about to square off against Democrat Mario Procaccino and Republican John Marchi. There was a sense that the political winds had begun to shift. His GOP primary loss to Marchi had made it easier for liberals to support him on the Liberal Party line. Procaccino's win meant that a highly conservative, backlash-embracing, pro-Vietnam War candidate would be the Democrats' standard-bearer--making defections to Lindsay the more likely. And fate--in the form of a New York Mets' World Series win and a perfectly timed visit by Israeli Prime Minister Golda Meir—had given Lindsay a run of benign media coverage.

So maybe it was a sense of optimism that gave Lindsay the idea of playing a mind game or two with his opponent. Whatever it was, he chose not to appear at the appointed time for a microphone check, but to remain out of sight, shooting the breeze with his campaign team. When Procaccino arrived, he was clearly put out by Lindsay's absence. We could hear him, in our Green Room, put off by the Mayor's absence.

"When I'm the Mayor," Procaccino groused, "I'm going to be on time!" With just a minute or two before the broadcast began, the Mayor sauntered onto the stage with a cheery wave of his hand. As the debate later showed, Procaccino was clearly out of sorts. It made me wonder where Lindsay had learned his skills at gamesmanship.

Jeff Greenfield, a Lindsay speechwriter, is a television journalist and author of 13 books. He has been a political commentator for CBS News, CNN and ABC News.

Joel Grey

John Lindsay was the classiest Mayor one could imagine in any city—totally committed to the work at hand and always ready with an encouraging, friendly smile.

We met when I was appearing in "George M!" at the Palace Theater. He was a great supporter of the theater and its community had enormous affection for him. During his mayoralty, John Lindsay and Hal Prince created "Broadway in the Streets," which brought performers from shows running on the Great White Way to the Bronx, Queens, Brooklyn and Staten Island on a Saturday or Sunday morning. We would put up a piano on a temporary stage and the neighborhood would show up en masse to watch us sing and dance at no charge, just as we would be doing a few hours later on Broadway for paying customers. Everybody—performers and audience alike—loved it.

Many years later, when I moved into the Hotel Des Artistes on West 67th, I got to know the Mayor personally because he and Mary lived there, too. He remained the charming, kind gentleman I remembered from that special time in the 1960s. ∎

Joel Grey, who originated the role of the Master of Ceremonies in "Cabaret" and the title role in "George M!," has won an Academy Award, a Tony Award and a Golden Globe Award. He has appeared in films, on television and on stage. Three books of his photographs have been published and the Museum of New York has exhibited his photography.

Judah Gribetz

I served as Buildings Commissioner at the end of Mayor Robert Wagner's third term. Soon after, Robert Weaver, the first Housing and Urban Development Secretary and a great New Yorker, asked me to be Regional Administrator of his new federal agency. So I was involved with Mayor Lindsay's housing team throughout his first term. In early 1969, I left the government to join the law firm of Shea and Gould.

Anticipating his re-election campaign, Lindsay established an innovative rent stabilization program to put a brake on escalating rents without extending controversial rent controls. To my surprise, the Mayor asked me to serve as impartial chairman of the nine-member Rent Conciliation and Appeals Board, which would adjudicate complaints from tenants against landlords. The board consisted of four real estate industry members and four public members. I had looked forward to becoming fully immersed in private law practice and was reluctant to take on so controversial a role. But the Mayor was persistent and my firm's two name partners—legendary lawyers and major public figures Bill Shea and Milton Gould—urged me to accept.

The rent stabilization legislation also created a second board to set the rate of rent increases. Lindsay selected Roger Starr, the respected housing expert, to chair that Rent Guidelines panel. We were all pleased that *The New York Times* praised the Mayor for choosing Roger and me.

I served as part-time chair for most of Lindsay's second term and thought the new board and the Rent Stabilization scheme worked surprisingly well. That basic structure is still in place.

When he was elected Lindsay's successor in 1973, Abe Beame asked me to serve as one of his three Deputy Mayors. With another nudge from Bill Shea, I returned to City Hall.

The next year, Hugh Carey was elected Governor and I accepted his offer to become his Counsel. Carey called the Mayor to explain why he thought I was right for this position. The Mayor graciously assented.

By 1975, I was on the frontlines of the Fiscal Crisis, advancing the Governor's heroic, creative effort to save the city from bankruptcy. By the end of Carey's first term I had been challenged and drained, and was ready to return to private law practice. I joined my dear friend Leonard Garment at Mudge Rose. Lindsay arrived there several years later.

On a trip to visit family in Jerusalem, I took my grandson to a small park where I was surprised to notice a plaque saying "John V. Lindsay Park dedicated in his honor by his Appointments Secretary Harvey Rothenberg." I took a photo and gave it to John who kept it in his office.

Near the end of his second term, as part of the Mayoral transition process, John invited Mayor-elect Beame to accompany him to his last meeting of the National League of Cities. Under pressure to form his government, Beame asked me to go as his representative. I met Lindsay at Gracie Mansion, where we boarded a police helicopter for the trip to the airport. To my astonishment, the police pilot turned the controls over to Lindsay as soon as we took off. When I served as an aircraft carrier gunnery officer in the 1950s, pilots told me that it was easier to land a jet on the carrier deck, yanked by a tail hook, than to fly a helicopter. Hardly reassuring.

When we landed, Lindsay explained that he decided to learn how to fly the chopper long ago in case something happened to the pilot in flight. A few months later, I was in a police helicopter again with Mayor Beame. During a sudden thunderstorm, we temporarily lost power and descended into Buttermilk Channel. I recognized the wisdom of Lindsay's precaution.■

Judah Gribetz has served in senior positions in city, state and federal government. As Senior Counsel to the law firm Morgan Lewis, he is currently the court-appointed Special Master in the Swiss Bank Holocaust Victims Asset Litigation.

David Grossman

City Planning Commission Chairman Don Elliott was firmly convinced that a South Bronx High School was desperately needed. He wanted funds be set aside for its construction promptly. Even if the school would not be built for several years, Don argued, such a commitment was important "to keep the community's spirit up." I disagreed strongly. In my view, allocating revenue for such a project prior to its going through the site selection process was no way to restore credibility in the capital budget whose reputation had been marred by years of inflated, unfulfilled promises. Don and I continued to squabble.

Eventually, the Mayor summoned us to his office to settle our dispute.

JVL put it bluntly: "I can't be called on to decide a technical issue between the two of you, but I'll tell you a story. During a campaign, a guy came up to a booth where my volunteers were gathering signatures on my petitions. They asked him for his signature. He opened his zipper, pulled out his pecker and proceeded to pee all over my petition forms. That's what I'll do to the two of you unless you settle this now."

—

Frederick O'Reilly Hayes, Mayor Lindsay's first Budget Director, had served in the Federal Bureau of the Budget (now the Office of Management and Budget) as well as other Washington agencies. Fred's only shortcoming was his narcolepsy, a relatively rare disease that causes its sufferers to fall asleep unexpectedly. Fred told some of us that he dropped off to sleep at his very first White House meeting, which was held in a stuffy basement room. He awoke to find the meeting over and the room empty.

For some commissioners, our weekly cabinet meetings at Gracie Mansion offered an opportunity to complain to the Mayor about what they regarded as the Budget Bureau's excessive questions about requests for "urgently-needed" staff and funding. Fred, slumped against the fireplace in the Cabinet Room, often appeared to be sleeping, another bout of narcolepsy, perhaps. But when a commissioner blamed the Budget Bureau for his agency's falling short of agreed-upon performance targets, Fred would suddenly rouse from slumber. "You turkey," he would growl indignantly. "Your requests haven't gone anywhere because you and your staff failed to provide us with the essential paperwork, despite our asking for it time and again." Fred would then explain in pungent detail just what the aggrieved commissioner's application lacked. The commissioner would blush and Fred would go back to sleep.■

David Grossman was Deputy Director and then Director of the Budget. He later served as a budget and policy consultant for public and non-profit agencies in New York and developing countries around the world.

Bruce Gyory

I was a very lucky young boy to have been involved in both Lindsay mayoral campaigns. My father Nicholas B. Gyory was Vice President of the United Hatters Cap and Millinery Workers Union and active in the Liberal Party. My mentor Alex Rose, the President of the Hatters and Chairman of the Liberal Party, was a key architect of those campaigns.

I recall two instances when John Lindsay displayed raw political courage.

My father and I attended a rally in front of Alexander's department store in the Bronx in October 1966 where the Mayor urged voters to oppose an upcoming ballot referendum to block the addition of four non-police officers to the Civilian Complaint Board. The panel, which reviewed citizens' allegations of mistreatment by the police, consisted then of three deputy police commissioners. My father had warned me that "some folks will be very angry with the Mayor," but I was unprepared for the vitriolic crowd that tried to drown Lindsay out whenever he attempted to speak. Despite the tension and jeering, the Mayor never lost his composure and persevered in making his case. The review board was defeated at the polls in a landslide a few weeks later.

The struggle to strike a balance that protects citizens' civil rights, especially in minority communities, and preserves the police's ability to fight crime in situations where a moment's hesitation can endanger lives is still playing out. Mayor Lindsay's sensitivity to the grievances of minority New Yorkers helped our city contain or prevent the sort of disruptions that plagued Los Angeles, Baltimore, Newark and Detroit during the long hot summers that loomed ahead.

In late afternoon on the day of the June 1969 primary, Alex Rose invited my father and me to his office. With a surgeon's attention to detail and a chess grandmaster's strategic thrust, he laid out his view of how those contests as well as the November election would turn out.

He predicted that the rise of Herman Badillo, then Bronx Borough President and the first Puerto Rican to hold that office, as well as the candidacies of author Norman Mailer and Bronx Congressman James Scheuer, would siphon off enough reform and minority Democratic voters to enable City Comptroller Mario Procaccino to defeat former Mayor Robert Wagner for their party's mayoral nomination. Mr. Rose also thought Staten Island State Senator John Marchi would beat Lindsay for the Republican nod because outer-borough Italian-American voters were the heartbeat of that party's primaries. With a twinkle in his eye, he explained that this defeat would be a blessing in disguise for Lindsay, enabling the Mayor to win running up the middle, while Marchi would undercut Procaccino's politically right-leaning flank.

Years later, Mr. Rose told me that political defeat is never easy for incumbents, but Lindsay had the mental toughness to win by projecting confidence as well as humility after being kicked in the gut at losing his party's primary.

John Lindsay's courage and determination in the face of obstacles and reversals are character traits that were and are all too rare in American politics.■

Bruce N. Gyory, who worked in Lindsay mayoral campaigns, is a political and strategic consultant at the law firm of Manatt, Phelps & Phillips and has served two Governors of New York as a senior advisor. He is an adjunct professor of Political Science at SUNY Albany.

Steven Haft

I first met JVL in 1964. I was a Queens high school student whose letter to Congressman Lindsay got me a meeting.

Arriving at his office, I met the Congressman's Executive Assistant, Barney Patterson, then his Legislative Aide, Connie Eristoff. Barney's a girl, Connie's a guy—progressive stuff for a Flushing kid. Then, ushered into his office, to meet the preppiest guy I ever laid eyes on—Robert Redford looks and Eleanor Roosevelt idealism. But he was nevertheless a Republican. Their last Presidential candidate was Barry Goldwater. Still, in the immortal words from the film *Some Like It Hot,* "Nobody's perfect" Only he kinda was. On the way out, Barney says, that if I am still smitten come spring, contact Mackie Arnstein to volunteer for Lindsay's next campaign.

Spring arrives. #7 train from parents' home to Grand Central. Cut to 60 East 42nd Street, near the Roosevelt Hotel, the Lindsay for Mayor HQ. And there is the leggy Mackie (my first Jewish Preppie) with a piece of desk-space just for me—and a stack of envelopes. I'm officially a volunteer. Lick & Stamp, in endless repetition. But scoping out 60 East provides ample distraction.

Now, right above my desk is a mezzanine with more desks—but no envelope licking and a buzzy kind of energy. This, I discover, is the domain of Sid Davidoff. Rapid-fire, high testosterone, distinctly less WASPY; even the girl-watching is different. It's not exactly sexy. Just sexier than the "Look at me. I look like you" preppy thing downstairs. After a while, I inveigle my way from the envelopes to the mezzanine.

And, while not instantly obvious, the entire trajectory of my young life changed the moment I joined the upstairs ranks. I am now part of the "I'm with Him" world of pols and their posses. Goodbye #7 train, hello Manhattan and daily life with Him. What an education. I can't get a good seat at my parents' synagogue on Parsons Blvd, but with HIM, the entire city is opened wide, best seats in the best houses. The Waldorf, Sardi's, Wall Street, the *New York Times*, the Knicks, Broadway, Brooks Brothers—an endless parade of the topmost stars, the boldest names and the toniest joints in town.

Even back in Queens, I've moved up from my Dad's Pontiac to riding in a mini-motorcade. In Brooklyn, rabbis lead us around in the daytime and these polite scary-looking guys show us the ropes after dark. We are after every vote. And Lindsay, without losing a button from his first or third shirt of the day, seemed to fit in everywhere. He looked like the aspiring Mayor of Manhattan, but he began to feel welcome in Rockaway, Harlem, Bensonhurst, Jamaica, and on Arthur Avenue.

And everywhere he went we went. And we began to feel part of the City too. The Ring around The Candidate—Sid, Norman, Shelley, Jimmy, Dennis, Chick, Arnie—was his hand-picked Secret Circus. But the tent was big. In the outer ring I reveled and watched and grew up. God bless those guys and girls—my inspirations.

THIS PICTURE says it all. It's a few years later…a line-up at the Plaza Hotel. John Lindsay, Andrew Heiskell (CEO of Time Inc.) Andrew Young (a hero of the civil rights movement), Ivy Leaguers and dignitaries, and at the end of the line, Ronald Ziegler, Press Secretary to President Nixon, followed by Steven Haft, Flushing High School grad now, a more regular part of the Traveling Circus and just passed my 18th birthday.

I know, Sid. I'm standing too close.■

Steven Haft is Senior Vice President for Innovation at Time, Inc. He created Indyworks, a media management consultant, and ran Haft Entertainment, whose films included "Dead Poets Society."

Edward K. Hamilton

Working for John Lindsay had never entered my mind before I got a call at my Brookings Institution office in early January, 1969—just before I turned 31—from his Chief of Staff Peter Goldmark, of whom I knew nothing. To my surprise, Peter asked if I would be interested in being considered for a senior job in the re-staffed Administration which Lindsay was assembling for his second term. I had only a *New York Times* reader's general familiarity with Lindsay's first term and little of the mental furniture needed to think knowledgably about urban government service. But I admired Lindsay's vigorous, progressive image and was persuaded by Goldmark to visit New York and meet the Mayor and some of his senior stalwarts.

The Lindsay aides I'd known—Health Administrator Gordon Chase, a colleague of mine in the Johnson White House, and Budget Director Fred Hayes with whom I worked in the federal Bureau of the Budget—stressed two points: First, making progress on problems they were addressing in New York was more important to the nation's future than anything else they could do with their precious time. Second, Lindsay was the only chief executive of a major public entity who had the guts, perseverance and deep appreciation of quality talent necessary to make such progress.

I first met Lindsay in his limo riding from City Hall to Gracie Mansion. He asked what I cared about most. I mouthed some generalities about advancing the public interest. What, he probed, was I best at? I described myself as a systems analyst who favored an economist's analytic tools, but noted that my career had been in international affairs except for a year as Staff Assistant to the Federal Budget Director. He waved that aside and drew a vivid topic-by-topic portrait of New York's dilemmas and the innovative ways his people were dealing with them. He declared that the only winning strategy was to recruit the very best young people and unleash them on these challenges. Convinced by this inspiring 15-minute soliloquy, the best I'd ever heard from an elected leader, I joined the Administration.

—

Soon after becoming Deputy Mayor, I was on Riker's Island when inmates revolted there. I understated the disruption's impact to reporters, hoping to prevent copycat episodes. A press account also revealed that I failed to don a mask when tear gas was released to quell the uprising. Lindsay called to say teasingly he was concerned that the public might question his judgment in appointing a Deputy Mayor who couldn't protect himself. On arriving at work the next day, I found a gas mask on the chair in my office.

—

Late in the term, the Mayor asked me to assess the city's prospects for state aid after he left office. I said Republican Governor Malcolm Wilson needed support downstate for his upcoming election bid, giving Abe Beame, the likely next Mayor, enough added leverage to hold the city's financial ground. Lindsay replied—I paraphrase—that if their pasts were any guide, neither would have the wit to carry that off. I doubt that he ever wished so much to be proven wrong.∎

Edward K. Hamilton, who held the posts of Budget Director and First Deputy Mayor, is a Founding Principal of HR&A, a full-service financial, executive search, litigation support, public policy and management consulting firm.

Sheldon Harnick

The Inner Circle, a New York City press corps organization, had a long-standing tradition of roasting the Mayor at their annual benefit dinner. The Mayor would strike back with a speech. When it was John Lindsay's turn to be the Inner Circle target, he chose to break tradition and respond with a song. Lindsay asked his friend producer Harold Prince to recommend songwriters for the assignment and Hal suggested composer Jerry Bock and me.

The Mayor asked us to write a duet because he planned to perform with Broadway star Florence Henderson. One of Lindsay's assistants told me what might be effective subjects. I wrote a lyric titled "It Must Be Fun To Be The Mayor Of New York" in which the Mayor, with Florence's assistance, poked fun at himself. Jerry Bock set it to music with a "soft-shoe" beat. To keep their upcoming performance a secret, John (which is what he told us to call him) and Florence rehearsed in the privacy of my apartment. My wife Margery, a professional singer/dancer/actress, staged the number, which included a modest tap dance routine.

In those days, women were not allowed on the main floor at Inner Circle events; they had to sit in the balcony. When John said that he was performing with a female partner, the reporters told him not to do so because that would undoubtedly antagonize his audience. (He identified his partner not as Florence Henderson, but as Mrs. Ira Bernstein, her married name.) The Mayor replied that unless he could present what he had rehearsed, he would not appear. "Be it on your own head," they told him.

On the night of the event, the master of ceremonies introduced the Mayor with a somewhat snide speech, hinting that what Lindsay was about to do might not please the audience. But when John and Florence appeared on stage, the crowd instantly recognized Florence and burst into surprised and delighted applause. Then John and Florence went into their song and dance. If John had sung well and been a graceful dancer, I believe the audience would have resented it, considering him a show-off. But since John didn't sing that well and danced rather clumsily, the audience appreciated his willingness to look foolish. Thank God, they enjoyed the song, especially this line: "It must be fun to know that when you go to bed at night/Not one single goddam thing you did was right." When John delivered that line, the audience erupted in laughter and applause.

The performance was so successful and so enthusiastically received that, as far as I know, all of John's subsequent Inner Circle appearances were musical. And my wife and I became both fast friends and admirers of Mayor John Lindsay.■

Sheldon Harnick has had a long career as one of Broadway and Hollywood's most successful composer-lyricists. Among his best known works are Fiorello! and Fiddler on the Roof, both with Jerry Bock.

Fred Harris

John Lindsay and I must have seemed to others as unalike as bagels, cream cheese, and lox are different from chicken fried steak and gravy. He was a big-city Republican Mayor when I first knew him. I was a Democratic U. S. Senator from small-town Oklahoma.

Yet, almost immediately after President Lyndon Johnson appointed us both to the President's National Advisory Commission on Civil Disorders—the Kerner Commission—following the terrible riots in the African American sections of so many U. S. cities during the summer of 1967, John Lindsay and I formed ourselves into a single-minded and very aggressive two-man team that led and guided the work of that Commission from first to last. We recognized in each other a shared and most sincere motivation to do something lasting about racism, poverty, and the problems of America's cities.

For weeks and weeks and months and months on the Commission, leading up to the blockbuster and bestseller Kerner Report of 1968 ("Our nation is moving toward two societies, one white, one black, separate and unequal") as well as when, two years later, we co-chaired the Urban Coalition Commission which updated that report, John Lindsay and I may have spent more time with each other than we did with our best friends, if not our wives.

So, I knew John Lindsay.

He was authentic, "the real article," as they say. He was exceptionally well-motivated, deeply committed and engaged. He was a person of uncommon courage, a fearless risk taker for right.

—

As the Kerner Commission began to get underway that summer of 1967, swarms of field investigators were sent out to get the facts about the riots and about the social and economic conditions where they had occurred. We commissioned numbers of informed studies—on everything from policing to segregated schools. We sat for days and days of hearings—listening to official and unofficial, expert as well as ordinary, views, opinions, and recommendations. And we spent day after day in meetings where we read aloud and then voted on every word in our eventual Report—and I believe that John Lindsay or I made every motion and second that was brought to vote. But before all that, Commission members paired off to go personally to the cities where the riots had occurred, to see those places for ourselves, and to talk with the people who lived there.

John Lindsay and I quickly agreed to become one of those Commission-member pairs. And for the first city we visited together, it took our advance staff three days to arrange a midnight meeting for us with a well-educated but highly militant group of African American young men and women. The group had demanded that the meeting be held in secret, and there were armed guards stationed just outside the doors when we met.

I don't think I knew any better, but John recognized the danger involved. Still, he never hesitated about going to the meeting. And he never flinched, either, when the first speaker at the meeting, a young black man with a PhD, said to us, "I can't even stand to look at your white shirts; white stinks to me. I didn't want to come here, it's too late for talking to you white people, and I'm gonna split as soon as I have my say. I am not gonna sit here and listen to any garbage you white people put down, man."

Nor did John flinch when another speaker in the same meeting, a young African American woman, said, "Why aren't you talking to white people, your fellow racists like Lyndon Johnson and Hubert Humphrey? You made this system, baby; you fix it up. We are tired of trying."

John didn't have to be there. He already knew that kind of hostility existed in so many African American communities. And the depth of it didn't shock him nearly as much as it did me. Nor did the personal attacks turn him away from his intention to help.

The next day after that secret meeting, John and I, in the company of a young black social worker, walked the "mean streets" of the black section of that same city. On one corner, we came upon a group of young black men shooting craps on the sidewalk in broad daylight. They stopped and stood up, wary. "Who are you, the FBI?" one asked us.

When our escort told the young men what John and I were there for, they all crowded around us and, all talking at once in a chorus, said, "We want a job, man. Get us a job, baby. Can't you get us a job?"

John calmed them by starting to ask the young men themselves some questions. And he didn't talk to them like a social worker or a police officer. He talked to them almost like he'd known them since high school. He asked questions like he wanted to know the answers—because he did. What kind of jobs did they want? Had any of them had jobs before?

The young men quieted down and let each in turn have his say. "I've got five kids, and I need a job," the first young man said. "Mr. Johnson got me a job this summer, but it ran out yesterday." (He was talking about President Johnson and a special federal summer program for young people in urban slums.)

I'm proud that jobs and training became a central focus of the Kerner Commission's later recommendations.

I well remember also—though this must have been two years after the Kerner Report, when John and I co-chaired the Urban Coalition's updating effort—an occasion when he and I presided at a public meeting, seeking local views, that we had arranged for in a rundown auditorium in East Los Angeles.

That session was barely underway and John and I were already being bitterly harangued and attacked by a local "Chicano" leader, as he introduced himself, when he, and we, were interrupted by a police officer who came up on the stage to privately hand John and me a written report of an anonymous telephone warning that a bomb had been planted in the auditorium and that it was set to go off at any moment.

Quickly conferring, John and I both agreed that we should go ahead with the meeting, though I don't think I was quite as sanguine about that decision as John was, but he and I also agreed that we should tell the audience about the warning, so that any who wanted to leave could do so. The crowd applauded our announcement that the hearing would continue. But the witness before us, the one who had been interrupted, was the first to leave. A few others left, too. John and I stayed, and the session continued.

—

While we went about our work in the summer and fall of 1967 and the spring of 1968, there was little news about what the Commission was doing. One day one of my best friends in the Senate and one of that body's most progressive Democratic members, came up to me on the floor and asked, laughingly, "How is it to work with John Lindsay?" He was obviously not, up to then, a Lindsay fan. The senator was surprised when I told him what a hard worker John was and what a progressive influence he was on the Commission. This senator, I may say, eventually became one of the most ardent supporters of the Kerner Report when it was released.

But while the Commission was in operation, President Lyndon Johnson came to believe that John Lindsay was too active and influential on the panel—and that he was using his Commission membership as a springboard to run for president, against Johnson.

The public had no idea about what the Commission was doing, but President Johnson did. Someone inside our panel was keeping him advised about our work and soon told him that John Lindsay and I were its two guiding leaders. So, once when I was in the Oval Office with constituents on a minor matter, the President turned to me, out of the hearing of the others, and said, "I'm surprised to see you up, Fred. I heard old John Lindsay had you down and had his foot on your neck."

The President asked me to stay on after that meeting to talk about the Commission's work. I told him what John Lindsay and I were finding and doing. I said that there had been no conspiracy or planning behind the riots, but that they had grown out of the great hostility so many African Americans felt because of their terrible conditions and bad treatment. Johnson disagreed, saying, "That's not what the FBI reports show." Another time, up in the White House family quarters, President Johnson opened an informal gathering of five or six of us senators by saying to me for all to hear, "Fred, tell us about your friend John Lindsay and his campaign for president."

I said, "Mr. President, John Lindsay's already got more on his plate than he can say grace over without thinking about running for president." The President was not dissuaded. I could have said that John's work on the Commission surely wasn't calculated to make him more popular. And who in the general public knew what John was doing on the Commission, anyway?

Back when President Johnson called to tell me in advance about the appointment of the Kerner Commission and that he was going to name me as one of its members, he wound up that telephone conversation by saying, "Fred, I want you to remember that you're a Johnson man; and if you forget it, I'm gonna take my pocket knife and cut your blank off!" He did not say "blank."

Sadly, by the time the Kerner Report came out, the President came to feel that I had, indeed, forgotten that I was "a Johnson man." Someone inside the Kerner Commission, probably the same one who'd told the President how John Lindsay and I were teaming up to shape its findings and recommendations, later told Johnson that our Report would ruin him, that it encouraged and condoned riots, and didn't have a good word to say about the President's recently enacted civil rights laws and great anti-poverty efforts.

All of that was totally false, of course, but Johnson believed it--without ever having read the Kerner Report himself. What a shame! I've always been sorry that this man, President Johnson, whose core desire, I know, was to do something about racism and poverty, and who actually accomplished more on those fronts than any president in history, turned his back on the Kerner Commission and its Report (though his push for civil rights and against poverty did not slacken).

Nor did President Johnson's attitude toward the Kerner Report deter John Lindsay from fervently advocating for full implementation of its recommendations—from the day the Report was released until the sorrowful day he died.■

*Former U. S. Senator **Fred Harris** is professor emeritus of political science at the University of New Mexico, where he continues as director of the UNM Fred Harris Congressional Internship Program. He is the lone surviving member of the Kerner Commission and its strongest living advocate.*

Frances E. R. Harrisingh

J. Lee Rankin, former U.S. Solicitor General, had also been John Lindsay's colleague in the Eisenhower Justice Department. During his first mayoral campaign, JVL said that, if successful, he would appoint Mr. Rankin New York City's Corporation Counsel. A few days before Lindsay was first elected Mayor Mr. Rankin interviewed and hired me to serve as an Assistant Corporation Counsel as well as his Law Clerk. An optimist, Mr. Rankin also hired 11 other young lawyers that week for the Law Department, an enormous law firm with but one client—the municipal government. Mr. Rankin told us, "If John wins we should be prepared to hit the ground running the day after the election."

I had a sense of what awaited me as a lawyer in public service. My father Scovel Richardson was a Federal Judge who sat on the U.S. Customs Court, known today as the U.S. Court of International Trade.

The day after the inauguration, we new hires were sworn in with Mayor Lindsay and Corporation Counsel J. Lee Rankin looking on. After the ceremony, the Mayor went down the line of new Assistant Corporation Counsels shaking our hands and asking us where we had attended law school. The first nine answered, "Yale Law School." "Wonderful, wonderful," exclaimed the Mayor, who had gotten his law degree there, too. I was one of the final three lawyers congratulated by the Mayor. The other two told him they'd graduated from Harvard Law School. When he reached me at last, I told him that I'd gone to Fordham Law School. JVL turned to Lee Rankin and said, "How did these three get in here?" We all had a good laugh and then went to work on the subway strike that confronted John Lindsay the moment he was sworn in. ∎

*Since serving in the Law Department, **Frances Harrisingh** has practiced law in Westchester.*

Stephen Heard

I talked my way onto the Lindsay Lancers football team by telling Sid Davidoff I had been a quarterback at Harvard. What I didn't mention is that it was for one of the worst junior varsity teams in Harvard's history. When Mayor Lindsay and Deputy Mayor Bob Sweet were told I was to be the quarterback, Sweet replied, "Well, we can't win 'em all."

Our game in Central Park was against the Bed-Stuy Restoration team, a bunch of do-gooders like us. But their defensive front line consisted of some of the largest human beings I've ever seen. Sid put himself, Ted Mastroianni and Dick Bell upfront against them, and while they were masterful, bloodied but unbowed, I saw so many stars from being flattened by our opponents that I could have been in the Hayden Planetarium. But we won on a last-minute circus catch of one of my passes by Ted Gross. It was one of the finest of my many fine moments with the Lindsay Administration.■

Steve Heard served as Assistant Administrator and General Counsel of the NYC Economic Development Administration. He practices law at the Venable firm in such areas as international litigation, corporate transactions, and white collar defense.

Susan Heilbron

W e were all so very green, filled with youthful exuberance and unbridled optimism. Our young, energetic and telegenic Mayor gave us a chance to make a difference and we didn't disappoint him.

The Office of Neighborhood Government was an innovative program designed to give local communities a say in their local governance by decentralizing the delivery of City services and affording them direct access to high-level decision-makers responsible for the delivery of those services. The experiment was widely studied by, among others, the U.S. Health, Education and Welfare Department and CUNY. In September 1972, at the age of 27, I was hired to supervise those external evaluation studies and to plan for the program's expansion if the experiment proved to be successful.

And successful it was! Everybody loved it. Local communities were getting the attention they hadn't even dreamed of in the past. Municipal workers got to talk to their constituents face-to-face for the first time. And best of all, City officials at the highest levels attended every meeting. Who can forget Corrections Commissioner Ben Ward's meetings with his Queens district service cabinet and all the projects he initiated!

Barely a year after I arrived, I became ONG's Deputy Director and Director of the newly-expanded program. Working with me were a slew of very young people, mostly in their early 20's, all very smart and similarly committed to making a real difference in the world. (A great many of them went on to stellar careers and continue their commitment to public service to this day.) They made sure that the projects which flowed from the district service cabinets were completed and their goals realized. We were overjoyed by the success of our efforts, but not surprised. John Lindsay made us believe that everything was possible. That if we were smart and worked hard we could meet—and even exceed—our goals.

Jay Kriegel played a key role in all of this, from helping to conceive of ONG, to his constant attention to its progress, and his care and feeding of his young proteges, which was critical to having it--and us--succeed.■

Susan Heilbron, a lawyer, served as Commissioner of the Department of Ports and Terminals during the Koch administration, was appointed Senior Vice President of the New York State Urban Development Corporation by Governor Mario Cuomo, was Executive Vice President of The Trump Organization and President of Lacey & Heilbron.

Marian Heiskell

I remember John fondly for how accessible he was. You could enter City Hall at the basement level and go up the flight of stairs leading to his office where a policeman stood guard. The officer would check to see if John was available and, if so, in you went. He always seemed to have time for me.

Soon after he was re-elected Mayor, I got a call from John who asked, "How would you like to help me clean New York?" "Anything to clean New York," I replied. We formed the Mayor's Council on the Environment to unite New Yorkers and their Sanitation Department. The Mayor was Chairman and I was Co-chairman.

I think we made a difference for the better. The Council once hosted a cocktail party attended by Sanitation Department officials. Also on hand was Paul Screvane, the agency's commissioner in the WagnerAdministration. He had been a sanitation worker on the Upper East Side in the early days of his career.

After the work we did, the sidewalks became much more attractive, and walking around the city became an even greater pleasure. ∎

Marian S. Heiskell was appointed by John Lindsay as the first Chair of the Mayor's Council on the Environment and has since co-created America's first urban national park (Gateway National Recreation Area); the first green markets (Grow NYC); and rejuvenated seven derelict 42nd Street theaters which was critical to the transformation of Times Square (The New 42nd Street, Inc).

Robert Heller

John Lindsay turned 50 on November 24, 1971, the day he interviewed me at City Hall, the final step in the vetting process for my becoming an Assistant to the Mayor. I had already been interviewed by Jay Kriegel—or sort of interviewed as he fielded and placed a flurry of phone calls—and Ed Hamilton. Nat Leventhal and I had been friends since our days together on the Columbia Law Review and he recruited me for the City Hall team. I'd never met the Mayor, but admired him from a distance for his vision, courage and integrity. Our first meeting was a blip on his schedule, but a momentous occasion for me.

Oddly, my lasting impression of that meeting is not of the Mayor's questions, which delved a bit into why I was interested in public service, my personal and professional background and the like. Nor do I recall in any detail our conversation about New York in particular and American cities in general and the scant national resources devoted to them. What I do recall vividly is the enthusiasm with which he embraced turning 50. As people stopped by to congratulate him on his birthday, his comfort with what in those days seemed like a major marker of aging was obvious.

Coincidentally, I had also served with another gifted man at the time he turned 50. The contrast was vast. That man couldn't bear to discuss the milestone, but the Mayor exuded a fundamental optimism about the future and his ability to help shape it. I can't imagine how anyone in my position could have left his office that day without wanting to enlist.

John Lindsay's character and outlook on life were important reasons why so many of us were inspired to serve with him.■

Robert Heller, *Assistant to the Mayor for housing, planning and related matters, was Managing Partner of the law firm of Kramer Levin Naftalis & Frankel. He has taught at Columbia University's School of Architecture and was the first Chairman of the Board of the Tannenbaum Center for Inter-religious Understanding.*

Joan Gregory Hendricks

After graduating from Dominican Commercial High School in Jamaica, Queens, I went to work at the Park Avenue law firm of Kelley, Drye, Newhall, Maginnes & Warren as a stenographer. I was assigned to Constantine Sidamon-Eristoff, a tax attorney at the firm. The following spring Connie decided to leave Kelley, Drye to set up his own practice. I asked if I could join him as his secretary and he said yes.

During that fall of 1964, we both worked on John V. Lindsay's congressional re-election campaign. The following spring, we enlisted in the Lindsay mayoral campaign, spending our days trying to win another election and our evenings and weekends managing the law practice. Connie "donated" my services to the Campaign Coordinator, Elizabeth Barnett Patterson. Barney, as everyone called her, had joined a few others from JVL's Washington congressional office staff to help him become Mayor.

Mary Lindsay, whom I'd met during the congressional campaign, had an office across the hall from ours in the Roosevelt Hotel. I knew her secretary Stephanie Fuchs. After the election, Mary talked with Harvey Rothenberg about hiring a second secretary. Stephanie would work at City Hall and she wanted to have someone with her at Gracie Mansion as well. Harvey was kind enough to recommend me. When Mary asked if I "would be intrigued at the idea of working for her and the family at Gracie Mansion," my answer was a resounding "Yes!!" That was the beginning of a wonderful journey and friendship that lasted forty years.

Mary toured Gracie Mansion after the election and found it in urgent need of repair and updating. The house had been used almost daily for receptions, tours and many of Mayor Wagner's meetings. She was determined to make it a home for her family. Mare's mother, Mrs. Randolph Harrison, suggested she consult with a friend of hers, Mrs. John Pemberton, who had done many restorations and decorated several homes of the mansion's era in Philadelphia and Williamsburg.

178 / JOAN GREGORY HENDRICKS

At Mrs. Pemberton's recommendation, the workmen took down the heavy drapes and let in the light. They also painted the walls brighter colors, including shades of yellow, which had been the style during the building's period.

While the workers refurbished the house, I got to join Mary, Mrs. Pemberton and her assistant on expeditions to the Metropolitan Museum of Art and the Museum of the City of New York to prowl through their collections and choose art that would hang in the Mansion. There were endless racks of incredible paintings in the bowels of the Met—Sargents, Cassats, O'Keefes, and on and on. We felt like kids in a candy store!■

Joan Hendricks worked for the House Judiciary Committee and the Carter White House's Congressional relations office. She retired after a career in the cable television industry and lives in Sacramento, CA.

George Hirsch

I worked in the Lindsay campaigns for Congress in 1964 and for Mayor in 1965.

New York Magazine was launched In April of 1968. I was its founding publisher.

Soon after, Clay Felker, *New York*'s editor, contracted with Elia Kazan to cover the upcoming Republican convention in Miami for the magazine. Felker asked Kazan, who had directed such masterpieces as "A Streetcar Named Desire" and "On the Waterfront," to write about the political gathering as if he were creating a film. Felker asked me to accompany Kazan during the convention and introduce him to as many people as possible.

John Lindsay agreed to talk to us in his hotel suite. When we left after a relaxed and candid conversation, Kazan said to me, "If I were casting this film he'd be the candidate for sure."

Of course the Republicans decided on Richard Nixon.■

Publisher **George Hirsch** *was a founder of the New York Marathon, a candidate for Congress and founding publisher of* New York *Magazine,* New Times *and* The Runner. *He is currently the Chairman of the New York Road Runners.*

Eloise Hirsh

I came to work in the Lindsay Administration in January 1968, my first real job out of college. I came of age in that optimistic time when so many young people felt drawn to public service, and, in New York City, to the Lindsay team. This was the place to be part of the crusade to make American cities better. I "signed on" and was lucky to find my way to Barry Gottehrer's office. That's where I wound up in the thick of urban action task forces, little city halls, and working with Abbie Hoffman, the Five Percenters, the Young Lords—that incredible mix of characters whose issues engaged the Lindsay people.

I had also become familiar with the issues and leaders in the North Bronx. Somehow, that made me Barry's expert on the borough. Going into the re-election campaign, the Mayor had an appearance there and I accompanied him. It was the only time I ever met John Lindsay and it was an exciting day for more than one reason. We traveled to the stop in a police helicopter. I was completely awestruck, of course—flying to the Bronx with America's most famous and glamorous Mayor.

Suddenly, Lindsay announced that he wanted to take a turn flying the helicopter. I thought, "Wow, this man can do anything!" The pilot obediently gave him the controls. We flew along for a few minutes, enjoying spectacular views of the city when, all at once, we were tipping onto our side! Not where helicopters should be! The pilot grabbed the controls back, and righted the ship.

It turned out that there was something that John Lindsay couldn't do!■

Eloise Hirsh is Administrator of the 2200-acre Freshkills Park on Staten Island, which is being transformed from the city's largest landfill into a recreational facility and nature preserve. She has also served as New York City's First Deputy Commissioner of Parks and Recreation and Director of the City's Labor, Management and Productivity Council.

Joan Hochman

"The Lindsay Years." Hazy at best. The subways are not air-conditioned. Climbing out of the Seventh Avenue IRT, on the northeast corner of Chambers and West Broadway on the way to the Muni building. Hit by the Greek deli's blast of fried oil. Makes me want to vomit. Or maybe it is the fear of the first day of work at the Project Management Staff.

"Good morning," I say, false cheery, to my German engineer office mate. "You have no right to be here, taking the job of someone supporting a family," he says back. Screw you, I think. At the women's college from which I had just graduated, they didn't tell me opposition would be impolite. Neither did my mother. Need a whole new way of operating, maybe a whole new way of being.

"Calculate the critical path of the PERT by hand," says Andy Kerr. What? Maybe he is right. Maybe "girls" can't do this job, as he said in my job interview. "When is the project due," asks our three-person team. "Tuesday" is the answer. "Tuesday next semester," I ask hopefully. "Next Tuesday," comes the reply. One teammate begins hyperventilating. She also graduated from a women's college.

Some Maximum Base Rent housing meeting. Going to see the "big client" at the Housing Preservation and Development Administration. Buttoned up McKinsey guys, very dapper, lots of data in big, greenish printouts. But the "big client" conducts the meeting lying on the floor from under his desk. I didn't see him the whole time. Wow. And I'm still wearing shirt-waist dresses and mary janes.

Later, in my evolving analyst-to-management role, I meet "citizens." I particularly like the ones who come to the local offices I set up in neighborhood preservation districts with paper clips hanging out of their ears. The clips sometimes dangle to the floor, to "ground" their wearers and block signals transmitted from CIA. They become regulars in our offices. I have them do chores. Not like the kind of "citizen interaction" simulated in Woodrow Wilson School policy classes.

We are making "change" inside "our" government. At least that is what we tell ourselves. Or "their" government. It wasn't ever clear to me who prevailed—the civil servants or "us". But I would come to understand—about change—that resource allocation is sexy, but execution is everything. Have you seen many organizations in the public sector, broadly speaking, that function that way? I haven't.

Actually, resource allocation and implementation aren't everything. The people with whom and for whom I worked are everything. My lifelong friends. The ones who smile knowingly when others in our midst talk about New York City, its government, its policies, its foibles. We don't need to be the source of the corrections. We know.■

Joan Hochman *served on the Project Management Staff in the Bureau of the Budget and as Deputy Assistant Commissioner, Neighborhood Preservation Program, in the Housing and Development Administration. She is a Managing Director of Fintec LLC, a management consulting firm.*

Malcolm Hoenlein

I first came to New York in 1971 to serve as the Founding Executive Director of the Greater New York Conference on Soviet Jewry. Soviet Jews striving to live fuller Jewish lives and emmigrate to Israel faced harsh oppression, suffering prosecution and imprisonment. Little information was available from a repressive Soviet government about allegations and often-unwritten policies and rules governing the dissidents' cases.

Mayor Lindsay was one American government official who actively supported our efforts early on. In 1973, we urged the Mayor to visit Moscow. He insisted on being able to raise both individual cases and the general issue of freedom of emigration to Israel. Mr. Lindsay applied to include former deputy Mayor Stanley Lowell, the chairman of our Conference, and me in his official party. The Soviet embassy approved the applications of everyone the Mayor wanted in his delegation but Lowell and me. The Mayor consulted the Conference for guidance. Following a special meeting, we urged the Mayor to make the trip without us, hoping he would be able to help some individuals and gain valuable intelligence. The Mayor then provided the Soviets with a new list that included Seymour Graubard, Chair of the Anti-Defamation League of B'nai B'rith, and Paul Sann, Executive Editor of the *New York Post*. (This was, of course, years before that newspaper's reincarnation under Rupert Murdoch's ownership, while the *Post* was still a respected voice of progressive values.) He also told the Russians that he would only go to Moscow if his entire reconstituted group were approved (it was). The Mayor also insisted on the right to meet with any non-official (meaning Soviet Jews) he chose, and requested a list of senior government officials responsible for emigration policy.

In preparation for his trip, the Conference also briefed Mr. Lindsay's accompanying staff, providing a detailed list of questions for senior Soviet bureaucrats.

The Mayor then briefed us on his return. He and his staff had met with every senior official on our list, including Soviet Premier Kosygin and Deputy Minister of Internal Affairs Shumilin, who administered emigration policy. Few Westerners ever had such extensive discussions with them. Mr. Lindsay probed skillfully, learning their unwritten guidelines. He also asked them about certain Soviet Jews whose emigration applications had been turned down. He asked why they had been rejected and objected to how they were treated.

Mr. Lindsay and his staff also met with Soviet Jews trying to emigrate. He hosted a dinner at the official government guesthouse with several of the most prominent "refuseniks" who had rarely been able to gather so openly, and at a government building no less. Paul Sann published their stories and photographs in the New York Post, dramatizing their plight and showing that they were neither alone nor forgotten. We published Mr. Sann's own account of the trip, along with the Mayor's comments, one of the earliest comprehensive reports of Soviet Jewry's situation.

Mr. Lindsay's journey spotlighted this cause. He provided critical information about Soviet emigration procedures, focused public attention on the travails those heroes of conscience endured, and inspired successful efforts to deliver our Jewish brethren to freedom.■

Malcolm Hoenlein has been Executive Vice Chairman of the Congress of Presidents of Major American Jewish Organizations since 1986. He is also Founding Executive Director of the Greater New York Conference on Soviet Jewry and the Jewish Community Relations Council of New York.

Martha Holstein

I came to City Hall from Helen Gurley Brown's *Cosmopolitan* Magazine in Mayor John V. Lindsay's second term to work in Deputy Mayor/Public Administrator Ed Morrison's office as a liaison to the City Council.

How important I felt to be helping develop positions on rent regulations, building code changes, the consolidation of departments into superagencies, fees and regulations on taxation, consumer affairs, and legislation affecting the Police and Fire Departments, education, and transportation. It was thrilling.

Not long after arriving in government, I was assigned to evaluate a City Council bill that provided supplemental pension benefits to surviving widows and orphans of deceased Police officers, and recommend whether Mayor Lindsay should sign or veto the measure. Its annual cost to the city would be about $250,000. That was a lot of money to me.

Taking my job very seriously, but having little knowledge of pensions and only a rudimentary understanding of municipal finance, I worried for over a week about what to tell the Mayor. I spent hours researching and reviewing legislative memoranda and other comments. I took the "approval or veto" papers home at night and debated in my mind the bill's merits and demerits. Finally, I decided to recommend approval, defending my conclusion with a strongly written argument.

Deputy Mayor Morrison, Council Vice Chairman and Majority Leader Tom Cuite and everyone involved in the process anticipated the bill being signed into law with a great flourish. The Mayor presided at the ceremony, putting his signature on the bill with lots of Lindsay pens, with its many Council sponsors beaming by his side.

With good reason, the Mayor and the Council periodically gave police officers' surviving widows and orphans much deserved small increases to their meager pensions. Only a dunce would have denied them such a benefit. There were many experts in the Lindsay Administration whose input was essential (mine was not), but that and other experiences taught me much about politics, and how and why a bill became a law.■

Martha Holstein, *Local Legislative Liaison in the Mayor's Office during the second Lindsay Administration, spent 20 years in municipal government in various positions before becoming Principal at Strategic Urban Solutions, an environmental and infrastructure consultant.*

Elizabeth Holtzman

On a recent hot Sunday afternoon, I found myself driving past the Thomas Green Playground at the edge of downtown Brooklyn. I stopped and got out, wanting to check on the local impact of a 1968-1969 Lindsay Administration program to rapidly build 50 mini-pools around New York City. This playground was one of its sites. I was very pleasantly surprised to see two pools there: one for teenagers and adults that was chock full, and another, smaller one for very young children that was rimmed with parents, dangling their feet in the water and carefully watching their charges splashing around. Everyone seemed to be having a grand time—and the pools looked clean and inviting.

Getting those pools constructed was a lot more complicated than this serene scene so many years later would suggest. I was an Assistant to the Mayor and his liaison to the Parks, Recreation and Cultural Affairs Administration from 1967-1969, and took my instructions to develop and implement new programs quite literally. But my determination created a problem for which I wasn't at all prepared. The head of the PRCA, a genteel, aristocratic, elderly man, was not accustomed, to say the least, to taking direction from a twenty-something-year-old woman like me on so major a program for his agency. He was equally resistant when I proposed putting safety matting under the swings and seesaws in all the city's playgrounds—an important, lasting safety advance. I remember endless meetings at City Hall with a very patient Deputy Mayor Bob Sweet who managed to soothe ruffled egos while gently but firmly ensuring that the programs got completed. Not surprisingly, when everything was done, I was shifted to a liaison position with another city agency.

Being part of the Lindsay Administration was—and still is—a tremendous source of pride to me. Although far from its inner circle, I was excited to be part of an Administration that thrived on innovation and change. Most of the Mayoral assistants were young, idealistic and energetic. And they were given tremendous responsibility. Those were heady days.

I was also proud to be working for a Mayor who believed in racial justice, and walked the streets of the city during tense and dangerous times to bring racial peace. Many of the programs he instituted were designed to remedy the problems of the inner city. Few Mayors of New York have had such a frank and open concern for the less fortunate and for basic civil rights.

It was a bit awkward in 1980—eleven years after I left City Hall—to find myself running for the US Senate against my former boss, John Lindsay. He was unfailingly gracious to me—as he had always been —and just as handsome as ever. It was an amazing irony that without his having given me a chance to work for him in City Hall, I would never have entered politics. He showed me that public service was a privilege and a precious opportunity to do good. For that I will always be enormously grateful. Although it had a bittersweet quality, I was still glad I won the primary.■

Elizabeth Holtzman was a four-term member of the House of Representatives, serving on its Judiciary Committee during the Watergate hearings. She was the first woman to serve as New York City Comptroller and as District Attorney for Kings County.

Edith Holzer

I have never forgotten the great privilege of serving in Mayor John V. Lindsay's Administration as deputy to his wonderful speechwriter the late Gordon Stewart. I worked at City Hall for the final year and a half of the Mayor's last term.

Our office on the second floor consisted of one medium-size room where Gordon worked and a small anteroom for his deputy and administrative assistant. The Board of Estimate chamber was located to one side and the Committee of the Whole meeting room to the other. Whenever officials from the Board of Estimate stumbled into our office we were never surprised to see their puzzled expressions or hear their inevitable question: "Why can't we take over this room?"

In late September 1973, Welfare Island was re-named in honor of President Franklin Roosevelt. The ceremony, one of the highlights of my time at City Hall, would take place on the island. A boat would ferry the participants across the East River. I felt so fortunate to be involved in preparing the Mayor's remarks for that occasion. Gordon must have bounded up and down the stairs between our office and the Mayor's more than twenty times, conferring with him and revising the speech. We worked hard to avoid the dreaded Lindsay verdict of "pedestrian," his customary criticism of a draft that failed to meet his standards. The Mayor wouldn't hesitate to strike out words or whole paragraphs that displeased him. We worked until nearly midnight on that speech. My reward would be a wonderful letter from Jay Kriegel saying that I did a good job for the Mayor.

The next day, as the press gathered to watch the dignitaries board the boat to the soon-to-be rechristened Roosevelt Island, Pamela Harriman, a future Ambassador to France, hiked up her skirt to stride across the dock onto the gangplank. Some male reporters whistled and commented, "Nice legs!" After all, it was the 70's!

Edith Holzer is the former public affairs director of the New York State Council of Child Caring Agencies.

Ken Howard

In 1973 I appeared on Broadway in "Seesaw." We had great reviews but no money to promote the show. The press was always commenting on my resemblance to John Lindsay, so one night, to drum up publicity, he was persuaded to come out on stage in my place for the musical number "My City" in which the character I played was surrounded by ladies of the night. The audience went wild and he had a terrific time standing in for me. It was a truly special evening and will always be a fond memory for me. Not to mention, it boosted ticket sales. I appreciate all he did for "Seesaw" and his deep love of theater and the arts. I was lucky to know him and his wonderful wife Mary. We became great friends over the years.■

Ken Howard is the National President of the Screen Actors Guild. Over a forty-year career on stage, screen and television, he has won two Emmys and a Tony.

Edward Hudaverdi

My friend and former student Lois Bernstein got married on February 9, 1969. I was one of about a dozen in the wedding party. The rehearsal dinner was held at Gracie Mansion, hosted graciously by Mayor and Mrs. Lindsay. Being with them felt like being "at home."

The reception was held Sunday at the Hotel St. Moritz. I looked out a window across to Central Park. It was snowing fiercely. The Mayor stood to my right. "If you weren't here next to me," I said kiddingly, "I'd think you were causing this storm." He smiled. "Don't worry Eddy. They'll find a way to blame me."

Of course, he did shoulder the blame for that storm, particularly in Queens. And now, in 2015, you can Google "Lindsay snowstorm" and there are dozens of commentaries. He handled it all with charm, humor and humility.

Perhaps he was less humble when it came to his height. The Mayor was proud of his stature and appearance. He had appointed a certain tall woman Commissioner of Consumer Affairs. She, too, took pride in her height, but since the Mayor didn't like to seem the shorter one, the Commissioner was asked not to wear her high heels when she appeared with him in public. Accordingly, she kept a pair of flats in her desk.

One of Mayor Lindsay's executive orders gave pedestrians the right of way. I've quoted that executive order—one rarely observed—to young policemen who never knew his name, nor were they aware of its directive. But John Lindsay wrote it into the books—or wherever executive orders go.

America had JFK and Camelot. New York City had John and Mary Lindsay.■

Edward Hudaverdi is a playwright, writer and editor.

Berna Gorenstein Huebner

I did opposition research in 1965 with Sherwin Goldman, who went on to become a distinguished producer. Chris Patten, the future Chancellor of Oxford University and Governor and Commander-in Chief of colonial Hong Kong, was visiting for the summer from England. He helped Jay Kriegel with research on the Chicago police commissioner and assisted JVL speechwriter Jim Carberry. What a campaign! ■

Berna Gorenstein Huebner *runs arts programs for people with dementia and is Director of the Center for the Study of International Communications in Paris. She was Research Director for Governor/Vice-President Nelson Rockefeller.*

Steven Isenberg

This is about the war JVL fought in and the one he fought against.

On my son Christopher's 21st birthday we had lunch with JVL at the Century Association. Christopher was born with six months left in City Hall, so we were two decades away from the mayoralty. I asked JVL if he could tell us something of himself at twenty-one.

He was a lieutenant in the Navy in the South Pacific. During a Marine island landing, his ship fired its guns to push back the Japanese. When the beach master, who directs ship fire from the shore, was killed, JVL replaced him.

He had never done the job: aiming from a ship is different than calculating fire trajectory from the target zone. The first rounds he called in almost landed on him. I eyed Christopher for his reaction, while imagining JVL in khaki uniform, thin, blond, handsome, fresh out of Yale, amidst chaos and death.

After the Japanese had been pushed back far enough, JVL and a young Australian officer found a deep ditch down the beach to sleep in. He was taking a risk because technically still on duty; sleeping on watch was harshly punished. Up so long, they could barely stay awake. They slept in the ditch, their heads at opposite ends. Sound asleep, he felt a touch on his leg. (I wondered where this story was going). He slightly opened his eyes and saw Japanese soldiers pointing their rifles. The only hope was to play dead. It worked: the Japanese thought it was a burial pit. They left.

JVL started to laugh: "I was so damn scared, I shit myself."

He had talked to me once about coming home from World War II, "naively believing we had made the world safe from war."

That was not to be. He kicked himself over his Congressional vote for the Gulf of Tonkin resolution that authorized LBJ to take action in Vietnam — "The worst vote I ever made." Despite his mayoral advisors, he came out against the war. He was among the earliest politicians to do so. He could have dodged the matter, but wasn't built like that. He saw the war as destructive of young lives, wrong in its rationale, and deeply corrosive on the home front.

I was strongly opposed to the war, and felt Bobby Kennedy's campaign would dislodge LBJ. JVL and Fred Hayes gave me leave from the Budget Bureau in 1968 to campaign in Oregon and California. After RFK's assassination, JVL invited me to coffee. He spoke of the sad and shocking course of that year, the loss of Martin Luther King and Kennedy, and the continuing toll of the war. He was deeply concerned about disillusionment among the young

Perhaps it was the cold showers and moral fiber of his days at St. Paul's, and the experience of war, that gave him resolve. When it came to convictions about our civic character and well being, his coda was "stand firm." Neither cold winds, nor standing alone deterred him.

His generation is almost gone, ours is autumnal. It is Christopher's generation's turn as beach masters. JVL would say to them, in the service of your beliefs and your nation, stand firm. In his memory, I would add: Stand tall.■

Steven Isenberg, the Mayor's Chief of Staff, has been Publisher of New York Newsday, *Executive Vice President of* The Los Angeles Times, *Chairman of the Board and Interim President of Adelphi University and a visiting professor at Berkeley, University of Texas at Austin, Davidson, Yale and Oxford. He was also President of the American PEN Center.*

Pazel Jackson

Throughout August of 1966, Democratic State Senator Seymour Thaler relentlessly criticized the Lindsay Administration's Health Department, alleging such improprieties as payroll padding and improper government sponsored research projects. Thaler also said Lindsay delayed the construction of several critically needed new public hospitals with a sluggish capital budget process. Streamlining the bureaucracy had been a Lindsay campaign promise. Thaler claimed that, after eight months in office, the Lindsay Administration had made no tangible progress in improving the delivery of needed public health services, especially to his Queens constituency.

Still new to the complex capital budget process, Lindsay and his aides were sensitive to such charges. In mid-August, Mayor Lindsay called a summit meeting of the Budget Director and all commissioners whose departments were directly involved in providing health services

William Mattison was Commissioner of Public Works. DPW was an 8,000-9,000-person agency responsible for the design, construction and maintenance of almost every public construction project in the city except highways. Bill Mattison was a brilliant lawyer and a trusted mayoral ally. His assignment was to shake up the construction bureaucracy. I was Secretary of the Department, the Professional Engineering Advisor to the Commissioner.

Walking to that summit meeting, Commissioner Mattison told me how frustrated he was about our situation. Out of some previously untapped well of knowledge it occurred to me that a Central Project Manager was required to bridge the divide between DPW, Hospitals and the Budget Office. This person might cut through agency red tape. The person appointed would need extraordinary authority from the Mayor's office. During that short ten-minute walk we refined the concept of a "Hospital Construction Czar." Mattison had his talking points for the meeting.

The following Monday at ten a.m., I received an urgent call from Bill Mattison in the Hamptons where I was vacationing for what I thought would be two weeks. Bill asked me to return to Manhattan immediately. The Mayor had liked our suggestion and planned to announce my appointment to the new position the next day. I would become both Assistant Health Services Administrator reporting to Dr. Howard Brown and Deputy General Manager in DPW reporting to Commissioner Mattison—a double promotion. My assignment was to " shatter the bottlenecks in the site selection, planning, budget approval and construction in the score of health and hospitals construction projects" having a contract value of half a billion dollars, exclusive of the cost of equipment.

During the next busy twelve months, many new procedures were implemented by several agencies. The Budget Director's Office introduced Critical Path Method (CPM) controls into the capital budgeting process. The Department of Public Works and the Hospitals Department successfully revitalized their hospital construction program, completing all the projects identified by Senator Thaler. Unfortunately, Bill Mattison never lived to see the results of his bold decision. Five months into the new program he had a fatal heart attack while speaking at a construction industry luncheon at the Waldorf Astoria hotel.■

Pazel Jackson, who held commissioner-level posts in three municipal agencies, was senior vice president of several major banks, a board member of the Urban Development Corporation and Vice Chairman of the Battery Park City Authority.

Anthony Japha

For reasons I don't recall, JVL had to meet with the Honorable Abraham Beame, his eventual successor. We probably needed the Comptroller's agreement to undertake a well-considered financial maneuver.

The mood was light in JVL's office as we awaited Beame's arrival. Jerry Kretchmer's jokes were the funniest. Several had to do with his brother Arthur, long-time editorial director of *Playboy* magazine.

Beame finally arrived. Before getting down to business, though, some of us tried to set an informal tone. (The issue to be dealt with could not have been all that critical.) A hilarious joke about the prospect of a pooper-scooper law broke everyone up—everyone but the Honorable Abraham Beame, who didn't even crack a smile.

Nevertheless, we did get what we needed from the get-together.

Following the 1973 mayoral election, the *Daily News* published a photo of the Lindsay/Beame transition committee. Each administration—incoming and outgoing--had five representatives at most. JVL's transition team had an average age of maybe 30 years younger than Beame's. Steve Isenberg clipped the photo and circulated it with this note: "The torch is passed to a new generation."■

Anthony Japha held several positions in the Bureau of the Budget, including Assistant Director for the uniformed forces and criminal justice. Most of his later career was spent in government, including the Health and Hospitals Corporation and the MTA. He was the first director of the East Side Access Project that will bring the Long Island Rail Road to Grand Central Terminal.

Vernon Jordan

In 1969, shortly after his re-election to a second term as Mayor, John Lindsay invited me to New York for breakfast at Gracie Mansion where he offered me the job of running the Model Cities Program.

He was gracious, charming and persuasive, and I was honored to be asked. But I knew it was not for me. "I'm not your man," I told the Mayor. "After all, when I landed this morning I just found out that Kennedy Airport was in Queens. All I know about the Bronx is that it has a zoo. And that Brooklyn once had the Dodgers and still has The Bridge."

And when I asked the Mayor if he had consulted with Manhattan Borough President Percy Sutton, the wise and respected black political leader of Harlem's Famous Gang of Four (along with Rangel, Paterson and Dinkins), or with trailblazing Congresswoman Shirley Chisholm from Brooklyn, he said he hadn't. I thought that would instantly put me between a rock and a hard place politically.

I rode down to City Hall with the Mayor in his limousine where he was going to hold a Cabinet meeting. En route, a staff member briefed the Mayor on what to expect, while being quite dismissive of certain Cabinet members. "He's not worth much," or "She doesn't know what she's doing," he said. It was a life lesson on the power of all those eager young staffers around the boss who can block access and poison the well for an agency head. It certainly taught me that it was less attractive to be the head of a program, than being on the inside with the boss.

I had lunch with some of Lindsay's top aides, including Jay Kriegel. One of them, perhaps Kriegel, tried to add pressure and urgency, "You need to get on this train, now, Jordan," I remember them saying. "Where's it going?" I asked. "1600 Pennsylvania Avenue," they answered. "I can't take that ride," I replied. "You all are going in the wrong direction."

After our visit, Lindsay soon appointed J.B. Williams, a Brooklyn judge, to lead the Model Cities program. A consummate New York street operative, fully plugged in and all-knowing, J.B. was the right man for the task and he thrived in this most difficult task.

As for me, I moved to New York in January 1970 to take over the United Negro College Fund. Lindsay remained a friend, and supporter, and I worked with him on the formation of the Urban Coalition. And whenever we saw each other, he invariably would tease me that I hadn't joined his team to be on the frontline, where John Lindsay indisputably built such an admirable record in dealing with racial tensions, and set an unparalleled example for officials across the nation.■

Vernon Jordan, adviser to several Presidents of the United States, is a Senior Managing Director of Lazard Freres & Company. He sits on many boards of major American corporations, was Executive Director of the United Negro College Fund, President of the National Urban League and Legal Counsel to the Washington, D.C. law firm of Akin Gump Strauss Hauer & Feld

James Kagen

I doubt that I had more than two meetings with JVL. Both were in the Blue Room and, as I recall, there had to have been at least twenty to thirty other people on hand. I think the conversations concerned kids "slangin' dope," kids throwing their sneakers over telephone wires to point the way and how awful the new drug of choice—barbiturates?—was. He might not have cared about such details, but I think the Mayor was bridling at criticism for setting up too many methadone clinics or drug programs. "I won't look another mother in the eye and tell her I'm not doing everything I can to help her child get treatment," he said.

I wish I'd had more contact with him. Nevertheless, I'm eternally grateful to JVL. Because of him, I found a way to turn an unfocused desire to help into a useful professional life.

Most of my time was spent with Health Services Administrator Gordon Chase and his aide Bob Newman. Naomi Feigelson, the press officer (who later married him), and Gordon were sucking all the publicity on health out of the air without giving the Mayor much, if any credit. Nat Leventhal, the Mayor's assistant assigned to cover our superagency, complained about that, but to no avail. When Naomi and Gordon were on vacation in Switzerland, however, they sent Nat a postcard saying they mentioned the Mayor's name everywhere they went.■

James Kagen is Consulting Director of The Chartis Group which serves healthcare organizations in setting and attaining their financial and strategic goals.

Jeffrey Katzenberg

The summer of '65 was my best summer ever. When school let out, my education really got started. I'd like to say that I volunteered in the Lindsay campaign for the most high-minded of reasons. But the fact is that I found myself with a lot of time on my hands after being thrown out of summer camp for gambling. So I thought it would be pretty cool (not a word generally associated with the 14-year-old me) to see if I could get involved with the campaign. I was politically aware enough to already believe that John Lindsay was everything a leader should be. A liberal Republican (before that became an oxymoron), he marched to his own drummer. And so I dropped by the campaign headquarters, and life for me was never the same again.

When I finally met John Lindsay face to face, I was not disappointed. He filled the room with his charisma. I was too in awe at that moment to recall anything he actually said to me. But I do remember his laugh. This was a man who loved what he was doing, and it all came through in that singular from-the-gut Lindsay laugh.

Once he had moved into Gracie Mansion, I had a choice between focusing on school or on being a gofer for the mayor. Easy choice! I went on to squeak through high school, while excelling at fetching coffee and collating press releases.

Why did I do it? Other kids' heroes were named Mantle and Maris. Mine was named Lindsay. The other kids could only see their heroes from afar. I got to see mine up close, and even work for him ... even if that "work" was photocopying a speech.

In many ways, my time as the short, scrawny kid in the Lindsay Administration (they actually nicknamed me Squirt) set the course of my life as the short, scrawny adult in Hollywood. I learned the supreme importance of minding the smallest details, of not accepting the bureaucratic "no," of being prompt, of returning calls, of staying focused on the big picture and, most of all, of always striving to do your very best to exceed expectations.

Now, 50 years later, I marvel at how lucky I was. To be a kid at that moment with that mayor in that city verged on the miraculous.

Thank you, John Lindsay.■

Jeffrey Katzenberg was Chairman of Disney Studios for ten years and is a Founder and CEO of Dreamworks Animation.

Robert Kaufman

My first recollections of working with John Lindsay antedate his election as Mayor. I was Legislative Assistant to Senator Jacob K. Javits when John was elected to the House of Representatives in 1958. When John came to Washington in January, 1959, Senator Javits sent me over to his office "to explain how the Congress REALLY works," and how to draft legislation so that it had a chance to pass.

I also remember sitting in John's Congressional office and telling "war stories" about legislation that Senator Javits had written. We stayed in touch off and on while he was in the House, particularly on election finance issues. I had become an expert in that field and, as a result, became John's election law lawyer after leaving Javits to join the Proskauer law firm. I advised John and Dick Aurelio, who had been Javits's Administrative Assistant, on election law matters during the Mayoral campaigns and his Presidential run. I always suspected that John knew as much or more on that subject than I did, but he did listen to my advice.∎

Robert Kaufman, a partner in the Proskauer law firm specializing in hospital and healthcare matters, also served in the United States Department of Justice's Antitrust Division. He is a past President of the New York City Bar Association.

Tom Kean

In 1965, I was a graduate student at Columbia living on West 74th Street, still a depressed neighborhood before Lincoln Center's completion. Every morning, I took the subway north to school at 72nd Street and Broadway, across the way from a drug needle "exchange center" later made famous by the movie "The Panic in Needle Park."

The city was in trouble and everybody knew it. My father had represented a New Jersey district in Congress so it was natural for me to follow politics, but I never expected to participate as other than a voter.

I was of the generation called to public service by John F. Kennedy. Inspired by that call, I volunteered for John Lindsay's first mayoral campaign. It turned out that thousands of young people like me did the same. My motives weren't purely idealistic. The word around Columbia was that the Lindsay campaign was a great place to meet nice girls. That turned out to be true.

John Lindsay just seemed so different and far removed from the average New York City politician. Clean-cut, well educated and liberal in outlook, he was a breath of fresh air. And he was a Republican, not part of the tired Democratic machine. Many people my age thought that this was a man who could lead the nation's greatest city out of its crisis, and whose election could change politics in New York and, maybe, in the country, too.

I was one of hundreds assigned to distribute campaign brochures on street corners, subway entrances and other gathering places. Every now and then, I convinced a voter to change his or her mind and vote for Lindsay. Most people were civil, but occasionally, I had brochures thrown back in my face. The overall experience, though, was challenging and fun. When Lindsay won, I was convinced that if enough people believed or cared, you could change the system. I still believe that.

Because I savored the taste of politics I got in the Lindsay campaign I volunteered in campaigns in my home state of New Jersey and eventually ran for office there. If not for that experience in the Lindsay campaign, I might have gone in a different direction.■

Tom Kean *served as the 48th Governor of New Jersey, 1982-1990 and later was Chairman of the 9/11 Commission 2002-2004.*

John Keker

Steve Isenberg and Peter Goldmark hired me, a first year law student and Vietnam veteran, to work in the Budget Bureau on police matters in the summer of 1968. Mayor Lindsay was all over the news because if the news media were sure of one thing, it was that New York and Oakland, not yet afflicted by race riots, would blow up that summer. The Mayor, handsome and brave as a Saxon Prince, walked the streets, talking to people, and to everyone's surprise New York made it through the summer.

And what a summer it was--following the Prague Spring and the MLK assassination. The summer of '68 began with another killing, of RFK, whose body lay at St Patrick's Cathedral with lines of mourners down Fifth Avenue. These tragedies were followed by the Republican Convention, with the Mayor losing the nomination to be Nixon's Vice President to the unknown Spiro Agnew. How JVL would have hated that job had it been his, but he, not Gerald Ford, would have become President when Nixon fled. The Democratic Convention in Chicago was held a few weeks late--rioting in Grant Park, cops in riot gear, Mayor Daly going crazy on national TV.

Jay Kriegel took me to the one intimate meeting I attended with the Mayor. David Garth, the political advisor, was the other person there. I can't remember the substance of what was said, but I recall being thrilled to be there with the Mayor, so thrilled that I tried to sit next to him, until Garth told me, rather abruptly, to get up and move.

The people I met that summer, loyal and admiring of the Mayor, were like him--idealistic and tough-minded. They became friends for life.■

John Keker, a founding partner of the law firm of Keker & Van Nest, was a Marine platoon leader in Vietnam and clerked for United States Supreme Court Chief Justice Earl Warren.

Raymond Kelly

When I was assigned to the NYPD Crime Prevention Section as a sergeant, I was charged with launching something called the Block Security Program. The department had never done anything like it before. Mayor Lindsay was planning to highlight the program in his upcoming presidential campaign as a fresh way of fighting crime. It made some sense, actually.

The Block Security Program called for local community groups to raise small amounts of money to pay for door locks, window guards, burglar alarms, security lighting, and other anticrime measures in their neighborhoods. The city would then match—or double or triple—those funds. The concept was promising, but no one had thought about any of the practical details. That was my job. I wrote the regulations, determined who was eligible, and established how the money could be used. I even called on my artistic talents to create a logo and draw the pictures that were used in the brochure. I was the Block Security Program, and City Hall couldn't get enough of it—or me. The experience gave me my first inside look at the upper levels of city government. And here was the best part: the program actually seemed to be working.

On September 13, 1973, Mayor Lindsay traveled to Washington to testify in front of the House Judiciary Committee about this wonderful new program of his, and I went along. I didn't get to say anything, but I sat behind the Mayor in the hearing room as he testified, knowing that much of what he was touting had originated with me. Over time, I got to know Counsel to the Mayor Jay Kriegel, mayoral assistant Steve Brill, and several of Mayor Lindsay's other "whiz kids." I saw Kriegel as the de facto mayor. He was amazing, making top-level decisions at City Hall, and he wasn't much older than I was. The crew around Mayor Lindsay showed me how bright, young, energetic people could have an impact working in government. That insight was genuinely inspiring. ∎

Raymond Kelly *joined the New York City Police Department in 1966 and rose through its ranks to serve as Commissioner during the Dinkins and Bloomberg Administrations. He has also been Director of the International Police Monitors of the multi-national force in Haiti, Undersecretary for Enforcement of the U.S. Department of the Treasure and Commissioner of the U.S. Customs Service. He is also a retired Marine Colonel.*

Andrew Kerr

I was recruited from the business world (I was a management consultant at Booz Allen) to be the first head of a new special Project Management Unit in the Mayor's Office, providing sophisticated scheduling and rigorous tracking of a select list of highly visible priority projects. Because these complex projects usually cut across multiple City agencies, they were afflicted by fragmented responsibility, with no single city official in charge. As a result, there was no overall schedule for the project, and each agency acted independently, often resulting in finger-pointing and tasks done consecutively, rather than simultaneously, which greatly lengthening the process.

Our team adopted the most advanced techniques being used in sophisticated federal agencies like NASA and the Defense Department to produce PERT chart schedules showing every review, approval, and technical step required, with a specific deadlines for each, and a single Project Manager to monitor progress daily. Since every agency received the complete schedule for all tasks, and received our detailed monthly report of every step taken and every delay identified, we eliminated many disputes about responsibility and imposed accountability for each delay or failure by an agency. For the first time, everyone involved in a project knew on any day who was responsible to take each action.

These management principles were applied to renovating hospitals, rehabilitating outdoor swimming pools, expanding methadone clinics and other municipal endeavors.

I reported both to the Mayor's Office and the powerful Budget Bureau, which gave our staff of project managers clout over every city agency. We recruited smart, aggressive young project managers, mostly from business, finally building a staff of sixty.

Aside from those two mentioned federal agencies, we were in the vanguard of project management techniques and discipline. Not surprisingly, we had a steady stream of visitors, both from governments and big corporations, who wanted to see how we operated. Many from the business world were startled to learn that New York City's government, which had generally been thought of as backward and inefficient, was now in the forefront of modern management.

To keep staff quality high, I resisted taking political referrals from Sid Davidoff's operation. One day, he sent over a young woman named Joan Hochman. She didn't say much, just stared with a slight smirk. I tried to provoke and discourage her by off-handedly saying, "Women just can't do this work." As soon as I said it, I realized my blunder. "Oh shit," I said. "You're hired." That turned out to be a blessing. Joan became one of our stars.

One day, after I had been there six months, I accompanied the Mayor to Gracie Mansion in his limo for a chat about odds and ends, but as we arrived, the Mayor said "Andy, you've been doing a great job, but there's one problem. You haven't made any mistakes." "Isn't that good?" I said with surprise. "No," he replied. "It means you're not doing enough, you're not stretching. You've got to do more and take more risks."

He was the ideal boss, both supportive and constantly pushing.■

Andrew Kerr was the first head of the Mayor's pioneering Project Management Office and then served as Housing and Development Administrator. He is founder and managing director of Boston-based Devonshire Partners, an investment banking firm with significant assignments and investments in software, information technology and cable and satelite communicatons companies

Bruce Kerr

I saw Man of LaMancha six times. What has that to do with John Lindsay? Like the Knight of the Woeful Countenance, but much more effective, the Mayor, too, was an idealist.

I will always believe in John Lindsay and Don Quixote.

I will forever be a Davidoff Raider and wish I had been allowed to take the field with the rest of the older Lancers when they played the Playboy Bunnies.

What I learned from members of the Lindsay Administration proved invaluable in my career and personal life.

I was a lucky kid who was able to hang around and work with the OLDER GUYS who made up the Lindsay advance team. I'll be forever grateful for the fun we had, the seriousness of our mission, and the sense of shared purpose and teamwork.

At a Lindsay reunion in 2010, my wife Rose (we've been married now for 38 years) got to meet many members of the Administration. From that day on she seemed to know me a lot better.

I only wish that I could explain to my children something of what Rose picked up that night.

My last boss, the executive director of a hospital, could never understand how I accomplished the things I did, connected with people the way I did regardless of title and level of government, or express my beliefs so firmly regardless of the situation. I owe all that to those wonderful Lindsay years. ■

Bruce Kerr has had a career in various aspects of hospital administration at the City's Health and Hospitals Corporation, Bellevue Hospital and Sea View Hospital.

Robert Kimball

After I served as a summer intern in his Congressional office in 1961, John Lindsay asked me to return as his legislative assistant. I was immediately struck by how kind, thoughtful, idealistic, and considerate he was. His interests as a Congressman were broad and varied, embracing foreign affairs, legal matters, and the arts.

One of the first things Lindsay told me when I joined his staff was that he did not think he could keep me out of the draft. He said that he could help only one person a year, that he had already aided the tuba player in the "My Fair Lady" orchestra, and that he didn't know if I was as valuable. Later he wrote an amazing letter on my behalf in which he claimed, among other things, that I was not only an expert on foreign affairs but also one of the leading authorities on Medicare! It did the trick.

When he was in Washington, which was most of the week, he put in long hours, often working well into the evening and generally avoiding cocktail parties and social gatherings. He always found time for constituents, lobbyists, members of the press, and, of course, his wife, Mary, and their four children. He took his responsibilities as a member of the House Judiciary Committee very seriously and was a friend to many of his colleagues on the committee, especially the ranking Republican, William McCulloch.

Lindsay accomplished many great things in his seven years in Congress. He played a leading role in the 1962 defeat of the Industrial Security Bill, the first major setback suffered by Chairman Francis Walter and the House Un-American Activities Committee, and was one of the leaders in forging the bipartisan compromise that led to the 1964 Civil Rights Act.

We stayed in touch over the years. We happened to sail together on the QE2 right after his twin brother, Dave, died, a loss that upset him profoundly. As a music critic for the *New York Post*, I had to review his performance with the New York Philharmonic in Copland's "A Lincoln

Portrait." Before the concert, Mary Lindsay told me that if I didn't give John an excellent review, she would murder me. Of course I gave him a well-deserved rave.

The last time we spoke was by phone, about two weeks before his death. He and Mary were living in Hilton Head, South Carolina, and he was gravely ill. I arranged to visit him but he died before I got there.■

Robert Kimball is a musical theater historian, compiler and editor of the lyrics or Ira Gershwin and Cole Porter and co-author of Reading Lyrics.

Arthur Klebanoff

I was a young aide to Deputy Mayor Tim Costello in 1968. One of my assignments was the preparation of a tract map matching census data with voter participation rates throughout the city. The map revealed a clear pattern of under-participation by blacks and Puerto Ricans at the polls, a disparity that triggered the arrival of inspectors from the U.S. Department of Justice under the Voting Rights Act.

These maps also drew the attention of *The New York Times*, which published them. In response, Mayor Lindsay launched a voter registration drive.

Minority group under-participation in the city's elections, as illustrated by the tract maps I produced, was selected as a topic for the Mayor's weekly television show. I was asked to appear on the program and discuss what the maps told us.

But another subject scheduled for discussion—new subway cars—also had some graphic backup. There were two photos showing crowding on subway platforms, one with the current cars and another with the new cars in service. The new, larger cars were intended to relieve congestion on the platforms by accommodating more riders, but, unfortunately, the photos were indistinguishable, suggesting that the new cars would not have their intended effect.

The Mayor took one look at those photos and said that he wouldn't appear with them on air. The "experts" there to brief him insisted that he use them. Impatiently, Mayor Lindsay said, "If you think these graphics do a good job of making your argument, you go in front of the camera and present it."

That segment was shelved.■

Arthur Klebanoff is Chief Executive Officer of RosettaBooks and owner and president of the Scott Meredith Literary Agency.

George Klein

In 1939, my father, Stephen Klein, started the Barton's Candy Company. In the late 1940s, we established our factory at a former Con Edison plant on Fulton Street at Flatbush and DeKalb Avenues with some 400 employees, many of whom were refugees from Europe or Holocaust survivors.

Lifestyles shifted after WW II. Much of the middle class left the borough for the suburbs. Downtown Brooklyn started to deteriorate, a situation aggravated by the departure of the beloved Dodgers in 1957. Many businesses fled the city for greener pastures as well. The city government seemed powerless to reverse the trend.

A new Mayor, John Lindsay, arrived in City Hall in 1966, committed to finding ways the government could intervene to retain and attract business, and stimulate new commercial construction.

Early on, Mayor Lindsay and his team focused on two of downtown Brooklyn's largest movie theatres—the Paramount and the Fox, both on Flatbush Avenue. The Paramount Theatre was sold to Long Island University. The Fox Theatre was on the verge of foreclosure. Our family owned several nearby properties, including our factory. Ken Patton, the Mayor's economic development czar, asked if we would be willing to pay off the mortgage, take over the Fox Theatre and redevelop the site.

Within weeks, we shook hands on a deal with the City. Iimagine that— no legal contract, just a handshake with government for a multi-million dollar deal. We would proceed with an unassisted urban renewal plan, the first of its kind in New York. We bought the Fox theatre property with our own funds and sold it to the city at our cost price. The city then gave us a long-term ground lease. On that site we built a 300,000 square foot office building for Con Edison, the first commercial space constructed in downtown Brooklyn in decades.

Ken and the Mayor kept all their promises; our handshake's terms were honored. I had no prior experience in commercial real estate, but wanted our project to be distinctive. We hired a leading American architecture firm, Skidmore, Owings & Merrill (SOM), giving them their first New York project since Lever House. Known for signature corporate headquarters, they had rarely designed traditional commercial buildings.

That was the beginning of Downtown Brooklyn's long revival. Two years later, we added a second commercial 350,000 square foot SOM building across Flatbush Avenue, which was occupied by New York Telephone. When we look at the booming development underway along Flatbush Avenue today, we're proud to know that it all began 40-odd years ago with John Lindsay, Ken Patton and us.

Those buildings launched my real estate career. We sold Barton's after my father passed away and devoted all our energies to Park Tower Realty. Our next project was a sleek black glass tower on Park Avenue and 59th Street in Manhattan, designed by the celebrated I.M. Pei. Using world-class architects like Edward Larrabee Barnes, Kevin Roche, Helmut Jahn, Philip Johnson and KPF, as well as I.M. Pei and SOM, became our trademark. These projects and our sponsorship of the Greenpoint waterfront mark a long journey from our candy factory on Flatbush Avenue.■

George Klein *is Chairman and Chief Executive Officer of Park Tower Realty, a major New York City real estate development concern.*

John Koskinen

I was young and intimidated by Washington in August 1967 when I showed up to work on the staff of the National Advisory Commission on Civil Disorders (The Kerner Commission). President Johnson had created the panel to find out why cities across the country were being torn apart by riots.

John Lindsay, the commission's vice-chairman, was impressive leading its discussions. The usual diverse sweep of Johnson appointees for such endeavors included Democratic and Republican members of Congress, a conservative businessman, a union president and a major civil rights leader. Supporting the Mayor was the ever-irrepressible Jay Kriegel, who became a friend of mine for life. The commission's report, published the following spring, famously warned that, "Our nation is moving toward two societies, one black, one white—separate and unequal."

After the report was issued, I was delighted when the Mayor asked me to join Peter Tufo in setting up and running New York City's Washington Office, the first of its kind. We embarked on what amounted to a graduate education in the Great Society's new programs, the challenges of running the country's largest city and the importance of leadership in achieving progress at all levels of government.

In those days, you could fly to New York from Washington on the Eastern Shuttle for $13 each way, an affordable regular commute to and from the Mayor's cabinet meetings. The cabinet's members were leaders from many different backgrounds, all of whom were dedicated to realizing John Lindsay's vision of a better New York for every citizen. They answered the call to public service from a Mayor whose personality, energy and enthusiasm made him a hard man to turn down.

Just last year, I acquired another insight into John Lindsay's unique character. I met for the first time as an Internal Revenue Service

Commissioner with then Senate Majority Leader Harry Reid. The first thing Senator Reid said to me was, "Anyone who worked for John Lindsay is o.k. in my book." He then told me that, years earlier, he had been a young Capitol policeman. His job was to guard the door of the House office building most of the day. The only Congressman who ever noticed him, he said, was John Lindsay who would always ask how he was doing and, on occasion, bring him something to drink on a hot day.

That genuine concern for others, even when cameras and the public were elsewhere, tells a lot about why the Mayor was successful in keeping New York "cool" when other cities were unraveling in violence. He created a sense of hope and optimism, even in difficult times. It was an honor and a privilege to spend time with this great man.■

John Koskinen, a Legislative Assistant to Mayor Lindsay, is the 48th Internal Revenue Service Commissioner of the United States. He has also served as Non –Executive Chairman of Freddie Mac and Deputy Mayor of the District of Columbia. He was also a member of The Palmieri Company for 21 years, rising to the positions of President, CEO and Chairman.

Jack Krauskopf

In Mayor Lindsay's turbulent first term, the Human Resources Administration (HRA) was created as one of his super agencies to bring together all social services and anti-poverty programs, with an emphasis on community participation that was one of the prevailing philosophies of the War on Poverty. There were times when "participation" was up close in the HRA office at 100 Church Street. Among many demonstrations in that first year (1966-67), I recall when Jesse Gray, who led rent strikes in Harlem and elsewhere, came to our office with chickens. He proceeded to scatter feed across the office floor to dramatize his point that the community would not accept anymore the "chicken feed grants" that were being offered to local organizations, and that more substantial funding was required. That may have also been the time when demonstrators cooked themselves dinner in a kitchen in the office (which previously had a corporate tenant), but I can't be sure it was them since such demonstrations were so frequent that memories run together.■

Jack Krauskopf was Deputy HRA Administrator and teaches at Baruch College.

Jerome Kretchmer

The Liberal Party's endorsement enabled Republican John Lindsay to be elected mayor in 1965. As an active and engaged Assembly member I wondered why the Republican governor, Nelson Rockefeller, and the Mayor were always at odds. Very often, the liberal (small l) Democratic members were on John's side and trying to improve the way the city was governed by providing him with the tools necessary to make changes.

In 1969, when Lindsay ran for reelection both on the Liberal party line and a "stopgap" Independent line, those same Democrats did something highly unusual. They endorsed him for Mayor, abandoning their own party's candidate to help him to win. As a result of Lindsay's victory, a Democratic Assemblyman—me—was destined to become a member of his administration.

I thought Dick Aurelio was calling for assistance in vetting prospective appointees, but he invited me to join the government. But I had a different ambition at the time—to run for Congress. I was uncertain about taking the City job. The legislature was in session and I was busy. Richard Brown, the city's Albany representative and a close friend, was among those encouraging me to accept the Mayor's offer to become the Environmental Protection Administrator,

At Dick's suggestion, I agreed to meet the Mayor in Albany when he was there on other business. John Lindsay, Richard Brown and I met in a hotel room, a setting that had become familiar to me during eight years in the state capital. This meeting was different, somehow. The Mayor filled the small room. I had seen a lot of politicians and officials close up. John was different. The times were different. The Mayor conveyed an excitement about government and believed that reform was possible. I don't remember how long we talked but I was convinced that he would give me a chance to do different and daring things in dealing with environmental issues.

The first Earth Day was held on April 22, 1970. The Mayor and the City led the nation in setting goals for environmental management. From a platform in Union Square Park, the Mayor declared a credo for the environment that, unfortunately, has yet to been achieved. I was fortunate to be there with him on that first Earth Day.

No matter what the issue—Con Edison burning coal to generate electricity on the East River, cars using leaded gasoline, or providing equal sanitation services to the Upper East Side, Bedford Stuyvesant and the South Bronx—the Mayor was there. The city was having a hard time but the Mayor never stopped trying to fix what ailed it. He attacked racial injustice, economic inequality and environmental pollution and their effect on the city at a time when few in municipal government anywhere addressed these issues. When I think about John Lindsay I think about a grand man who always was trying to make the city better.■

Jerry Kretchmer, Environmental Protection Administrator in the second Lindsay administration, has been a real estate developer and restauranteur.

Jay L. Kriegel

In my years at City Hall, I took pride in being available around-the-clock. One summer night, after I had watched the Late Show movie on Channel 2, then dozed off during the Late, Late Show, the phone rang. I bolted up to answer.

"Jay, did I wake you?" It was the Mayor, who slept little and fitfully during those long, hot summers and sometimes looked for excuses to commune. "Of course not," I said, trying to sound alert. I glanced at the clock. It was 3:15 a.m.. "I need to consult you on a very sensitive matter," the Mayor said.

Hearing the Mayor ask, "So what do you think," I realized that I'd fallen asleep again while he was talking. Caught off guard, I muttered, "Let me think it over." "Okay," he said.

Relieved to escape embarrassment, I slipped back into a deep sleep. Then, the phone rang again. Bolting up a second time, I saw it was 5 a.m. "Did you think about it?" the Mayor asked. Panicked, I blurted out, "Sounds okay to me." "Good," he replied. "Let's go ahead."

After we hung up, I was gripped with guilt that I had agreed to something horrendous, like endorsing the bombing of Cambodia.

When I got to City Hall that morning I waited anxiously outside his office. When I finally got in, I asked, "Mayor, do you remember our discussion last night?" "What discussion," he replied. "The thing we agreed to about four hours ago," I said. "I have no idea what you're talking about," he answered.

And I still have no idea either.

—

On those hot summer nights when Lindsay walked the streets, he directed the police to stay away. Despite the obvious risks, he wanted no visible evidence of patrol cars, watchful officers or plainclothesmen. Just his personal bodyguard and Sid's advance men.

Business leaders and celebrities often wanted to walk with the Mayor to see what he saw, as with the photo of the young Marlon Brando with JVL and Teddy Gross striding up 125th Street.

I was with JVL on that street one night when an odd-looking guy started walking toward him. Suddenly, I felt anxious and sensed Pat Vecchio, the Mayor's bodyguard, coming up from behind. As the man got close, he took his hat off and spit the toothpick he held in his mouth into the hat. Every movement seemed stranger and less predictable than the one before.

"Hey, Mayor," he shouted. "Why are you wearing a green tie with a blue shirt?"

Things were never quite what they seemed or we feared on those streets. Lindsay's fearlessness and fundamental trust were borne out again and again.

—

Early in my time at City Hall, I made a terrible mistake. Distraught, I went to tell the Mayor. I even thought this might be the end. I entered his office and walked up to his big LaGuardia desk where he was writing in his shirtsleeves. He pushed his glasses up onto his forehead, listened to my confession, then roared, "Go back and do it again...And again, and again, until you get it right."

He loved his youthful staff, and it is difficult to imagine that a young staffer could have had a better boss.

—

One fall afternoon while walking down a bombed-out desolate street in Brownsville, JVL came upon a free-standing tenement where a young black woman stood holding a baby.

"Can I come in," he asked. He followed her into the house and down the hall where two other small children were playing in front of an open oven that was heating the room.

"Where are you from," he asked.

"Mississippi," she said.

"Why did you come here?"

"To find a better life."

"Did you," he asked.

"Yes," she said.

Looking at the squalor inside and out, we wondered what it must have been like down there.

—

In 1971, I was called to testify before the Knapp Commission, appointed by the Mayor to investigate police corruption. The hearing was held in the ornate Great Hall of the Chamber of Commerce near Wall Street, with a gaggle of press and cameras, and carried live on public television.

For several tough hours, I was grilled by Commission Chief Counsel Mike Armstrong. When it was over, drained, and self-conscious, I took a subway home. After sitting in front of those hot bright lights, constantly observed by press and cameras, I felt that everyone on the train was staring at me. At my station, I went to a different liquor store than usual, where I hopefully wouldn't be known. Picking a bottle of scotch, I got in line to pay, keeping my head down.

Suddenly the woman ahead of me turned, stared at me, and loudly exclaimed, "I know you." She paused to remember, as I tensed, then continued triumphantly: "You were singing on the Johnny Carson show!" "I was singing," I said, half regretting the notoriety, though relieved at the misidentification. "But it wasn't on Johnny Carson." ■

Jay L. Kriegel, who served as *Chief of Staff and Special Counsel, is senior advisor to The Related Companies, one of the city's largest real estate developers. He was co-founder of The American Lawyer, senior vice president of CBS, and executive director of NYC2012, New York City's Olympic bid. He ran the national campaign with Lewis Rudin to save the deductibility of state and local taxes*

Robert Krulwich

Here's what I saw once: John Lindsay standing in the corner of a hotel room, being greeted by fans, voters. Up they'd come, he'd smile, put out his hand, call them by name. This is what politicians do.

"Jerry…So nice to see you."

"Benito! What 's going on with Dominic? Did you get my note?"

That kind of thing. It's basic.

But Lindsay? He'd stand there. The person would approach. And then Mary would say, brightly, as if thrilled, "Oh, John, you remember Mario DiVota and his grocery store, the one you visited last year?" The Mayor's eyes open wider. "On Kissena Boulevard," Mary reminds him. He smiles, but tentatively. She goes on, "…when you cut the ribbon at, what? Was it your tenth store, Mario?" And before Mario can answer, Lindsay is calling out "Mario!" and bending down.

Because the Mayor was taller than pretty much everybody, he's pumping the man's hand, while Mary, looking over Mario's shoulder, is already saying, "John, you remember Felix, right? Felix Latoya? Who threw us that party in Howard Beach?" and Lindsay, picking up the beat, says "Felix!" and that's how it went. Mary would ID whoever approached, without using any notes I could see, or the help of a whispering assistant. She just knew. John just didn't.

I don't know how they did it. The Mayor always got the name in the nick of time. Mary pitched, he caught and the visitor was "recognized." They never missed. Watching this, I wondered how a guy who can't remember names put himself in a business where names are flying every which way, where you've got to know who you're talking to, where if you don't, you lose, so you fake it, and faking it must be incredibly dangerous, but that's how John Lindsay worked the room. It was seamless, but dangerous.

Lindsay was good. I'll give him that. But on the day I watched, Mary was better. She pitched a perfect game.■

Robert Krulwich *is senior science correspondent for National Public Radio and host of Radiolab. He has reported for PBS, ABC and CBS.*

Diane Lacey

I came to work at City Hall following a successful campaign organizing poor South Bronx residents who wanted better health care and more effective drug treatment programs. The health care center I helped create, supported by empowered community members, still serves that neighborhood.

Although having a health agency portfolio was my first choice, I was assigned to Parks, Recreation and Cultural Affairs and the Addiction Services Agency. The epidemic of heroin addiction was at its height and there were no easy solutions. The Mayor was very concerned about these problems. At task force meetings he was patient, attentive and willing to provide resources to agency heads who presented reasonable proposals.

As drug affected communities began to receive services, proposals came in from everywhere. One day, when I was in my small office not too far from the Mayor, I heard a commotion at the police desk. A man from Harlem was demanding to meet the Mayor. Jay Kriegel and Gordon Davis were out, so security ushered him into my office. He was a big man who looked like Mr. T, but without the jewelry. He carried a large walking stick of the kind Moses must have used to part the Red Sea. He did not expect to meet a black woman with a large Afro who was not "scared." His proposal did have some merit and was eventually funded. I don't think John Lindsay would have been scared of him either.■

After serving as Assistant to the Mayor, **Diane Lacey** *researched drug treatment programs nationally and internationally. She served on the Board of the Health and Hospitals Corporation for almost three decades and now is a pastor of the Presbyterian Church in Park Slope.*

Michael Lacher

On a beautiful Saturday in late fall of 1965, JVL was campaigning around town and drawing huge crowds everywhere. But Terence Smith of *The New York Times*, covering us that day, was skeptical about a portion of the Lindsay stump speech.

In the South Bronx before an overwhelmingly Hispanic crowd, John mounted a festooned flatbed truck to ear-splitting shouts of "Viva, Lindsay." He promised to give this community direct contact with him. "I promise you that the only thing between you and me is…US!!!," he said. The ovation was deafening, but Terence Smith turned to me and observed, "Impressive, but just what does that mean?" "Oh, Terry, John tapped into their innermost feelings," I replied. Smith smiled…benevolently.

In Rego Park, Queens, we found a very different demographic, to be sure—middle class, mostly Jewish, and virtually all white. JVL drew a rock star's greeting from the very large throng on Queens Boulevard. He closed with same line about "the only thing between you and me is us" and that crowd went wild, too. Terry Smith, increasingly perplexed, said, "But that doesn't mean anything." "Maybe not to you," I responded, "but the people understand him." "Okay," Smith conceded, "Maybe I just don't get it." But Smith's quizzical reaction worried me. What kind of article would he write about JVL's campaign?

Our last stop was Douglaston, Queens, then as now a politically conservative area generally populated by New Yorkers of Irish and Italian descent, and home to many active and retired police officers. Although Douglaston, like Rego Park, was an educated, striving and thriving community, its residents were uneasy about a "fusion" candidate from Manhattan's Silk Stocking District. Polls told us that JVL's alliances with the Liberal and Democratic parties diminished his standing there. We didn't expect an enthusiastic reception. On the way to the stop in the press car, Terry Smith told me that the Lindsay campaign should write Douglaston voters off.

He also predicted that this otherwise successful day would end on a low note.

It was late afternoon by the time we arrived and the sun had gone down. JVL remained good-humored, however, and was determined to stick to his message. He mounted that flatbed truck one last time and launched into his speech. The crowd was respectful, but silent and somber. JVL did his best to present the issues that concerned his audience most—crime, schools and public transportation. But nothing seemed to move these listeners. As he approached the end of his speech, Terry jabbed me in the ribs and said, "The line won't work here," but John had decided to try it once more, this time to no effect at all. The crowd was silent and Smith smirked. Then, John added another touch. At the top of his lungs, he shouted, "US! ALONE!!! TOGETHER IN THE STREETS...IN THE CITY...IN THE SUMMERTIME." Finally, the crowd broke into a great cheer. Terry Smith said he'd never seen anything like it in his years of covering campaigns. It was John Lindsay's special chemistry. He was an electrifying speaker and a great Mayor. It was a privilege to serve in his Administration.■

Michael Lacher is a partner in the law firm of Eaton & Van Winkle, LLP where he practices trial and transactional law.

Philip Lacovara

Recent events in Ferguson, Baltimore, Cleveland and elsewhere across the country recall challenges that Mayor Lindsay faced five decades ago in dealing with persistent problems of crime and racial polarization. As Special Counsel to Police Commissioner Patrick Murphy, I watched the Mayor respond with experimental policies to narrow the gap between the police and the community and transform the force from an army of occupation to a service organization that was part of the urban fabric.

Some of these initiatives were symbolic or cosmetic—re-painting police cars a more visible, less ominous white, instead of traditional dark green and changing the police garb from black uniform blouses for patrolmen (and they were almost all men then) to a less intimidating powder blue. Some in the department's rank-and-file said these changes reflected a softer attitude toward crime.

But the underlying goal was to reduce crime through new substantive measures in the department's protocols and administration. We stressed better continuing education and training for officers from the entry level on, making supervisors accountable for the actions of their subordinates, promoting the recruitment of blacks and Hispanics, especially from communities where crime had been endemic for decades, opening the patrol ranks to women and expanding their career opportunities beyond the limits of the restrictive, traditional "Policewomen's Bureau" and rooting out corruption.

When Commissioner Murphy and I met with him to discuss our progress and consider new strategies, it was clear that Mayor Lindsay had a lawyer's sense that it would be unwise and impractical to combat crime or terrorism (which even then was a palpable problem) while riding roughshod over civil liberties, a tension that posed the most vexing dilemma for a municipal chief executive and his police department. It was not for lack of leadership, determination or creativity that success occasionally eluded our grasp.

On my last day in the Administration, the Mayor invited me to his office. I was on my way to Washington to serve as Deputy Solicitor General of the United States in charge of the government's criminal and national security cases before the Supreme Court. Mayor Lindsay presented me with a green leather-framed engraving of a view of City Hall as it appeared in the early 19th century. He inscribed it with thanks for the time that we spent together "in this old building." I have taken that gracious memento from one office to another over the past forty-plus years.■

Philip Lacovara *also served as Counsel to the Watergate Special Prosecutor. He is Senior Counsel to the law firm of Mayer Brown where he became a partner in 1993.*

Robert Laird

On a brutally hot afternoon in July of 1970, a Brooklyn cop shot a black teenager to death. He thought the boy was waving a gun. He wasn't. It was just the flash of silver foil from a candy bar wrapper. Lindsay rushed to the scene with a small team of aides, myself included.

A good-sized, increasingly angry crowd had gathered by the time we arrived. Lindsay plunged right in, though, looking for friends. And he found them. All the walking tours he'd taken in this African American neighborhood had put him on a first-name basis with community leaders, many of whom were in the crowd. Lindsay asked for their help, and they agreed. Next, he told his advance men to locate an indoor space to get everyone off the street. They quickly found an empty room in a nearby public housing complex. Somehow, with much coaxing, Lindsay and the leaders convinced the reluctant crowd to head there.

As everyone jammed into the sweltering room, I began wondering how this would turn out. There was just one exit, and a lot of bitter, scowling people stood between it and us. But Lindsay showed no hesitation as he climbed up on a chair and started talking. He spoke in a strong, passionate voice for about five minutes, all ad lib of course, yet astonishingly eloquent—a stirring appeal for restraint in the face of tragedy, an urgent plea to keep the peace for the community's sake.

There were some shouted responses and emotional questions, but Lindsay's message took hold, and everyone finally filed out, many promising him they would help keep the lid on that night.

After checking some quotes with me, the handful of print reporters (no TV crews had appeared) rushed off with what seemed to me a terrific story: Mayor Averts Violent Outbreak. The next day, however, not one word appeared in the papers. What's going on, I wondered. And then it hit me. No riot, no story.

—

Early one day in 1969, in the midst of a tough reelection campaign, an opposition politician hurled what appeared to be a sensational accusation at Lindsay. The press office was quickly flooded with queries, an obvious signal the media thought a big story—maybe even, gasp, a scandal—was brewing. We needed to defuse the situation, fast.

Fortunately, Lindsay had a news conference scheduled that morning, which meant he could respond in a formal setting rather than an impromptu media scrum. That also gave him time to work out an answer that would put this ridiculous slander to rest without appearing defensive.

The news conference was packed—City Hall's Blue Room was SRO—and, as expected, the first question was about the sensational charge. With just the right tongue-in-cheek aplomb, Lindsay responded with a line that —as far as we could determine in those pre-Google times—dated back to a mid-19th century congressional debate:

"I deny the allegation, and I defy the alligator!"

The press corps erupted in laughter, and that was the end of that. Once again, Lindsay had warded off a potential disaster.■

*Robert Laird was deputy press secretary, 1966-73. He served as Gov. Hugh Carey's press secretary, 1974-76, and worked at the **Daily News** (1977-2005) as chief editorial writer and op-ed page editor. He now works part-time with the Dilenschneider public relations firm and the Hunter College Communications Department.*

Edgar Lampert

I served three years in the Lindsay administration as Deputy Director of the Mayor's Office of Lower Manhattan Development (OLMD) and as General Counsel to the Housing Development Administration.

At the age of 28, I was the "business person" and attorney for the talented young architects the Mayor had appointed to direct his special development offices. Richard Weinstein ran OLMD and Jaquelin Robertson headed the Midtown Office. I negotiated the complicated transactions creating the South Street Seaport, worked with Senator Moynihan's staff to prepare legislation for the City to obtain the Custom House from the General Services Administration, and prepared the Battery Park City ground lease with the State, writing the City's first "Air Rights Transfer" District—WOW!

At HDA, I had equally exciting work. I focused on rebalancing the City's housing program with rehabilitation initiatives—establishing the state's first mortgage insurance program for housing rehabilitation and collaborating with the city's major commercial and savings banks to establish the Community Preservation Corporation (CPC), which became the most significant lending organization for residential rehabilitation.

I remember most vividly a group of young people led by Donald Elliott, Chairman of the City Planning Commission, who were intent on "pushing the envelope", and the Mayor, who thought much could be accomplished and achieved a reasonable portion of what we had set out to do.■

Edgar Lampert is Vice Chairman of The Georgetown Company, a development concern. He was President of the Community Preservation Corporation.

Moon Landrieu

I was elected Mayor of New Orleans in 1970, a time when the nation's cities were deeply troubled, especially following the violent outbreaks of the summer of 1967, and then the spontaneous disorders in May 1968 following the murder of Dr. Martin Luther King, Jr. Virtually every city was tense. Uncertainty and fear prevailed among residents (black and white) and the police. We also confronted a terrible shortage of financial resources to improve conditions and services.

John Lindsay had just been re-elected to a second term as Mayor of New York. He had earned a national reputation for his outreach to minority communities symbolized by his walks in troubled neighborhoods. His courageous presence had a dramatic impact and set an example for leaders in every city.

A new breed of mayors was emerging—younger, more innovative and responsive to the needs of these deprived communities. But we desperately needed revenue. So Lindsay formed a special Legislative Action Committee of 17 mayors, including Joe Alioto of San Francisco, Kevin White of Boston, Pete Flaherty of Pittsburgh, Ray Gribbs of Detroit, Sam Massell of Atlanta, Ken Gibson of Newark, and me.

Our first goal was to build awareness across the country of our cities' common plight and shared problems, the result of national forces that demanded federal action. John led us on trips around the country to visit each other's cities and meet with the local media, business leaders, and elected officials to make that case. Lindsay, being talked about as a possible presidential candidate, appeared frequently in the newspapers across the country, on magazine covers and television. He attracted broad coverage wherever we went, which he skillfully used to help us publicize the urban crisis. When the group came to New Orleans, it was enormously helpful for our leaders and journalists to hear from other mayors that we weren't alone, and that each of these cities faced similar pressures.

We visited Detroit, which had the worst riot in the nation in 1967, with 43 people killed and massive damage. Our mayoral delegation toured the devastated area by bus, followed by a large national press contingent. Eventually, the seventeen of us lined up for a photo at a now vacant block that became a powerful two-page spread in Life magazine. We all knew that never would have happened without John.

To get additional federal support, we also mounted an aggressive campaign to lobby Congress, testifying together to show our common need, and meeting with key members. Lindsay led all this. He was handsome and articulate; gracious and attentive to be sure that we each got our time in the spotlight and that our local needs were considered.

All of this work culminated in 1972 when Congress enacted Federal Revenue Sharing, which was enormously valuable to all our cities. We took great collective pride in this achievement, which our sustained efforts, under John's tireless leadership, had helped bring about.■

Moon Landrieu *was Mayor of New Orleans for eight years and served as Secretary of Housing and Urban Development under President Jimmy Carter.*

Albert *and* Stephanie Lasher

On June 11, 1967, Mayor Lindsay was to address a large audience of Israel's supporters in mid-Manhattan. The Six Day War had just ended with the encircled, besieged Jewish homeland emerging victorious. Pride in Israel and anxiety about its future were running high in New York, which had a larger Jewish population than Jerusalem's.

That same evening, though, John and Mary Lindsay were among the 200 guests invited to attend our wedding at the Reform Central Synagogue in Rockville Center, Long Island.

The Mayor was eager to declare his allegiance to Israel at that historic moment. But the Lindsays were also longtime friends of Stephanie's family and she had worked for JVL since his days as a Congressman.

To ensure that he could be on hand for both occasions, JVL commandeered a police helicopter. Being Mayor has its privileges. Following his speech, he could fly above the traffic on the Long Island Expressway faster than any car could travel "the world's longest parking lot" and arrive in time for our wedding. But where could the Mayor's party land? We had no airport across the street from the temple, but, ironically, there was a restricted country club. Jews were barred from membership, but there was more than enough room on its golf course for a helicopter to put down safely.

John and Mary loved the idea of using a restricted country club's facilities to enable them to attend a pro-Israel rally in Manhattan and a Jewish wedding in Nassau County during the same evening.■

*Stephanie Lasher was Mary Lindsay's press and scheduling secretary in City Hall. She then got an MBA and passed the CPA exam and started a business with her husband **Albert**, in which she is still active.*

Simon Lazarus

My stint as General Counsel to the Department of Consumer Affairs, then just established by Mayor Lindsay, was brief—January 1969-June 1970—and a very long time ago. But the memory still glows—one of the very brightest spots over all those decades—when we made a lot of noise, did some good, made worthwhile changes some of which remain in place, and, most of all, had a ton of fun doing it.

That job was only my second after law school. From the beginning, as I watched the Mayor swear in my new boss, Commissioner Bess Meyerson, I was, to be candid, taken as much as anything by the reflected glamor of working for and with these two startlingly charismatic characters. A photo of that occasion appeared in Bess's obituary in the Times. Beautiful people for sure, but also tough and canny New Yorkers.

Especially Bess. Presumed, as a former Miss America with zero political experience, to be destined for service as an ornament, she brought to her job an understanding of what the people she knew growing up in the Bronx needed and expected from a consumer advocate. And she also brought the street smarts she acquired there to help her deliver, and to become a political force in the City. She made the front page of *The New York Times* business section with her first speaking engagement, before the Better Business Bureau of New York, when she "criticized her hosts," dismissing their "industry self-policing plans [as] seals of approval based on advertising budgets rather than product quality," and urged the business leaders in the audience to help her draft new consumer protection laws that would "hit only their intended targets." That set the tone, and she stayed on pitch.

From time to time, there was friction with the Mayor's team at City Hall. The Mayor was probably as surprised by that first speech as everyone else in the audience. But in that administration, as I recall, the sparring and gamesmanship always twinkled. I remember Bess and her team debating whether Mayor Lindsay would be very angry if she committed the cardinal bureaucratic sin of going public to attack—and overturn in the City Council—his proposed budget cuts for the Consumer Affairs Department. She finally ended the debate by saying, "Of course, he'll be angry, but [smiling at me] he'll think it was your idea!" She was right, as I recall, on both counts. But she also got the cuts canceled.

And I like to think she and our work were assets in the tough, but victorious 1969 re-election campaign.■

Simon Lazarus is Senior Counsel to the Constitutional Accountability Center, a public interest law firm and think tank. He was Associate Director of President Jimmy Carter's White House Domestic Policy Staff.

David Lebenstein

I had the good luck, as a 20-year-old college student, to work at City Hall for Assistant to the Mayor Ed Skloot. Ed's responsibilities included serving as JVL's liaison to the Parks Department. Three weeks after I arrived, though, Ed went off on vacation, leaving me to mind the store.

One day, while Ed was away, a mayoral secretary came by and said JVL wanted to see me. I entered Mayor Lindsay's office to find him alone and cradling a telephone. He looked up at me and said, "I'm talking to Jon Barnett (his representative at the Art Commission) who wants to know how he should vote on the Metropolitan Museum of Art's proposed expansion into Central Park for its new American Wing." This was a politically charged matter. Demonstrators protesting the museum's incursion into the park had attracted considerable television news coverage. Intimidated in the Mayor's presence but not wanting to look stupid, I blurted out, "He should vote yes." "Vote yes," Mayor Lindsay repeated decisively into the telephone before hanging up on Barnett.

As I turned to leave his office, JVL said, "And have that memo on my desk tomorrow about the Boathouse in Prospect Park." Of course, I answered, "Yes, sir." All I knew about Prospect Park was that it was located somewhere in Brooklyn. On returning to my desk, I called Donald Simon, Executive Assistant of Parks Commissioner August Hecksher, to find out what the Mayor might have wanted. He told me that JVL was scheduled to tour the new boathouse with City Council Majority Leader Tom Cuite whose district included the facility.

Even though he had called for my advice, I'm not sure Mayor Lindsay even knew who I was at that point. Perhaps he thought I was Ed Skloot.

When John Lindsay decided to run for President in 1972, I thought America's Mayor was an excellent alternative to Richard Nixon and those running to unseat him. I was asked to draft a position paper on national policy toward Cuba. I summarized Senator Ted Kennedy's enlightened view on the subject—lift the embargo, open the trade lanes, exchange ambassadors, take Cuba off the list of terrorist havens, and permit travel to and from the island.

But JVL was announcing his candidacy in Miami, home of many embittered Cuban refugees who would never vote for anyone recognizing the Castro regime's legitimacy. Florida is always a major force in the electoral college. In 1972, 1992 or 2008, what happened in Florida made a significant difference.

I watched the Mayor's announcement on television in New York. The first reporter to question him after his statement predictably asked JVL what he thought America's policy toward Cuba should be. Here was his answer:

"I don't think we should recognize Cuba nor lift the embargo. Cuba is a threat to our country and we should continue the tight embargo on trade until there is a new, very different kind of regime and Castro is gone."

My heart sank, but I understood political reality. Four decades later, Barack Obama became the first American president to try another approach.∎

*After having worked in Lindsay congressional and mayoral campaigns as a high school and college student respectively, **David Lebenstein** served in City Hall as an aide to Assistant to the Mayor Ed Skloot. He went on to found what became the Educational Priorities Panel, a public policy think tank, with Stan Litow, another Lindsay alumnus, before embarking on his current, longstanding career as a real estate advisor to non-profit organizations.*

Gerald Lefcourt

When, as columnist Murray Kempton wrote, everyone else was tired, Barry Gottehrer, barely 30, was hired as a mayoral assistant, joining Jay L. Kriegel, Sid Davidoff and other brash beginners whom Mr. Lindsay was attracting to his administration. Though his methods were sometimes called unusual—Barry was accused of coddling black militants and consorting with revolutionaries like Abbie Hoffman—the City stayed cool during the long, hot summers of the late 1960s when other American cities burned. Barry described himself as "a white in a world of black and brown, a moderate in a world of revolutionaries, trying to bring change where change seemed needed most, trying to buy time until the change would come."

Abbie Hoffman, my client, came up through the civil rights movement where he organized voters in the South, to become a leader of the anti-war and civil rights movements of the '60s and '70s. He organized the "exorcism of the Pentagon" demonstrations and the protests at the Democratic convention in Chicago. For those and many other protests he received subpoenas to the House Un-American Activities Committee and an important place at the table in the Chicago 8 trial.

One day, on his way to court in Manhattan to appear in a case where he was charged as part of the Columbia Student strike, he arrived to see a large demonstration for the Black Panther 21 case (also my clients). The police saw him coming into the courthouse and, of course, thought Abbie was part of the demonstration for the Panthers. They overreacted and grabbed him. He tried to explain that he had to be before a judge, but chaos ensued and Abbie had a broken nose and a new arrest.

When I got him out, he said, "Call Gottehrer." I asked why. He begged me to call him. "I've had enough," he said. I pleaded with Barry, "Please come talk to him." Abbie was in a bad way, broken nose and yet another case. Barry liked Abbie a lot so he came to his apartment. Abbie said he had thought long and hard about this and threatened that unless Lindsay got rid of this new charge for resisting arrest when he had done nothing wrong, he would announce his support for Lindsay and campaign for him in Queens where residents were still furious at Lindsay over the failure to plow the streets after the great blizzard of February 1969. Abbie said that his support would ensure Lindsay's defeat in the '69 election. Barry froze, not knowing whether to laugh or freak out.■

Gerald Lefcourt is a prominent criminal defense lawyer.

Ilene Leff

My journal notes on Mayor Lindsay's memorial, held on January 26, 2001 at the Cathedral of Saint John the Divine, are another reminder of why working for a leader of such high principles was so wonderful. During the service, his daughter Kathy told us that John Lindsay taught his children to judge people by who they were, not by the wealth they had accumulated, or by their race or religion. She might have added gender.

During an era when few women held professional positions in companies or government, the Mayor judged the qualifications and work of both men and women by a single standard. When thousands marched down Fifth Avenue one August evening in 1970 to celebrate the 50th anniversary of women's suffrage and to mark the Women's Strike for Equality, Eleanor Holmes Norton, appointed by Mayor Lindsay as Chair of the city's Commission on Human Rights, addressed us at a rally in Bryant Park. She called on the U.S. Senate to pass the Equal Rights Amendment. "Give us the right to compete. Give us the right to live, the right to a job, regardless of sex," she said. We marched that night for equality in the workplace and in domestic and social relationships. Today the world is better for the progress we've made since our movement took hold in those years.

Sitting at meetings with Mayor Lindsay as one of his advisers was a high point in my life and career. Tall and handsome as a movie star, he was, nevertheless, very down to earth. He focused intently on the task at hand and the substance of what people said. I think I became only the twelfth female management consultant at McKinsey & Company in part because clients like the Mayor hired and took advice on the basis of merit alone.

Speakers at Mayor Lindsay's memorial also recalled how he made serving in city government exciting and worthwhile. His Administration launched the careers of so many men and women who have achieved great success in in the public and private sectors. The hopes that President Kennedy and

Mayor Lindsay stirred drew many of us to public service and convinced us that we could change the world. More important, he gave us a chance to start doing so.■

Ilene Leff, who worked at the Budget Bureau as part of the McKinsey & Company group, was one of the first female management consultants. She headed Revlon's worldwide Human Resources office and served as Deputy Assistant Secretary of the Department of Housing and Urban Development in the Clinton administration.

Joan Leiman

I was working in my office in an old building at the corner of Worth and Church Streets. Across the street, construction workers were building the very large AT&T telephone tower. In the distance, I could hear some shouting and sirens. Then, someone shouted, "FIRE." Suddenly I heard an explosion and looked behind to see flames coming through the roof. I rushed down the stairs and reached the street safely.

Fireballs rained down from the AT&T tower. Sirens were screeching. Firemen were everywhere. People were screaming. Terrified, I inched my way along the sidewalk, clinging to the sides of the buildings, anxious to get up the block and away from danger. All at once, someone grabbed my shoulder and shouted, "WATCH OUT!!" Sure that I was about to be struck by a falling firebrand, I looked over to see two very high boots. I continued looking up and found myself staring into the concerned, but broadly smiling face of John Lindsay. "You all right, Joan? Do you need my help?" I hadn't worked for the Mayor directly yet. Aside from my relief, I was astonished that Mayor Lindsay even knew who I was. "Oh, Mr. Mayor, I'm fine. Thank you," I managed to say. He released his hold on my shoulder and I went on my way.

Why have I chosen this anecdote from my seven years in the Lindsay Administration? First, because it reveals his warmth and caring nature, qualities not sufficiently recognized by the press and public who often saw him as a somewhat aloof WASP patrician. Second, it shows his boyish sense of humor; he got a kick out of surprising me even as he was genuinely concerned. Third, it calls to mind his height; terrified as I was, I was so conscious of those tall boots stretching toward the sky. His height was part of what made him a charismatic presence. When accompanying him on field trips to one program or another, he would look to me to run interference when that charisma caused him to be greeted and treated as a rock star. I'm afraid I wasn't all that good at it. On one occasion, he berated me gently for not being Steven Isenberg, his then Chief of Staff, who was very good at it.

Finally, his being on hand that day calls to mind the side of him that took a young man's delight in going to fires. Throughout most of his Administration, the Mayor retained his youthful openness to experience. He brought a sense of possibility to the city and its problems, a belief that changes could be made. That conviction carried him through the streets of Harlem and enabled him to bring New York City into the second half of the twentieth century despite punishing setbacks and vicious criticism.

Understandably, John Lindsay left office tired. But thinking of him at that fire—those tall boots, the broad smile, his delight in surprising me, and the warmth and concern in his greeting—will always remind me of what made him an exceptional Mayor and a wonderful human being.■

Joan Leiman is Chief of Staff to the President and Chief Executive Officer of New York Presbyterian Healthcare Center and Special Lecturer at Columbia University's Mailman School of Public Health. She also served as Executive Director of the Commonwealth Fund's Commission on Women's Health

Nathan Leventhal

I was flying down to Washington, D.C. with JVL who was going to testify that day on health care issues before a congressional subcommittee. As he read over the speech that had been prepared for him, the Mayor asked me why there was no mention of abortion. New York had just become the second state, following Hawaii, to legalize abortion. I replied that I didn't know, but assumed that it was omitted because abortion was still a very controversial issue. At that, he took out his black felt-tip pen and inserted the following sentence in his speech: "The New York City Health and Hospitals Corporation has performed 18,000 abortions legally and safely." Then he turned to me and said, "Let's shove this down the throats of those goddamn Southern Democrats." ■

Nathan Leventhal was the Mayor's chief of staff and Commissioner of Housing, Preservation and Development during the Lindsay Administration, Deputy Mayor for Operations under Mayor Edward Koch, served a four-year term as a City Planning Commissioner during the Bloomberg Administration, has been Chairman of the Mayor's Committee on Appointments for 13 years and for almost 17 years was President of Lincoln Center for the Performing Arts.

Mark L. Levine

The 1965 mayoralty campaign was a magical event for all of us who worked on it. Having finished my junior year at Columbia only days after Lindsay announced his candidacy, I went to the 4th floor of the Hotel Roosevelt looking to help.

I was initially hired, along with Dick Sauer and Al DelliBovi, to drive Lindsay and the press to his daily campaign stops. My duties quickly shifted, however, after an accident while driving Harvey Rothenberg's car during a dry run in the Bronx to make sure the following day's directions were correct. Wise heads understandably decided I was not someone who should be driving the candidate or the press.

My new job, which I had through election day, was fantastic—but we all thought that about whatever job each of us had that summer, didn't we? I was Gil Robinson's assistant and one of the small entourage (Gil, me, Jim Smith, Pat Vecchio and Harry O'Donnell or Ollie Pilat) that traveled with Lindsay to virtually all his campaign stops.

My duties were varied: making sure there was always food in the car for JVL while traveling; that the battery for the car's sound system was charged every night in our office bathroom so it would work the next day when Lindsay mounted the platform atop the car to address crowds during the daily walking tours; and seeing that no reporter was left behind at any campaign stop.

I also walked in front of JVL on his walking tours, using a bullhorn and repeatedly announcing, "Here he is, John Lindsay, right here on [Flatbush/ Flushing/Baychester (or whatever)] Avenue. You've seen him on the cover of Time, you've seen him on the covers of Newsweek and Life. Now, right now, meet John Lindsay in person…"

One memory illustrates my willingness to give all for the campaign: We had stopped for lunch at a popular restaurant in Coney Island. John Jr. ("Don't call him John-John!" we were told) was with us that day. No one had noticed that while JVL was having only a bite or two of whatever hot dog, knish or ice cream someone handed him as he walked, others were giving the same treats to his 5-year-old son. Seated for lunch at the same table as John Jr., I suddenly noticed a desperate look on his face and immediately stretched out my hands and cupped them right below his mouth. "I hear you had your hands full yesterday, Mark," Mary Lindsay said when she saw me at headquarters the following morning.

I also smile when I look at the cover of Ollie Pilat's *Lindsay's Campaign* (Beacon Press 1968). It's the photo Dave Garth used, slightly cropped, in the "He is fresh and everyone else is tired" poster that was everywhere that summer. Cropped out of the poster image, but walking nearby in the cover photo, is a 20-year-old college student from Columbia.

Fifty years later, I too am no longer fresh, and more than a bit tired. But happy and proud—as is everyone still alive who worked in that campaign, whether at the Roosevelt or one of the 122 neighborhood storefronts—to have been a small part of that remarkable adventure of a remarkable man at a remarkable time in a remarkable city.■

Mark L. Levine is a corporate, banking and publishing lawyer in New York and the author or editor of three books.

Norman Levy

In 1972, my childhood friend John Scanlon took a leave from the Lindsay Administration to be Representative Hugh Carey's press secretary in his final congressional campaign. John asked me to round up volunteers. In a weak moment, I said yes.

Eventually, I had over one hundred volunteers, provided by the Lindsay borough coordinators, working in that race's last month. Carey was trailing badly when we came to his rescue because he had stayed in Washington and ignored the district for three years. A few days before the election, the polls said that the Lindsay forces had helped to put him ahead of his opponent by about two percentage points.

With his chances for victory improved, Carey called me to a last minute meeting and asked for the Lindsay troops to leave the campaign because he feared that his conservative Bay Ridge voters would discover the "John Lindsay" support.

Angered by that request, I told the Congressman that you can't take volunteers' support and then discard them so near the end of a campaign. After all, they had done an amazing job of turning his district around. We had a heated argument, and I told him that either he lets the volunteers finish or our volunteers would put on their LINDSAY buttons and ring every doorbell in the district, starting with Bay Ridge!

At that, Hugh Carey stormed out of the room. John Scanlon asked me why I had provoked the Congressman. I simply replied, "Screw him!"

The volunteers stayed and Hugh Carey won another term in the House of Representatives. The rest is history, and remarkable history at that. Carey went on to be a two-term governor. His leadership in Albany and his knowledge of Congress saved the city and state from bankruptcy. The former Brooklyn-Battery Tunnel now bears his name. ■

Norman Levy is a government, business, and community relations consultant.

John Lewis

I never knew New York Mayor John Lindsay well, but I first met him in 1971, shortly after he switched to the Democratic Party and announced that he was running for President. I was no longer the chairman of the Student Non-Violent Coordinating Committee and had begun serving as Director of the Voter Education Project (VEP) based in Atlanta.

One day Lindsay's office called and said he wanted to meet, so on one of his campaign trips to Florida, an important early primary state, Lindsay stopped off in Atlanta, and we met at the airport. I was impressed by his deep personal knowledge and passion about the battles for civil rights. He had been intimately involved in the passage of the most influential legislation in the last 50 years, the Civil Rights Act of 1964 and the Voting Rights Act of 1965. I had spoken at the March on Washington, been arrested and taken to jail, and marched on the front lines in Selma while Lindsay was serving in Congress. He had been one of the lead Republicans who marshaled bi-partisan support in Congress for both bills, during another era when moderate Republicans made up more than half of the Republican conference. He and I had played very different roles, but we shared a common bond as advocates and participants who helped to create those two legislative milestones. Later, I followed Lindsay's activities when I served on the board of the African American Institute with his older brother, George, a leading lawyer of the time.

More than his legislative record, his national reputation was built upon his unique willingness to spend time in New York's minority communities, in an effort to come to know and understand the people living there. His compassionate leadership helped keep New York calm when many other cities erupted in violence shortly after Martin Luther King Jr. was killed. He also used his knowledge of America's racial conditions to lead the National Advisory Committee on Civil Disorders, known as the Kerner Commission, whose 1968 report spoke so bluntly about the existence of two American societies, words largely attributed to Lindsay.

Some years later I was at an auction and bought one of the Nov 1, 1968, *Time* magazine covers of John Lindsay. It was a photo collage created by one of my favorite artists, Romare Bearden. It still hangs in my home today.

John Lewis has served as a Member of Congress from the 5th District of Georgia for 28 years. As Chairman of the Student Nonviolent Coordinating Committee (SNCC) in the 1960s, he was one of the Big Six leaders of the Civil Rights Movement and is the only surviving speaker of the 1963 March on Washington. He was in the forefront of the marchers in Selma on Bloody Sunday which led to enactment of the 1965 Voting Rights Act.

Lance Liebman

In 1968, I was finishing my clerkship with Associate Justice Byron White at the U.S. Supreme Court. That term ended with the shocking retirement of Chief Justice Warren followed by the Abe Fortas scandal. Months later, incoming President Richard Nixon would start replacing the departed members of the Warren Court with more conservative justices, a trend that led to the rightward-leaning court now sitting a half-century later.

I was preparing to take a position in the Civil Rights Division of the Justice Department. We had a baby (now 47) and a $200/month apartment on Capitol Hill. My wife Carol and I talked obsessively about whether it was moral or ethical to work in the Johnson Administration in any way—even in Justice's Civil Rights Division—given the Vietnam War. Finally, we decided that I shouldn't. That so many of us regarded LBJ's Administration as immoral is intriguing in light of what has happened in Washington since.

Somehow I was put in touch with Jay Kriegel and eventually appointed an Assistant to the Mayor with a salary in the vicinity of $5,000 per year. Soon enough, we settled into an apartment on West End Avenue and had a second child.

Now, at the age of 73, I still recall extraordinary experiences I had working with an exceptional team at City Hall.

Politics, of course was part of all that. Before the 1969 Republican primary, which JVL had the good fortune to lose, resulting in a three-way race in the general election that enabled him to win with little more than 40 percent of the vote, Carol and I held a reception for Republican voters at our West Side apartment Surprise: the turnout of Republicans in our neighborhood was tiny and the people who showed up might make parents of small children uneasy. But the evening passed uneventfully.

Because of some leg problems, I now spend a lot of my life in cabs and am frequently reminded of my role in coordinating taxi policies for the Lindsay Administration. When I concluded that it would only make things worse for us and for riders if we tried to change existing taxi regulations, however imperfect they were, the Mayor and his staff gave me their full support. How could we have predicted Uber?

The subsequent careers of so many Lindsay team members, including a large cohort of distinguished public servants, make me proud to have served among them for two years, even if I never became a full-time government employee again.∎

Lance Liebman, *Assistant to the Mayor, became a law professor at Harvard and Columbia. He was Dean of the Columbia Law School for five years and Director of the American Law Institute, a legal reform organization, for fifteen years.*

Elizabeth Lubetkin Lipton

I have so many memories of John Lindsay. I worked in his campaign office on 86th Street when he first ran for Mayor (the only time I worked for a Republican). I met with him, Ed Hamilton and Jule Sugarmen to decide how to divvy up the Community Employment Training Act jobs. We were both on hand at the opening of the movie "Hospital." But my warmest recollection is of his appearance at Mitch Ginsberg's funeral.

I graduated from the Columbia School of Social Work, where Mitch was my mentor. When Mitch went to work for the Lindsay Administration, I felt it was "legit" to work for government too.

Until Lindsay became Mayor, municipal administrations did not actively recruit graduates from the best schools, but JVL took a page out of JFK's playbook, and brought in some dynamite people to work for him, young and old. Mitch was one.

By the time Mitch died, he and the Mayor had been out of government for a long time. John Lindsay was half blind by then and I had to give him my name when I went up to talk to him at Mitch's memorial. He was as gracious as ever to everyone who approached him that day, whether he knew them or not. Many had not worked in his Administration, but who just wanted to say hello to "the people's Mayor."

It impressed me deeply that even though his frail health was a more than acceptable reason for not being there, it was clear that John Lindsay wanted to come and pay his respects to an old colleague, supporter and friend. He was loyal that way. And those who saw him there, including Ida (Mrs. Ginsberg) were so pleased he had come.■

Elizabeth Lubetkin Lipton, a labor arbitrator and mediator, is on the labor panels of the American Arbitration Association and the New York City Office of Collective Bargaining.

Stanley Litow

I was in grade school when I first met John Lindsay. He visited my parents' apartment in Stuyvesant Town as a candidate for Congress. In those days, he campaigned by going door-to-door in the district and introducing himself to voters. Mom asked if he wanted anything to eat or drink. He declined, but charmed us all. My folks were impressed and I was totally blown away.

I met him next as a volunteer in his second mayoral campaign. I rang doorbells on his behalf in Manhattan, which was great, and in Forest Hills, which is another story.

After he was re-elected, I worked for Mayor Lindsay as Associate Director and then as Executive Director of the Urban Corps, our municipal version of the Peace Corps. Created by the Mayor during his first term, approximately 10,000 students from over 100 colleges and universities worked for the city at the program's peak as Urban Corps interns. They had full-time assignments during the summer and part-time duties during the school year. Ranging from freshmen to graduate and professional school students, interns were posted in virtually every City department and, in some instances, managed or expanded municipal services. Law students, for example, staffed borough offices of the Department of Consumer Affairs and handled shoppers' complaints.

The Urban Corps model leveraged federal college work-study funds to pay students' salaries. As a result, these internships cost the City only twenty cents for every dollar paid in student wages. All interns were paid and eligible for financial aid. Based on the success of New York's Urban Corps, over 100 other American cities launched such efforts following our innovative model.

Several effective approaches to enlisting young people in public service were derived from Lindsay Administration programs, including the

Corporation for National Service and the University Year for Action. In 1972, to cite a case in point, New York City became the first non-university to receive a competitive federal University Year for Action grant to augment our community health services via a student intern five-borough endeavor known as Mobilization for Adolescent Student Health, or MASH. MASH interns helped young people navigate the healthcare system.

A Nixon Administration grant to support a Lindsay initiative was, to say the least, unusual. I reported to Deputy Mayor Ed Morrison who shared the Mayor's feeling that our application was a long shot, at best. When the grant was awarded, the Mayor asked to see me. As a very junior member of the Administration, I rarely saw him and was thrilled at the prospect. While clearly not a big fan of President Nixon's, Mayor Lindsay said it was likely we were funded "on the merits" and expressed his deep appreciation for our success. My feet barely touched the ground as I returned to my office from City Hall.

One of my assignments was responding to unsolicited mail from students pursuing internships or jobs with the City. We averaged a few hundred such letters a week. John Lindsay inspired these young men and women, as he inspired me and countless others, to consider entering public service. Transformative Lindsay Administration experiences shaped my career.■

Stanley Litow is President of the IBM International Foundation and IBM's Vice President for Corporate Citizenship and Corporate Affairs. He has also served as New York City's Deputy Schools Chancellor.

William Maloney

I n 1970, I was working for Dick Brown as one of NYC's Albany lobbyists when Commissioner Bess Meyerson came north to press the legislature on behalf of the City's consumer affairs proposals. Since that
agency was my responsibility, I had the pleasure of squiring her around
for the day. When our rounds were concluded, I asked her if she would
like to join Dick, the rest of our staff and me for dinner. Bess graciously
declined, saying she was quite tired and would be going to bed early. She
added wittily that she enjoyed spending the day with a man taller than she.
I was flattered.

In 1972, I resigned my City job and ran unsuccessfully for the State Senate against Roy Goodman. I found myself unemployed and nearly broke
when, to my delight, Dick Brown called to ask if I would accept the job
of First Deputy Commissioner of Consumer Affairs. The relationship
between the Mayor and Commissioner Meyerson had soured and the
appointment of an insider closer to the Administration was thought to be
desirable. Several names had been suggested to Bess by City Hall. She
had rejected all but mine.

I said that I would consider the offer and met with the Mayor to discuss
the position. He, in turn, asked me to meet with Dick Aurelio to work out
the details. I told Dick that I would accept the job on the condition that I
be paid one dollar a year more than Deputy Commissioner Henry Stern,
one of the best "inside government" manipulators I had ever seen. Henry,
I was sure, would see to it that I was consigned to Siberia if there was the
slightest indication that I wasn't actually his superior.

Dick asked what I was making when I resigned in June; I told him $20,000,
and since Henry was making $35,000, compliance with my request would
have meant that I would be getting a 75% raise. The *Daily News* had recently raked the Administration over the coals for giving Ronnie Eldridge
a similar increase. Dick acknowledged that while a nice raise was in order,

75% was out of the question. *Sic transit gloria Mundi*, I went on to seek employment elsewhere.■

William Maloney served as the Mayor's Deputy Legislative Counsel and then as General Counsel of OTB. He was subsequently in private law practice.

Ann Manwaring

Mayor Lindsay had the sagacity to surround himself with exceptionally smart and skilled people, all of whom were fiercely loyal to him. I was fortunate to work for one of them, Jay Kriegel.

After working for Jay for a few months, I realized that he was perpetually late for his appointments by at least an hour, even for such high-level agency people as the Police Commissioner. Even though Jay might be delayed because he was involved in policy discussions with the Mayor and other staff, I thought Mayor Lindsay was not well served when important senior officials were left to cool their heels waiting for a staff person, so I began to run Jay's calendar 45 minutes ahead. As a result, he ran late by a more respectable 15 minutes. After a year, Jay caught on to my chicanery. I hope this subterfuge, presumptuous as it might have been, served both Jay and Mayor Lindsay well.■

Ann Manwaring has served as a member of the Vermont Legislature since 2006..

Julie Marenghi

I worked for Deputy Mayor Robert W. Sweet. Each day was full of challenging work. The hours were long.

While planning to receive the King of Norway and his retinue of officials, we learned that His Majesty's party would be unaccompanied by spouses. Mary Lindsay decided, however, that a group of women representing her husband's Administration should attend the formal reception to be held at the Brooklyn Museum. Mrs. Lindsay thought each Norwegian visitor should have a lady from the City Hall office staff at his side during the dinner there.

The entertainment at the reception included a performance by the New York City Ballet. I was seated next to a Norwegian journalist who spoke excellent English. The event went off without a hitch. At 11 p.m. the King arose, thanked the Mayor and left with his entourage in tow.

The ballroom was emptying when I caught sight of the Mayor sitting alone and sipping coffee. I assured him that the dinner was a great success. He surprised me by asking how I was getting home. When I replied that I would ask someone on the office staff to give me a lift, JVL told me to inform his chauffeur that I was to be driven home with the Mayor's group. I did as he instructed.

I was seated in the car along with singer/actress Kitty Carlyle, her escort and Mary Lindsay. JVL sat beside the driver. It was a warm, sultry May evening. When the Mayor's long black limousine stopped at my brownstone, the driver got out to open the front car door for JVL and then the rear door for me. I told the Mayor that my family would never believe who took me home. He said, "In that case, let me say hello to them." I entered my home with him and called out to my mother, "Mom, the Mayor is here." She was in the kitchen and dressed in a vintage frock. My dad was in the living room watching TV in his undershirt. Neither was exactly dressed for a Vogue or GQ photo shoot. JVL greeted my mom and proceeded to the living room to say hello to my dad, who offered the Mayor a drink. JVL thanked him, but declined because he had people waiting outside who had to be driven home. My sister, my brother-in-law, who was an attorney for the city's Department of Markets, and their recently born son were also on hand. The Mayor chatted briefly with them, too.

My parents were overwhelmed and thrilled to have JVL in their home. Their intense stares taught me, though, not to surprise them like that again on a hot evening in May.

I've never forgotten that night nor Mayor Lindsay's graciousness and kindness, but, most of all, I'm so grateful to have had the opportunity to serve in his Administration.

By the way, my nephew is now a 50-year-old anesthesiologist.■

Julie Marenghi *was City Council President Sanford Garelik's Administrative Assistant, then held public relations posts at the Transit Authority and the MTA. She lives in Litchfield, Connecticut.*

Victor Marrero

John Lindsay was often accused of displaying his patrician background and Ivy League education when dealing with some of the earthier government officials and union leaders.

We were in Queens to launch a pilot program to improve the Department of Sanitation's trash collection services. The experimental program would enable sanitation workers to perform their garbage pick-up rounds faster, with less noise and more efficiency by encouraging residents to store their rubbish in large plastic bags to be placed on the sidewalks, instead of in corrugated tin cans, as had been the practice for years. The City would obtain the bags from major companies in the waste hauling industry and distribute them free-of-charge to homeowners in several neighborhoods for a trial period long enough to get these New Yorkers accustomed to this new approach.

On the outdoor platform were several local officials and community leaders, among them Sidney Leviss, the Queens Borough President who was seated alongside the Mayor. After Lindsay spoke, extolling the major innovation and the many benefits it would yield for the city, Leviss stepped up to the platform and proceeded to attack the Mayor's record for what the borough president characterized as JVL's indifference to the delivery of public services to the people of Queens. He also reminded the audience, on this hot summer day, about the Sanitation Department's slow response to the infamous snowstorm of February of 1969.

By the time Leviss finished, Lindsay was fuming. As they stepped down from the stage, the Mayor turned to the borough president and whispered, "You know, Sidney, you are an oaf." Leviss asked Lindsay, "I'm a what?" "An oaf, Sidney…O—A—F." ■

Victor Marerro was appointed a judge in the US District Court for the Southern District of New York by President Bill Clinton in 1999. He also served as US Ambassador to the UN Economic and Social Council and US Permanent Representative to the Organization of American States. He was co-founder of the Puerto Rican Legal Defense and Education Fund.

Ted Mastroianni

I joined JVL's mayoral campaign in May of 1965. Someone at our Hotel Roosevelt headquarters assigned me to an advance team—a squad of aides that made arrangements for stops the candidate would make as he campaigned. My task was to find an apartment house in a poor neighborhood whose courtyard was full of rats, and ask the superintendent to let then Congressman Lindsay, accompanied by television news crews and other journalists, inspect the premises. Our objective for this "spontaneous visit" was to demonstrate the city's deterioration and show that New York needed a vigorous new mayor to reverse this decline and bring us better days. I found just the sort of property our strategists had in mind. The super was cooperative. The rats in the courtyard were huge and fearless. I call the Hotel Roosevelt with the good news.

As John Lindsay and the press corps arrived at the selected scene of urban decay, he told the reporters that there were rats running wild through this part of town. When we entered the building, though, the superintendent proudly announced that he had shot six rats formerly residing on the property in order to help us make New York more livable. JVL was furious. Instead of staging such occasions, we found other ways to convince voters that our candidate should be the next mayor.

—

John Lindsay loved to ask odd questions that required detailed answers He might point to a building, for example, and ask how many people lived there, or inquire how many dogs—pets and strays—lived in the city. He wanted an accurate answer. If we didn't have one, and few of us did, he would order us to research the matter.

While I served as Deputy Parks Commissioner, the Mayor often toured our agency's domain. Strolling through Central Park with him one autumn day, JVL noticed some of our workers gathering up the fallen leaves. "How many leaves were there on a typical tree, and how much do they weigh?" he asked me.

Fortunately, Jim Linden, my Director of Operations, was with us. Jim told the mayor that there are about thirty thousand leaves on an Oak tree. The mayor repeated his question about how much the leaves weighed. "Well, it depends on how much water they've absorbed," Jim said, "how long they've been on the ground and what kind of tree they fell from."

Satisfied with those answers, the Mayor moved on. Later that day, I asked Jim how he came up with that information. He laughed and said, "I've been in this department for thirty-five years and have met a lot of mayors."

—

When I accompanied John and Mary Lindsay in the Mayor's car during the first administration's early years, they would speak of personal matters—finances, how the children were doing—as though I weren't there. Mary did not like large crowds. She and JVL tried to arrange events she was involved with to minimize that possibility. Sometimes, though, I could see the Mayor's attention shift from his wife's concerns to his preoccupations with the city.■

Ted Mastroianni, campaign aide and First Deputy Commissioner of New York City's Department of Parks, Recreation and Cultural Affairs, also served as Atlanta, Georgia's Director/Commissioner of Parks, Libraries and Cultural Affairs, on President Jimmy Carter's Intergovernmental Affairs staff, in senior posts at the United States Department of Labor's Employment and Training Administration during the Clinton administration, and has been a consultant to schools, governments and various non-profit organizations.

Robert "Josh" Mazess

We had between 21 and 36 volunteers in Tampa at any one time—some from Tampa/St. Pete—but most from NYC. I finally had to rent a one-bedroom apartment so that everyone had a flat space to sleep at night. Once that problem was solved, we had to figure out how to feed a swarm of young people. I've no idea what was happening in other areas of the campaign but we had no money to work with. Our volunteers began to get out of hand. Some took to stealing bread and lunch-meat from local grocery stores. I worried how this swarm of Huns descending on the innocent people of Tampa would look on the front page of the Tampa papers.

Mary Lindsay came for a day. We did four or five stops and took Mary back to the airport to await her flight. She had a pass to one of the airlines' special waiting rooms and invited all the volunteers to join her there while she got ready to board. There was a small bowl of peanuts on a coffee table. They disappeared in a minute. The hostess re-filled the bowl. Again, the nuts were gone in a flash. After the fourth bowl, Mary asked me, "Don't you folks have any money?"

This problem was solved when I discovered that Gordon Davis had a brother that owned a deli in Tampa. After that we ate pretty well.■

Robert "Josh" Mazess was Chief of Staff to Congressman Fred Richmond of Brooklyn, later followed by appointments as Special Assistant to the Chief Executive for School Facilities at the Board of Education and Special Assistant to the Deputy Comptroller for External Relations under City Comptroller Bill Thompson.

Carl McCall

After graduate school, I went to work for the Taconic Foundation, which was a major funder of civil rights activities and innovative urban projects. I worked largely on organizing clergy in Brooklyn to participate in education and voter registration programs.

When John Lindsay was elected in 1965, Taconic joined the Ford Foundation in funding a study of the city's human services, manpower and welfare programs, headed by Mitchell Sviridoff of New Haven, whom Lindsay was trying to attract (and did) to head the City's new Human Resources Administration. Taconic donated me to the task force as well.

Lindsay and Sviridoff's HRA included the relatively new Council Against Poverty, created as part of LBJ's War on Poverty in 1964, and I became its third Chair (following two legendary leaders, Arthur Logan and James Dumpson). HRA had a terrific staff of exciting community-experienced leaders, including Major Owens as Commissioner of Community Development, Cyril Tyson, Stan Brezenoff, George Nicolau, and John Edmunds.

After two years, I moved over to become a Deputy HRA Administrator under Mitchell Ginsberg (who had succeeded Sviridoff) and the brilliant Henry Cohen.

I remember one day in 1967, following the shock of the devastating riots in Newark, Detroit and other cities, flying to Washington with the Mayor and Time Inc. CEO Andrew Heiskell for the founding of the National Urban Coalition.

When we returned, Lindsay asked if I wanted a ride home. "Sure," I said, and went with him to a police helicopter. When we boarded, he said, "I'll be flying—and doing my first landing!"

When we took off, Lindsay took over the controls and flew over parts of Manhattan, which he obviously loved to do, and then finally made his first landing on an East Side waterfront helipad. I was relieved when we landed.

After HRA, which gave me the grounding in government services and citywide politics and community dynamics, I went to work with the great Percy Sutton on the founding of his Inner City Broadcasting Company, then made my first successful run for office for the State Senate from Harlem.

Those were years of challenge and testing, unequaled since in their pressures and explosive tensions, which provided essential experience in the frustrations of communities and both the capacities and limits of government to meet human needs. And the camaraderie of a great team, with mixed backgrounds and skills, inspired by a courageous Mayor determined to reach the disadvantaged and alienated, was a life lesson in finding and using talent to pursue worthy goals.■

Carl McCall served as Chairman of the City's Board of Education and was elected New York State Comptroller. He is now the Chairman of the State University of New York (SUNY).

Paul "Pete" McCloskey

In June,1963, I was a young small-town lawyer in Palo Alto, California. One day, an unexpected telegram arrived: "Would you please join me and other distinguished members of the Bar in the East Room of the White House on Wednesday at 3 p.m. John F. Kennedy."

"Would I?" I was the first to arrive at the East Room. As the 300 seats filled, it was clear that these men were leading lawyers from around the country. There were no women lawyers present. I recognized a few titans of the San Francisco Bar and realized that I had no business being there

It turned out my fellow Marine platoon leader from the Korean War, Chuck Daly, a member of Kennedy's Irish Mafia, had heard Bobby Kennedy talking with his brother about their forthcoming White House conference for lawyers on the Administration's civil rights legislation: "These are all Democrats," the Attorney General said of the prospective attendees. "Doesn't anyone know a Republican civil rights lawyer?" Daly said, "I know two." That got me on the list at the last moment.

Daly and I had been wounded the same day in Korea exactly 12 years earlier. He was famous as the only Marine rifle platoon leader to have overrun a North Korean regimental command post shortly before he was hit. He would spend a year in the Bethesda Naval Hospital, griping at doctors who wanted to amputate his left arm.

JFK appeared right at 3 p.m. His words were powerful: He observed that as President he could not be as effective on this matter as lawyers in their own communities. Would we do what he could not by returning home and making sure that the black people in our communities had access to local political and business leaders when they had problems?

He referred to the Birmingham riots of three months earlier. He predicted that black unrest would spread throughout the nation if African

Americans' legitimate grievances weren't redressed. His civil rights legislation, unfortunately, was going nowhere because the powerful Southern Democrats opposed it. It took Kennedy's tragic assassination and LBJ's legislative wizardry to finally secure the passage of the Civil Rights Act of 1964 and the Voting Rights Act of 1965,

I walked out of that meeting on Cloud Nine. The President had asked for my help. I was so moved that, when visiting Daly in his West Wing office, I asked whom I might talk to if I wanted to run for Congress someday. Politics was a profession that previously had been repugnant to me.

Daly's response was terse: "You're a goddamn Republican. No Democrat will talk to you." Then, after a moment, he said, "Well, wait a minute. There's one Republican around here who may someday give us trouble." I assumed the long-range future he contemplated envisioned Bobby's succeeding Jack to the White House, to be followed by Teddy.

Chuck made a call and handed me a note with a name and office number on it. "If you hang around until tomorrow," he said, "this guy will see you at 4 p.m."

At the appointed time I found myself in the Longworth House Office Building where a lanky, handsome man in his shirtsleeves welcomed me with a big smile. He said that if I was really interested in a political career, I should do three things: First, read a good newspaper every day that published the full texts of presidential speeches. Second, subscribe to the weekly *Congressional Quarterly*. Third, and most important, get involved in every issue affecting your community, from old folks to health issues to kids' problems.

So I started reading the L.A. *Times* every day and got six friends to join me in subscribing to the *CQ*. I was already doing what young lawyers do to build a practice, but also started a legal aid clinic for blacks in East Palo Alto, our one minority community; worked to implement fair housing policies, helped Hispanic mothers see to it that their children learned English, tried to conserve the foothills behind Palo Alto, and pursued other public objectives.

Four years later, when our congressman died suddenly, former child movie star Shirley Temple was the odds-on favorite to win the special election to replace him. At the time, Ronald Reagan was our Governor and Hollywood tap dancer George Murphy was one of our U.S. Senators. Something in me snapped. I entered the race, won unexpectedly, thanks to a bunch of good friends who worked their tails off, and joined the House as the first Republican elected to the House opposing the Vietnam War. I would serve there for 15 years.

In the late 1960s I visited John at Gracie Mansion to thank him for his help. He opened a closet door a few feet behind his desk where he had installed a life-size paper poster of Shirley Temple. He told me that when he wanted to relax, he would throw a few darts at her image. John also invited me to join him and U Thant in his limousine while he and the UN Secretary General discussed how to end the terrible war in Southeast Asia.

I visited John again in 1971, hoping to persuade him to challenge Nixon on the war issue in the upcoming Republican primaries. Two other moderate Republican congressmen, Don Riegle of Michigan and Tom Railsback of Illinois, and I also urged him not to leave the Republican Party. He didn't take our advice. Ultimately, Don Riegle left the Republican ranks in 1973, followed by me in 2007.

One of the few things I did in the House was to co-chair the first Earth Day with Senator Gaylord Nelson of Wisconsin in 1970. Mayor Lindsay closed Fifth Avenue to vehicular traffic and held rallies all over city. Today

Earth Day is celebrated in every state and in many countries.

I would never have gone to Congress to confound conservative Republicans by seeking to end the Vietnam War, making the first floor speech suggesting the impeachment of Richard Nixon and fighting to save Justice Douglas from impeachment but for the generous encouragement and guidance of John Vliet Lindsay, a truly great American public servant and a worthy descendant of the Dutch forbearers who purchased Manhattan.

John would roll over in his grave today if he could hear the oratory of the modern-day Republicans running for the White House, a place he would have graced with honor, humor and humility.■

Paul "Pete" McCloskey, *a decorated Marine Corps Korean War veteran, represented California's 12th District in the U.S. House of Representative. He is co-author of the 1973 Endangered Species Act and ran for the Republican Presidential nomination in 1972 as an anti-Vietnam War candidate.*

Steven McDonald

W hile involved in banking, I became interested in politics and was inspired by the 1965 Lindsay campaign poster with the Murray Kempton quote, "He is fresh and everyone else is tired."

My first foray into politics had been running the upstate campaign for Senator Jacob Javits' re-election, and also doing fund-raising.

In 1969, I got a call from Gus Levy, the head of Goldman Sachs, who had agreed to chair Lindsay's re-election finance committee. He asked me to join his team, along with Fergus Reid.

Gus was a Wall Street legend, a powerful business-getter and prodigious fund-raiser. His southern accent and gracious charm were traceable to his New Orleans roots. He employed a range of styles. For those few of his own stature in the financial community, Gus could play humble and say, "I'm doing the best I can, but I need help." For those who worked for him or owed Gus favors, he could just bark out, "Goddamn, I need $5,000 by tomorrow," and those checks would roll in.

After Lindsay lost the June 1969 Republican primary, we were concerned about the reaction among Lindsay's base of traditional Republican donors. Gus quickly convened a high-level meeting of influential and loyal supporters. He made a forceful case that they had to support John to ensure that his campaign would be well funded. At that one meeting, he raised over one million dollars, mostly in $100,000 contributions from Paul Mellon, Jock Whitney, Arthur Houghton, John L. Loeb, William Burden, Dick and Bruce Gelb and, I believe, some of Nelson Rockefeller's brothers.

As the campaign progressed and the line between Lindsay and his two ultra-conservative opponents became clearer, others came on board.

One day, Sam Lefrak, the celebrated developer, walked into our office in the campaign headquarters carrying a shoebox; he said it was filled with $2,000 worth of postage stamps. "Hope you can use these," he said. Those stamps were used to mail pleas for support to our most affluent prior donors. The Lindsay campaign must have been looking increasingly strong. Lefrak returned a few days later with ten checks, each for $3,000.

Under Gus's leadership, we raised a record amount for a local campaign.

Two years later, after Lindsay had switched to the Democratic Party and announced his candidacy for President, I was made campaign finance chairman. While I didn't have the clout usually required for that position, this was an unusual situation. Lindsay had one major backer—J. Irwin Miller, Chairman of Cummins Engine—who deeply believed in his candidacy and message. Miller and his sister essentially agreed to underwrite the campaign's initial phases. Lindsay and campaign manager Richard Aurelio decided to test his candidacy's viability in the early primaries. If the Mayor did well, a full fund-raising effort would be mounted. But that was not to be. The Millers largely funded the fledgling Lindsay presidential campaign.

Working for John Lindsay was a wonderful experience. I probably learned more than I contributed, but I developed a perspective that has lasted. It was a time I will always cherish.

John gave us the feeling that pitching in to help New York City was a noble cause. He was right.■

Stephen McDonald served as Deputy Finance Commissioner in the Lindsay Administration and is now Executive Vice President of the Trust Company of the West and President of TCW Middle East.

David McGregor

In the late 1990s, long after we'd all been together at City Hall, Warren Wechsler, Jaque Robertson and I had breakfast with John Lindsay at the Regency Hotel to consider whether the Mayor should write a book on urban design, one of his Administration's major commitments and successes. We had a fine reunion, but decided not to proceed with the project. Leaving the hotel we saw that the mayor's car was double-parked on Park Avenue. As JVL walked between the parked cars to get to it, a bicyclist blasted down the street between the mayor's car and those parked close to the curb, nearly hitting him. The bicyclist skidded to a halt, looked around, shouted "Top of the morning, Mr. Mayor" and rode on. The broad smile on his face told us that our man was thrilled. ∎

David McGregor was Chancellor of Vermont State Colleges, Acting President of Southampton College and is Managing Director of the architecture and design firm of Cooper, Robertson & Partners.

E.J. McMahon

As a kid growing up in northern Westchester, I was a precocious news junkie, devouring New York City papers and the New York-based TV news, which meant I grew up closely (often literally) tuned in to John Lindsay's tumultuous heyday as mayor. To be sure, I was a Buckley guy, not a Lindsay fan, and as a policy analyst in recent years I've been critical of JVL's legacy. Nonetheless, when "The Lindsay Years" ran on our local public TV station a few years ago, it was a nostalgic must-see for me.

The documentary had been running for a while when my visiting daughter Rosemary happened to pass through the room. Rose—a married mom in her 30s, born and raised upstate many years after Lindsay left office—is a distinctly no-nonsense type of person. Her head is not easily turned. But as footage of the mayor in his prime filled the screen, she stopped in her tracks.

"Who," she asked, "is that?"

That's charisma for you.■

E.J. McMahon has been a journalist, staff member of the NY State Assembly, and is now the President of the Empire Center for Public Policy.

Jerry Mechling

Missed garbage collections, overflowing cans and filthy streets were important problems for the Mayor. He complained about the Sanitation Department's poor performance in an early *Playboy* interview, offending many in the agency.

I ran the Environmental Protection Administration (EPA)'s new PPBS office that provided policy analysis. Much of my time went to "translating" information traveling between the Sanitation Department, EPA, the Bureau of the Budget and the Mayor's Office.

My pitch to the Sanitation Commissioner and his bureau heads was simple: "Look. You don't need to like me, or EPA. Or the Budget Bureau. Or the Mayor. But to get what you need, you have to speak their language. My staff and I speak it."

We met often at department headquarters, digesting Sanitation reports, analyzing data, and talking things through.

Their first PPB submission included three "fact-based" ideas:

• Legalize paper and plastic garbage bags to reduce the weight to be lifted.

• Reallocate staff to bring in more workers to match the collection load on peak days (Mondays and Tuesdays).

• Elevate productivity by improving vehicle maintenance to ensure that workers would not be idled by outages and too many trips to the dump.

These proposals won us critical support from Budget Director Fred Hayes and his analysts. Fred—in what I think was a first—visited the EPA's office to review our proposals (Carter Bales was able to wake Fred up from a narcolepsy spell before anyone saw he had fallen asleep).

Even more important, we brought top-line Sanitation staff to Gracie Mansion to meet with the Mayor. That gave us LOTS more credibility.

But the better-maintained trucks didn't improve productivity, at least not immediately. And the bags weren't legalized immediately. And the union wouldn't go along with the reallocation of manpower.

Our analysis was sound, but not our implementation.

In the second term we got much better, making new findings and developing new support:

• To legalize paper and plastic garbage bags, we ran tests in different neighborhoods evaluated by the National Sanitation Foundation. The union loved this project for lightening their load while gaining it recognition as a national leader. Union head John DeLury appeared in a video to publicize the new code (it needed multiple takes because of his dyslexia, but he had become a solid JVL supporter).

• We reallocated staff to peak days in negotiations with the union. An unforeseen issue was preserving three-day weekends (computer analysis helped here). To calm union anxieties, the new schedule was introduced one district at a time to enable us to work through such sensitive issues as redesigning carpools.

• To get greater productivity from the new trucks, we lengthened collection routes on a district-by-district basis. The union distrusted many district managers. Its priority was equity, not productivity. We succeeded because Walter Scharaga, a tough but respected Bronx commander, put a team together that methodically worked through and changed each of the city's roughly 1,400 collection routes.

When we were done, we had improved "tons per truck shift" by more than 20% and—more important—virtually eliminated the "missed collections" that had been such a problem. "Garbage time" had once again become a reliable and basically invisible daily routine.■

Jerry Mechling *ran the PPBS Office at EPA and has since taught at Harvard's Business School and Kennedy Institute. He is now with Gartner, the consulting firm.*

Tanya Melich

We were the New York liberal Republicans. In 1958 we elected John Lindsay to Congress and Nelson Rockefeller Governor. With our help four years later US Senator Jacob Javits was re-elected by nearly a million votes.

The political landscape seemed to favor our kind of politics—conservative on fiscal matters, liberal on social issues and internationalist on foreign policy.

I arrived in New York City for Columbia graduate school that fateful year Lindsay and Rockefeller were first elected. I wasn't sure I'd stay after I'd earned my doctorate. I was a westerner and naïvely believed that easterners were snobs and valued government over individual freedom.

My Dad had been a Utah Republican State Senator and became the 1964 Republican nominee for Governor of Utah. My grandfather, a mining engineer, had been a professional colleague of Herbert Hoover's. I'd been an officer for the University of Colorado Young Republicans and the National Federation of YRs. You couldn't have found a more loyal Republican.

I talked to Lindsay not long after arriving in New York and found him to be smart, personable and no snob. I liked these New York Republicans and realized that my earlier prejudice against easterners came from ignorance. Some of the local YRs told me that someday they would elect Lindsay President.

In 1965 Jack Wells hired me as research director for the Republican City Campaign Committee for Lindsay. He'd managed campaigns for been Javits and Rockefeller. Jack told us to get Lindsay got every Republican vote we could find. William Buckley was in the race to help Goldwater conservatives prove they still had influence within the GOP.

During his 1965 fusion campaign, Lindsay took positions that seemed more Democratic than Republican. Should Albany make decisions on rent control? Was the state or city most responsible for housing production?

Would the state give the city more governing power?

I prepared position papers that tried to fit a New York liberal Republican framework. Well aware that the Governor was funding our operation, we had to be sensitive to City and State authority. Our balancing act was intended to keep peace between the Governor and the soon-to-be Mayor.

Election Day affirmed Wells' GOP strategy. Lindsay won by only 102,407 votes. The consensus was that the 281,796 votes on the Liberal line had elected him. But Wells kept a close watch on the Goldwater movement, which predicted its mayoral candidate, William F. Buckley, would win 800,000 votes; he got only 341,226. Lindsay's 865,433 NYC votes on the Republican line were more than Goldwater's New York City's presidential GOP numbers.

Wells understood that the Lindsay Republican strategy was also the foundation for Rockefeller's forthcoming re-election campaign and would affect both Lindsay's ability to govern and to win the Republican mayoral nomination in 1969.

He also knew the fight for control of the national Republican Party and its 1968 presidential nominating contest was underway. Getting Republicans to vote for Lindsay in 1965 was part of a grander vision than many in the Lindsay campaign were willing to acknowledge.

Many of us hoped John Lindsay would be our party's next presidential candidate.■

*Political analyst, writer and election reform advocate **Tanya Melich** is co-founder of the National Women's Political Caucus and led the National Women's Education Fund. She is a Visiting Woodrow Wilson Fellow.*

Ruth Messinger

In 1968, I had recently returned to New York City after a stint in the Midwest and became involved in setting up a parent-controlled open classroom on Manhattan's West Side that was entirely integrated with equal numbers of black, white and Hispanic students. It felt like a truly new time in the city, with a mayor who cared about people and neighborhoods, and a general climate that was ripe for innovation, despite the flurry of campus takeovers and strikes.

As we launched our effort it turned out, no surprise, that we needed all kinds of help from the government--access to City-owned buildings and storefronts, help in explaining our existence to the local school authorities, recognition of our effort that might provide assistance to us in pursuing private funding and other support.

The urgently needed help came from a unit that Mayor Lindsay had established to help activists and community groups trying to achieve positive change. How notable that such a unit had been set up to encourage and support efforts like ours. Its staff was excited by what we were trying to do, eager to cut through red tape whenever possible and always reachable.... and that made a difference!■

Ruth Messinger is President and Chief Executive Officer of the American Jewish World Service. She served as a member of the New York's City Council and as Manhattan Borough President.

Philip Michael

I traveled to NYC from San Francisco in the fall of 1972 to pursue my Department of Justice anti-racketeering assignments and visit my close college friend, Steve Isenberg, the Mayor's Chief of Staff.

Steve brought me in to meet Mayor Lindsay for a short visit, without agenda. Meeting the Mayor was thrilling. I told him I had just concluded a bribery and racketeering case against his good friend, San Francisco Mayor Joseph Alioto, who called me a "psycho" when we crossed paths after the case, a case which Alioto won, by the way (in a miscarriage of justice, I might add). I also informed the Mayor that I had recently convicted Joe Bonanno's Sr.'s two sons of drug dealing. Nevertheless, his eldest son Bill gifted me with his book, *Honor Thy Father*, and inscribed it," To an honest prosecutor." Its jacket claimed revelations from inside the most powerful Mafia family—but the book contained none.

The Mayor reminisced about his early career at Justice Department. When I told him I was a fourth generation Californian, he said, "Come here and start a new streak," and assured me he was not concerned about Alioto's bluster, given Steve's endorsement. He said Police Commissioner Murphy was his next appointment, and that he fully supported Murphy's insistence on strict anti-corruption measures and tough discipline.

By pure happentance, Steve also introduced me to Police Commissioner Patrick Murphy who arrived at the Mayor's office as I was leaving. During our very brief conversation, one of the most important of my career, as it turned out, I mentioned that I was a senior government prosecutor.

I flew home later that day. The next morning at 7:00 a.m. (Pacific Standard Time) Steve's telephone call awoke me. "What did you guys talk about," he asked. "The Police Commissioner is going to call and offer you a job." Murphy called as Steve and I hung up. He asked me to move to New York and become the NYPD's Trial Commissioner.

Within a month, Jean and I, with two infants, arrived in New York, expecting no more than a year's work before returning to California.

One of my first major cases concerned an officer who shot a fleeing thirteen-year-old African American boy in the back, killing him. Like all too many tragedies that still plague us, the youth was running away from a plainclothes cop in pursuit who thought he was a criminal. The officer and his partner were fired. Around that same time, a complex hostage situation in Brooklyn led to the death of a fine police officer before the perpetrators fell asleep and the hostages escaped. Regrettably, Mayor Lindsay's term ended soon thereafter.

We're still here, our oldest "infant" having recently celebrated his 45th birthday and the anniversary of my 1993 retirement from the city after working in four mayors' administrations. John's was the best.∎

Philip Michael was also First Deputy Commissioner of the New York City Department of Investigation, Finance Commissioner under Mayor Edward Koch, Executive Director of the New York State Financial Control Board for New York City, and Budget Director of the New York City Office of Management and Budget. He is of Counsel to the law firm of Troutman Sanders.

Harriet Michel

On the Mayor's 50th birthday my assistant and I wanted to give him a token gift. Knowing we couldn't compete with the larger offerings from others, we went to a tiny shop in Times Square, Headlines In Print, and had a mock copy of the *Daily News* printed with the cover blaring " Holy Shit! Lindsay Wins Democratic Nomination." We were enormously pleased with ourselves because he appeared to get such a kick out of it.

There was always a scramble to get the Mayor's attention when he came out of his office to go to the bathroom on the first floor behind the police gate. At times it got so hectic staff members would shout his name and wave papers just to get a few minutes of time on his the way to the head. I was frustrated that my bid for attention had to end at the bathroom door while people like Jay would charge in right behind him. Talk about gender discrimination!■

Harriet Michel runs the National Minority Supplier Development Council. She was President and Chief Executive Officer of the New York Urban League and a Fellow at the Kennedy School of Government's Institute of Politics at Harvard University.

Thomas B. Morgan *(by Kate Tarlow Morgan and Nicholas Morgan)*

My brother Nick reminds me that our father had a hand-drawn caricature of a man bending over a percussion instrument with a determined, but crazed look on his face. Beneath the image was written, "All I do is beat this damn drum!" This and other souvenirs recalling his years as Mayor Lindsay's press secretary donned the walls of all of my father's workspaces as the years marched on.

In 1968, I was entering high school and my parents had just separated. Under no uncertain terms, my father's new home in 1969 became New York's City Hall. I expect that Dad spent more time there than anywhere else. I recall the place as the great white granite "waiting room," because my brother and I watched the heart of city government pump along, while we waited to "see" our father.

My brother recalls, "going down to City Hall to have lunch with our father and ending up having a midnight snack at Blimpie's!" I remember visiting Dad in anticipation of a dinner out, but being suddenly spirited away in a black limo instead, shoulder to shoulder with city officials, and following behind a line of fire engines headed to a huge blaze in Queens.

I remember, too, the readily accessible entry to City Hall—climbing the long, white terrace of steps of this 1812 structure and passing through the front doorway that leads to the central dome. Just before reaching the arched stonework that cast in so much light, we would be greeted by Pat Vecchio, the Mayor's security officer, and others who, as my brother recalls, would parody a "frisk" and send him on his way. There were no electronic or magnetic sensors at City Hall in those days.

Hanging a sharp left down the western arm of the building, we'd arrive at our father's office, which preceded Mayor Lindsay's. There was always light shining through that far room, which makes me think that much of the time Lindsay kept his door open. Does the current Mayor?

Dad's office was, as my brother says, a "veritable newsroom" with several desks, one belonging to our father, another to his deputy Robert Laird, and a third to the indispensible secretary. There was also the BLACK couch-- a broad, soft, shiny piece of furniture into which my brother and I would sink, as we waited for our father while he did the work that he was so very, very proud of doing.■

Thomas B. Morgan, who died in 2014, was press secretary in Mayor Lindsay's second term and had been a campaign aide to Ambassador Adlai Stevenson and Senator Eugene McCarthy. The author of over 200 articles and several books, he was also a magazine editor, editor of The Village Voice, *President of the United Nations Association and President of WNYC.* **Kate Tarlow Morgan** *is a choreographer, New York City historian and author of* Circles and Boundaries *(2011).* **Nicholas D. Morgan** *is an entrepreneur and avid supporter of animal rescue.*

Robert Morgenthau

During 1969, my ninth year as U.S. Attorney for the Southern District, the newly-elected Republican President Richard M. Nixon repeatedly tried to force me out of office. While I refused to succumb for a year, the pressure ultimately became unsustainable and I submitted my resignation effective January 15, 1970.

Meanwhile, New York City Mayor John Lindsay, just re-elected as a moderate Republican with the support of many of my Democratic friends and colleagues, approached me about joining his second term Administration. John and I already shared some common experiences. We had served in the same destroyer group during WWII in the Mediterranean, John on the USS Swanson, me on the USS Lansdale. We then both went to Yale Law and each went after to a major law firm where we became partners.

John's call to me in 1969 was timely since I was still stunned about leaving the U.S. Attorney's Office and had no idea what to do next.

I had been impressed by John's first term, especially his handling of the racial tensions and community unrest during the turbulent summer of 1967, with the violent upheavals experienced in Detroit and Newark. And we had personally interacted when he wanted to learn about PAL (the Police Athletic League, which I chaired) activities in disadvantaged neighborhoods. John also visited a PAL play street with me. He was enthusiastic about the program and made our play streets eligible for the Mayor's Office business community fundraising for summer programs. PAL play streets became a visible part of the Mayor's outreach in minority neighborhoods throughout the five boroughs.

On January 6, 1970, John announced my appointment as Deputy Mayor, with a charge to focus on drug treatment and enforcement. I brought four of my top lieutenants from the U.S. Attorney's Office with me—Elkan Abramowitz, Paul Rooney, Frank Turkheimer and Paul Galvani. Their level of energy and talent matched what we found in the Mayor's own well-regarded staff. My team provided extensive knowledge and capability in the area of criminal justice reform, one of John's strong personal interests and an area where he was already establishing a record of innovation.

While my tenure in Lindsay's City Hall was brief, our team attended first to the problem of minor drug arrests that were clogging the court system and deflecting scarce police and prosecutor resources. Working with these agencies and Phoenix House, we developed a pilot program to divert minor drug offenders from overcrowded courts to treatment. The effort was badly needed then, and sadly, still is.■

Robert Morgenthau was appointed United States Attorney for the Southern District by President John F. Kennedy and served nine terms between 1975 and 2009 as New York County District Attorney. He is Chairman of the Police Athletic League, Chairman Emeritus of the Museum of Jewish Heritage and of Counsel to the law firm of Wachtell, Lipton, Rosen & Katz.

Dick Morris

S ometime in 1970, my political buddies and other friends were invited to Gracie Mansion for drinks (sodas for us) with Mayor and Mary Lindsay. We had just won a trove of primary fights on Manhattan's West Side making us—the West Side Kids as we were known—a new force to be reckoned with, having successfully challenged the Reform Democrats who had been in power for more than a decade. Our group included Congressman Jerry Nadler as well as Richard Gottfried, who would soon be elected to the State Assembly. He still holds that seat forty-five years later.

John Lindsay was so charismatic. You couldn't help but be awed by his good looks, his patrician bearing and his attractive style of speaking. I had to forget what he looked like and just concentrate on what he was saying. I don't remember the content of the talk, but I do recall my circuits being jammed as they never have been before or since.■

Dick Morris *has been a political consultant, campaign manager, author and commentator.*

Edward Morrison

The City Charter revision approved by New York's voters in 1989 was the most extensive re-structuring of municipal government since the five boroughs were consolidated ninety-one years earlier.

For nearly a century, the Board of Estimate, consisting of the mayor, the comptroller, the president of the City Council and the five borough presidents, was the most powerful body in that government. The board shared the right to approve the budget with the Council, and had final say on land use decisions and city contracts.

The Board of Estimate, however, posed a political problem for Mayor Lindsay and a constitutional problem for the City government.

The political problem stemmed from pressure on the borough presidents exerted by Democratic Party country leaders to deliver satisfactory results in terms of municipal jobs, real estate development and other benefits. Sometimes, but not always, the mayor and borough presidents negotiated successfully to accommodate neighborhood aspirations, political objectives and citywide needs.

The constitutional problem would not be resolved until Mayor Lindsay was long gone from City Hall. On the Board of Estimate, each borough president had the same voting power. Staten Island's vote counted for as much as Brooklyn's even though it had far fewer people than Kings County. This arrangement violated the U.S. Constitution's one person-one vote provision. The 1989 Charter Revision dissolved the board and re-distributed its powers between the City Council and the executive branch.

Mayor Lindsay insisted, of course, in being involved on all significant Board of Estimate actions. As a matter came up for public comment from the audience on hand in its chamber, the Mayor's representative on the board—a role I played—would walk down to his office from a stairwell behind the desks where its members sat and get him. On the way up the stairs, I would brief him on the issue. Invariably, on arrival in his chair, the Mayor would deliver a brilliant speech on the subject. His ability to absorb information and present a logical, compelling position was consistently impressive.

The City Council had exclusive jurisdiction over legislation. Democrat Thomas Cuite, the council's Majority Leader, was a reserved man, compared to the ebullient Mayor. He and his party's county leaders controlled the fate of laws sought by the mayor and his commissioners, but exempt or appointed jobs in the agencies not covered by Civil Service regulations were bargaining chips in negotiations between the legislative and executive branches. Jobs of that kind were often given in exchange for council passage of laws and budgets proposed by the Mayor and his team.

Tom Cuite was a tough negotiator, who often extracted major concessions from the mayor, but he was also an "old school" politician; his word was his bond. And he was respectful of John Lindsay and the mayoralty.

Unfortunately, the same could not be said of some other city legislators. Councilman Matt Troy of Queens appeared with me on a radio show where he admitted telling lies to get elected. He also attacked Mayor Lindsay for opposing the Vietnam War.

Under the Board of Estimate/City Council system, the Lindsay Administration operated well and relatively scandal-free.■

Edward Morrison was Deputy Mayor/City Administrator and Chairman of the Liberal Party.

Gregory Mosher

In 1984, after years of struggle and mostly empty houses, the theater component of Lincoln Center was known as the Troubled Beaumont. The Beaumont's board and the parent Lincoln Center board were having what diplomats call full and frank discussions over their corporate relationship. Into this unseemly tangle stepped former Mayor John Lindsay who was charged with setting a new course for the theater.

Among John's tasks was to find an "artistic manager." And so I found myself coming in once a week from my job at Chicago's Goodman Theatre to meet various board members and, almost always, have dinner with JVL. But I had no intention of taking the job. Several men I admired had failed at the Beaumont, and there was no reason to think I'd succeed. Besides, we were having a great time at the Goodman.

But those dinners with JVL were irresistible. And, long story short, after about twenty of them, John said the wine wasn't going back in the bottle, that I'd committed myself. There still wasn't any money and the problems hadn't gone away, but it was John, and I couldn't say no.

John rallied the board, and found some operating capital. He engendered, by putting his credibility at stake, considerable good will around town. He supported my wish to bring Joseph Papp's longtime associate Bernard Gersten aboard. New York finally wanted the theater to succeed, and John both mustered, and was the public face of, that good will.

Because we didn't have enough money for a season, we started with a single show, a pair of one-acts by David Mamet. Critics hooted. I called JVL the next day, thanked him for all the great dinners, and released him from any obligation to me. He laughed and said, "I liked the show. Can't win 'em all. You said it would take a few years. What's next?" Almost anybody else would have accepted my resignation or, more likely, grabbed the chance to amend my authority over the theater's direction. Indeed, some of John's major donors wanted to rein me in. But John rebuffed them. The next show ran for a few years and we were out of the woods.

If the Beaumont had shut its doors in 1985, New York would have let out a mighty shrug. It had never had a clear identity. Was it to be European style art house? A place for the new plays from the country's finest playwrights? A "national" theater? Arguments raged. This carping was absurd but became addictive. John's genius was to not get caught up in it. For him, the idea of theatrical art that Broadway wouldn't try, and which therefore deserved subsidy and correspondingly modest ticket prices, was mission enough. Taking chances was the name of the game, and the box office was only coincidentally related to value. This, too, is the politician's insight. John bought completely into the idea, as uncommon as it is obvious, that the theater is what happens at 8 p.m., not its press clippings, awards or annual reports, let alone the producer's "vision." His joy infused the whole enterprise. John got true and deep pleasure out of people. This too infused the board and everyone he touched with the only sensible attitude with which to create, or enable the making of, theater: It's supposed to be fun.

In the nearly 25 years since John and I left the Beaumont—in together and out together—millions of people have seen its shows. Thousands of artists received a decent wage to ply their craft. The Troubled Beaumont is as established as an arts institution can be. Many people worked very hard behind the scenes to make this possible, and all deserve credit. But we should remember that it wasn't always thus, and John was, more than any individual, the person who made it all possible.■

Gregory Mosher has produced and directed multiple plays as well as film. His recent stage productions include "Love Letters," "That Championship Season," "A View from the Bridge" and "A Streetcar Named Desire." He headed the Arts Initiative at Columbia University.

Lawrence Moss

Lindsay '65 was my first campaign, and marked the first and last time I supported a Republican candidate for any office. Still seven years away from being old enough to vote, I began my active political life by handing out Lindsay flyers on the boardwalk in Rockaway Park. Frankly, I don't remember feeling passionate about any of the three candidates in that race.

After the election, though, many New Yorkers became quite passionate about some of Mayor Lindsay's progressive initiatives, particularly his appointing four civilians to the reconstituted Complaint Review Board that investigated police conduct. In a high school debate, I opposed the ballot referendum to forbid direct civilian oversight of police officers. Both the class and, later, NYC voters overwhelmingly supported the referendum. The civilian-augmented board was dismantled.

Out of sync with my neighborhood again, I favored Lindsay's experiment to strengthen community involvement in public schools. In September of 1968, the Ocean Hill-Brownsville school district dismissed several teachers and administrators. The city's teachers' union called a strike. To show my solidarity with the community control effort and counter, somewhat, the teachers strike, I organized tutoring sessions in math and science at a public housing project in Arverne.

1968 was an especially tumultuous year. As opposition to the Vietnam War mounted, I organized 150 high school students to elect a slate of delegates supporting Eugene McCarthy's antiwar campaign for President, and led Far Rockaway High School students in a one-day strike against the war. Our strike presaged the 1969 Vietnam Moratorium.

Off to college in Rhode Island, I was sorry to have missed the exciting 1969 campaign, when Lindsay triumphed as a Liberal-Independent candidate in a three-way race after losing the Republican nomination to Staten Island Senator John Marchi. I was still too young to vote in either state, but, without doubt, the Lindsay years were my initiation to politics and movements for social change.■

Lawrence Moss was in high school in the Rockaways and now teaches at CUNY's Hunter College.

Mitchell L. Moss

I grew up in Forest Hills, the community where John Lindsay actually built low-income housing in a middle class neighborhood, a battle that launched the political career of Mario Cuomo who forged a compromise that has resulted in affordable housing that has not disrupted the local neighborhood, despite the intensity of the conflict at the time.

Lindsay, in fact, is far better known by the people he attracted to government. That's his legacy, not the strikes, not the scatter site housing, not even the slow pace of removing snow in Queens.

Ambitious young men and women flourished in New York City government.

John Lindsay did not draw on the traditional Democratic Party clubhouses when he assembled his team in 1965. He made municipal government exciting, a chance to take on big challenges; the individuals he recruited have built careers that endured far longer than his mayoralty.

Simply put, Lindsay's impact should be measured by the the people he lured to city government who then went on to even greater success under other mayors and governors.

Nat Leventhal, a graduate of Forest Hills High School, got his start in the Lindsay Administration as an Assistant to the Mayor, then went on to be Housing Commissioner, Chief of Staff and First Deputy Mayor under Ed Koch, President of Lincoln Center, Chairman of Michael Bloomberg's 2001 transition committee and then head of his appointments committee for all twelve years of his mayorality.

Peter Goldmark, Lindsay's Assistant Budget Director and Chief of Staff, went on to serve as Governor Hugh Carey's Budget Director during the fiscal crisis, Executive Director of the Port Authority, Publisher of the *International Herald Tribune* and President of the Rockefeller Foundation.

Especially noteworthy are the cadre of African-American appointees in the Lindsay Administration who successfully pursued careers in appointive and elective office, long after Lindsay's terms ended.

Eleanor Holmes Norton, Human Rights Commissioner under Lindsay, went on to serve as Jimmy Carter's chair of the federal EEOC and then became the first elected member of Congress from the District of Columbia, now in her thirteenth term.

Major Owens, a librarian from Brownsville, was appointed by Lindsay to head the Community Development Agency, and that became the stepping-stone to election to the US House of Representative where he served for 20 years.

H. Carl McCall, a minister, served in Lindsay's Human Resources Administration, and then went on to serve in the State Senate, as Chair of the Board of Education and as the first African-American elected to statewide office as Comptroller of New York. He is now the Chairman of the State University of New York.

Gordon Davis, initially hired by Lindsay's Chief of Staff Jay Kriegel, worked first in the Budget Bureau, and went on to be Assistant to the Mayor and a principal speechwriter for Lindsay, before being appointed to the City Planning Commission by Lindsay, and Parks Commissioner by Ed Koch.

Amy Betanzos, Lindsay's Executive Secretary, then served as Commissioner of both Youth Services and Relocation, and then went on to have appointments from the next four mayors, including serving on the Housing Authority.

The longevity of Lindsay appointees in the public sector is especially striking—and has endured well into the 21st century.

Nicholas Scoppetta, Commissioner of Investigation under Lindsay, went on to be a Deputy Mayor under Mayor Beame, was the first head of the Administration for Children's Services created by Mayor Giuliani, and then served as Fire Commissioner for eight years of the Bloomberg Administration, successfully rebuilding the FDNY after the devastating losses on September 11, 2001.

Stan Brezenoff, started in Lindsay's Human Resources Administration under Mitchell Sviridoff, then forged an all-star career as President of the Health and Hospitals Corporation, Administrator of HRA, First Deputy Mayor under Ed Koch, Executive Director of the Port Authority and most recently as a leading hospital executive.

John Zuccotti, Chairman of the City Planning Commission under Lindsay, served as First Deputy Mayor under Abe Beame and has subsequently served as Chairman of Brookfield Properties and as a key leader in the renewal of lower Manhattan after 9/11.

Dick Brown, currently in his sixth term as District Attorney of Queens County, was hired by Lindsay to be the City's lobbyist in Albany, and then went on to work for Governor Carey, and serve in many senior judicial positions.

One of the city's most seasoned political operatives, Sid Davidoff, started as a volunteer worker while a Young Republican at City College. Davidoff, Lindsay's driver when he served in Congress, continues to be the sage of local lobbyists, 50 years after Lindsay's election to the mayoralty.

Lindsay also provided a launching pad for the city's first two city-wide female elected officials. Carol Bellamy, who served in the Health Department, became a State Senator and City Council President, and Betsy Gotbaum, who started as an assistant to the Mayor for education, was appointed to be Parks Commissioner by Mayor David Dinkins, and successfully ran for two terms as Public Advocate in 2001 and 2005.

New York City government has always been a terrific place for young professionals. You get serious responsibilities at an early age, experience the constant rush of action that makes a difference, and build relationships that last a lifetime. The Lindsay team has shaped city and state government for 50 years. Quite a run for a guy who just served eight years in City Hall.■

Mitchell Moss is Henry Hart Rice Professor of Urban Policy and Planning and Director of the Rudin Transportation Center at New York University.

Ira Mothner

I first saw John Lindsay in the fall of 1960 in a public school auditorium on Manhattan's East Side. He was then Congressman Lindsay, representing New York's 17th Congressional District, the city's traditionally Republican "Silk Stocking District" and there to debate his Democratic challenger William vanden Heuvel. I was there, seated behind my candidate's wife, as the newest member of vanden Heuvel's campaign team. It would be my first paid political gig and I was moonlighting from my day job at *Look* Magazine.

Eleven years passed before I saw John Lindsay again, when Tom Morgan brought me to Gracie Mansion soon after *Look* had folded, and I joined the City Hall staff as executive assistant to the Mayor and Lindsay's latest speechwriter.

I never did tell John how sharply I recalled the telling moment of that earlier evening as he and vanden Heuvel squared off over many of the same issues that Kennedy and Nixon were then disputing in the nation's first set of televised presidential debates. Kennedy's positions were put forth by vanden Heuvel and Nixon's by Lindsay, a difference that gave vanden Heuvel a substantial advantage when the issue of Quemoy and Matsu was raised. They were two islands in the Strait of Taiwan that lay right off the coast of mainland China and had been fortified by Chiang Kai-shek's Nationalist forces on Taiwan. From Taiwan, the Nationalists exchanged long-range artillery fire with communist forces on the mainland.

In the debate at the top of the ticket, Kennedy clearly seized the advantage when he rejected use of the Seventh Fleet to defend the islands, which were, he pointed out, both plainly indefensible and in no way essential to Taiwan's security. Moreover, President Eisenhower had urged Chiang to give them up rather than risk a major confrontation with China. After vanden Heuvel made the practical case put forth by Kennedy, John failed to parrot Nixon, who had argued that we should defend "on principle" the islands he called "an arena of freedom."

John nodded agreeably as vanden Heuvel spoke. Then, he paused and asked innocently, "So if we give the islands to China, Bill, what do we get?" After thinking for a moment, vanden Heuvel suggested that, since the Chinese were holding a number of American citizens, it should be possible to arrange for their release in exchange for the islands. "I see," said John. "And tell me," he asked, "If they get hold of any more Americans, do we give them Staten Island?"

At that point, I realized I was about to enlist in a campaign that was clearly a lost cause.■

Journalist **Ira Mothner** *is the editor of Folio, the magazine of the Graduate Center of the City University of New York (CUNY).*

Diana Murray

One night, after working late at the Budget Bureau, I told my colleagues, as I was about to go home, that I wasn't sure the Mayor would appreciate my memo on the importance of the methadone drug maintenance program. About to walk out the door, I wondered why everyone was smiling broadly. When I turned to leave, two inches from my nose was the knot of a blue-and-white tie. I looked up and there was JVL looking down at me. I explained, most unprofessionally, "My God, you are gorgeous!" While recovering my equilibrium, he smiled at me with those deep, blue eyes and said softly, "I will most definitely appreciate your memo." ■

Diana Murray has held senior financial positions at the Metropolitan Museum of Art, Columbia University, the New York City Health and Hospitals Corporation, the Emergency Financial Control Board of New York and the Office of the Secretary of Health, Education and Welfare.

Frederic S. Nathan

John and I met at Yale Law School where on occasion we sat alphabetically: Lindsay, Morgenthau, Nathan. I would later serve as John's First Assistant Corporation Counsel under J. Lee Rankin, whom John had served under when Rankin was U.S. Solicitor General.

Today on the walls of my home are photographs of John at the parties we gave every two years before his next Congressional election to introduce him to our friends and neighbors. There was one party he could not attend, but he phoned from Washington to talk with the guests. After most of these gatherings, Mary would arrive the next morning to pick up his forgotten coat.

Looking at the pictures, you can see our children grow from the age of 2 on.

The most prized picture may be the one from a 1967 *New York Times* article about Mayor John Lindsay's weekly early morning meetings with City officials on the lawn at Gracie Mansion.

When my father died, John hand-wrote a three-page letter to me which I still have.

Our children now remind us of the occasion when the Mets won the World Series and were then entertained at Gracie Mansion. John stood by and cheered when the children of his administration officials took turns batting to the Mets.■

Frederic S. Nathan, serving in the office of the Corporation Counsel, became a partner at Kelley, Drye and Warren.

Harriette Silverberg Natkins

When working at the Economic Development Administration, I wrote a press release for the opening of the Hunts Point Warehouse. As usual, John Scanlon, the agency's public information officer, had me take my draft to City Hall for the Mayor's press secretary, Tom Morgan, to review and add a headline. Tom gave it to his aide Carlotta Maduro who prepared it for the mimeograph and wrote the "head."

She ran off a dozen copies and I ran one down to the press corps in Room 9,where I handed it to a friendly reporter.

"Signed off by Tom?" he asked.

"Absolutely," I replied.

"Well, I am about to save your butts," he said. "Take it back and have Carlotta fix the typo."

I looked at the release, turned purple and gave that journalist a big kiss on the cheek.

The headline of what I had handed him read: "Lindsay Opens Hunts Point Whorehouse."

Of course the reporter kept that version pinned to his bulletin board for a long time. I should have kept one too.

After that, I always proofed any document just one more time.■

Harriette Silverberg Natkins served in EDA as the first director of Japanese Affairs, then worked in marketing and development, including for the NYC Bicentennial Commission, and spent over 30 years at MetLife.

James Nespole

The times were turbulent, characterized by municipal union labor disputes, student sit-ins at colleges and universities and provocative appearances on campuses by controversial figures. In that volatile climate, the Mayor's office told the Law Department to obtain injunctive relief when necessary to restore order. The City's lawyers were often called upon in the middle of the night to pursue such relief. We would meet on the 16th floor of the Municipal Building to draft papers and look for a judge who would sign a court order barring violations of the Taylor Law, seeking the removal of students who defiantly occupied university property, or prohibiting someone from disrupting a campus by giving an inflammatory speech.

A Taylor Law injunction was triggered on an oppressively hot summer day when Barry Feinstein ordered a work stoppage of the bridge and tunnel workers and caused widespread chaos. Ambulances were unable to cross bridges that remained raised. Police and fire vehicles were stranded.

Judge Gold, a stalwart notwithstanding his advanced age, signed an injunction ordering the rank and file back to work. We arrived at the union's 14th Street headquarters with the injunction in hand to find that our entry to the building was barred. Not to be deterred, we called the local firehouse and commandeered one of its trucks. One of us read the injunction sitting on the end of its elevated engine company's extension ladder, which was poised outside the union office's window. Then we taped the papers on the window, completing the injunction's service. The union told its members to comply with the judge's order.

On another occasion, Rabbi Meir Kahane, leader of the radical Jewish Defense League, spoke at Brooklyn College inciting a small, but violent riot. Kahane insisted on returning the next day to continue what he called the "dialogue." At midnight we got an injunction barring his encore and set off on a merry chase to find and serve the Rabbi. Escorted by the police, we visited half a dozen locations, including one in Rochdale Village, where an elderly man, also named Kahane, opened the door to us at 3:00 a.m. The numerals on his arm marked him a survivor of Hitler's death camps. Finally, a police radio call directed us to an address in Borough Park, Brooklyn. When we arrived there, the Rabbi met us at the front door; he had been expecting us. We told the cops to wait outside. After debating Meir Kahane for two hours about whether the First Amendment afforded him an absolute right to make his presentation, we left. He did not appear the next day at the school. Mission accomplished.■

James Nespole is *Of Counsel to the law firm of Norton Rose Fulbright US LLP* .

Robert Newman

I have many reasons to be in awe of Mayor John V. Lindsay—and enormously grateful to him. He was a man of exceptional commitment and conviction.

He pursued objectives relentlessly, yet was willing to be flexible and innovative to a degree unimaginable among most elected public officials.

It was apparent that the NYC agency responsible for dealing with the addiction crisis of the late 1960s was incapable of thinking and acting on the scale necessary to have an impact. Lindsay asked his newly appointed Health Services Administrator, Gordon Chase, to tackle the problem. Chase recognized that methadone maintenance treatment offered the only hope of a reasonably adequate response. The urgency of our crisis required that the program be established with unprecedented speed. The affected population also called for a much larger patient capacity than had ever been provided for methadone maintenance. Virtually every "expert" in the field believed it couldn't be done.

And who was this man who Mayor Lindsay made his "health czar," responsible not only for building a huge addiction treatment program but for all City hospitals, Mental Health Services, and the Department of Health as well? Thirty-seven-year-old Gordon Chase had no experience or education in any field of health care. His only academic degree was a bachelor of arts in political science. His appointment was greeted with consternation by the local and national healthcare establishment.

Mayor Lindsay also made no effort to dissuade Chase from appointing a physician with essentially no clinical or administrative experience in any field of health care, let alone addiction medicine, as head of the planned program—me. I was a resident in Public Health at the time. Lindsay simply accepted Chase's judgment—a judgment ridiculed by most health leaders at the time. Chase's judgment and Lindsay's support were vindicated. Within eight months, the new methadone maintenance program had an active census of approximately 6,000. It would grow to some 12,000 in two years. A parallel short-term ambulatory detoxification program was admitting some 20,000 patients annually.

Here's another example of John Lindsay's exceptional courage and his readiness to support key staff regardless of possible political consequences. In 1972, I was issued—and refused to honor—a subpoena from the Manhattan District Attorney to "produce photos of all Black patients" in one of the city's methadone clinics. A witness to a murder told police she had seen the perpetrator running into that clinic. The Corporation Counsel's office insisted Lindsay order me to comply or be fired. Lindsay rejected that demand and allowed me to resist the subpoena. My brother, attorney Thomas Newman, represented me before the New York State Court of Appeals, which upheld my authority as Program Director to refuse to provide the photos. The US Supreme Court denied certiorari, refusing to consider the case further. This victory on behalf of patient confidentiality led directly to the federal government's promulgating privacy protections for addiction treatment patients throughout the nation, protections that were —and remain to this day—unparalleled!■

Robert Newman, M.D., is President Emeritus of Continuum Health Partners and the Director of The Baron Edmond de Rothschild Clinical Dependency Institute of Beth Israel Medical Center.

Eleanor Holmes Norton

Fifty years ago, I was fortunate to begin my career as a public official as John Lindsay began his Administration as Mayor of New York City. I had admired Lindsay as a congressman, who regularly broke with his Republican colleagues to support passage of civil rights and other progressive laws. The start that John Lindsay gave me in public life was to buoy me for the rest of my professional career.

As a young woman who had been a member of the Student Nonviolent Coordinating Committee (SNCC) and was then an American Civil Liberties Union (ACLU) lawyer, I was an outsider most comfortable when criticizing and protesting the actions of public officials—and suing them. A lawsuit with Mayor Lindsay as defendant is how I came to the attention of John Lindsay. In 1968, George Wallace was gaining ground in the Democratic primary. His outspoken segregationist views were anathema to New Yorkers. Yet, Wallace was popular in some pockets of Northern states, including New York. When Wallace sought Shea Stadium, a public facility, for a rally, the Lindsay Administration denied him a permit.

I was asked by colleagues at the ACLU if I wanted to represent George Wallace in Queens Supreme Court. It was an easy First Amendment case because access to a public facility must be permitted regardless of viewpoint. A Mayor generally does not ask a lawyer who sues and wins a case against his administration to join his administration. It helps to understand John Lindsay the man and the Mayor that he viewed my lawsuit not as a personal attack but, perhaps, as an opportunity to help the Mayor with his own larger vision.

The turbulent Ocean Hill-Brownsville school decentralization crisis had seriously fractured Black-Jewish relations. When Lindsay saw me represent Wallace despite my profound disagreement with his views (and Wallace was not my first), he may have believed that the New York City Commission on Human Rights needed a chair who would be inclined not to represent her own views but to resolve issues. John Lindsay gave me the opportunity to do human rights work in the world's most polyglot city. He supported and empowered me every step of the way, later making me his executive assistant in addition to my duties as chair of the commission.

My work in the Lindsay Administration has been instrumental in everything worthwhile I have done professionally. My appointment by President Jimmy Carter to chair the Equal Employment Opportunity Commission was the direct result of the opportunity and latitude Mayor Lindsay gave me to carry out his policies at the New York City Commission on Human Rights.

Today, as a Member of Congress, who fights for equal citizenship for her constituents in the nation's capital, I am following in the footsteps of Congressman John Lindsay, whose service has been a guidepost for me in the House of Representatives. John Lindsay's principled service, which demonstrated that a Republican could be elected and reelected in a Democratic city, speaks volumes to this country to this day. ∎

Eleanor Holmes Norton has served as Delegate to the United States Congress representing the District of Columbia in the House of Representatives since 1991. Appointed by Mayor Lindsay as the first woman to chair the New York City Human Rights Commission, she held the first hearings by a public body concerning discrimination against women. President Jimmy Carter appointed Ms. Norton the first female chair of the U.S. Equal Employment Opportunity Commission. Under her leadership, the commission issued the first regulations defining sexual harassment and categorizing it as a form of sexual discrimination in violation of federal civil rights law.

Charles Ortner

I first encountered John Lindsay—the Congressman—when I attended Washington University in St. Louis. As the university's first Congressman-in-Residence, he spent a weekend on campus meeting with students and faculty, laying out a thoughtful and inspiring vision for the constructive role of government in dealing with the dangerous physical and spiritual decline of America's cities. After returning to New York following graduation and finishing my first year of law school, and still resonating from the message he had delivered a few years earlier, I signed up to be a summer volunteer on the Mayor's re-election campaign. After he won, I joined the City Hall staff.

It wasn't easy being the Mayor of New York City. When he ran for re-election the Mayor's campaign slogan was "The Second Toughest Job In America". At a campaign event at the Felt Forum in Madison Square Garden, which was hosted by the comedian Alan King, King asked, "Do you know who has the toughest job in America? Spiro Agnew's wife."

When the Mayor was elected he made clear that he was going to be hands-on, and City Hall would never be without a mayor present. So he created the "Night Mayor" program. I thought that was a great idea, until my time to serve came up. It was the night of the first anniversary of the assassination of Dr. Martin Luther King. I was in a near total panic, worrying that the City might erupt in violence and I would be in charge of saving the City.

However, I was assured that the Night Mayor position was really a symbolic thing—the Police and Fire Departments had developed extensive plans and would handle all emergencies. I could sleep peacefully in the City Hall basement with a phone nearby, comforted by having been told that in the unlikely event that I received a report of trouble, all I had to do was pick up the phone, call the Police Commissioner's office, and go back to sleep. That sounded fine to me, and I happily headed down to the basement and opened the fold-out bed.

Then I noticed that there were mouse traps against the walls and in every corner. Panic returned. This time it was not the fear of having to manage the Police and Fire Department's response if the City blew up. Worse, it was the fear of a mouse appearing. I survived the night. As did the City.■

Charles Ortner, an Aide to the Mayor, is a partner of the law firm of Proskauer Rose, specializing in music, and a board member of the Kennedy Center in DC and the Grammy Museum in LA.

Elizabeth Palay

I worked as assistant to Harry O'Donnell, Lindsay's second press secretary, for several years. Harry came to the Lindsay Administration from the Republican State Committee, had been a journalist, was a veteran of many campaigns, and served as press secretary to Governor Thomas Dewey. I can only imagine the disappointment he felt that fateful day when the Dewey presidential landslide failed to materialize.

Harry was a large man of jovial demeanor who always wore a newsman's hat. No matter what the crisis, the tension or the unhappiness (even anger) of others on the Mayor's staff (or even of the Mayor himself) about some article or negative coverage, Harry never changed his tone. The only time he displayed anger was when he clashed with others on the staff over whether Lindsay should seek the Senate seat left vacant after Robert Kennedy's death. Harry favored that course. He believed that Lindsay would never be able to realize a potentially great future in national politics if he was pinned down by the daily woes of City Hall, but Lindsay didn't follow his advice.

Any reporter who entered the press office would always find a warm and respectful greeting from Harry, often followed by a personal story, or a question, a current baseball statistic and, most certainly, the offer of a look at a recently acquired picture of a steamship for his treasured, growing collection. Finally, he would get to the business at hand, but always with a twinkle in his eye and a smile on his kind, rotund face. Harry was the consummate professional with the easiest style imaginable and a true gentleman, beloved by all.

David Garth, Lindsay's media consultant, was a frequent visitor to our office and Harry's stylistic opposite. Short, high-wired and pugnacious, David was a force of nature. He was enormously proud of his work and enjoyed bragging about its impact and the role he played with candidates. This was understandable because the television commercials he did for

Lindsay and so many others were distinctive, powerful and incredibly effective. Despite all the bluster, David's work did indeed shape elections and make careers.

On the surface David was almost always combative, challenging, defensive. He took offense easily and willingly provoked disputes. He almost dared you to like him. (He used to say that he had no friends, only employees.) But beneath his bravado, David was sweet, generous and thoughtful. He was a genuine and good friend and mentor, taking great pride not just in the work but also in those who worked for him. His encouragement and good counsel launched and furthered the careers of many and provided personal support in times of doubt and need.■

Elizabeth Palay is an exhibiting artist, now living in Madison, Wisconsin.

Victor Palmieri

I first had the privilege of serving with John in 1967 when President
Johnson appointed him Vice Chairman of the National Commission
on Civil Disorders (known as the Kerner Commission). I had joined
the commission as staff director under David Ginsburg, its executive director. We began work as the nation faced its third consecutive long, hot
summer of racial unrest. After Los Angeles' Watts district burned in 1965,
Chicago's Division Street went up in flames the following year and the
Newark riots lay ahead. Ghetto arson and violence had scarred almost 100
other American cities.

LBJ named a distinguished group of leaders to the commission, nicely
balanced between representatives of various interest groups and political
views. The panel included I.W. Abel, President of the US Steelworkers of
America, Tex Thornton, CEO of Litton Industries, Roy Wilkins, Executive Director of the National Association for the Advancement of Colored
Peoples, and Fred Harris, U.S. Senator from Oklahoma.

The President directed the Commission to determine "what happened,
why it happened and what could be done about it."

LBJ did not foresee, however, that from the start of our work, John
Lindsay, along with David Ginsburg, would replace Governor Kerner as
the politically polarized commission's driving force in the heated debate
over our draft report's tone, findings and conclusions. When the President
realized that he had transformed the articulate, photogenic Mayor of New
York into a national political figure and potential Republican challenger,
he turned his back on the Commission, cut off further funding, and ignored
our report. That report drew newspaper headlines across the nation with
a memorable sentence which I had borrowed from a draft by Lindsay's
staff: "Our nation is moving toward two societies—one black, one white,
separate and unequal."

Another episode in my relationship with John began when he called me in California in 1985. He had become Chairman of the Board of the Lincoln Center Theater and asked me to serve as the board's President. Our task was to bring the theater, which had been closed for the past seven years, back from the dead. I still marvel at the way John's charm and good humor mesmerized our new board as he led us toward restoring that exceptional institution, one of the great success stories of the American theater.■

Victor Palmieri served as Deputy Director of the Kerner Commission, then Ambassador-at-Large and U.S. Coordinator for Refugee Affairs in the Carter Administration. He was Chairman of the Palmieri Company specializing in restructuring troubled companies and president of the Lincoln Center Theater when Lindsay was chair.

Leon Panetta

For over fifty years, I've drawn inspiration to serve the public from my immigrant parents, two years in the United States Army, and two youthful political leaders—President John F. Kennedy and Mayor John V. Lindsay, both of whom spoke eloquently about what citizens owe to their communities and the nation.

The last time I saw the mayor was in my office in the Clinton White House, where I was chief of staff. Although he was dealing with health issues, John Lindsay wanted to continue serving the nation as he always had. Having been a World War II veteran, congressman, mayor, vice chairman of the Kerner Commission on Civil Disorders and presidential candidate, he yearned to do still more for his country.

I recall Congressman Lindsay visiting the Senate side of the Capitol to plead with Tom Kuchel of California, like JVL at the time, a moderate, Eisenhower-style Republican, to join Democratic Senator Abe Ribicoff of Connecticut in pushing for hearings on the recent urban riots. I was Kuchel's legislative assistant. Lindsay did persuade Kuchel to add his voice to those urging that the Senate address the plight of America's large cities.

As mayor, JVL brought gifted young men and women into a municipal government whose policies had previously been shaped by the party politics of an entrenched machine. Although he ran into a wall of labor strikes and civil strife, he symbolized a new spirit of leadership. Along with such leaders as Richard Daley of Chicago and Joseph Alioto of San Francisco, he organized the nation's mayors into a powerful lobbying force.

When I lost my job in the Nixon Administration for enforcing civil rights laws that ran counter to The White House's "southern strategy," Lindsay's Deputy Mayor Dick Aurelio offered me a job at City Hall. Dick and I had been friends since we worked in the U.S. Senate, he as administrative assistant to New York Senator Jacob Javits.

Mayor Lindsay was locked in perpetual combat with Albany and Washington. The brutal fact is that all mayors must go hat-in-hand to the state or federal government for the funding necessary to carry out their most significant initiatives. Frustrated, but ingenious, Lindsay asked me to write a memo on the potential consequences of New York City's declaring itself the 51st state. Although he relished the idea, the Mayor realized that, as a practical matter, he was stuck with Governor Rockefeller and President Nixon.

Whatever his faults, Mayor Lindsay was essential to his city's survival and renewal in its moment of great crisis. He calmed a turbulent New York while riots wracked other major municipalities. Whenever disaster struck, he was on hand, responsive to peril and acting to ensure that New Yorkers could walk their streets and enjoy their neighborhoods to the fullest, enjoying the city's unique diversity.

John Lindsay's total devotion to public service throughout his career and so memorably in his effective leadership of the greatest city in America is perhaps his greatest legacy.■

Leon Panetta was Secretary of Defense and Director of the Central Intelligence Agency under President Barak Obama and Director of the Office of Management and Budget and White House Chief of Staff under President Bill Clinton. He also represented a California district in the U.S. House of Representatives.

Christopher Patten

In the late summer of 1965 I found myself in New York City at the end of a long trip around the United States on an Oxford scholarship paid for by a wealthy benefactor of my college. When the friend who accompanied me had to return to Oxford to take an exam, my benefactor suggested that I stay in New York where a friend of his was heavily involved in raising funds for the mayoral campaign of a moderate Republican candidate, Congressman John Lindsay. He also suggested that I try to get a job on the campaign.

While I had no previous political experience, or, to be honest, political interest, I went down for an interview at the Lindsay campaign headquarters in the Roosevelt Hotel. Slightly to my surprise, I was deemed fit for duty and joined a glittering talented and eclectic group of the congressman's supporters.

My task in the Research Department, working under Sherwin Goldman, who became a lifetime friend, was to dig up information on the somewhat eccentric politics of the right wing candidate William Buckley. With my English accent and vocabulary, I seemed to have become a sort of campaign mascot, a living embodiment of the fact that Britain and the US are two countries separated by a common language. Everybody, including and especially the candidate, was very kind to me. John Lindsay was unfailingly courteous, treating me with a sort of amused benevolence. He exuded loads of charm.

I have a great deal to thank him for. He set me on the road to a political career, which in due course took me to the Cabinet, Hong Kong and Brussels, diverting me from a life in broadcasting back in London, my previous intention.

I have worked for many people over the years. I have seen politicians of all sorts and qualities take part in and run campaigns, but I don't believe that

I have ever seen a more natural campaigner than John Lindsay. I cannot speak for his qualities in office; after his election I was back on the boat to Britain. But as a campaigner he was one of the very best with a natural articulacy, enthusiasm and relaxed grace, all related, perhaps, to his actually liking people, which is, oddly, not a trait that you always find in politicians. You would have backed him against most opponents in a campaign, though you might have wished him a rather easier constitutency that the New York of the 1960s.■

Lord Patten, Chancellor of the University of Oxford, has been Chairman of the BBC Trust, the last Governor and Commander-in-Chief of Hong Kong, a Member of Parliament from Bath and a member of the European Commission.

D. Kenneth Patton

The mayor and I were crossing over the East River in his car when I pointed out a stretch of land under the Brooklyn Bridge that local longshoremen were using as a parking lot. "If we build a container port for them further down the waterfront," I told him, "they'll park elsewhere and we can give that part of the city's shoreline to Buzzy O'Keeffe who wants to park a new floating restaurant there. We don't have to acquire or lease land to do it," I went on, "so the deal is essentially 'off the books.'" JVL got it immediately. What a splendid site for a restaurant, which would command a view of the harbor and the Statue of Liberty to the south, and further north the eastern face of Manhattan's skyline. "Just make sure it isn't some chain," he insisted. "Make it a real restaurant." For decades now, the world has come to the River Café, where it twinkles just north of a spectacular park in a reclaimed, blooming district that offers some of the best of New York living—further lasting evidence of John Lindsay's vision for a city with all the urban graces. ■

Ken Patton served as Economic Development Administrator. He was then president of the Real Estate Board of New York (REBNY) chief operating officer of the real estate firm Helmsley Spear and Dean of NYU's Schack Institute of Real Estate.

Nicholas Pileggi

John Lindsay did not play ball with the city's power elite. They sabotaged him on his first day in office with a massive transit strike. Lindsay would also face three UFT school strikes opposing community control of the arthritic Board of Education. Following a winter storm, piles of snow were shoveled slowly, and mounds of garbage were left piled up for viewing on the evening news during a nine-day sanitation union strike. Waste disposal workers walked off the job allowing raw sewage to flow into city waters and operators left their posts with the city's drawbridges locked in the "up" position, creating traffic chaos.

Lindsay paid a political price for not playing ball with the city's entrenched power brokers, but only by not playing ball was he able to make changes the city desperately needed.

For instance, under previous Administrations, police routinely chased minority youngsters out of upper-income neighborhoods. "You live around here?" they'd ask. That was the drill. Even peaceful protests were treated harshly and a brick thrown from a rooftop would be returned with a fusillade of bullets turning Harlem and Bed-Stuy into Omaha Beach.

Lindsay, however, removed the wooden barriers outside precinct houses. He sent his closest aides, Barry Gottherer, Sid Davidoff and Teddy Gross, into the city's most volatile neighborhoods to connect with not only the traditional clergy and local politicians, but the local street gang leaders, civil rights militants and the youngsters who had never met with anyone from the city besides cops, judges and parole officers.

Lindsay created the Urban Action Task Force and insisted it operate in these neighborhoods on a daily basis. At one point, Gottehrer met with Allah, the head of the Five Percenters, one of the city's most dangerous gangs. Despite the Police Department's warnings that the First Percenters were mostly "perps," Gottehrer established a relationship with Allah by supplying city buses to take the group's youngsters to Rye Amusement Park on hot summer nights. The surprise that Lindsay's City Hall kept its promises allowed Gottehrer to slowly develop connections to not only Allah, but to some of the most alienated, angriest New Yorkers.

Lindsay was berated editorially for "reaching out" until April 4, 1968, the day Martin Luther King, Jr. was assassinated. That night, cities throughout America erupted in violence, looting and burning. Shops and restaurants within walking distance of the White House were robbed, then set ablaze. It took thousands of National Guard troops, as well as Army and Marine units, weeks to restore peace to hundreds of smoldering downtowns.

When Lindsay emerged from his car at 125th Street and Eighth Avenue, he was a familiar face to the furious crowds that had already gathered there. He had been walking those streets and meeting with some of these people before. They knew he was not there as a "photo-op" mayor.

Jimmy Breslin wrote: "He looked straight at the people on the streets and he told them he was sick and he was sorry about Martin Luther King. And the poor he spoke to who are so much more real than the rest of us understood the truth of John Lindsay. And there was no riot in New York."∎

Journalist and author **Nicholas Pileggi** *has written two books and several screen plays, including those for the films "Goodfellas" and "Casino," both directed by Martin Scorsese. He was also executive producer of the film "American Gangster," directed by Ridley Scott.*

Gabe Pressman

It was January 1, 1966—and the city was paralyzed by a subway and bus strike. It was also the first day of a new Administration at City Hall.

John Lindsay, the charismatic new Mayor of New York, appeared on Madison Avenue just outside his campaign headquarters at the Roosevelt Hotel early that morning and told a cluster of reporters, including me, that he was going to march all the way down from 45th Street and Madison to City Hall. I had a crudely put together "mobile unit," a Cadillac with a big, lumbering studio camera on the back seat.

We couldn't transmit a signal to get the picture on live unless we had line of sight to the roof of the RCA building. It looked as though we could follow him for just a few blocks and then we'd lose the line of sight picture. So I hustled to get with the Mayor before he disappeared into electronic limbo. There were two major problems. The camera was not wireless. So an engineer had to schlep the camera cable alongside the Mayor and me. Also, Lindsay was 6 foot four inches tall and I was just over five foot seven. And this guy wouldn't slow up! The long-legged Mayor and the short-legged reporter were quite a sight. I chased him for about two blocks. And the interview went something like this:

Q. Do you intend to walk to City Hall every morning? A. Yes. And I would encourage all New Yorkers to walk to work as long as it's necessary.

Meanwhile, Lindsay was waving and smiling at crowds of people who thronged the sidewalks. I was soon out of breath—and the line of sight to the roof of the RCA building was soon severed. I grabbed a cab to ride down to City Hall. I met another crew down there. I was huffing and puffing still—but I had scored the first interview with the new Mayor of New York. And I guess we were both happy with the outcome. ■

Gabe Pressman, a pioneer in American broadcast journalism, is Senior Correspondent for WNBC-TV. His career spans over six decades.

Robert Price

John Lindsay and I first met in the early 1950s through the Young Republican Club. In early 1965, Lindsay asked me to organize his likely Mayoral campaign. (I managed his first congressional campaign in 1958 as a third-year law student, and his next three re-election campaigns.) To ensure we had the needed resources, I negotiated with Republican leaders until we received a personal contribution of $500,000 from Governor Rockefeller. In May, Lindsay announced his candidacy with the enthusiastic endorsements of Rockefeller, popular State Attorney General Louis Lefkowitz and US Senator Jacob Javits.

But he faced a steep challenge to win in this overwhelmingly Democratic city, folk hero Fiorello LaGuardia being the last Republican to win the mayoralty twenty years before.

The endorsement of the then-influential Liberal Party, led by the brilliant political strategist Alex Rose, was critical, giving us an essential election line on which liberal Democrats would be comfortable voting only one year after Barry Goldwater's ultra-conservative campaign severely damaged Republican credibility. (Lindsay refused to endorse Goldwater.)

To overcome prevailing skepticism about Republicans, Lindsay favored the three hallowed pillars of middle class New York: rent control, free tuition at the City University and the 15-cent transit fare. Those positions were essential to secure the support of Jewish Democratic voters. So was the endorsement of the liberal flagship *New York Post* under owner Dolly Schiff and Editor Jimmy Wechsler. Greenwich Village Democratic District Leader Ed Koch's breakout endorsement two days before the election, amplified by the tabloid press with front-page coverage on Election Eve, helped seal the deal.

To reach equally important minority Democratic voters, Lindsay vigorously called for a Civilian Complaint Review Board, spoke forcefully to their feelings of exclusion, and made regular appearances in their communities.

Lindsay ran the most aggressive, visible campaign in the City's history. We sent him out on the streets every day from morning till night. He was tireless, going to every corner of the five boroughs. People became accustomed to seeing him walking in their communities. Complementing his personal presence, we mounted a massive grassroots effort, opening 122 storefront headquarters in every neighborhood, recruiting tens of thousands of volunteers. This was both the most ambitious part of my campaign strategy and the riskiest. We had a field organization whose power was based on a volunteer response that far surpassed every expectation.

Finally, powerful cinema verite commercials created by 35-year old David Garth, brilliant but mercurial, contrasted the telegenic Lindsay with grim images of a bleak city.

After Wagner decided not to run for re-election, Comptroller Abe Beame became the Democratic nominee. While this complicated our efforts to appeal to Jewish voters, his old-fashioned, uninspired, Democratic-machine image paled beside Lindsay's bravura.

It was always an uphill struggle given the 5-to-1 Democratic registration edge. Discouraging early October polls showed us trailing by 8-10 points. But campaigns are complex organisms; they build slowly. Ours came together right on schedule, driven by a reform movement's momentum. We captured major shares of the traditional Democratic constituencies—Jewish and minority voters--to win a three-way race (Bill Buckley ran to the right for the new Conservative Party), eeking out a 45-41-13 percent triumph. It was an historic campaign and victory.■

Robert Price, Deputy Mayor in the Lindsay Administration, has been an attorney, investment banker and media executive.

Harold "Hal" Prince

One morning in 1965, John Lindsay called to invite my wife Judy and me to join him and Mary in front of St. James Church on Madison Avenue, just blocks away from where we lived on 81st Street. He sounded very excited.

We dressed quickly and went off to meet the Lindsays. He told us that he was going to run for mayor and wanted us to accompany them to the Roosevelt Hotel downtown to look at potential office space there. As we made our way south, he discussed his plans for the campaign but interrupted the narrative every few minutes to introduce himself to New Yorkers walking in the opposite direction. Although he was our district's congressman, I'll bet that seventy-five percent of the people we passed did not recognize him. When the four of us arrived at the Roosevelt we checked out the empty rooms there on offer for a campaign headquarters.

Of course, we reassured John that we would work for him. When he asked if I would take the honorary position of Arts Representative to the Mayor, I accepted proudly.

That summer I suspended my office's theater business activity and devoted my time to his mayoral campaign. We commandeered flatbed trucks and enlisted musical groups and Broadway stars to canvass the five boroughs on John's behalf. The theater industry was on fire with passion for his election. John was its perfect candidate.

He remains the only political figure in my memory—and I speak not only of mayors, but of governors, senators and presidents of the United States—who loved the theater and attended regularly.■

Harold "Hal" Prince has had one of the most distinguished careers in the American theater as a director and producer, including the productions of Fiddler on the Roof, Cabaret, Company, Evita *and* Phantom of the Opera, *and has won a record 21 Tony awards, including.*

Jennifer Raab

I was the valedictorian of my sixth grade class at PS 173 in Washington Heights in June 1968. My speech was a call to action to my fellow twelve year olds on our responsibility to help create a more just society. I spoke about Martin Luther King's assassination and how inspiring it was that our Mayor had kept the city calm when there were riots in cities all over the country. When another parent asked my mother who had helped me with the speech, she reported that I had not only written it myself, she had never heard it before.

I was prematurely obsessed with government and politics. I loved the handsome Mayor of our city who had kept the streets calm and really seemed to care about people. He was a leader who wanted to improve life in the city, especially for lower income citizens. It was an exciting time in New York City...even for a kid in elementary school. I remember the drama of the transit strike and Mike Quill dying in jail. I was out of school for weeks during the teachers' strike. And then, of course, we missed more school during the blizzards. I remember Mayor Lindsay on the 6 o'clock news (what seemed to be every night) standing up for a principle or trying to respond to a crisis.

I was inspired by all the dreams and passion of the Lindsay Administration. By the time I started junior high, I knew I wanted to go to law school and have a career helping people who needed government assistance. I wanted to be like the exciting people I watched on the news who worked for Mayor Lindsay.

During the 1969 mayoral election, I was old enough to volunteer on my first political campaign. I found my way to a Lindsay campaign storefront on Broadway, somewhere between 170th and 181st Street. We were given flyers and assigned to give them out on a corner of Broadway.

Soon thereafter, my second cousin, Carl, whom I idolized, went to work for my other idol, Mayor Lindsay. He was one of the few people in our extended family who went to college and graduated from law school. I aspired to do both. And then I wanted to follow in his footsteps and work for an exciting New York City Mayor.

During the second Lindsay term, I babysat for Deputy Parks Commissioner Ted Mastroianni's children. I quizzed the Deputy Commissioner about Mayor Lindsay when he drove me home from babysitting. I grew even more taken by the glamor of the Lindsay Administration and by the young idealistic people who worked in city government. I was particularly interested in Lindsay's vision of how parks should serve the city and provide arts and recreation to citizens who would otherwise not have those opportunities.

Of course, reader, the rest is history. I followed my favorite cousin, Carl Weisbrod, into a career in city government (serving in the Koch and Giuliani administrations) and public service, fulfilling the dream of making a difference in society—a dream that began when I was a kid in Washington Heights, inspired by Mayor Lindsay. ■

Jennifer Raab is the President of Hunter College. She was Chairwoman of the New York City Landmarks Preservation Commission in the Giuliani Administration and the City Planning Commission's Director of Public Affairs during the Koch Administration.

Edie Radley

I can't say that working for JVL was all that glamorous. It took me about five years after the Administration ended before I could begin wearing a watch again. And oh, his handwriting! But I wouldn't trade the experience for anything in the world.■

Edie Radley served as Appointments Secretary.

Charles Rangel

In 1969 I was a member of the State Assembly and New York was in the midst of an exciting Democratic primary for the upcoming mayoral race. Bronx politician Mario Procaccino, then the city's Comptroller, called me to ask for my endorsement in that contest. Mario had made his way working for the notorious, nefarious Tammany Hall machine. I thought to myself, "Oh, God, anyone but Procaccino."

So after the primaries, I went against my party's line, reached over to the other side of the aisle and endorsed John Lindsay for mayor. Having lost the Republican primary to State Senator John Marchi, John remained a Republican—for a while, at least—but ran on the Liberal Party ticket. He beat Procaccino and Marchi in the general election.

Despite some partisan differences, John and I went on to have a great working relationship during his years in City Hall. When I ran for Congress in 1970, both John and Governor Rockefeller, another Republican, endorsed me. As a former member of the House of Representatives, John's support meant the world to me. I will never forget him for that and much more.■

Charles Rangel has represented Manhattan's 13th District in the U.S. House of Representatives since 1971 and is the second longest currently serving member of that body. He was the first African-American to chair its Ways and Means Committee and was a founder of the Congressional Black Caucus. A veteran of the Korean War, he was awarded both the Bronze Star and the Purple Heart.

Richard Ravitch

I met John Lindsay in Washington DC in 1959. I had finished Yale Law School, spent six months in the Army at Fort Dix and then got a job working for the Government Operations Committee in the House of Representatives. The son of a friend of my mother's was the administrative assistant to the new Republican Congressman from the East Side of Manhattan who invited me to dinner. I was impressed with his energy and idealism but wondered where a Republican could go in New York City politics.

I was a fan of Robert Wagner and thought that the campaign launched by Lindsay and the newspapers was unfair and cheap politics. Public employees had earned the right to bargain for their wages and benefits. Government's role in providing services had expanded geometrically because of the Great Society's programs and the civil rights revolution had instigated justifiable efforts to rectify unacceptable practices of the past.

I came to learn that John Lindsay was the right person to be the chief executive of the City of New York during the next eight years. His party affiliation had nothing to do with his convictions or his actions. Although I disagreed with his plans for community control I admired the people he brought into government, his sensitivity to changing demographics and the unquestioned integrity of the expanding city government

He asked me to be Commissioner of Public Works but I was in the middle of building a career as a developer of affordable housing. I also had a dream about building a racially and economically integrated housing development on the East River in full view of the United Nations. I showed Mayor Lindsay the model for that plan and explained that the City had never leased waterfront property for a sufficiently lengthy term to make a new development there eligible for long-term financing. Lindsay was enthusiastic about the idea and indicated that the City would enter such a lease and, furthermore, provide the mortgage financing through the issuance of tax-exempt bonds. Unfortunately, the City ran out of debt capacity and, with some embarrassment, the Mayor told us that they could not provide the mortgage loan. I then sought the help of the clearinghouse banks of New York who ultimately agreed to make the loan on the condition that the Mayor committed to replace their loan with City money when the construction was completed. But once again, because of growing deficits, the City could not keep that promise. Lindsay, however, was determined to honor his obligation, even though it was not legally enforceable. He did so by creating the New York City Housing Development Corporation which repaid the banks and made Waterside an exciting addition to the landscape of the city that he cared so much about. Today, HDC is the nation's largest financing institution for affordable housing.■

Richard Ravitch has been a real estate developer, the Owners' Representative for Major League Baseball, Chairman of the Metropolitan Transportation Authority, the New York State Urban Development Corporation and the Bowery Savings Bank, NYS Lieutenant Governor under David Paterson.

Chip Raymond

I was 23 when I joined an amazing collection of young people who, like me, dreamed that with a leader like John Lindsay and a lot of hard work, we could change the world. My first job was with the Human Resources Administration headed by Jule Sugarman. I was asked to take a position as head of the Neighborhood Youth Corp Payroll Division. The summer before I was hired, a $6 million fraud had occurred. A set of fake agencies were created along with fake social security numbers for fake kids that were submitted on fake time cards, and the City paid. We implemented a program that prevented fraud from occurring again. It was a great introduction to working in government.

After a year, I became the Deputy Director of a brand new initiative, the Methadone Maintenance Program under the Health Services Administration led by Gordon Chase. Having the City distribute methadone began a new phase in the city's attempt to help addicts kick the heroin habit. We set up distribution centers around the city, including one on a mothballed ferry boat, the Gold Star Mother, moored on the Hudson River. It was cutting-edge and controversial. The program was short-lived but we learned a lot about treating addictions and dependencies.

For my next assignment, I was recruited by Herb Elish, Commissioner of Department of Sanitation, to run the Sanitation Police Force. The former head of the Force had resigned under fire and I was asked to "undertake a complete re-evaluation" of the troubled agency. Based on our review, we restructured the operations, reporting structure and chain of command. This is another example of the kind of exciting opportunities available to some of us within the administration. We were presented with new challenges and we generally met them. Some members of the Force thought I should carry a .32 caliber pearl handled pistol in an ankle holster. I was content just to have a badge.

I ended my career in the Administration as Director of the Mayor's

Single Room Occupancy Task Force, another innovative program that turned out to be very effective in providing on-site city services to occupants of SROs. This was a precursor to my becoming the first Commissioner of the Department of Homeless Services during the Dinkins Administration.

I was proud to be one of those who were thrown into roles that, at least going by our resumes, we never should have had. This administration set my moral compass and gave me the ability and confidence to take on numerous challenges in areas that even surprised me.

A week after we all packed our belongings and left City Hall, my family along with my in-laws, set off for several weeks in Grenada in the West Indies. The Mayor, his wife Mary and son Johnny, were headed to the same island. We all had a great time with the Lindsay family on and off for a week, sailing, swimming, eating and talking. There was very little conversation about the city or politics. The sublime admiration I felt for the man was right on the money. He was the best.■

Chip Raymond's *multiple city positions included becoming the first Commissioner of Homeless Services under Mayor Dinkins and has since been director of the New York City Ballet and President of The Citigroup Foundation.*

Robert Redford

I met New York City Mayor John Lindsay through our mutual friend Steve Frankfurt, the president of the Young & Rubicam ad agency. In the early years of Sundance, John became a fairly regular visitor. We enjoyed skiing together and he even purchased a lot high up on the mountain. During a visit in early 1971, when I was filming "Jeremiah Johnson," speculation was growing that John might run for President in 1972, and media interest in him, while always high, was heightened. One photo of the two of us on the ski hill, somewhat unshaven, went out on the wire services and was carried by hundreds of newspapers across the country, giving Sundance (as well as John) an airwaves boost.

There was considerable speculation when I made the film "The Candidate" in 1972 that the character of Bill McKay had been patterned after John (who had just ended his unsuccessful presidential run), though others suspected that Bobby Kennedy had been an inspiration. But that was just speculation (in truth, it was patterned after Senator John Tunney). One clear linkage with John was that we retained his political consultant David Garth as a technical advisor for the film, and the portrayal of media hustler Howard Klein undoubtedly had elements of Garth.

After John's time as Mayor, I enjoyed quieter times together with him and his wife Mary, including dining, going to the theater and a memorable Frank Sinatra concert in New York.

Importantly, we shared a concern about the environment, with John building a strong record as Mayor including leading the first Earth Day in 1970, while I was growing Sundance's role as a center for environmental innovation.■

*Actor, director, environmental advocate and philanthropist **Robert Redford** is founder of the Sundance Film Center and the winner of two Academy Awards.*

Richard Reeves

"**B**liss was it to be alive in that dawn. But to be young was very heaven." Well, Mr. Wordsworth, it seemed something like that to me in the dawn of November 3, 1965. I was a 29-year-old reporter on the *New York Herald Tribune*, the late edition closed, running and skipping along an empty West End Avenue with a laughing, yelling gang of my colleagues Dick Schapp, Mickey Carroll, and Don Forst, the night city editor. Our coverage of the first election of John Lindsay as Mayor of New York was over and we were headed for a late, late supper prepared by Forst's talented wife, the food critic Gael Greene.

The morning after came on January 1, 1966, when Lindsay was sworn in as the first Republican mayor since Fiorello LaGuardia. That dawn I was walking across the Queensboro Bridge to the city's traffic headquarters in Long Island City. The Transit Workers Union had called a citywide strike of the subways and buses. Nothing, nothing was running, at least on wheels. What the *Trib* used to call a "City in Crisis" was a city in chaos. As I walked along, the new mayor was in a helicopter, telling the city by radio and television that he was in charge. One of Lindsay's many celebratory celebrity friends, the multi-talented Sammy Davis, Jr., said, "What a Mayor. Less than 24 hours in office and he has eliminated crime in the subways."

Its work done, the Republican *Trib* fell to the same angry unions in April of 1966. I was lucky enough to catch on with our hated rival *The New York Times*. For a year I had the time of my life doing investigative reporting around the country. More bliss, that. But there came a day when my bosses, city editor A.M. Rosenthal and his deputy Arthur Gelb, called me in and said they wanted me to be City Hall Bureau Chief. I did not want the job but was informed that what I wanted was not the issue. I have always suspected that I was chosen because I was one of the few WASPs—White Anglo Saxon Protestants—on a staff heavy with Jews and Irish Catholics. I think Abe and Artie believed Lindsay and I shared some kind of secret

WASP handshake.

I did my job, with the usual ups and downs. The big up was the impossibly handsome mayor walking, again and again, into truly dangerous minority neighborhoods, to calm potential unrest, the plague of the 1960s. Charisma and courage were potent weapons and Lindsay had them. Management skills: Not so much. Drama, yes. I was with him when he spotted a garbage truck parked outside a bar. He stormed in, trapped the surprised sanitation men and told them to get the hell out of there and clean up the city. He had his faults, but he was a man.

But he did become a talent magnet, particularly after the assassination of Robert F. Kennedy, then New York's junior senator, and one of Lindsay's few glamorous rivals. Even today, I am in awe of the young talent he attracted to the dungeon-like basement of New York's stunning City Hall.■

Journalist and author **Richard Reeves** *is a syndicated columnist, Senior Lecturer at the University of Pennsylvania's Annenberg School of Communications, and author of several books, including biographies of Presidents Kennedy, Nixon and Reagan.*

Fergus Reid

I was John Lindsay's campaign treasurer. In the late afternoon of November 9, 1965, a week after JVL's election, I had a date with the Mayor-elect to review and seek his signature on some outstanding financial documents. It was time to put such matters in order and close our books.

At about 5:30 p.m., I set out to hail a taxi at my apartment on East 67th Street and head downtown to meet with JVL at the Roosevelt Hotel. Suddenly, New York was hit with a major power failure and the entire city was shrouded in darkness. I decided to walk to the Roosevelt.

On arriving at the hotel I climbed six or seven stories up the fire stairs to JVL's suite and knocked on the door. The voice inside said, "The door is open. Come on in."

Sitting there alone, with only a single candle illuminating the room, was the newly elected Mayor of New York. John looked up at me, smiled and said, "Fergie, it's great to see you. Better days are coming!" ∎

*Campaign Treasurer **Fergus Reid** was Chairman of the JP Morgan Mutual Funds Complex and the Morgan Stanley Mutual Funds Complex. He has also served as Chairman of the Hudson River Valley Commission and was Vice Chairman of the New York City Educational Construction Fund.*

Suzie Rentschler

I set up a small runway show of models to display clothes that JVL might consider buying for Mary as Christmas presents. I'd always hoped that a friend or acquaintance would see me getting out of the Mayor's limousine at the end of a day working on this delightful assignment. Unfortunately, that never happened, even though I had this assignment for more than one Christmas season. The Mayor was unfailingly gracious and appreciative.■

Suzie Rentschler has been a philanthropist and entrepreneur in Columbus, Indiana.

Alice Richmond

I was a Sloan Urban Fellow on leave from Harvard Law School when I arrived at the Lindsay Administration. For about the first eight months I worked for the City, I made $87.50 a week, not much, even in 1969. When Budget Director Fred Hayes found out what Sloan Fellows earned, he insisted on putting me on the Budget Bureau payroll.

I became the program analyst for the MCAD (Manpower Career & Development) agency. Cyril Tyson, its commissioner, regularly gave Human Resources Administrator Mitch Ginsberg, his boss, a headache. Intriguingly, MCAD was the only municipal operating agency funded by the capital budget on the truly creative theory that an investment in man-power training was a long-term capital investment. This funding format required MCAD's program analyst to work with the capital budget examiners who, to put it mildly, were a breed apart. Even in the 1970s, they were still very 19th century in their thinking.

Fred Hayes, optimist that he was, hoped that I, a very young Harvard Law student, could communicate with the budget examiners, Commissioner Tyson and Mitch Ginsberg, bringing greater glory to his program planners. Gordon Davis, the mayoral assistant in charge of human services, was my supervisor.

In the middle of a budget process under stress for lack of money and too many priorities, Ginsberg and the Mayor took comfort from knowing that the vast sums sought by Commissioner Tyson could be drawn from the well-funded capital budget.

Fred told me several days in advance that I would be making the MCAD presentation to the Mayor, and that Gordon would be there in case I needed support. The day arrived and despite being February-frigid, I wore my best mini skirt. As I look at pictures now, I wonder what I was thinking.

After waiting for what seemed like forever, I was finally called into the room where the Mayor was reviewing the budget requests. When Gordon introduced me to him, I tried to avoid making eye contact with the Mayor and immediately launched into my well-rehearsed presentation. When I finally looked up, the Mayor and Gordon were chatting softly and laughing. I became flustered. Gordon passed a napkin toward the Mayor, who wrote something on it and passed the napkin back to Gordon. They continued communicating this way this way until I was almost finished with my presentation.

When we left the room, I exploded at Gordon, asking him what was so funny that he needed to be sending notes to the Mayor while I made my case. He took the napkin out of his pocket and handed it to me. It said "Nice Legs. John V. Lindsay". "I gave it back to the Mayor to sign his name," Gordon told me.

I still have that napkin. It's framed with a picture of Mayor Lindsay, the handsomest man I've seen, and the Sloan Urban Fellows. And, boy, there was and is a lifetime of lessons in that experience.■

Alice Richmond, *a program planner in the Bureau of the Budget, became a lawyer, bar association leader and law professor*

Joseph Riley, Jr.

John Lindsay's terms of office did not overlap with mine. I knew about him as a young person who was very interested in American government and politics. I admired his leadership of New York during a time of change and challenge.

I had the pleasure of meeting John Lindsay a few times, most memorably at a conference entitled "The Politics of City Design" at the University of Virginia. Jacque Robertson, a close friend of Lindsay's and a former colleague as his Director of the Mayor's Office of Midtown Planning, was dean of UVA's School of Architecture. I had heard so much from Jacque about their time together and John's visionary leadership. I had the great pleasure of spending time with the Mayor at the conference sessions. We discussed the importance of quality urban design and the need for a sound strategic plan and vision for one's city.

I called John Lindsay a few times over the years. He always supported what I was doing in Charleston and generously contributed to my campaigns. I was honored to have his support and friendship.

John Lindsay was a defining figure in the modern history of the American city.■

Joseph Riley, Jr. has been Mayor of Charleston, South Carolina, since 1975.

Eileen Robert *and* Jane Shalam

Eileen Robert (née Levin): I worked for John Lindsay in the 1964 Congressional campaign. Back in those pre-Internet days, politics was very retail-based and campaigns gave loads of responsibility to people like me who were barely able to vote. I was charged with organizing a Building Captain's network throughout what was then the 17th Congressional District. I must have done an OK job, as Bob Price asked me to stay on and work part time afterwards, keeping in contact with many of these supporters on John's behalf.

When the combination of finishing college and getting married interfered with my Lindsay duties, I found an able replacement: my cousin Janie Bishop (now Shalam), who was excited to work for John, one of the most glamorous politicians of that era. I literally handed off a shoe box full of the information for all the Manhattan building contacts into Janie's most capable hands.∎

Jane Shalam (née Bishop): I was attending the Neighborhood Playhouse of the Theater when my cousin Eileen Robert, a student at Sarah Lawrence College, asked that I finish her job of canvassing for John Lindsay's Congressional campaign. With lots of trepidation I went to pick up Eileen's shoe box full of names. I was so overwhelmed with my performance schedule, I didn't know if I could do this.

The shoe box sat on my desk for a week, staring at me, until I had an epiphany. I made a list of private and public schools in the 17th Congressional District, and I contacted each of the schools and told the student body presidents that I was starting "High School Students for John Lindsay" and that I would need students to canvass the shoe box full of index cards of the Manhattan building contacts.

I also promised that if John Lindsay got re-elected, on election night there would be a big pizza and soda party at campaign headquarters at the Roosevelt Hotel. Hundreds of students joined. It took me days to organize and photocopy the information for my new canvassers. I gave each of the students a list of names by building and asked that each of the people be canvassed twice and their visits documented.

I realized there was a problem, I didn't want to lose face because I promised a huge party so I went to the Campaign Headquarters for the first time and met Barnie Patterson, John Lindsay's Administrative Assistant. I told Barnie about my promise, and she asked me to wait. So there I sat, with my shoe box full of names on my lap.

The campaign headquarters was full of commotion with other issues happening by the minute, and she forgot that I was sitting in the office. Then in came the candidate, John Lindsay. I was very nervous. After an hour of watching Congressman Lindsay, Bob Price, the Campaign Manager and Barnie walking in and out, John Lindsay stopped abruptly and said to me "Hello, pretty girl, have you been taken care of?" I said, "No."

I explained that I had started "High School Students for John Lindsay" and that I would need a ballroom for the pizza party I'd promised them if he won. He said, "You're hired!"

And that's why I continued working for Bob Price on the mayoral campaign, then became his Administrative Assistant when John Lindsay became Mayor. John Lindsay was one of the most charismatic politicians. Working in his campaign and Administration was one of the greatest experiences of my life.■

After working in John Lindsay's congressional office, **Eileen Robert** *went on to sell townhouses and luxury properties in New York, now at The Corcoran Group.,* **Jane Shalam** *has been married since 1969 to John Shalam, Chairman of the Board of Audiovox and VOXX International Corp.*

Sam Roberts

For decades, "the unrepentant, the unindicted and the unappreciated," as John V. Lindsay's press secretary, Tom Morgan, once called them, who enlisted in the Mayor's children's crusade have striven to redeem his legacy and, with it, their own.

"Remember those good old days in New York City," Barry Gottehrer, City Hall's balm-thrower recalled, not without irony, "when we all were young, beautiful, invincible and we all really cared."

Time usually heals. But fully 50 years since Lindsay was first elected, for those who can even remember or who still care, the challenge of recasting his two tumultuous terms into a gauzy reverie of the good old days has demanded more than mere nostalgia.

Time provides sufficient context in which a mayor can best be judged: By the handicaps he inherited, the resources he was able to muster to meet those hurdles, and whether, in fulfilling his agenda, he left a better city to his successors.

Fifty years is a long time to forget just how formidable those handicaps were. New York in 1965 had already endured the arrival of the Beatles, the murder of Kitty Genovese, the racially-riven opening of the World's Fair, summer riots in Brooklyn and Harlem and a costly political alliance between Lindsay's predecessor, Robert F. Wagner, and liberals and organized labor against the decaying Democratic machine.

The city was the epicenter of a national schizophrenia. The same John Lindsay who seconded Spiro Agnew's nomination at the 1968 Republican National Convention sparked a hard-hat riot by lowering City Hall's flags to honor the victims of Kent State and who won a second term by making his re-election a referendum on the war in Vietnam.

No surprise that three weeks after Lindsay was first elected, "Man of La Mancha" opened at a theater in Washington Square. For the next eight years, Lindsay would shatter his lances jousting with power brokers, real, imagined and self-created, in pursuit of his anthemic Impossible Dream.

The omens were not promising. On Lindsay's first visit to City Hall, he found a tiny metallic shamrock on his desk, a gallows-humor reminder that his baptism as mayor would be performed by a volatile Irish-born transit workers labor leader in whom he had already evoked historic distrust. "One day on the job," Sammy Davis, Jr. joked at an inaugural ball, "and John Lindsay has ended crime in the subways."

Yet for all the hypocritical claims to being above old-fashioned politics and for all the catering to opportunists who would later be denounced as poverty pimps, at least the Administration was not afraid to fail. Much of Lindsay's legacy remains the talent he attracted to government and the hope he instilled. And if City Hall pandered too much to save the city, at least Lindsay's successors, unlike some of their counterparts elsewhere in the country, inherited a city that had been largely saved.

"One does not mock the innocent and the brave," Murray Kempton wrote.

I remember that Lindsay looked teary when he left his desk for the last time, shortly after 6 p.m. on Dec. 31, 1973. "New York," Pete Hamill recalled, "broke his heart." He was wearing his long trench coat and broad-brimmed hat as he posed for a photograph for the *Daily News*. He was clutching his brass desk-lamp, not so much to shut it off as to continue carrying the torch.■

Sam Roberts *has been the Urban Affairs Correspondent of* The New York Times *since 2005. He is host of* The New York Times Closeup, *a weekly program on Channel One, and author of several books, recetnly* A History of New York in 101 Objects, *and edited* America's Mayor John V. Lindsay and the Reinvention of New York..

Jaquelin T. Robertson

When John Lindsay announced that he was running for Mayor, we thought we should first test the waters in unlikely places —working-class neighborhoods that didn't typically receive much attention from Republican candidates. I believed it would be helpful to generate the kind of "hands-on" information that could be useful politically in precisely those places, like Coney Island, which most thought him unlikely to visit. We went to work quickly, gaining local insight; and we drew maps of the neighborhoods identifying their concerns, where traffic accidents occurred, which streets were dangerous after dark, or where people felt safe and liked to walk.

The real question was, could a Republican politician ever do well there? John decided to take me along to meet with members of that community where typically, Democratic pols visited, promised to help improve things, but never did. The locals in this community were curious to see what this WASP running for Mayor was all about, and John prepared by memorizing the material we'd put together for him on local issues. At the conclusion of his remarks, the audience stood up and clapped and came up to touch John, to see if he was "for real." During the election Coney Island showed unexpected support for Lindsay.

Soon after his election Mayor Lindsay persuaded a small group of high profile civic leaders including Bill Paley, chairman of CBS, Walter Thayer, chairman of the *Herald Tribune*, and others, including me, to lead a task force recommending the addition of urban design professionals as part of the City Planning Commission staff. The Paley Report, issued in early 1967, came at a time when fresh thinking was required to revitalize downtowns and recognized the city as an important development partner to private interests. It led to the creation of the Urban Design Group within City Planning as well as district development offices reporting directly to the Mayor (five were created in Midtown, Downtown, Downtown Brooklyn, Jamaica and Staten Island). These became the places in city government where the Mayor's urban development agenda was at the forefront.

Together with Don Elliott, the newly appointed Chair of the Planning Commission, the cast of architect/planners in this newly established mission included Richard Weinstein, Jonathan Barnett, Alex Cooper and myself. After my appointment as Director of the Office of Midtown Planning and Development, our mandate implemented new strategies designed to attract investment capital back to the city; comprehensive planning to inform development decisions; and new concepts of vertically mixed-use development.

Most importantly, we initiated the use of incentive zoning to induce developers to achieve the Mayor's public objectives, like the creation of a series of innovative special zoning districts, such as the Theater District. With the Mayor's personal interest and intense involvement, we were able to persuade developers to build new theaters in Times Square, and Olympic Tower, an innovative mixed-use building next to St. Patrick's Cathedral, as well as numerous other important projects. Under Lindsay, architects and urban designers became centrally involved in the politics of New York.

John Lindsay became the strongest advocate for his city as it faced unprecedented social and political challenges in the 1960s and beyond. Lindsay was one of two great Mayors I worked for, the other being Joe Riley of Charleston, S.C. I feel privileged to have worked for both of them.

Jaquelin T. Robertson was a founder of the architectural firm of Cooper Robertson and former Dean of the University of Virginia School of Architecture.

Gilbert A. Robinson

In early spring of 1965, I helped form a group to draft John Lindsay to run for mayor. Three weeks after telling me to stop the draft effort, he called to say that he would run—in fact, he seemed to have no recollection of our prior conversation—and asked me to work on the logistics of announcing his candidacy.

Connie Eristoff and I wanted to try something different. Although mayoral candidates traditionally declared at a Manhattan press conference, we arranged for JVL to make his announcement in each of the five boroughs on a single day. We began at 9 a.m. in the Bronx near Yankee Stadium, moved on to Queens, then announced in Brooklyn, in Staten Island and, finally, in Manhattan in late afternoon. All these events were covered in the evening television news programs.

The next day John called and said, "Where are you?" I said "What do you mean . I am working in my office." He then said "But I need a whole campaign entourage and we need to campaign in all the boroughs. Will you be my Campaign Field Manager and ride with me all the way?" It was hard to say no since I really wanted him to be Mayor. Therefore, I volunteered for the campaign.

To manage the candidate's time as efficiently as possible throughout the campaign, we purchased "walkie-talkie" portable radios—cellphones were far in the future—to keep the advance staff in touch with one another as they moved JVL around the city. I met with engineers from the Motorola Corporation at the Empire State Building to see how we might set up a communications apparatus on its tower. The property manager approved our plan and we had the first network of its kind. Our arrangement was a well-kept secret.

I could step outside a meeting, point my hand-held Motorola radio at the city's tallest building and its signal would be bounced to my advance man.

Using the radio, I could ask staff on the scene if the crowd was big enough at the next stop, or whether JVL should be prepared for a debate if an opponent or an opponent's representative was expected to be on hand. This technology, primitive by contemporary standards but state-of-the-art back then, enabled us to maximize the number of our campaign engagements—we were hitting five or six a day, the competition managed two or three—and make the most of them. As we approached Election Day, I leaked the story of our "network" to *The New York Times*, which published it with a beautiful photo of the Empire State Building on the front page. There wasn't enough time left in the campaign for our opposition to create a similar system.

Soon after the election, Lindsay invited me to discuss, what position might I have in the new Administration? I had always been interested in foreign affairs, and up in his transition office at the Roosevelt, we were thinking, perhaps, city representative to the United Nations?

Then the lights went out. The biggest power failure in U. S. history, to that date. By this time, as Mayor-elect, Lindsay had an official police detail, which had flashlights, and led us down the stairs. As we parted, our "business" not completed, John said, "We will get together later.' I don't know where he went. I walked 20 blocks to my apartment.

In the meantime, quite by accident, I teamed up with a friend (another PR professional), Bill Safire, to form a political-consulting company. As Bill put it, "Why should we be giving all of this great advice, for free?" Our first project was to manage the New York City component of Governor Rockefeller's successful re-election campaign—for a comfortable fee. And we were off and running. Win a few, lose a few, but along the way, Bill moved into the Nixon Administration and then became a columnist for the *New York Times*, and soon enough I was working with Ronald Reagan.

Life is interesting. I never completed that talk with John Lindsay.■

Gilbert A. Robinson is chairman of GAR, an international firm advising companies on trade, government relations and communications. He has served as Deputy Director of the USIA, and Ambassador and Special Adviser for Public Diplomacy to Secretary of State George Shultz, and was the first President and CEO of The Center for the Study of the Presidency.

Robert Rosenberg

For reasons which now completely elude me, I spent my teenage years in the Bronx as a teenage conservative Young Republican. Worse yet, I spent some of my early adulthood as an insurgent fighting for control of the borough's GOP organization. Why bother? For the privilege of always losing the Bronx? JVL's decision to become a Democrat persuaded me to bolt the Republican Party as well. I had been disgusted by the Vietnam fiasco and Nixon's moratorium on federal subsidies for residential construction. Housing production, after all, was my profession.■

Robert Rosenberg authored and implemented the Rent Stabilization Law as well as the 421a residential tax abatement statute, and oversaw the Mitchell-Lama housing construction program. He was General Manager of Starrett City in Brooklyn, the nation's largest federally assisted housing development.JUkie

Mitchell Rosenthal

Phoenix House was born in the Lindsay Administration. In 1967 the Mayor mounted an effort to combat drug addiction in New York using funds provided by the State's Narcotic Addiction Control Commission, created by Governor Nelson Rockefeller. The Governor believed that controlling drug addiction was essential to dealing effectively with New York's raging crime problem. With a Republican Assembly and Senate behind him, Rockefeller secured hundreds of millions of dollars to build a statewide treatment network and contract for addiction services with the city government.

On the advice of Nancy Hoving, wife of his Parks Commissioner, Lindsay hired Effren Ramirez, an energetic, imaginative psychiatrist who had devised a model treatment program in Puerto Rico. Ramirez entered the Lindsay Administration as director of what would become the city's Addiction Services Agency.

At the time, I was finishing my tour of active duty as a Navy psychiatrist in Oakland, California, where I had developed a pilot program to treat the drug and alcohol abuse of returning Vietnam veterans. Before this program began, these users were medically discharged as unfit for military service. Our program—the 49 Project—provided peer-driven treatment that enabled most of its patients to resume active duty after three-to-six months of therapy.

When I met with Dr. Ramirez and Nancy Hoving in 1967, he asked me to become his Deputy for Rehabilitation. I moved back to New York to take the assignment. Jack Aaron, a far-sighted philanthropist, helped to set up a non-profit foundation that partnered with the City (not unlike the Central Park Conservancy created some years later) that enabled us to accept donations and buy property for our residential treatment facilities. The network became known as Phoenix House, named for the bird that rose from its own ashes.

Lindsay's deputies had a "can do" attitude and strongly supported the Phoenix approach. In our early days, Lindsay held a Criminal Justice Co-ordinating Council (CJCC) meeting at our first residence on the Upper West Side. The Mayor's aides were impressed with our restoration of a former SRO as shiny, yet comfortable temporary living quarters as well as the residents' esprit de corps, determination and optimism.

The program grew rapidly and we opened new Phoenix Houses in other parts of Manhattan, as well as Brooklyn, the Bronx and on Hart Island, the latter borough's most eastern point. Within a year of the CJCC's meeting we had almost a thousand men and women in treatment.

Lindsay's thoughtful Human Resources Administrator Mitch Ginsburg and his deputy Bernard Shiffman were instrumental in making it possible for residents to pool their individual welfare checks to pay for their treatment. David Garth and Dan Melnick, two members of Lindsay's "kitchen cabi-net," became Phoenix House board members. We also enjoyed a warm, productive relationship with Mike Dontin, the Mayor's liaison with the Addiction Services Agency. Later on, mayoral aide Harriet Michel took on that role.

The public/private partnership between the City and our private sector supporters enabled our programs to grow rapidly and become the Lindsay Administration's most visible treatment initiative. This alliance also made it possible for the Phoenix House Foundation to take control of Phoe-nix House operations, replacing the City in that role in 1970. Since then, Phoenix House has become a leading national behavioral healthcare orga-nization with 120 programs in ten states.■

Mitchell Rosenthal, M.D., is Founder and Executive Director of the Rosenthal Center for Clinical and Policy Studies and Advisor to the Phoe-nix House President and Chief Executive Officer.

Bill Roskin

There was a meeting at Gracie Mansion of Commissioners. My boss, Harry Bronstein, City Personnel Director, asked me to drive up with him so we could work in the car there and back. It seemed that every Commissioner took his own limo to the meeting, so that the last chauffeur, who was driving a Chrysler, could only get his limo just inside the gate. When the meeting ended, all the Commissioners got into their respective vehicles ready to go. The Chrysler blocking the exit, however, stalled. No one could move. All the drivers got out and offered fruitless advice on how to start the limo. Being a suit, I hung back, but I had had some experience starting Chryslers that had stalled, so I stepped forward, removed the air filter, stuck a pencil into the carburetor, and to everyone's amazement, the car started. The Mayor had come out to see what was going on and after observing my miracle, shouted, "How would you like to be Commissioner of Engine Repair?" Harry Bronstein shouted back "He has a job!" The Mayor said "I'll throw in Car Czar!" Harry said, "Get in the car," and waved good-bye to the Mayor. Thus was my career cut short.■

*After serving as Counsel to the Department of Personnel, **Bill Roskin** was a vice president of Warner Communications and then Viacom and serves on the board of Martha Stewart Living.*

Laura Ross

If you didn't have a sense of humor, you would have been terrified of Jim Carberry, John Lindsay's first speechwriter. He was gruff, sardonic, spoke in clipped sentences, and didn't suffer fools. He owned newspapers in Penn Yan, NY, and was a whip-smart political pro. He was also going through a divorce, stayed out late, and swam at a gym each morning. "If anybody calls for me tomorrow morning, tell them I'm working from home," he'd bark at the end of each day.

It was the summer after my first year in college when Mr. Carberry hired me to be his "secretary." I have only fond and funny memories of him. Shortly after I arrived, by some odd quirk of fate, he hired my cousin, who had just graduated high school, to be his research assistant. Mr. Carberry never called us by our first names. I was always Ms. Gore and Robert was always Mr. Krulwich and he was always Mr. Carberry.

When Lindsay was preparing for his first debate, Mr. Carberry wrote a memo on how to appear on television. "The best answers to any question," Mr. Carberry advised, "are, in the following order, 'no,' 'yes,' and 'maybe.'" End of memo.

Another cousin was also working in the campaign. Each night, the three of us would ride the IRT while our campaign enthusiasm got the best of us. From somewhere we learned a song, lyricist and composer unknown, which we would perform nearly nightly on the subway—replete with gestures worthy of Broadway.

> Say hello to Lindsay
> Say hello to a better New York.
> After years and years of fooling around
> All over the town
> We're going to get down
> To bus-i-ness.

Say hello to Lindsay.
Say good-bye to care and woe
He's going to be the new attraction
For the folks down at Gracie Mansion
So come on, Hooray, let's go
And tell John Lindsay
John V. Lindsay
Tell John Lindsay,
HELLO!

My cousins and I suspect, on no evidence whatsoever, that repeatedly singing the "Lindsay Song" on the uptown IRT local, sometimes adding a small soft shoe interlude, probably narrowed the election ever so slightly. Lindsay won with 44.99% of the vote. Had we not sung, he might have finished a wee bit stronger. (45% maybe?)

But you can't worry about these things. He ran. We danced. He campaigned. We sang. That's politics. Everybody does what they can. ■

Laura Ross served in the U.S. Department of Justice, as a Congressional staffer, and on the staff of NYS Attorney General Robert Abrams and has been active in Democratic politics.

Harvey Rothenberg

S oon after John Lindsay was elected Mayor in 1965, he called from Arizona, and asked: "Harvey, how would you like to be my Appointments Secretary?"

"But I've never been one," I replied.

"Harvey, I've never been Mayor!"

So I left my business and moved into City Hall for the next five challenging years.■

Harvey Rothenberg *served as John Lindsay's Appointments Secretary (1966-70) and then moved to Sarasota, FL, where he assisted teaching school for twelve years.*

Howard J. Rubenstein

John Lindsay was the most atypical mayoral candidate since that charismatic rascal Jimmy Walker.

Telegenic, elegantly groomed, sophisticated, with chiseled features that made many a woman voter rush across the street to shake his hand when he was campaigning, Lindsay was as different from the traditional mayoral hopeful as porterhouse steak is from a pushcart veggie burger. He also became Mayor as the city was experiencing seismic changes in its demography, economy, racial relations, labor negotiations and policing.

For those of us in public relations during the mid-1960s, he was also something of an enigma. While you could probably predict how the traditional politician would interact with the press and public, Lindsay had a profoundly unprecedented kind of relationship with the local media. He leveraged his Kennedy-like charisma and ease before the cameras to score points and project his message. He was calculating about his appearance, literally rolling up his sleeves and shedding his tailored suit jacket to wade into a crowd. To use today's expression, he was a "rock star," although most of us didn't appreciate the transformative effect he was having on politics.

While representing the Uniformed Sanitation Workers Union, I arranged a meeting of key union delegates with candidate Lindsay, who sought their endorsement. Grizzled and wise in the way of bareknuckle New York City politics, the delegates were nevertheless unsure of what to make of this liberal Republican a Yale-educated patrician, who had represented the prosperous "Silk Stocking" district in Congress.

The sanitationmen's endorsement would demonstrate Lindsay's abilities to attract support from a politically astute union and communicate effectively with working men and women. His speech received polite applause, but the leadership reserved its decision and we retired into executive session.

Although we couldn't come to a consensus about the endorsement at first, some of us understood that Lindsay represented a new generation of politician, one we would have to learn how to deal with. You could sense a shift in opinion in his favor as we debated the pros and cons of giving him our nod.

When the smoke lifted and the half-full cups of coffee were cleared away, John V. Lindsay had won the endorsement of the 7000-member Sanitation Workers Union. A marriage of new age politics and good old-fashioned political pragmatism had begun, a relationship that continues today with different partners in these same roles. ■

Howard J. Rubenstein founded Howard J. Rubenstein Associates, a major public relations concern, in 1954. He has counseled New York's corporate, civic, governmental, philanthropic and corporate leaders.

Lewis Rudin *(by Beth Rudin DeWoody and Bill Rudin)*

Beth: My memories are personal, as I wasn't involved politically then. My brother Bill and I were taken to Washington in the 1960s by our Dad, Lew Rudin, and visited John Lindsay when he was a congressman. I remember thinking how handsome and friendly he was. I loved when he became Mayor and we had Fun City. We had a little glamour in the city. I remember Dad's surprise to learn about John's immigrant background. Dad had always thought he was a WASP from Puritan background, when in fact his father's side of the family had only come relatively recently to the U.S.

What was amazing also about John were all the people who worked under him and what they all accomplished later. His administration became a training ground for amazing talent. And I loved to visit John and Mary in Bridgehampton in the summer. Very cool house. Very relaxed! ∎

Bill: I was fourteen years old when my dad Lew Rudin first invited me to join him at Gracie Mansion for dinner with the Lindsay family. As I stepped over the threshold, Mayor Lindsay shook my teen-age hand firmly and said, "Welcome, Billy, to the People's House." I don't recall what was served, or even how long we were there, but I do remember this first glimpse of what it means to be a leader.

My dad and the Mayor discussed the economy, politics, and what they considered priorities for the city—cleaner, safer streets, creating more and better jobs, stemming the then current trend of corporate flight. They agreed that government alone could not solve the city's problems and explored what the business community could do to help.

Brainstorming together during that and many similar conversations, my dad and the mayor devised a new kind of partnership between the public and private sectors—a collaboration that brought every stakeholder to the table—government, business and labor—to address critical issues facing the city. They recognized that such cooperation was key to getting New York back on it feet.

Their conversations planted the seed that grew into the Association for a Better New York (ABNY), which my dad formed with his colleagues in business and labor, who included Bob Tisch, Victor Gotbaum, Alton Marshall, Howard Rubenstein and Jack Bigel. One of our city's most successful public-private partnerships, ABNY, under my dad's leadership, supported innovative public safety programs, worked with owners of properties on major commercial corridors to clean and maintain sidewalks and promote New York City worldwide.

My dad led ABNY from its founding in 1971 through his death in 2001. Those challenging thirty years were an era of amazing progress for the city. I believe that my dad learned much of what he knew about politics, governing and public service from Mayor Lindsay. They shared the mission of making the city a better place, but they were also good friends who greatly respected one another.

I was fortunate to have seen Mayor Lindsay and my dad during their intimate, unguarded dinners together. ■

*Real estate executive **Lewis Rudin** was founder and chairman of the Association for a Better New York (ABNY). During the fiscal crisis, he spearheaded the pre-payment of $600 million in real estate taxes. He also led the successful national campaign to preserve the deductibility of state and local taxes. On his death, he was succeeded as chairman of ABNY by his son **Bill Rudin**, chief executive office of Rudin Management, one of the city's prime real estate companies, who also serves as chairman of the Battery Park Conservancy. His sister **Beth Rudin DeWoody**, executive vice president of Rudin Management, is on the board of the Whitney Museum and the Brooklyn Academy of Music.*

Deborah Sale

We were in Bridgehampton riding on the back roads in a Mustang convertible---four 20-something women. Coming upon a group of bicyclists, we warned our driver, "Watch out for the bikers. Watch out for the bikers."

Then one of the bikers turned to look at us with his big blue eyes and every young woman squealed,

"It's John Lindsay!"

Mary Lindsay, cycling alongside her husband, seemed most amused. ∎

Deborah Sale ran the City's high school volunteer and internship program, initiated as a parallel to the successful Urban Corps. She was Executive Vice President, External Affairs, for the Hospital of Special Surgery, and is an independent director of Blue Wolf Healthcare Services Group..

Stephen Salup

Lynda Gould, JVL's Administrative Assistant, and I led Mary Lindsay's advance team during the 1972 Wisconsin Democratic presidential primary. We flew around the state in a six-seat private plane and arranged her speaking engagements in mostly remote towns.

One day, we were caught in a unseasonal snowstorm and had to make an emergency landing in Madison, the state capital. As luck would have it, Senator George McGovern, the eventual Democratic nominee, and his campaign team had just been forced to land at that airport, too. The senator's party was rushed into a private waiting area, but Mary and the rest of us had to wait out the weather in public view.

With downtime on our hands, I suggested to Mary that we accuse Senator McGovern of ducking debates and have her challenge the senator to one right there in the airport with the stranded press corps looking on. Not sure if Mary was ready to be her husband's surrogate but eager to make mischief, I knocked on the door of that private waiting area and demanded that Senator McGovern's chief of staff produce his candidate. However reluctant the senator might be to debate Mrs. Lindsay, I told his aide, she might be more than a match for him. The aide slammed the door in my face.

Moments later three offensive linemen from the Washington Redskins football team appeared. Members of the Athletes for McGovern contingent, they threatened to take me out of commission. I informed them that in 1960 I had been an undergraduate track star at the University of Maryland and the fastest Jew in America. The sight of them chasing me around the Madison airport, I said, would delight television audiences and newspaper readers. And an account of them beating me senseless, I pointed out, would hardly reflect well on Senator McGovern.

The McGovern campaign was stymied. Mary thought about taking a hotel room in Madison to keep our opponent "under siege" but we'd had our fun at their expense and when the weather cleared were on our way. Word got back to us that the McGovern group lingered a while before departing to be sure the coast was clear, throwing them even further behind schedule.■

Stephen Salup was Assistant Administrator/General Counsel at New York City's Economic Development Administration. He is Chief Legal Officer and Executive Vice President of Starrett Companies, a Blackstone affiliate that develops, owns, and manages affordable and market-rate housing in the Greater Metropolitan Area.

Marvin Schick

It was mid-January 1973 and my wife had given birth to a boy about a week before. I had accompanied the Mayor on a visit to the home of the Bobover Rebbe, Rabbi Shlomo Halberstam, who resided several blocks from our home.

At the conclusion of our meeting with the Rebbe, I telephoned my wife Malka to inform her that the Mayor would be coming to our house for coffee within the next five minutes. Rushing to get ready, my wife neglected to inform our baby nurse Mrs. Carmichael that the Mayor was on his way.

When Mrs. Carmichael answered the doorbell with a broom in one hand and a dust shovel in the other, she was shocked to see the Mayor of New York City standing on the doorstep. When she could finally speak, Mrs. Carmichael exclaimed: "My oh my, Mr. Mayor. I have seen your picture many times, but I never thought I would get to shake your hand. My oh my, my oh my!"

Throughout the rest of her stay at our house, the lovely Mrs. Carmichael could not stop talking about that occasion, always introducing the subject by exclaiming again, "My oh my," in semi-disbelief that she actually met Mayor Lindsay. The Mayor's impromptu visit and the memorable moment it afforded our baby nurse has become a favorite anecdote in our family.

This anecdote has a footnote. My wife, no less thrilled than Mrs. Carmichael to meet the Mayor, told her proper European aunt about his time with us. "I hope you served him coffee in your dining room," her aunt said. Malka then realized that she had committed a *faux pas* and had served the Mayor and his party coffee in the kitchen. She brooded over this for some time.

In every way, the Mayor's visit was unforgettable. ∎

Marvin Schick served as Assistant to the Mayor and liaison to the Jewish Community, then returned to teaching at Hunter and the New School. He has been the long-time volunteer President of Rabbi Jacob Joseph School, the oldest Jewish Day School in the U.S.

Robert Schiffer

I first met John Lindsay as a 15-year-old working for him on the Independent Citizens line. The future Mayor was the first Republican I had supported. I spent a day with him in Brooklyn, joining him and his staff for lunch at Lundy's. I sat next to his twin brother who I really thought was a great guy. The Mayor spent a few minutes talking with me. He had the gift of making you feel very special. I was at the Roosevelt Hotel the night he won.

—

I got to know Ronnie Eldridge and worked for her during the summer of the 1969 mayoral campaign when I saw the Mayor a few times. I was attending college in Tennessee when he was re-elected in November.

My first real job was in the Bureau of Lead Poisoning. During the summer of 1971, I saw first-hand how the Mayor's program to test for lead among youngsters, eliminate the use of lead-based paint and manage its abatement saved lives.

Ronnie recruited me to organize Tennessee students for the Mayor's Presidential campaign. We got started but then shifted our activities to Florida.

Years later I was working on Wall Street and had come to know the Mayor very well. He visited MaryAnn, my two-week-old daughter and me at our home. The Mayor and Mary also joined our family at the Saratoga Racetrack. They were such warm, appreciative people.

—

My firm Drexel Burnham faced a looming setback when the state legislature bill prohibiting savings and loan banks from buying "junk" bonds for their portfolios. Drexel funded these bonds to capitalize the growth of new innovative companies. I convinced our Chairman Bob Linton to call Governor Mario Cuomo and ask him to hear both sides before deciding what to do on this legislation. I also told Bob that John Lindsay was the best person to represent Drexel on the matter. The editorial boards of all New York's papers called on the Governor to veto the bill and the pension fund managers opposed the legislation too. We had a chance.

The Governor called a special hearing to hear both sides of the argument. John Lindsay spoke first and obviously made a deep impression on the Governor. Although the bill passed with only two assemblymen and one state senator voting against it, the Governor vetoed the measure. John Lindsay made the difference.

—

As we considered the potential Democratic Presidential candidates in 1988, Jay Kriegel and I agreed that U.S. Senator Dale Bumpers of Arkansas was the star of the field. We introduced Senator Bumpers to John Lindsay who tried to persuade him to enter the race. Though Bumpers ended up deciding not to run, he and John Lindsay became good friends. I took great satisfaction from their fine relationship.

So many of the best people I met in and outside government first worked for the Mayor. It was a privilege to have him as a friend as well as a colleague. He made me believe in government.■

Robert Schiffer is Managing Director of Indochina Renewable Resources Management. He has been Chief Executive Officer and Executive Director of the U.S.-Vietnam Trade Council and had a long career in finance with several leading Wall Street firms.

Charles "Chuck" Schumer

I went to college thinking I would play basketball, but when I tried out for the team, the coach saw my height—I was 6'1"—and asked me if I could dribble. I said it was not my strong suit and he sent me home without ever seeing me touch a basketball.

I was distraught. But as fate would have it, that night somebody knocked on my door and said "How would you like to join the Harvard Young Democrats? We're working for this slate of candidates." I didn't have a political bone in my body, but the next morning I went down with a group of kids and we went around knocking on doors and having a great time. I spent the whole weekend doing it and was bitten by the political bug.

Had someone knocked on my door that night and said, "Would you like to join the Harvard Seashell Collecting Club" I wouldn't be where I am today. But I got involved in politics that summer and remained so throughout 1968. Eventually, I changed my major from Chemistry to Government and started seeking out opportunities to break into politics professionally.

In 1969, I had the opportunity to meet Mayor Lindsay. Having been transformed into a political soul, I was excited by the prospect and went to Lindsay headquarters hoping to join his re-election campaign.

I met Mayor Lindsay, shook his hand, and thought, "Gee, he seems like a nice guy but he sure ain't from Brooklyn."

That was the extent of our meeting; he was a busy guy. Then I was sent to interview with someone who actually did seem like he was from Brooklyn. Everyone called him "Squirt." Many more people know him now as Jeff Katzenberg, but he had started working for Mayor Lindsay at age 14, so "Squirt" he was to everyone in Lindsay's orbit.

Anyway, I thought I had a good interview, but nothing ever came of it.■

Charles Schumer is the senior United States Senator from New York and the third ranking Democrat in that legislative body. Previously he had served in the House of Representatives between 1981 and 1999. He had also been a three-term member of the New York State Assembly.

Nicholas Scoppetta

As an Assistant US Attorney, I was intensely involved in a celebrated police corruption investigation that was made into the movie, "Prince of the City." As a result, I tended to avoid going to police-sponsored events.

One police promotion ceremony included several of the terrific officers who had worked with me on the investigation. One of my colleagues came by and asked if I was ready to go over to Police HQ for the event. "I don't attend those," I said. "C'mon," he replied, "these guys deserve it."

So I went with him to the ceremony.

Arriving early, we were in a holding room with Police Commissioner Patrick Murphy. When Mayor Lindsay arrived the commissioner introduced me. By coincidence I had seen the Mayor on the Carson Show the night before. He had been hilarious and I told him so. We went on to have a warm conversation.

The position of City Investigation Commissioner was vacant and I had sent my resume in, unsolicited, for the position without much expectation of being appointed. (I had served on the staff of the Knapp Commission, appointed by the Mayor, to investigate police corruption and gained a feel for the complexities of city government). However, I had no political advocate, background or rabbi.

After the ceremony, the Mayor came over to me—he obviously now knew who I was—and asked to talk privately. He asked if I was interested. "Definitely," I replied. "Then get me your resume quickly," he said.

I almost ran back to the office and delivered my resume to City Hall.

The following Sunday evening, I got a call from the Mayor asking me to come to breakfast the next morning with my wife. He would send his car. Unable to get a baby sitter for our two young children, Susan bowed out and I went alone, picked up by the Mayor's stretch limo. (I had never ridden in one).

When I arrived, it was just the Mayor and me in the Gracie Mansion dining room.

Breakfast consisted of poached eggs. Now a foster kid like me, from the Lower East Side—didn't know from poached eggs. Indeed, I had never seen one. I struggled to get an egg onto my plate. After several futile attempts to get it onto my spoon, I simply smacked it onto my plate. I then saw the toast left on the platter, which was obviously how the egg was to be picked up. I was certain that I had embarrassed myself and probably lost the job. However the Mayor never seemed to notice. He just continued talking about the position. Its responsibilities were obviously important to him—and, finally, he offered me the job.

I was proud to become Commissioner of the DOI and to work with this gracious mayor who obviously hired without regard to politics, and took issues of integrity most seriously. So I am grateful for the opportunity he gave me which led to other challenging positions under several mayors.■

Nicholas Scoppetta also served as Deputy Mayor for Criminal Justice under Mayor Abraham Beame, Administrator of Children's Services under Mayor Rudolph Giuliani and Fire Commissioner under Mayor Michael Bloomberg.

Anthony Scotto

C argo in the New York City port, and the jobs that go with it, had been slipping for some time when John Lindsay became Mayor in 1966. There was a widespread belief that Governor Rockefeller had made a private agreement with New Jersey officials that, in return for their agreeing to build the World Trade Center in Manhattan, he would allow the bi-state Port Authority to grow port operations mostly on the Jersey side of the harbor, diminishing the future of our piers.

Lindsay, however, was committed to build the city's economy with a new government aggressiveness and saw the port as a vital component. He was the first mayor in modern times to invest in expanding the City's port facilities. So the city built the Red Hook Containership Terminal and the Northeast Marine 39th St. Terminal in Brooklyn and started work on Howland Hook in Staten Island, all of which offered longshoremen hope that the New York side of this great port would remain vibrant.

Lindsay also emphasized the need for rail connections to the Brooklyn waterfront, through the New York Dock Railroad.

All this attention and activity gave new energy to the New York City Port Council, which I co-chaired as head of the International Longshoremen Association (Local 1814) of Brooklyn and Staten Island, along with Frank Barry, a great gentleman and the powerful head of the Circle Line and a legendary leader of the city's tourism and port industries. This flurry of projects gave the waterfront industries an optimism they hadn't seen in years. This included a deliberate effort by the Mayor to promote the port. He and his staff organized Port Day to trumpet the new projects along the waterfront and to show the strength of the City's shipping industries.

Simultaneously, the City also asked the ILA to support its agenda in Albany and I agreed to join with Victor Gotbaum, head of DC Council 37, the largest union of municipal workers, in advocating the Mayor's program for expanding welfare benefits and other social services. Gotbaum's and my members seemed to have little in common, his largely the clerical and administrative city workforce and mine blue collar dock workers, but this only seemed to make our coming together around this legislative agenda more impactful.

And this new attention to the port broadened relationships, as Marion and I built ties with Barry Gottehrer and Jay Kriegel from City Hall, as well as with Loews Hotel chief Bob Tisch, the great leader of the tourism industry, and his wife Joan.

Yet despite these efforts, the trends were negative and with the rapid rise of containerization, and automation, employment in the port overall continued to slide from about 25,000 to just a few thousand. It was never the same. But John Lindsay helped move us into a new era and to recognize the vitality and importance of our work.

John Lindsay genuinely cared about working people and their families. ■

Anthony Scotto was head of local 1814 of the International Longshoremen's Association for Brooklyn and Staten Island.

David Seeley

M y tenure in the Lindsay Administration was relatively brief. Yet, my appointment drew a story and photo on the front page of *The New York Times*. They were exciting times full of crises, including the early stages of the Ocean Hill-Brownsville disaster. But from my family's point of view the most thrilling event of that period was my serving as "Night Mayor," bunking in City Hall for an evening and taking calls to the Mayor's office and routing them to the appropriate official or department. Assigning appointees to a turn on the night shift was one way the Mayor projected his Administration's being on duty 24/7.

My five small children had little understanding of why I suddenly uprooted them to move to New York in the summer of 1967, or what I was supposed to do when we got there, but they were very excited that I was going to be mayor for a night. They came over to help me get bedded down in a basement room in City Hall to be available for whatever emergencies might arise.

Luckily for me and for the city, I slept peacefully through the night with no emergencies to deal with (unlike the case in my day job), but from my kids' point of view, there was something concrete for them to contemplate in having a father with an important post in the Mayor's Administration.■

David Seeley was Director of the Mayor's Office of Education Liaison. He has since been executive driector of the Public Education Association, professor at the College of Staten Island/CUNY and at the CUNY Graduate School focusing on redefining school reform.

Arnie Segarra

In the summer of 1967 a riot broke out on 111th Street and Third Avenue in East Harlem over a police incident involving a local resident. Sid Davidoff and his staff asked some of my young friends and me to meet with Mayor Lindsay at Gracie Mansion. Also on hand were some older Puerto Rican leaders, most of whom represented various community organizations.

After the meeting, I was asked to assist the Mayor in bringing peace to the neighborhood. We had a storefront and I organized twelve teenagers, four Puerto Ricans, four Negroes (as they were called then), and four Italian-Americans. We were called The Dirty Dozen. We cleaned the streets, organized tenants, and did other highly visible jobs that improved conditions in the neighborhood. I worked closely with Sid and Barry Gottehrer who made sure City Hall provided the resources we needed.

I especially remember helping to organize the Mayor's walking tours and how easily he related to individuals in our community. The Mayor's presence told our people that City Hall cared about them.

These efforts on the streets of East Harlem helped keep the peace when many other cities were exploding. Sid, Barry, and many others deserve credit for following the Mayor's lead. But it was John Lindsay's frequent appearances that showed New Yorkers who might be frustrated and angry that ours was an inclusive city, and that the doors of City Hall were open to all. ■

Arnie Segarra has been an aide to Mayors Lindsay and Dinkins and a campaign aide to President Jimmy Carter.

Robert Selsam

As a mayoral intern in 1968 I had limited contact with Mayor Lindsay, but remember that he was a-larger-than-life character whose charisma penetrated walls. Everyone felt the palpable excitement when he entered a room. The Mayor offered a vision of a better city and inspired young people like me to join the city government. That's just what I did after getting my Master's degree in urban planning from Columbia, working in the Department of City Planning under Donald Elliott. I got to collaborate with many of the top Lindsay people as a transportation planner.

I staffed the task force that advised Mayor Lindsay on the Port Authority's expansion of runways into Jamaica Bay, chaired by Don Elliott. The group included Connie Eristoff, Steve Isenberg and Jerry Kretchmer. Our meetings were always fun and jocular and I felt very privileged to be in the room.

We finally concluded that expanded runways weren't needed because bigger planes like the DC-10 and L1011 were making their appearance. The task force was taken for a one-hour trip around the city in one of these much quieter planes. One stood at the end of the runway as another landed, and we learned that microwave instruments landings systems (ILS) would soon enable curved landing approaches that would spread out the noise impacts. (In 2015 we are still waiting for a new national air traffic control system.) We all got an education in NEFs or Noise Exposure Forecasts. Based on our findings, I drafted a report to the Mayor. I gave it to Don Elliott on a Friday and Monday morning he called me to his office and gave me a totally rewritten and much improved final version. It was an important lesson about taking all the time available to do the best job possible. Mayor Lindsay accepted our report and came out against the expansion noting that the capacity constraints were actually on the ground and not runway related.■

Robert Selsam *remained at City Planning until 1978 and became Director of the Transportation and Regional Planning Division, under Directors John Zuccotti, Victor Marerro and Bobby Wagner Jr. He founded and led the Metropolitan Transportation Administration's planning department. After six years there, he joined Boston Properties where he headed the New York office.*

Marilyn Shapiro

I graduated Wellesley in 1962. While studying for my Ph.D. in Public Law and Government at Columbia University, I worked for Nancy Hanks at the Rockefeller Brothers Fund on their study of the economics of the performing arts. Through my research on the foundation paper for the study I met Joan Dunlop, a close friend of Deputy Mayor Robert Sweet. I asked her help in possibly working for the Mayor, and she introduced me to Bob.

During my interviews with Jay Kriegel and Wyn (Werner) Kramarsky, each warned me about how fragile government employment was—I could be fired at any time!

My initial responsibilities included working with Corporation Counsel Norman Redlich, one of the most distinguished public servants I've ever known on budget matters and legislative proposals that would be resolved in Albany.

Another important assignment was following up on promises made in the Lindsay 1965 campaign White Papers—50 or so goals for new housing starts, additional police officers and other improvements in municipal services and productivity. I learned much about the relationship between campaign promises, government policy and re-election strategies. I recall visiting a dusty library to review clippings of the Mayor's statements.

So many memories:

• Because I was paid from a budget line in the Environmental Protection Agency, sanitation vehicles sometimes took me home to Brooklyn and picked me up in the morning.

• Media guru David Garth called me "that broad who killed my advertising" because I fact-checked his commercials. Yet, watching David operate was an education in political public relations.

- Harry O'Donnell, the Mayor's Press Secretary, a true pro, and Jeff Greenfield, distinguishing himself as a speechwriter, were other models of how to do their jobs.

- I also admired Wyn Kramarsky's management of Board of Estimate initiatives and the way Peter Goldmark and Fred Hayes navigated the state legislature and the city bureaucracy in shaping the municipal budget.

- John Lindsay was ahead of his time in making so many younger people, women in particular, Assistants to the Mayor. Elizabeth Holtzman, Sally Bowles and I were in that fortunate group. Other assistants included Lance Liebman, who went on to become Dean of Columbia Law School.

- John Lindsay always "sucked the air out of the room" when attending meetings or making speeches. We were all proud of his work to further civil rights and improve living conditions for the least fortunate New Yorkers. His charisma attracted an army of very talented young people, who went on to important careers in government, journalism and business, including the young Jeff Katzenberg who ran errands.

I'm so grateful to Bob Sweet, Jay Kriegel and Wyn Kramarsky and others who made it possible for me to join John Lindsay's Administration. What I learned there equipped me to help Elizabeth Holtzman run successfully for Congress, head up her office, and support her service on the House of Representatives Judiciary Committee when it considered impeaching President Nixon.■

Arts consultant **Marilyn Shapiro** *has served as Executive Director/External Affairs for the Metropolitan Opera and Executive Vice President of the Los Angeles Opera.*

Hank Sheinkopf

It was bad enough that two major league baseball teams had taken the city's heart out. Worse, there was more bad news to come.

With the postwar out-flow of blue collar jobs, many workers followed jobs to the suburbs. A sizable community of longshoremen living in west midtown Manhattan watched helplessly as the Port Authority shipped waterfront jobs off to New Jersey. The city's rising taxes burdened small businesses, particularly small manufacturers who had formerly thrived in lofts. As they folded, thousands were left unemployed.

Tammany Hall, increasingly inept, lost some of its power to deliver public sector jobs; as a result, essential services like sanitation started to decline, an additional reason for residents to flee.

The needs of the city's newest immigrants increased the pressures on municipal government. More than 750,000 Puerto Ricans, many of them poor and unskilled, came to New York during the thirty-year postwar period. They faced discrimination, a dwindling job base and deteriorating neighborhoods. African-Americans fared little better. The welfare-receiving population swelled.

Then heroin arrived. Heroin meant addicts, and addicts meant crime. No one knew what to do. Cops would arrest the addicts and the courts would send them to jail for a while. After serving their sentences, those same addicts would return to the streets and support their habits by committing more crimes. It didn't help matters that an exemption from the Lyons law's permitted police officers to live beyond the city line. Many now returned each morning to preside as part of an occupying army over the poor, crime-ridden neighborhoods they once called home too.

Municipal unions, granted collective bargaining power in 1965 by Mayor Wagner, were the new political bosses. New York just wasn't working and the city needed some light, some hope, some dreams, and a break from the aching and painful transition that would take another 25 years to conclude.

The right figure for the moment was the handsome congressman from Manhattan's Silk Stocking district, John V. Lindsay. Murray Kempton wrote, "He is fresh and everyone else is tired." Lindsay had ideas and energy. He replaced the wax-faced men lingering in political clubhouses awaiting their pensions with young professional managers. He gave life to a city that was near death.

My first paid political job was working in Bronx Borough President Herman Badillo's 1969 Democratic primary campaign, which he lost to Comptroller Mario Procacciino. My mother lived in a fifth floor walk-up on 58th Street in Lindsay's old congressional district. She was a big fan and danced when he ran for mayor and partied each time he won. For all of us dreaming of being political consultants, Lindsay's media guru David Garth was the model whom we aspired to be like

Was it the best of times? No. But Lindsay tried to right wrongs, to include those left out, to give hope to a tarnished Gotham. He was the mayor we needed at that moment, He will be remembered for giving up a safe congressional seat for City Hall's battles, taking on the imperial Governor Rockefeller, seeing government in modern terms, and compassionately empowering parts of the city that had been made to feel they didn't belong. In most of that he succeeded.

He shined the Big Apple as best as he could while many others were kicking this beautiful town hard and often. And for that we owe. Each and every one of us.■

Hank Sheinkopf is a political consultant and commentator. His clients have included President Bill Clinton and Mayor Michael Bloomberg. He is Principal of Sheinkopf Communications.

Jonathan Shils

I was the "unaffiliated liberal" on the Columbia student strike commit-tee. The episode began with a student rally at the Sundial. For the first time in my Columbia experience black students and white students joined together at such a gathering. About 150 of us marched to one of the immediate objects of our ire—the site for the new gym in Morningside Park. After a scuffle and a few arrests, we adjourned to Hamilton Hall, the College's administrative and classroom center and the office of Dean Henry Coleman. We all sat down. Dean Coleman, a nice man, stayed put.

Over the next 14 hours, black students held Hamilton Hall. Other students, white, Hispanic, and Asian, took over President Grayson Kirk's office in Low Library.

By the time the Mayor's team arrived on campus, three other Columbia buildings were occupied by between 1,000 to 2,000 students and remained so for several days.

Various student constituencies—anti-war activists, civil rights types, Maoists, black students, a women's group, university reformers, stoners, art history majors, and philosophy students, and some "joiners" from other city schools—created individual cultures and "demands" on a building-by-building basis. The self-selected students leaders had little real influence. The University's leaders proved dumber than a box of rocks and remained tone deaf to the campus and community.

Although some of us harbored the illusion that the academy's "town/gown" tradition would keep the NYPD off campus, City Hall told us that would not be the case much longer.

The students' concerns—the war, the draft, the University's ties to the Institute for Defense Analysis, Columbia's relationship with New

York City, its treatment of black students and the institution's sclerotic governance—were beyond a mayor's control. Desultory efforts by various groups—faculty, administrators, mayoral aides—went nowhere. Negotiations ended when some student leaders demanded amnesty.

City Hall realized that the University administration's fears of the black students calling on "community support" to come up the hill from Harlem were delusional. But those anxieties brought us extra time and saved black students' heads from being cracked.

The Mayor could not end the war, stop the draft, derail the gym, or reform the University. All we had were City Hall's assurances about the high quality of police leadership in Manhattan North, despite what we heard about the NYPD's Red and Tactical Squads.

I knew the Mayor wanted to keep the city from exploding over Columbia. Although he succeeded, the Lindsay Administration couldn't control the 1,000 police who entered the halls of the academy to accomplish what the University was unable to do—empty the buildings and return the campus to their control.

Badge numbers were covered with black tape. Cops wielded nightsticks and brass knuckles to crack students' heads. The Mayor's power to control officers in the field eager to dispense some "class justice" proved limited. Still, nobody died or was shot, and injuries healed. The riot occurred during the 60 days between the assassinations of Martin Luther King, Jr. and Robert F. Kennedy. The war did not end for another four years and racial justice still eludes us as a nation.■

Jonathan Shils, a member of Columbia Strike Steering Committee, is a partner in the law firm McGuire Woods in Atlanta, Georgia. .

Robert Shrum

Before I arrived at City Hall as the Mayor's speechwriter, John Lindsay held New York together while other cities were burning in the race riots of the 1960s. He did it by walking all but alone into the tinderbox of angry crowds and persuading them to go home.

I witnessed a memorable reprise in the fall of 1970 when the inmates seized the city's jails, and guards were held hostage. The staff moved into Gracie Mansion for all-night meetings. I drafted appeals to the prisoners to be broadcast on the radio by the Mayor, and caught catnaps on a sofa in the first-floor ballroom.

Corrections Commissioner George McGrath argued the only choice was an all-out armed assault on the prisons. Lindsay refused; he wasn't going to kill the inmates and see the guards get killed, too. Instead, he issued an ultimatum demanding the release of the hostages but promising that as soon as that happened, he would go to the jails personally to discuss the inmates' grievances. McGrath was appalled: What if the Mayor was taken hostage or shot? Lindsay said he'd take that chance—and if it went wrong, he didn't want anyone negotiating for his release.

He was driven to the Tombs, the city's most notorious prison; he was inside from shortly after midnight until 3 a.m. As prisoners yielded at jails across the city, some force was used but with no loss of life. Then, while Lindsay was inside the Queens House of Detention, the enraged police and correction guards conducted their own riot, clubbing and kicking the surrendering inmates. The spectacle was brutal—and shocking. Afterward, Lindsay was as angry as I ever saw him, even though he had averted the kind of tragedy that a few months later left twenty-nine inmates and ten hostages dead when Governor Nelson Rockefeller ordered an all-out attack, shotguns literally blazing, in reaction to an inmate takeover of Attica State Prison.

John Lindsay had courage, both the courage of his principles and genuine physical courage.■

Robert Shrum, Carmen H. and Louis Warshchaw Chair in Practical Politics and Professor of the Practice of Political Science at Dornsife College of Letters, Arts and Sciences at the University of Southern California, has been a political consultant whose clients have included Al Gore, John Kerry and Ted Kennedy. He served as a speechwriter for Mayor Lindsay, Senators Edmund Muskie and George McGovern.

Constantine Sidamon-Eristoff (*by Anne Eristoff*)

L indsay's first campaign for Mayor was perhaps one of the last major old-fashioned campaigns in America. No fancy electronic devices, just person-to-person contacts, door to door, in all five boroughs.

My husband Constantine Sidamon-Eristoff, known as Connie, was a Georgian prince by inheritance, but also a down-to-earth American lawyer who had worked as an assistant during Lindsay's last year as a congressman. He was chosen by Campaign Manager Bob Price to head the Borough Coordinators.

Assisted ably by Ruth Adler, Connie appointed the twenty Borough Coordinators whose teams of volunteers covered the city's neighborhoods from storefronts reaching many potential voters who had never before been involved in politics.

The campaign was headquartered in the Roosevelt Hotel. Connie's office was a scene of intense, precise organization marked by an ever-growing optimism, an optimism which proved justified when Lindsay was resoundingly elected.

On election night, the hotel corridors were so jammed with excited supporters that it was almost impossible to move, and I shall always remember Sid Davidoff's brilliant method of getting through the crowd. He carried a tray of cups high overhead, shouting "Hot coffee! Hot coffee!" and people moved, if ever so slightly, out of his way. Whether or not there was coffee in the cups, I shall never know.

Before the second mayoral election, Mary Lindsay thought of a good way to capture the interest of woman voters. Knowing that most women were curious about houses, she decided to open Gracie Mansion to busload after busload of women. She also asked the wives of Lindsay's appointees to help greet them.

We addressed invitations by hand. When we didn't know whether to put Miss or Mrs. before the name, we scribbled Mus, which could be read either way.

We learned about the history and furniture of Gracie Mansion, and we gave tours. At first, each of us took groups all the way around the Mansion. Later, we decided it would be more efficient to station a person in each room and let the groups move themselves from one room to the next. It was fun. And it worked.

Sometimes, the Mayor was there, too, to meet and greet. He was the icing on the cake.

—

The night of the Kent State shootings in 1970, Connie and I were at Gracie Mansion. After dinner we were invited upstairs to the Lindsays' bedroom to see the television coverage. It was incongruous, almost unreal, to be sitting on the Lindsays' bed to watch such grim, far-reaching events.■

Constantine Sidamon-Eristoff, who passed away in December 2011, served as Highways Commissioner and Transportation Administrator. He subsequently served on the MTA board and as the federal Regional EPA Administrator. Anne Sidamon-Eristoff was Chairwoman of the American Museum of Natural History and has served on the boards of WWF and The Conservation Foundation.

Jonathan Siegfried

In October of 1970, I had been working in the Mayor's Office for four months for Lew Feldstein, JVL's Executive Assistant. It was my first job after graduating from college.

One day Lew called and said, "Jon, I need you to represent the Mayor tonight at the Council Against Poverty. The Council meets at six." That was heady stuff for a 21-year-old—my first chance to join the War on Poverty, and as the Mayor's representative, no less. There was one small problem, however. I had no idea what the Council Against Poverty was. Rather than admit my ignorance to Lew and risk having him change his mind, I said, with all the confidence I could muster, "Great. Anything special you want me to do or read for the meeting?" In those days, Lew spoke in the rapid 30-second bursts typical of the Mayor's most senior aides. "No," he said. "Just follow Major Owens (the Community Development Agency's Commissioner). Do whatever he does at the meeting." I had my marching orders.

I arrived at the Human Resources Administration's headquarters to find a small crowd outside the building and rushed by to a conference room on the first floor where Major Owens was sitting in front of a window looking out on Barclay Street. David Billings, the Council's chair, mentioned that the now chanting crowd, whose numbers had swelled, was protesting some of his organization's recent actions. Owens remained silent. A security guard appeared to tell us that the protesters had pushed by the guards at the front door and were on their way down the hall.

At that report, Owens stood up, turned around and, without a word to anyone, jumped out the window. Lew had said I should do whatever Owens did and who was I to argue? I followed Owens out the window and the other Council members followed right behind me.

I caught up with Major Owens as he was racing toward a cab. "Does this happen often," I asked. He smiled at me as he jumped into the cab. "Son, why do you think I sit by the window?" And with that he was gone.

A few years later, Major Owens left the administration to become a state senator and later a distinguished congressman. I left to attend law school.

Although I never got to ask him, I am sure John Lindsay must have attended a meeting or two of the Council Against Poverty. I doubt, however, that he ever left through the conference room window.

Thus was the War on Poverty waged.■

Jonathan Siegfried is a partner in the law firm of DLA Piper specializing in commercial litigation and arbitration.

Hildy Simmons

I arrived in New York City in early September 1972, part of the third class of New York City Urban Fellows, a Lindsay Administration initiative begun in 1969 that still provides young people with extraordinary opportunities to work in city government.

Our fellowships paid a weekly salary of $95.00 for nine months. The schools we attended decided how many credits they would allot toward our undergraduate or graduate degrees for our stint in public service.

New to the city, the day before reporting to 250 Broadway for our welcome and orientation I made a trial run by subway to be sure I'd arrive there the following morning. As I wandered around Lower Manhattan, a passerby asked if I was lost. After directing me, she offered a vital piece of advice: "Never go north of 96th Street!"

Early on, Mayor Lindsay hosted the Fellows at City Hall. He seemed to have all the time in the world for us. I was awestruck and could barely shake his hand.

We all vied for positions in the Mayor's Office, rather than at the agencies. During a round of interviews, however, mayoral aide Nat Leventhal gave me some valuable advice. Although many Fellows wanted to work for him because of his portfolio of agencies, Nat suggested I look for an agency position and serve with a Commissioner to get a better sense of municipal service delivery. Manny Carballo, another highly respected mayoral aide, agreed. I took their advice and worked for John Lotz, Commissioner of Commerce and Industry, and learned a lot—little of it enthralling--about implementing policy.

This experience served me well, though. After the Fellowship ended, during the Administration's last year, I worked in the Office of Neighborhood Government (ONG) with the South Jamaica District Service Cabinet. Our mission was to ensure that municipal government kept the community's streets safe and clean.

One night, the Fellows attended a special dinner at Gracie Mansion. How could this 21-year-old keep up? After cocktails, we sat down to dinner. I found myself next to Mayor Lindsay and barely managed to nod when he asked if this was my first visit to Gracie Mansion. He told me about its various rooms and memorably described his son's treehouse. His engaging style put me at ease. He wasn't some distant political idol but a colleague whose company I enjoyed. There was no reason to feel intimidated. That "aha moment" has served me well throughout my career.

Through ONG, I worked with many wonderful people, most notably, Benjamin Ward, the Traffic Commissioner, who would go on to become Corrections Commissioner for both the state and the city and under Mayor Koch the first African-American Police Commissioner. Ben and I kept in touch and he gave me my first job after graduate school.

I helped open new correctional facilities across the state. In the mid-1970s no community wanted a prison in its backyard. Representing the New York State Correctional Services Department didn't make me very popular. Local officials and residents preferred not to deal with a young woman from downstate and let me know it. But I wasn't intimidated—then or ever again. The Mayor taught me an invaluable lesson.■

Hildy Simmons is an adviser to philanthropies and serves as a brand ambassador to Popinjay, which promotes the manufacture and sale of artisanal goods made in Pakistan. She has been Managing Director and head of the Global Foundation Group at JPMorgan and was Program Director of the Norman Foundation. She is a former Chairman of the New York City Board of Corrections.

Edward Skloot

It was September 1972. Bobby Fisher had just trounced Boris Spassky in Reykjavik, Iceland, to win the World Chess Championship. The Mayor wanted to give him the Key to the City (Bobby was a Brooklyn boy) and he accepted the invitation.

Fisher was notoriously unpredictable and uniformly unpleasant. He made repeated demands and constantly threatened to walk out during the seven weeks of the face-off. He had allegedly broken a contract for exclusive television coverage and had been threatened with a law suit.

I had assembled eight chess Grand Masters to greet the champion when he landed at JFK. We arrived at midnight and waited in a distant building. The Grand Masters busied themselves by playing chess with each other on palm sized chess sets.

The charter landed around 3 a.m. Fischer was whisked through a near-empty US Customs facility, then nudged into a waiting car and taken to an unidentified location in New Jersey.

Why New Jersey? Well, the threatened law suit was real. We'd heard, credibly, that Fischer would be slapped with a complaint at the earliest opportunity. We couldn't let that happen; so we had to keep him "sequestered" in New Jersey until the Friday ceremony at City Hall.

Sportscaster-writer Dick Schaap, who knew and was trusted by Bobby, found the place in Jersey. He also found the lawyers, ready to pounce, and we made a deal: If they stayed away from Bobby until after the ceremony they could serve him as soon as they could get to him, off camera.

On Friday morning, Bobby was ushered into the Mayor's Office where about 25 VIPs waited. Outside, dozens of TV cameras from around the world faced the stage in front of City Hall and 3,000 wildly cheering spectators mashed into the plaza.

It was a glorious, warm day. The Mayor greeted Fischer and placed the City's medal around his neck. Fischer responded with some hard-to-understand words and stepped quickly back to his seat.

Shortly thereafter, as podium guests surrounded him, two plainclothesmen spirited Fischer out a back door and into a waiting limo. He was gone, and no papers were served.

—

Attendance and revenues at Broadway theatres were declining in the early 70s, seemingly irreversibly. Many shows were playing to less than half-full houses. Many closed a lot earlier than they should have. Most of the City's 20+ live theaters were run with an iron fist by Gerry Schoenfeld and Bernie B. Jacobs, one argumentative and the other dour, who had recently taken over The Shubert Theatre empire.

Lindsay loved the theatre. He wanted to promote Broadway as the life blood of the City's romantic past and vibrant future. A simple proposal had emerged: Why not take unsold tickets and sell them at half-price on the day of the performance? That could easily boost audiences and theatre financials, and would enable young people, particularly students, to see performances cheaply, introducing a new generation to Broadway.

But the Shuberts were opposed, arguing that the plan would only cheapen their product.

At the Mayor's request, Mary Lindsay and I met with the Shuberts twice, along with Anna Crouse, musical theater stalwart and trustee of the Theatre Development Fund (TDF). After months we had a deal. The Shuberts agreed to a brief trial run to test out the idea. But we needed a place to sell the thousands of half-price tickets.

One day, before dawn, Deputy Parks Commissioner Ted Mastroianni arranged for an old rip-rap metal Quonset hut, probably once used for construction, to be dropped into Duffy Square at West 45th Street, in the middle of Broadway. Sales windows had been cut out. TDF named it TKTS, and has run it ever since.

More than four decades later a modern iconic structure, with the Times Square Bleachers on its roof, now stands where the first hut sat. It continues to be startlingly successful, having sold millions of tickets and bringing $1.5 billion into theatrical productions.

—

It was my first trip as a new staff assistant to the Mayor. We were heading to the Bronx, for the public groundbreaking of what was to become a 25 acre park on the Harlem River.

The place was bleak. About a dozen park maintenance workers were picking up trash and broken glass, trying to look busy. A few reporters and one TV camera were on site, along with some local residents.

I gave the Mayor prepared notes on index cards— and stood on the sidelines in case he needed something more.

When time came to deliver his remarks, he unexpectedly motioned to me to come over. "Yes, Mr. Mayor?" "How many trees are there in the City?" he asked. I was dumbstruck. I had no answer, or even a vague idea, about such a simple question. "Well," I stuttered, "it…it depends what you mean by trees." "That's not good enough, Ed, I want to know how many trees."

I was in panic. I ran over to Frank Maunton, a 35-year veteran of Parks, then the Bronx parks manager. "Frank, FRANK!" I pleaded, "The Mayor wants to know how many trees there are in the City. How many are there?"

"Well," he said calmly, "it depends what kind of trees you're talking about…" I pleaded, "No, NO, that's not good enough, Frank. You've got to know!" He thought for a moment and said, "Tell him a million. I don't know and he'll never know either."

I ran back to the podium and handed the Mayor an index card with "ONE MILLION" written on it. The Mayor nodded and, sure enough, began to wax eloquently, telling the small gathering that the City was proud to be adding to its one million trees.

From that day on, the media used the number "one million trees" in countless stories, over decades. It was repeated enough to become a fact.

(A tree census done in 2006 revealed that the City has a total of 5,200,000 trees.)■

Edward Skloot was Assistant to the Mayor and then Deputy Administrator of Parks, Recreation and Cultural Affairs, 1970-1974. He was the first President of the Surdna Foundation and Founder and professor at the Center for Strategic Philanthropy at Duke University.

Charles "Chic" Slepian

In May of 1968 I was assigned to be JVL's advance man for a speech he would give at the University of Oregon on behalf of Nelson Rockefeller's run for president. I flew to Portland and the following morning drove to Eugene, home of the school, to meet with my contact who, as it turned out, didn't know I'd be coming.

In the following panic-filled hours, I could find no one on the campus who knew anything about JVL's speech, which was scheduled for the next day. That evening, I found the student who had reserved the school arena some weeks earlier, but she had heard nothing about the engagement since. After pleading for mercy, she agreed to recruit a few other students to visit the school's sororities, fraternities and residence halls to "remind" the students that JVL would be speaking the following morning at 11:00 a.m.

When we arrived at the hall with a standing-room-only audience, JVL's constant NYPD companion and security officer Pat Vecchio asked how I was able to pull off such a crowd on short notice. I introduced him to the student who, I said, deserved all the credit. He advised me to take her home with me. I took his advice and brought her back to New York where we were married two years later.∎

After serving on the Mayor's advance staff, **Charles Slepian** *established the Foreseeable Risk Analysis Center in Oregon and New York providing security services and training. He specializes in aviation security and also serves as counsel to the Hunts Point Produce Market. He is married to Patricia Muray, a psychologist practicing in New York.*

Anthony Smith

Sometime in the early fall of 1972, when I had been an Assistant to the Mayor for about six weeks, Steve Isenberg called me to his office. He told me I was to be at the downtown heliport the next morning to accompany the Mayor to several appointments in Brooklyn. Sounded like fun.

As I turned to leave with the list of sites and groups we would be meeting with in hand, Steve said: "By the way, Lindsay likes to take control of the [police] helicopter right after takeoff." I turned back and said, "Not this time!" Steve just looked at me with a bemused sneer.

I spent the next couple of hours creating documents for the next morning.

As Steve had predicted, shortly after reaching altitude, JVL started to lean toward the pilot; I was sitting directly behind him, watching and waiting for this to happen. He had moved about an inch when I leaned forward, tapped him and shouted I had a memo about the group we would be meeting at touchdown. I handed it to him. He read it, handed it back, and started to lean again. I told him there was a slightly difficult political complexity at the next meeting—now he got my second memo; then my third; this was repeated one more time. He finished the 4th memo just as we touched down.

As we walked away from the chopper, JVL turned to me and said, with a wry smile, "You did that pretty well." The rest of the trip was in his limo. i was relieved—and alive.

Final thought: At the St. John the Divine Memorial after JVL's death, Charlie Rangel asked all those who had worked for JVL to stand. Some 300 or more of us stood, and Charlie said to us and the hundreds of others assembled: "Many of those standing in front of you have gone on to major, successful careers. I doubt any of those standing, however, have ever done anything they cherish more than working for John Lindsay." True then, still true today!■

Anthony Smith was President/CEO of the New York Horticultural Society, served in senior posts under five New York mayors and two New York governors, was a member of the Central Intelligence Agency for 16 years and an officer in the United States Air Force.

Jeffrey Solomon

As an assistant to the Commissioner of Social Services, I have wonderful memories of meetings at City Hall. But one night stays particularly embedded. I only tell it to special friends.

On September 14, 1969, I was the Night Mayor, sleeping at City Hall as part of a Lindsay initiative to have some officer responsible around the clock. Earlier in the evening, our family celebrated my new son's bris, the Jewish ritual circumcision ceremony. At the end of the ceremony I was handed a piece of gauze used by the moel, the "surgeon" performing the circumcision, to staunch the wound. He said it was my duty as the father to bury it in earth. Later, at 10 o'clock I climbed the steps of City Hall and was greeted by the detective guarding the door. Reaching into my jacket pocket for a cigarette lighter, I felt that piece of gauze. A light bulb went off. I told the detective I'd be right back, walked around the corner of the building and buried that precious piece of cloth in the earth below the Mayor's window.

A few weeks later, the Mayor met with a group of welfare rights activists. Some of us in the department didn't think this was a great idea, but, nevertheless, joined him for that meeting. The welfare advocates, as they often did, gave the Mayor a hard time. In his gracious, patrician way, he didn't react to their haranguing. At one point, though, the Mayor called for a pause and walked over to the window. My friend and colleague, Bob Carroll, Deputy Commissioner for Public Affairs was one of very few people in whom I'd confided about what I'd done. Bob moved over to the Mayor and told him what was buried under his window. Few in the room could understand why, given the tension, the Mayor was suddenly smiling broadly. It was an unforgettable New York minute.■

Jeffrey Solomon is President of the Andrea and Charles Bronfman Philanthropies.

Micho Spring

The survival of American cities was in doubt when John Lindsay became Mayor in 1966. He inspired an army of young people to do battle, as well as a new generation of charismatic Mayors in Boston, Newark, San Francisco, and Detroit. Eventually, I heeded his call and dropped out of college to join in that fight. I have never regretted it.

By 1968, Lindsay was a larger than life figure on campuses around the country for the courage and grit he displayed in holding his city together after the Martin Luther King, Jr. and Bobby Kennedy tragedies. As a relatively recent Cuban exile whose life had been upended by Castro's revolution, I was keenly aware of the importance of politics. But I had never worked in a campaign.

In the summer of 1969, following my sophomore year, while impatiently awaiting a summer internship at the Metropolitan Museum of Art, I decided to volunteer in JVL's re-election effort. I asked to be assigned where my Spanish could be useful. Within a few hours, Teddy Mastroianni, the Bronx borough coordinator, drove me to the Bronx, and put me in charge of the local headquarters there. The Bronx was key in Lindsay's ill-fated effort to win the Republican primary. After, I was given a staff job and helped Teddy cut our losses up there in the general election. When the Mayor was re-elected I cancelled my plans for a junior year abroad at the Sorbonne and proudly joined his Administration.

I worked first at the Parks Department helping to reclaim the city's parks as gathering places for concerts and recreation, organize the first Earth Day, and negotiate demonstration permits. The Mayor tried to protect activists' right to denounce the Vietnam War while maintaining order on the streets. Later I worked in the Office of Neighborhood Government, where I got the equivalent of a PhD in public sector organization, as we boldly experimented to decentralize the municipal bureaucracy.

In between these assignments, I worked on the Lindsay presidential campaign. In Florida, our Cuban press secretary turned out to be one of Nixon's Plumbers. In Wisconsin, I learned about advancing a candidate from the legendary master Jerry Bruno. I filled a hall on three days' notice with buses of nuns, who were mortified when Lindsay passionately defended abortion rights. JVL appeared before gun advocates and called for gun control. To a farmer's horror, he exposed the fake coloring of his tomatoes to television reporters. Not surprisingly, we were chased off the property.

New York in that era was a cauldron of causes—civil rights, gay rights, women's rights, and the peace movement. John Lindsay bravely championed them all and led his city toward better times.

I left for Harvard in 1973 and later joined Boston's city government where I served as Deputy Mayor to four-term Mayor Kevin White. Kevin was close to John Lindsay and had better luck establishing a network of Little City Hall. But the lessons I learned in New York and the incredible talent I worked with there has served me well for life. I am grateful for the privilege and the memories.■

Micho Spring served in the Parks Department and City Hall and was later Deputy Mayor of Boston. She is Global Practice Chair and President—New England for Weber Shandwick, a marketing, corporate communications and government relations firm.

Kathy St. John

During my four years sitting outside the Mayor's office in the Red Room at City Hall, strikes blew in like angry tornadoes. They often blindsided everyone involved and no one escaped untouched. When the Mayor moved his operations to Gracie Mansion, I went too.

That's where I found myself during the taxi strike. Tempers were hot and the Mayor was steadfast in working out the differences. He and Mrs. Lindsay were scheduled to go to the opening of "Love Story" that evening, but he canceled going to the movie premiere so I got to use his ticket. Joan Gregory and Mrs. Lindsay were there too, huddled with the film's star Ali McGraw. I cried like a baby as did most of the audience and went right home—still in tears to get ready for a big day back at City Hall.

The next morning, while the Mayor was in his car, I took a phone call for him from Ali McGraw. I couldn't control myself in telling her how much I loved the film. She had to listen to me ooh and ahh about the movie. After listening to me patiently, she still wanted to talk to the Mayor. In that era, way before cell phones and other gadgets were available, we used a plectron radio receiver when we had to reach the Mayor. His 'handle' was 'Winston' and I never gave out the number to anyone. But she was so sweet that I relented and gave it to her. Then I called 'Winston' to tell him he was about to get a call that would brighten his day.

After he strode into his office, I poked my head in and chirpily asked if the phone call was all he expected. "Yes, Kathy. But that was not Ali McGraw on the other end—it was a taxi driver's wife who had a lot to say to me."

He didn't raise his voice—probably because I had turned ashen. Embarrassment doesn't even come close to what I was feeling. But it was a very good lesson that I pass on: If you have to take a taxi to City Hall, ask to go to the Municipal Building across the street. You'll have a peaceful ride with out any harangue.

—

The Mayor invited powerful labor leader Harry Van Arsdale for lunch at City Hall—just the two of them. We would order from Longchamps Restaurant across the street and they would bring over the dishes covered with those silver domes to keep the food hot. I called Mr. Van Arsdale's secretary for his preferences. Since it was on a Friday, she made it clear that he didn't eat meat on Friday and would like fish. Having been brought up as a Roman Catholic, I was well aware of the rule and we decided to get him broiled scallops. I don't remember what the Mayor had, but when the dishes came and I lifted the dome covering Mr. Van Arsdale's plate to check—it had beautifully broiled scallops covered with bacon!

My head was spinning. In the 60s it was still a sin to eat meat on Friday. There was no time to send it back. I did the only thing I could do. I threw the bacon in the garbage and proudly served the plates. If St. Peter disagrees with my solution, I'm the sinner.

—

One day I got a call for the Mayor from Marlon Brando. I couldn't believe it. I had fallen in love with him when I was nine after I snuck into his first film, "The Men." He wanted go on the Mayor's next walking tour. I told him the Mayor was walking in Harlem the next day and he asked if he could he get back to me later that evening.

He took my home phone number and I collapsed.

Later that evening, he called and agreed to meet the Mayor at Gracie Mansion the next afternoon I arranged to be at the Mansion to greet him. He was still gorgeous and I was besotted. When we were introduced he said, "Ooh, I knew you would have dark hair, but I thought it would be longer."

That was it. He left with the Mayor to go walking on 125th Street in Harlem (there is a terrific photo of them in a crowd with mayoral aide Teddy Gross), and my fantasy ended. He had my phone number, but didn't call.■

After serving as Executive Secretary to the Mayor for four years (1967-71), **Kathy St. John** *co-founded Clinton Vineyards in Dutchess County and has been in non-profit development.*

Lesley Stahl

I worked for Mayor Lindsay from 1965-1967 as his speechwriter's researcher, a job I got by answering an ad in *The New York Times*

The speechwriter's researchers worked in a boiler room in the Municipal Building across from City Hall. Our one and only perk: an executive sink! While I was the only one full-time, other young people headed for careers in journalism rotated in and out of my corner of the Lindsay Administration there, including Don Graham (who would become the publisher of *The Washington Post*) and Robert Krulwich (now an economics correspondent for NPR).

I did not have what you might call a lofty position from which to observe the comings and goings, but you couldn't miss the air of idealism. It infused the Administration.

To get my job, I was interviewed by Lindsay himself. He was the handsomest man I had ever seen—in person dashing and patrician in appearance, looking like someone on a coin. But loose and fun. It seemed to me that everyone around him loved him, and worked hard to protect him.

I would go on to cover the White House for CBS News and saw a similar dynamic—all the aides vying for the attention and affection of the king, and walking on egg shells when it came to the First Lady. My boss, Jim Carberry, and Jay Kriegel were like sibling rivals in an ongoing battle for Lindsay's approval.

Just about everyone there felt they were working for a hero. John Lindsay had been the first member of the House of Representatives to come out publicly against the war in Vietnam. He was attracting the best and brightest young men eager to work in government and politics, especially those who were reform-minded.

This was just two years after JFK's assassination. There was a feeling that John Lindsay was "the next Kennedy." We all felt it was a privilege to be there.

By the way, the reason I left was because, from time to time, I would wander into the press room at City Hall across from Carberry's office. One day, I asked one of the reporters what he did all day. As he told me, I was hit by a thunderbolt: I had to do what he did. Not long after, I got a job as a researcher at NBC News.■

Lesley Stahl has been a correspondent on CBS News' "60 Minutes" since 1991. She has also been moderator of "Face the Nation," anchor of "America Tonight" and host of "48 Hours."

Peter Stangl

Soon after Abe Beame was elected mayor, Transportation Administrator Manny Carballo and I went over for our final meeting with JVL. When we reported on the pothole situation and how successful we'd been in repairing so many of the city's streets, the Mayor said, "Make sure to leave one pothole about five feet deep for that f%#*ing Beame."■

Peter Stangl was President of Bombardier Transit Corporation and of other divisions of that company. He served as Chief Executive Officer and Chairman of the Metropolitan Transportation Authority and as President of Metro-North Commuter Railroad

Toby Ann Stavisky

Mayor Lindsay invited my husband Leonard and me to Gracie Mansion to watch Neil Armstrong walk on the moon that unforgettable, hot summer evening in July of 1969. It was my first visit upstairs in the mayor's house, although Leonard had been there often when he was deputy to the City Council president during the Wagner Administration. We thought it was so cool to be watching this historic event with the Mayor, Mrs. Lindsay and members of his campaign staff.

Leonard and I were both involved in JVL's re-election campaign. Early on, Leonard decided that JVL was the better candidate and was one of the first elected Democratic officials to endorse him. We were among the people wearing FLBG ("For Lindsay Before Goldberg") buttons. They referred to Arthur Goldberg, the former Supreme Court Associate Justice and Ambassador to the United Nations. As one of the state's most prominent Democrats, Goldberg's support for JVL made it politically safer for other members of our party to do likewise.

The campaign was memorable. My son was a toddler. I set up a portable playpen in our storefront headquarters in downtown Flushing. I never had to find a babysitter. Instead of computers, we used long sheets of paper, index cards and pencils with very large erasers. Attracting volunteers was easy. High school students, undergraduates, senior citizens—everyone wanted to be part of the Lindsay team.

We were young, idealistic and believed that John Lindsay represented our best hope for the future. While my hair has turned gray, I try to retain the idealism, enthusiasm and belief in reform that we had all those years ago.■

Toby Ann Stavisky has been re-elected to the New York State Senate seven times. She was the first woman to be elected to the State Senate from Queens County and the first woman to chair its Committee on Higher Education.

Terry Strauss

Just out of UC Berkeley's School of Criminology, where I'd worked with the American Friends Service Committee in fledgling self-help initiatives for former convicts and drug addicts, I was fortunate to be hired by Henry Ruth for the Lindsay Administration's Criminal Justice Coordinating Council (CJCC). The council funded programs aimed at reforming practices throughout the criminal justice system—courts, police, and correctional institutions. We also studied alternatives to incarceration for defendants who posed little if any risk to society.

Grants from the federal Law Enforcement Assistance Administration jump-started these experiments. Some veteran bureaucrats, of course, were resistant to new approaches. The Release on Recognizance Program in the courts, eliminating juvenile status offenses and some community-based programs run by the Addiction Services Agency, for example, required unfamiliar or complicated budgetary maneuvers. But we saw some amazing results. In selected cases, courts issued deferred sentences to convicted juveniles and adults and made provisions for drug treatment and job training, assistance that offered an unexpected second chance for a decent future. We also launched a supported employment program through the U.S. Department of Labor that became a national model.

David Rothenberg founded the Fortune Society, one of New York's first self-help organizations for ex-convicts. We gave them a CJCC grant to expand their services. Two of its members, Ken Jackson and Mel Rivers, became friends and allies of mine. One day, Ken got a call from City Hall telling him that Mayor Lindsay wanted to tour the Fortune Society, meet some members and learn about its programs. The Mayor was impressed by what he saw and eventually appointed Ken to the New York City Board of Corrections. No ex-con had ever sat on that panel, but Mayor Lindsay recognized Ken's merit and the value of having someone with a convict's perspective help shape correction policy.

I remain so grateful to John Lindsay and Henry Ruth for giving an optimistic young woman the opportunity to play a role in improving the criminal justice system and see how ideas inform government action. Both the Mayor and Hank are gone now and so is Ken. I continue to be an optimist.■

Terry Strauss has been a consultant to the governments of Wisconsin, California and Alaska on alternative criminal justice programs for youth, as well as a sculptor, potter, and television producer.

Richard Streiter

Joining the Lindsay administration in July of 1968 was one of the most critical, positive, and life-changing decisions I've ever made. It involved giving up a full-time and secure position to work for the Office of Education Liaison as a temporary consultant at the request of Dave Seeley, Director. The end product six months later, an extensive paper on "Education and Social Services for Children on Welfare" received much praise and circulation.

However, at that important personal juncture, Seeley left to head the Public Education Association and was replaced by Henry Saltzman. During my first meeting with Henry, I pointed out that there were a significant number of boxes filled with unanswered citizen complaint letters to the Mayor regarding the Board of Education that were sitting unread in a closet down the hall. Several days later Henry called me into his office and told me that the Mayor had approved the concept I had suggested of creating an "unofficial ombudsman" to deal with Board of Education-related citizen complaints. Within a few months, every letter was dealt with and answered and the Mayor began to receive correspondence from parents, teachers, and principals, thanking him for the work his Office had done in responding.

It was then in early 1969 that I was asked to serve as Director of the "Mayor's Special School Task Force." The genesis was a series of meetings in January during which a number of senior Mayoral Assistants (including, I believe, Barry Gottehrer, Sid Davidoff, Lew Feldstein, Sally Bowles, and Gordon Davis) reviewed the protracted tensions in the City following the Fall strikes in the school system. Of special concern, was student unrest and the very real threat of overt student disruption. Student leaders were promising a "Spring offensive" that probably would result in massive police intervention and the closing of high schools throughout the five boroughs. With this in mind, the Mayor approved the creation of the School Task Force.

In the months following, the racially-mixed Task Force teams worked tirelessly in the high schools and communities where tensions and unrest were considered most threatening. And while it was impossible to predict how many schools would have experienced far greater disruption and dislocation had the Mayor not chosen to intervene in a politically risky environment, it was not difficult to document the positive impact of his actions and leadership.

In summary, not only did the President of the Board of Education and Superintendent of Schools request continued assistance of the Mayor's Task Force in early May of 1969, but principals and District Superintendents praised the services rendered by the different teams. On May 4th, a New York Times article "Task Force Acts to 'Cool' Schools" showed how much worse the situation could have been had the Mayor sat back and simply watched events unfold in the city's high schools.■

Richard Streiter has served as Dean of Students at Pratt Institute and the Fashion Institute of Technology, was a consultant to the government of India and executive director of the Education Foundation of the Fashion Industry. Since 2001, he has been president of Art Asia NYC

Herbert Sturz

Howard R. Leary was Mayor Lindsay's Police Commissioner from 1966-1970. He came to New York at JVL's invitation from Philadelphia where he was Police Commissioner from 1963-1966. Howard began his career in that city as a foot patrolman; he also acquired a law degree at night school. Howard's tenure as New York City' commissioner was marked by student unrest, racial unrest, synagogue bombings, and charges of bribery and corruption that scarred the department's reputation...the fare that characterized policing in the 1960s.

Working at the VERA Institute (a think tank founded by philanthropist Louis Schweitzer and myself that devises and promotes reforms in the criminal justice system), I got to know some of Howard's eccentricities and foibles, as we became friends. For example, one morning he unexpectedly boarded a flight to join my wife and me on a holiday in Mexico to inspect Mayan ruins. There he was, seated toward the rear of the airplane wearing a Cheshire cat-like grin.

Knowing him as I did, it was not difficult to discern Howard's growing anxiety following Lindsay's re-election about whether the Mayor would re-appoint him. Having heard nothing from City Hall, he became increasingly upset as the tabloids and *The New York Times* reported successive reappointments of what Howard considered "lesser" commissioners for such departments as Housing and Corrections.

But, as I saw it, something else was going on. Howard was 58. John Lindsay was ten years younger. Yet, I felt that the Adonis-like Mayor had become a father figure for the older man, who had arrived in New York largely friendless. With his professional future uncertain, Howard now felt abandoned by his "father," the Mayor. Howard was proud and he felt spurned.

Finally, Mayor Lindsay made up his mind and offered Howard a second term, but Howard was deeply hurt by the delayed reappointment process and the accompanying rumors. It had been a tenuous, fraught situation. The Mayor phoned me several times over several days, first wanting to know whether Howard would accept the job, if offered, then urging me to persuade Leary to take the second term. With good reason, the Mayor wanted a decision promptly.

On the night before the deadline, Howard and I drank a lot of red wine. I did my best to reassure him that the city needed him and, indeed, that the Mayor loved him.

Around midnight Howard and I went our separate ways. In the morning I learned that he had let it be known that he would not serve a second term. He never gave a reason for his departure and refused to provide City Hall with a formal letter of resignation.

All this led, of course, to Pat Murphy becoming New York City's next Police Commissioner. I had failed to talk Howard into signing on for a second term and he returned to Philadelphia. While a good man replaced Howard, I still felt I had disappointed the Mayor and Jay Kriegel, who enabled VERA to flourish and make lasting improvements in the criminal justice system, and had let Howard down, too. To this day, I believe Howard Leary wanted the second term, but didn't know how to say yes.■

Herbert Sturz has been Deputy Mayor and Chairman of the City Planning Commission under Mayor Koch, and was a member of The New York Times *editorial board.*

Ken Sunshine

I just missed the Lindsay era, but have always felt that he affected my generation of NY political activists and me profoundly.

Charging out of pristine Cornell University to end the horrific Vietnam War, remake America to benefit the poor and attack the pervasive scourge of racism, I was almost immediately caught up in liberal Democratic politics—and have been frustrated with the Democratic Party ever since.

Progressive New York politics was exciting in those times—full of larger than life characters like my mentor, the great Bella Abzug; the brilliant and principled Mario Cuomo; the inspirational Ted Kennedy, who showed how an old fashioned liberal could form coalitions with Republicans and pass legislation; my first boss, then Bronx Borough President Bob Abrams; the Harlem Gang of Four—Sutton, Paterson, Rangel and especially Dave Dinkins. All of them became important figures in my life. I got close to the great tabloid writers—Jimmy Breslin, Pete Hamill and particularly Jack Newfield who taught me about in-your-face journalism, sticking up for the little guy, and always resenting power and phony privilege.

I got to dislike Ed Koch in those years. I spent many years trying and finally helping to succeed in getting him out of power. Much later, I came to enjoy his company and arguing with him. I liked Herman Badillo's early, but not later life politics. I got to know Jesse Jackson, who introduced me to my friend Al Sharpton.

I only met John Lindsay a few times, but his courage in confronting the issue of race impressed my comrades and me. Politics and race were raw in those days. America had achieved great legal and legislative civil rights victories, but remained a long way from being a truly just society. Many members of the white working class—often described as "Reagan Democrats"—started voting against their own interests. When blue-collar whites align with economic interests inimical to their survival, race is at the core.

Why should poor and near poor Southern whites vote overwhelmingly Republican? What sense can it make to vote for the economic policies of Romney, the Bushes or the rest of the current crop of Republican presidential candidates, each outdoing each other in poisonous bombast at the expense of immigrants, the poor, or the culturally alien?

John Lindsay suffered politically because he confronted racism by seeking coalition with our African American and Latino brothers and sisters rather than exploiting racial antagonisms. And he did it with style, grace and class---qualities so lacking in today's political climate.

Many years later, as I keep trying in my small way to make the Democratic Party address the issue of race squarely, several of Lindsay's disciples, especially my friends and mentors Davidoff, Kriegel, and Eldridge, remain among the sharpest political minds around.

History should and hopefully will be kinder to John Lindsay's reputation. He inspired my generation.■

Ken Sunshine was Chief of Staff to Mayor David Dinkins. He worked in campaigns for Bella Abzug and Mario Cuomo and was a delegate for George McGovern in 1972. He is founder and co-chief executive officer of public relations firm Sunshine Sachs Consultants

Robert W. Sweet

As David McCall's campaign slogan—taken from a Murray Kempton column—put it in 1965 when John Lindsay first ran for mayor, "He is fresh and everyone else is tired." He was also tall and movie star handsome.

John and I spent many years together—as undergraduates at Yale, Naval Reserve officers, roommates at Yale Law School for a while, young lawyers and fathers in New York, Young Republicans (John was President of the club), one of his campaign aides, his Executive Assistant and his Deputy Mayor. He remained fresh, an impressive symbol of hope and progressive policy.

John discerned the fundamental principles of a matter and was not distracted by confusing details. Some of his policy goals were difficult to achieve. Scatter-site housing to mingle different income groups in the same neighborhood, for example, generated great controversy and opposition. Its resolution in Forest Hills, however, also gave political birth to Mario Cuomo, John's selected mediator. His aspiration to increase community participation in public education exacerbated tensions in demonstration school districts and led to three teachers' strikes. Other efforts were indisputably successful. Most important, perhaps, he kept the peace in disadvantaged areas of the city with regular nighttime walks on their streets, and displayed great personal courage and commitment during his visit to Harlem the night of Rev. Martin Luther King, Jr.'s assassination. Because of his presence, attention to civilized policing techniques and long record as a champion of civil rights, New York never suffered the severe disorders that permanently scarred so many American cities.

John was also mindful of his city's future. Where infrastructure was concerned, for example, he launched the third water tunnel, a can that had been kicked down the road for decades. Its construction promised no immediate political benefit, but he went ahead with the project to ensure the fitness of New York's water system. He also recruited some of a generation's best and brightest to serve the city. Many of his appointees went on to become mainstays of subsequent municipal, state and federal administrations.

Had John accepted the recommendation to conduct a floor fight against Spiro Agnew for the vice presidential nomination at the 1968 Republican National Convention, he would have been the shining star in the political firmament, whatever that contest's outcome. Consider the fate of that convention's nominated ticket.

Finally, the fisc sorrows that befell the city later on were not the result of bad decisions or mismanagement so much as the consequences of an economic downturn that closed the door on previously accepted short-term financing.

As mayor, John Lindsay remained fresh, principled and a symbol of hope.■

Robert W. Sweet, Deputy Mayor in the first Lindsay Administration, was a partner at the law firm of Skadden Arps Slate Meagher & Flom from 1970 until 1978 when he was appointed United States District Judge for the Southern District of New York. He sits on that court today.

Ann Thayer

I answered the phone in campaign manager Bob Price's office. It never stopped ringing. Our Transportation Department, run by Sid Davidoff, was next door. And I recall a 14-year-old who everyone called "Squirt" (Jeff Katzenberg) who was always hanging around and probably skipping school. Little Johnny Lindsay, who was about three, or five at most, ran up and down the halls.■

Ann Thayer worked for Robert Price in the 1965 mayoral campaign and was an executive in banking and finance.

Thomas "Toby" Thacher

When I first heard John Lindsay speak in 1969 at a Riverdale fundraiser in my parents' home, I was blown away, indeed almost star struck.

Some of my friends and classmates had died in Vietnam. Having just graduated from college, I was filled with anger and disillusionment over the national and local politics of war and greed. Listening to Lindsay talk that evening so articulately and passionately about the good that government could and must do, I was filled with awe and admiration for his plans to bring City Hall into the neighborhoods where government and politicians would serve rather than be served. Only two other politicians ever hooked me that way—John Kennedy and Mario Cuomo.

I immediately joined the campaign and worked with June Eisland and Oliver Koeppel in the Riverdale storefront to help re-elect the Mayor.

After the November election victory, I had the opportunity to help run the Neighborhood City Hall in Washington Heights with John Van Putten, under the incredible leadership of Lew Feldstein. The program was part of Lindsay's effort to bring government closer to communities, especially those that felt neglected and remote from City Hall.

As we dealt with local problems involving the police, schools and housing, I often saw a gap between policies made at City Hall and how they were implemented on the streets. In many cases, municipal officials working in these communities lacked the authority to modify rules to make city services more responsive to local needs. All too frequently, the government had difficulty monitoring service delivery in these far-flung neighborhoods. And I saw agency dysfunction and opportunities for corruption, observations that influenced my work since in law enforcement, private security and integrity monitoring.

Lindsay was determined to use the Neighborhood Government Office to change these conditions. He made city agencies more accountable and empowered local agency officials to act faster and more aggressively to meet community needs. He knew that creating this non-partisan administrative framework was necessary to replace the political clubhouses—then in terminal decline--that had traditionally performed these functions, but favoring those who helped get out the vote.

It was gratifying to be part of this experiment as City Hall reached out to neighborhoods across the five boroughs. The Office of Neighborhood Government set a standard for the basic approach of delivering city services still followed today.■

*After serving in City Hall, **Toby Thacher** was an Assistant District Attorney in Manhattan, Deputy Assistant Attorney General on the NYS Organized Crime Task Force, executive director of Governor Mario Cuomo's Construction Industry Strike Force and Inspector General at the School Construction Authority. He is president and chief executive officer of Thacher Associates, an investigative and integrity risk-management firm.*

Franklin Thomas

The 1965 mayoral campaign was an intense one for NYC and, in particular, for the NYC Police Department, where I had been hired by Commissioner Vincent Broderick to serve as Deputy Commissioner for Legal Matters. Candidate John Lindsay challenged us by calling for modernization of the force's antiquated support systems and proposing a Civilian Complaint Review Board (CCRB), until then a cause advanced primarily by civil rights leaders.

Commissioner Broderick was a principled public servant, but because Lindsay's campaign was perceived as critical of the department and its leaders, he was expected to replace the Commissioner when he won the mayoralty. When a new Commissioner was named, my fellow four deputy commissioners and I followed custom and submitted letters of resignation.

My somewhat awkward task during the transition was to work with the incoming Mayor's staff to draft the order creating the Civilian Complaint Review Board, an assignment that required carefully balancing the interests of citizens and officers and providing adequate protections for both. The board's structure and guidelines were announced in May 1966 to the consternation of many police officers and their commanders.

Lindsay's sensitivity to all concerned was in many ways ahead of its time, but the Review Board was overwhelmingly rejected at the polls by a 2-to-1 margin in 1966.

Later that year, Senator Robert F. Kennedy (with the support of Senator Jacob K. Javits) asked me to become President of the Bedford-Stuyvesant Restoration Corporation. Here was an opportunity to contribute to the revival of the neighborhood where I was born and had grown up. It was a challenging period, trying new tools and innovative approaches with substantial government and private resources to energize an important minority community with improved housing, amenities, employment opportunities, social services, and education.

The Mayor was always gracious and, despite potential political rivalries, was personally available, encouraging and supportive. In fact, he authorized and approved direct funding from the federal government to the Bedford-Stuyvesant Restoration Corporation over the objections of some anti-poverty officials and the advice of some of his senior advisors.

We had one additional shared chapter in our careers when the Mayor asked me to serve on the five-member Knapp Commission he appointed in 1971 to investigate police corruption, a difficult and sometimes unpleasant mission that included examining the highly sensitive issue of City Hall's role. But our work was central to ensuring the department's integrity and public credibility. Serving on the commission felt like fulfilling a necessary obligation.

The Mayor appointed a group of strong commissioners and accorded us full independence. He was always respectful of our responsibility even when our hearings must have been uncomfortable for his Administration. As with the CCRB, he obviously believed deeply in the need to establish credible procedures and strictly adhere to them.■

Franklin Thomas was the first president of the Bedford -Stuyvesant Restoration Corporation and then president of the Ford Foundation for 17 years. He is head of the TFF Group, a non-profit promoting development in South Africa, and Chairman of the September 11 Fund.

John Thomas

I became Andy Kerr's partner when he managed Lindsay's Project Management Office. We took on some major performance problems—notably trash collection, snow removal and Parks Department maintenance. In the face of negative publicity regarding Lindsay's use of consultants, our contract was terminated and our staff converted into City employees. The conversion made a *Daily News* headline: "City Hires Two Once-Secret Consultants".

During the second term, the Lindsay/Kerr Productivity Program became recognized nationally when Deputy Mayor Ed Hamilton produced a conference on municipal productivity improvement. One department chief after another proudly stepped up and explained to the nation's local government managers how to make municipal operations more productive and cost-effective.

Proof of our program's success was evident in the grudging acknowledgement of Governor Nelson Rockefeller. Subsequently Congress created the National Commission on Productivity and Quality of Work Life, chaired by none other than Vice President Nelson Rockefeller. I became a consultant to this commission and authored "So, Mr. Mayor, You Want to Improve Productivity . . ." which was published jointly by the Commission and the Ford Foundation.

Those were indeed challenging times. I am proud to have been a small part of this long stride forward in public administration.■

John S. Thomas served as Deputy Director of the Budget Bureau and later became a partner with Andy Kerr in Devonshire Associates of Cambridge, Massachusetts.

P. Robert Tisch *(by Jonathan Tisch)*

B ob Tisch's love of New York City was evident in his sense of responsibility as a business leader and his desire to be in the mix. Those attributes made him an important voice in how the city was run and the way it met its challenges.

And he really enjoyed both working with John Lindsay and being one of the Mayor's friends.

JVL's first day in office, January 1, 1966, was marred by a transit strike. The contract negotiations were held at The Americana Hotel on Seventh Avenue, which my father and his brother Larry had just built. During that tense period we never saw my father. He was in the middle of the action at the hotel and he loved it.

Throughout John Lindsay's tenure at City Hall, my father cherished being part of his "kitchen cabinet" and offering advice to members of his inner circle, such as Jay Kriegel and Barry Gottherer. Also on hand was Jeff Katzenberg, a younger staffer whom he befriended and would go on to great success in Hollywood.

Our family lived in Scarsdale during those years. When he received a phone call there from the Mayor or one of his deputies, Bob Tisch was in his glory.

My father's generation of civic leaders highly valued their relationships with major elected officials. In that select group, John Lindsay occupied a special place for him. ■

Bob Tisch, who died in 2005, built and ran the Loews Corporation with his brother Larry. With a special affinity for its hotels, he long-served as chair of the city's Convention and Visitors Bureau. He served as U.S. Postmaster General and was co-owner of the New York Giants football team. His son Jonathan Tisch has succeeded him as Chairman of Loews Hotels and is co-chairman of the Loews Corporation. He was first chairman of NYC & Company, the city's official marketing and tourism agency

William Toby, Jr.

I served as Federal-State Liaison Officer for the Model Cities Administration during Mayor Lindsay's second term.

In 1971, David Shipler of *The New York Times* reported that New York was lobbying Washington for more Model Cities funds despite failing to spend its annual $50 million dollar allotment within the fiscal year as required by law. The roadblock had been our own Budget Bureau's rigid spending controls. Soon after Shipler's front-page story was published, the U.S. Department of Housing and Urban Development, the agency funding Model Cities, put a hold on the city's monthly drawdown of our grant.

Mayor Lindsay was livid. At a meeting with his aide Gordon Davis, Model Cities Director Judge Joseph Williams and me, he asked who had leaked the story to the *Times*. None of us knew. After much discussion, the prevailing view was that the Mayor should call HUD Secretary George Romney and plead for relief.

When the Mayor asked if everyone agreed I shakily raised my hand and suggested another option. Considering how things worked in Washington, I said, it would make more sense for him to phone David Grossman, head of HUD's regional office located just a block from City Hall. If he telephoned Romney, the Secretary would only call Grossman for a briefing before returning the Mayor's call. I noted that talking to Grossman might also yield a political dividend because New York City mayors rarely made such overtures to regional federal officials and Grossman's good will could be useful. The Mayor agreed and asked me to prepare talking points for his upcoming conversation with the regional director.

The next day Mayor Lindsay, my points in hand, dialed David Grossman's office himself. When Grossman's secretary answered the phone, Lindsay, said, "This is Mayor John Lindsay. May I speak to David Grossman?" The secretary responded, "Oh, yes. I'm President Nixon" and hung up.

The Mayor, keeping his cool, redialed the number. "Look I am really the Mayor," he told the secretary, "and I need to speak to your boss David Grossman about a vital matter." She put him through.

David told the Mayor that if the city did not spend all the funds during the federal fiscal year, the money would revert to the Treasury. He pointed out, however, that if the Administration could prove that Model Cities funds had been allocated for, say, nursing training and contracts had been signed between Model Cities and local contractors providing that service, HUD would consider those funds to be in a "spent column or be deemed spent."

The Mayor thanked Grossman profusely. Our problem was solved. Later, he also wrote David a note of gratitude and telephoned HUD's Neil Guiney, the city's Model Cities Representative, to express his appreciation. Guiney later told me the Mayor's call left him in shock.

David Grossman and Neil Guiney became advocates for the Lindsay Administration to the great benefit of our Model Cities programs.■

William Toby, Jr., was Lindsay's Federal-State Liaison Officer for the Model Cities Administration. He later served as a Regional Administrator for HEW and HICFA, and is now a private consultant focused on Medicare and Medicaid financing and policy issues.

Michele Cohn Tocci

During my first year of graduate school, I worked for Barry Gottehrer as one of his many assistants. Barry was an Assistant to the Mayor and I was an assistant to the Assistant.

Barry led the Urban Action Task Force and attended meetings with community leaders, elected officials and policemen. I was responsible for his schedule: making and breaking dates, meetings and appointments. Under Barry's excellent tutelage I learned to lie with conviction and curse with abandon.

Barry was pleased with my work and gave me the opportunity, on one occasion, to serve the Mayor directly--my only "one on one" with John V. Lindsay. I was an advance man for a morning. I rode with the Mayor in a limo to a ceremony inaugurating a fireboat, I think. I had made notes about the boat, the Fire Department staff, water pressure from the boat's hose and other details in order to brief the Mayor who, it turned out, wasn't nearly as interested in my notes as he was in Barry's dating life. I knew way more about that than I did about fire-fighting equipment and statistics, so I happily filled him in on the actresses, singers, and other ladies who Barry squired around when he wasn't spending time with gang leaders.

When Barry left the Administration for a post at Madison Square Garden, I was assigned to work for Jay Kriegel, another mayoral Assistant. Jay's office was in City Hall, a big move up for me from 51 Chambers Street. Jay screamed a lot but gave me some interesting work and protected me from a mean, pencil-throwing intern.■

Michele Cohn Tocci is President of the David Berg Foundation.

William vanden Heuvel

After Robert Kennedy's assassination, his people had to determine how they would stay involved in politics. In 1970, I ran for the Democratic nomination for Governor. I didn't win, but John Lindsay, who had defeated me in a Congressional election in 1960, was apparently impressed enough because when the crisis erupted in the prisons, particularly in the Tombs, he asked me to become Chairman of the Board of Correction, a moribund group of citizens with designated responsibility for monitoring that system. John was a prison reformer, intent on making fundamental, much-needed changes, but recognizing that it would be very difficult. I accepted the appointment. Our re-constituted board launched new programs to achieve those changes. John followed our work closely and I had ready access to him. Knowing that I would be attacked by change-resistant elements of the criminal justice system, he always supported me. I don't think we ever had a mayor who was better informed about that system and more eager to reform it. He paid particular attention to the various studies that we published. In three years, we never had a meaningful dispute.

—

In 1971, Governor Rockefeller, feuding with the Mayor, appointed a commission to study the relationship between New York City and New York State and recommend ways to manage the former better. The Governor was out to embarrass John Lindsay. The Mayor responded by asking me to chair a commission to study the city-state relationship and make recommendations for improving both coordination between Albany and New York and the state government's Administration. Rockefeller was furious. I suggested to the Mayor that I meet with the Governor and assure him that our commission was substantively committed with no political agenda. The Mayor was delighted with the suggestion and I met with Rockefeller to discuss how we would proceed. Commission member Mario Cuomo and I reviewed all the papers written about State/City relationships during the past two decades, four or five of which had great quality. I'd been

Vice President of the 1967 State Constitutional Convention, which produced valuable work on these subjects as well. Eventually, the work of Rockefeller's commission got lost in the morass. We conducted some excellent studies, but the State/City relationship remained essentially as it had been.

—

My deep involvement in the criminal justice system sharpened my determination to run for Manhattan District Attorney when Frank Hogan, the immensely popular and respected DA, retired in 1973, as he announced he would. John Lindsay, knowing that Hogan was going to reverse his decision and run for yet another term, called me to his office and asked if I would succeed August Heckscher as the city's Parks Commissioner. He wanted to spare me a brutal campaign I was highly unlikely to win. He cordially accepted my decision to oppose Hogan anyway.

—

The Democratic Party had a multiplicity of candidates and did not need John Lindsay. His historic role was to lead and preserve the moderate Republican Party that was still a major force in the country. He walked the streets during the most dangerous times and gave courage to everyone, reminding us of what citizenship is in a democratic society.■

William vanden Heuvel has held many posts in government, including Special Assistant to U.S. Attorney General Robert Kennedy and Ambassador to the European Office of the United Nations and U.S. Deputy Ambassador to the United Nations under President Jimmy Carter. Ambassador vanden Heuvel, a past chairman of the Roosevelt Institute, is a senior advisor to Allen & Company and senior counsel to the law firm of Stroock & Stroock & Lavan.

Robert Vanni

In late 1968, I was invited to attend a reception at Gracie Mansion hosted by the Mayor and Mrs. Lindsay. I was working at the City Commission for the United Nations with Commissioner Frances Loeb, so I presume it was a reception for UN officials and the wider diplomatic community. For me, an impressionable young staffer, it was a grand evening - limos and luminaries, politics and diplomacy. The festivities were held in the impressive, recently completed Susan B. Wagner Wing.

As the event was to begin, the Mayor and his introducer were standing on a low platform. The room was aglow. The spotlight seemed to be trained solely on the Mayor. His smile matched its radiance. By chance, I was standing next to Mrs. Lindsay.

The introductory remarks were eloquent, if perhaps a bit too long. Just as they were ending, Mary Lindsay turned to those around her and said, "Gee, that's not the same man I go to bed with!!!"

It was a special evening. Mary's comment made it all the more unforgettable.■

Robert Vanni is Vice-chairman of the Nonprofit Coordinating Committee of New York and Vice President and General Counsel Emeritus of the New York Public Library.

Patrick Vecchio

JVL visits Japan accompanied by Jay Kriegel, Tom Morgan, the President of the City Council, someone from state government, Mrs. Lindsay and me. Everyone finds a gift in their room but me; I'm not listed as part of the official entourage. Jay tries, but fails to get a gift for me, and informs JVL.

Later that day, the Mayor emerges from a meeting with the head of Sony followed by a man carrying a shopping bag containing a very expensive camera. JVL hands the bag to me and says, "That's for you." He gives me a camera that is intended for him so that I don't go home without a gift.

—

JVL is taking an evening flight to Oregon in 1968 to campaign for Nelson Rockefeller, who is running for President. He is not happy about making the trip. I arrive at Gracie Mansion at 9 p.m. to get him to the airport for a 10 p.m. charter departure. Oregon Congressman John Dellenback, who is to accompany JVL and his press secretary Harry O'Donnell on the trip, waits for the Mayor with me. JVL and Harry, however, don't join us until close to midnight. As we pull out of the mansion's driveway, ten demonstrators protesting the Forest Hills housing proposal rush our car, pounding on its hood and screaming at us. Not surprisingly, JVL's mood worsens.

We board a Lear Jet at LaGuardia. Sitting next to the pilots in the jump seat, I hear a radio message from Chicago advising that we will have to descend to refuel. When told why we are landing, JVL is very displeased. Then, off we go again. Approaching Great Falls, Montana, the pilot radios the tower to have someone with a key to the fuel tank meet our jet. The tower answers that no one is available. Hearing about the second landing and refueling, JVL becomes truly angry.

Like it or not, we are staying in Great Falls for a while. Soon after landing, JVL storms into a small wooden building where an elderly man is polishing the floor and yells, "Where is the key?" The man ignores him. JVL grabs the phone book yellow pages, searches for a hotel and finds one.

A yellow cab sits on the tarmac. JVL tells its driver to take us into town. The driver says, "Oh no, you can't! This car is on a mail run!" Back to the building and the yellow pages to look for cab service. Finally, we reach an old, but serviceable hotel. We each get a room, but before I go to mine I ask JVL when he wants to be awakened. It is probably four or five in the morning, New York time. JVL looks at his watch, then blurts out, "Cancel the press conference." Dillenback panics. What to do?

I call Sid Davidoff in Oregon and tell him JVL has cancelled the press conference. He replies, "You get him here! I am not cancelling." I report to JVL and say I'll wake him at seven. We have breakfast and fly to Portland.

JVL is a big hit and all his anger and frustration are gone.■

Pat Vecchio has been Smithtown's Town Supervisor since 1978, making him the longest-serving official to hold that post in Long island's history. Smithtown's Town Hall is named in his honor. He was Mayor Lindsay's chief security officer.

Cynthia Wainwright

I began working for Dick Aurelio, manager of the second Lindsay mayoral campaign, at the end of August, 1969. My desk was in Dick's office only footsteps from his. I reported for work on my first day with the campaign at 8 a.m.. I was more than surprised to see John Lindsay standing at my desk, which, at that point, was entirely bare except for a telephone. The Mayor, tan, wearing a blue shirt and dripping perspiration on that desk, was using the phone and using the F word in, seemingly, every sentence and conjugated in every form. Soon enough, I would be a "potty mouth," too, having learned that you can't survive in New York politics without the liberal use of curse words and obscenities.■

Cynthia Wainwright, campaign and City Hall aide to Richard Aurelio, worked on criminal justice matters for the state government, served as Deputy Commissioner for Corrections in the Koch administration and headed Chemical Bank's Office of Corporate Social Responsibility.

Martha Wallau

I joined the Office of Neighborhood Government at the beginning of Lindsay's second term as Mayor. We were part of an exciting experiment that sought to link City Hall to various neighborhoods in the five boroughs, some of which seemed quite distant from Manhattan. We established a direct channel to the government by creating District Task Forces chaired by a senior member of the government who had status at City Hall. We also coordinated services at the local level by assembling local police, sanitation, parks, traffic and other officials and making them members of the local District Service Cabinet.

Our team served as the coordinators. My areas were in South Brooklyn, including Coney Island, Canarsie, and Flatbush.

It was a challenge to work with alienated communities on solving small problems in ways that could promote government's credibility and build relationships that would generate local support and leadership when needed in times of crisis.

I am proud that the system we built by trial and error for City Hall's dealings with local communities still exists 45 years later. I also made friends in the Lindsay Administration who remain some of my closest to this day.■

Martha Wallau is Chief Administrative Officer and Senior Managing Director of Eastdil Secured.

Warren Wechsler

The week they won the 1973 National Basketball Association championship, New York Knickerbocker coach "Red" Holtzman, and two of the team's stars, Willis Reed and Dave DeBusschre, were invited to join JVL as guests on his television program. As they prepared for their on-camera conversation in the "green room" adjacent to the studio where the show was taped, Holtzman sensed how little the Mayor knew or cared about basketball. Nonetheless, he appreciated Lindsay's gratitude for what the Knicks' success meant to so many New Yorkers. Searching for something in common to talk about, the coach asked JVL, "How do you put up with all the guff you have to take every day?" Both Holtzman and Lindsay were, after all, high achievers in a city with no shortage of second-guessers. "I don't mind a bit," he answered, smiling mischievously. The Mayor's zest for defending his programs, debating his opponents and carrying his case to the public was compelling, a quality that—like his idealism—energized supporters and fastened their loyalty. No less than his guests, John Lindsay savored and excelled at competition.

Before another television program, the Mayor anxiously awaited news of a hostage negotiation at a sporting goods store in Brooklyn. As his make-up was being applied, JVL received a telephone call informing him that the hostages had been freed and their captors arrested without loss of life or injury to anyone involved. He was also advised that Police Commissioner Pat Murphy was on his way to the studio to report. When Murphy arrived, the Mayor stood up and applauded. Everyone else in the room followed suit. He told the Commissioner how proud he was of the Police Department's performance in that perilous, uncertain situation. Unspoken, but no less evident was his feeling for the gravity and value of what government does.

In his last summer as Mayor, John Lindsay visited the Brooklyn Navy Yard with Mary. That morning, she christened the tanker *T.T. Brooklyn* by shattering a jeroboam of champagne against its hull. The *Brooklyn* was the first ship assembled in the Yard since the city acquired the facility as surplus federal property in 1967. Lindsay had been briefly stationed there as a young Naval lieutenant during WW II.

Following the ceremony, the Mayor, as usual the tallest and most vivid figure in the crowd, mingled with some of the 2,700 people who had earned their livelihoods building that ship. The workers and their families, mostly from local minority communities, were dressed for church services or a wedding. They were thrilled to see him and knew he was on their side. JVL had delivered solid, steady employment where jobs had long been scarce. Looking on was a longtime member of the Democratic Party machine that would re-possess city government after the Lindsay Administration's impending departure. He called me over. "Your guy," he said with a mixture of admiration, puzzlement and envy, "he's still got it."

Many years after leaving City Hall, John Lindsay told me, "You know, I was never tired a single day when I was Mayor."■

Warren Wechsler *served as a press spokesman and speechwriter and produced Mayor Lindsay's television program. He has been a public affairs executive and is a consultant on such matters to universities and nonprofit organizations, a broadcaster, writer and musician.*

Richard Weinstein

After helping to elect John Lindsay Mayor, fellow architects Jonathan Barnett, Jaquelin Robertson and I became founding members of the Urban Design Group under City Planning Commission Chairman Don Elliott.

Preserving the unique character of the Theater District was one of our priorities.

Developer Jerome (Jerry) Minskoff presented us with our first project in Times Square. He and his brothers owned the block front from 43rd to 44th Streets facing east onto the square. Their property included a theater slated for demolition. The Zoning Ordinance permitted "as of right" development for the Minskoffs' planned office building, meaning that no additional government reviews were required.

When Minskoff confirmed his intention to demolish the theater, we asked how it might be preserved. Could a new theater be slipped in under the back of the tower? Calculating our suggestion's cost, Minskoff looked indignant,.

Then we proposed placing the theater in the back of the tower with a lobby facing Times Square on the second floor. Under the Zoning Ordinance's 1961 revision developers who provided a plaza could add another 20% in floor area to their building. In this case, we would substitute including a theater instead of a plaza to earn the 20 % bonus. Although skeptical, Minskoff and his architect agreed to study our proposal.

Meanwhile we had obtained a grant from the Ford Foundation to create an advisory panel of theater luminaries to advise us on types of theater configurations. Producer-director Harold Prince, the Mayor's friend, led the panel. We also hired a real estate economist to study theater construction costs and the financial benefits developers might realize from various zoning variances.

Chairman Elliott and his chief counsel Norman Marcus helped write the language for the resulting Special Theater District Zoning and presented the initiative to civic groups, the local planning board, and the theater community.

The powerful Shubert Organization owned most of the Broadway theaters. The US Supreme Court had ruled that the corporation constituted a monopoly. The court issued a consent decree allowing the Shuberts to operate, but barring them from acquiring any more theaters. Understandably, the Shuberts were opposed to any one else building new ones over which they had no control.

Minskoff continued to balk. When the Mayor, Elliott, and I met with him at his Essex House apartment high above Central Park, he apologized for being unable to accommodate us. His reservations about our plan's feasibility convinced him to proceed as of right. The Mayor, equally apologetic, commiserated with Minskoff about the unprecedented back up of permits at the Building Department. How discouraging it must be, Lindsay said, for a developer with so much at risk to be delayed because of a sluggish bureaucracy the Mayor hopelessly fought every day. But then, Lindsay changed course and spoke eloquently about the theater's importance to New York, pleading for Minskoff's leadership as a citizen. "I may regret this," Minskoff finally said. We all smiled.

Our final hurdle was the Board of Estimate hearing. Hal Prince lined up such theater celebrities as Diahann Carroll and Angela Lansbury to testify for our theater zoning. The chamber was full. As we began, I received a note from the Mayor telling me the board's members had to leave soon to attend Cardinal Spellman's funeral at St. Patrick's Cathedral. With no time for testimony, Prince asked each of those theatrical stars favoring our zoning to simply rise when he called their names, a memorable roll call that still recalls the heart and soul of Broadway. The Mayor's eyes misted over as each actor, director, producer, and playwright stood in dignified silence.

Producer David Merrick's many hits, including "Hello, Dolly," had long runs in the Shubert theaters. Rising to represent their interests, Merrick said that he couldn't go against the wishes of so many of his colleagues in the room and withdrew his objections. There was a cheer and a few hats were thrown in the air.

This victory and the Special Theater District Zoning enabled us to induce the construction of two large musical comedy houses, and two experimental theaters as part of and paid for by office buildings.∎

Richard Weinstein is a Professor Emeritus at the UCLA Graduate School of Architecture and Urban Planning where he served as Dean from 1985 to 1994.

Carl Weisbrod

I got my start in government at the age of 25, three years after my graduation from law school. In the heady days of the late 1960s as a young legal services lawyer on the Upper West Side of Manhattan, I was representing squatters who were taking over city-owned buildings slated for demolition in the West Side Urban Renewal Area and displaced families housed in squalid hotels along Broadway.

I found myself constantly bringing lawsuits against Mayor John Lindsay's Commissioner of Relocation, Amalia Betanzos—an extraordinarily smart, savvy woman who had a strong relationship with the Mayor. "Amy," as she was known to just about everyone, could always find an answer to any challenge. She called me one day after my umpteenth lawsuit naming her personally as a defendant, and said: "If you really want to solve these problems come join the government and solve them."

So began my love affair with local government and my decades-long association with Amy Betanzos. She was an unusual role model for those times—a Puerto Rican woman from the South Bronx who was a confident and forceful presence. A biologist by academic training, and a community organizer by emotional commitment, Amy was the founding President of the Puerto Rican Community Development Corporation. In an era when few women and even fewer Latinas held command positions in government (or anywhere else), she was a natural trailblazer.

Amy believed in both the responsibility and joy of public service, displaying a skill, creativity and ease that inspired Mayor Lindsay and his next four successors to entrust her with ever more demanding challenges. She would serve as Relocation Commissioner, followed by Commissioner of Youth Services, and as a Member of the New York City Housing Authority. Although five mayors each appointed her to important posts, she never forgot her community roots or abandoned her commitment to the least powerful.

And she inspired young people like me--pushing us to develop our skills, to have confidence in our own judgment, and to be guided by fundamental values. While I, too, have been proud to serve several mayors, I still credit Amy more than anyone with teaching me how to balance competing interests, make tough decisions and lead others.■

Carl Weisbrod serves under Mayor de Blasio as Director of the Department of City Planning and Chairman of the City Planning Commission. He administered the Times Square rehabilitation program under Mayor Koch, was Founding President of both the New York City Economic Development Corporation and the Alliance for Downtown New York, Executive Director of the City Planning Commission, Chairman of the New York City Loft Board and President of the real estate division of Trinity Church

Steven R. Weisman

A walking tour of the leafy Yale campus was not exactly high on Mayor Lindsay's priorities in the spring of 1967. New York City was enmeshed in labor crises, budget battles and anti-poverty disputes. My first encounter with him (while serving as campus correspondent for *The New York Times*) made clear that his mind was back at City Hall.

At age 45, Lindsay was the youngest member of the Yale Corporation, which oversees the university's affairs, and he was in New Haven for a trustee meeting. "I try never to miss one," he said, "I feel that way about Yale." He told a Yale history class that municipal government was the place to go for young idealists. But as I struggled to keep up with him as he loped across the campus, nodding hello to excited students, he was muttering about how he had to get back to City Hall to negotiate "the damned capital budget."

I joined the *Times* the next year after graduating from Yale. The paper let me cover some of his tough re-election campaign. By 1969 I had made friends with several young advisers on Lindsay's team. But what I remember most was his dogged tours of synagogues in Brooklyn and Queens in the evening hours, looking improbable in his yarmulke, trying to shore up the core of his base among middle and working class Jews. The joke among political reporters was that at City Hall, when Lindsay—not the biggest baseball fan himself—was told he would be meeting with Ralph Kiner, the Mets announcer, in that storied year for the team, he said, "Kiner...Kiner...yes, I know Rabbi Kiner."

My final conversation with Lindsay was wonderful and poignant. I was serving as Tokyo Bureau Chief for the *Times* in the early 1990s, and Lindsay came to see if his law firm should open an office in Tokyo. Some of my friends on his old staff told him to look me up. We met at his hotel room, where he talked as he changed hurriedly for another round of meetings. He wanted to know all about Japan, the future of its economic boom, the role of lawyers, how I was enjoying Tokyo. He had the same restless curiosity, intellect, generous spirit, and commitment that inspired so many New Yorkers in one of its most trying eras.■

Steven R. Weisman is Vice President for Publications and Communications at The Peterson Institute. Over a long career with The New York Times, he was bureau chief in Tokyo and New Delhi and senior White House correspondent. He has written several books and edited the correspondence of Senator Daniel Patrick Moynihan.

Basil Whiting

I spent my few months in the Lindsay Administration as a Special Assistant to Mike Sviridoff, designer and first Administrator of the Human Resources Administration. I also had a few writing assignments from the Mayor's Office. I was pretty good at longer stuff, drafting Lindsay's review of "Cities in a Race With Time" for the first page of *The Sunday New York Times Book Review*. But I was not good at speeches and the calls from the Mayor's staff stopped coming.

At HRA, I was assigned to a team that was writing a proposal to the Office of Economic Opportunity (OEO) for a youth employment program in East Harlem.

We were working on the proposal in the wee small hours of the day before it was due when someone screamed, "Oh, shit! Omigod! Look at the project's title. Its acronym is S-P-I-C!" (I forget the actual title but not the acronym.)

"So we are having the Mayor propose a youth employment program for Puerto Rican kids in East Harlem named 'Spic,'" someone responded. "Oy! How did we get this far without someone noticing this?"

"I don't know," I said, "but we can't use this. We have to change the title."

Silence.

We had two choices.

First, come up with a new title, then use "white out" fluid to erase the offending title wherever it appeared in the 50-odd pages of proposal. Remember that this was back before computers and laser printers had been invented. We would have had to very carefully position each page in a typewriter and enter the new title on top of the whited-out old one. That arduous procedure would produce a messy result.

Our second choice was to retype the whole 50 pages or so. We divided the proposal up and each of us retyped a portion. Later that morning, one of us jumped on the train and hand delivered it to OEO in Washington. The renewal proposal was funded. I understand that the program almost named "SPIC" served the East Harlem kids, the Mayor and the city very well.■

Basil Whiting was on the staff of The Ford Foundation, served as Deputy Assistant Secretary of Labor in the Carter Administration, and as Vice President for Human Resources at the Long Island Rail Road.

Robert Wilmers

A s Finance Commissioner, I oversaw the City's vast revenue collection operations—voluminous transactions entailing extensive paperwork, but not very dramatic or newsworthy. So I was rarely with the Mayor or at City Hall.

But then, one day a large group of the parking meter collectors were arrested on charges of stealing funds and we had a major scandal on our hands.

I was called to City Hall to brief the Mayor before his press conference. As I walked him through the details of the charges, how our operation worked, and how the theft occurred, he didn't seem terribly interested. Moreover, I got the sense that he didn't fully understand what had happened.

But when he went before the press corps in the Blue Room, it was as if a magic transformation had occurred. He exuded self-assurance and handled every question with a mastery of the facts and a persuasive narrative. While I was never sure how much of the briefing he had absorbed, it didn't seem to matter. He was such a natural that he effortlessly conveyed total command. It was a lesson for those of us confident in our intelligence that outstanding presentational skills and political instincts often have the greatest impact and value.■

Robert Wilmers has been Chief Executive Officer of the M & T Bank Corporation for the past eight years. He has also served as Chairman of the NYS Development Corporation and the New York State Bankers Association, and as a director of the Federal Reserve Bank of New York..

Joan Ransohoff Wynn

During John Lindsay's Administration, I ran the Budget Bureau's Housing Unit. I worked with a few colleagues in a small room in the Municipal Building painted the standard bureaucratic green. Our ancient grey metal desks were well-worn and dented.

Occasionally, I would be aware of someone unfamiliar sitting next to me and look up to see the Mayor. He was, by turns, intense and relaxed, but always impressive. His questions were probing and focused: What was I working on? What would I be doing next? What were our most perplexing problems? What work and what results were we most proud of?

Over time, I became less startled when the mayor dropped by, but his interest in our efforts and his sincerity made us deeply loyal to him. In those years, when so many of us were full of idealism and hope, we believed that certain public policies and governmental actions would improve citizens' lives. That cause and personal identification with the Mayor and his goals inspired us to spend countless hours at our assignments, working through the night in our cramped quarters.

John Lindsay was piercingly smart, closely attentive throughout highly detailed capital and expense budget meetings as he ate a peanut butter and jelly sandwich and drank milk from the sort of small carton so familiar from elementary school.

On the night of Dr. Martin Luther King, Jr.'s assassination, John Lindsay walked the streets of Harlem to offer compassion and consolation. He encouraged a sense of solidarity throughout the city and sealed my enduring admiration for him, a feeling that has not diminished and never will.■

*After running the Lindsay Administration's Housing Planning Unit at the Bureau of the Budget, **Joan Wynn** was a researcher at the University of Chicago for sixteen years and has been a sculptor for the past decade.*

John Zuccotti

After graduating law school in 1964, I went to New York to practice at the firm of Davis Polk, where Congressman John Lindsay's twin brother David was a partner. So in 1965, when Lindsay ran for Mayor, and the campaign opened over 120 storefronts in every neighborhood across the city staffed by thousands of volunteers, my wife Susan and I, along with two other couples (the Tufos—a law school friend, and Carter and Amanda Burden) ran the Lindsay storefront in the 65th Assembly District in South Ozone Park, Queens. For months, the six of us coordinated schedules to ensure that at least one or two of us were able to travel to our distant Lindsay outpost every day and every night to provide coverage and share staffing responsibilities of recruiting, outreach, speaking, and advocating.

I also remember a night at Richmond Hill High School when Lindsay debated the Conservative candidate William Buckley in a dramatic showdown. As one would expect from two Yale men, it was a serious, thoughtful, articulate, and respectful exchange between two figures with deep convictions and strong views, often in sharp conflict—it makes today's version of political debates seem pale by comparison. Lindsay had arrived at the debate with his aide Sid Davidoff, while Buckley was escorted in by the Police Precinct Captain and six cops, indicating their hostility to Lindsay's plans, especially to create a Civilian Complaint Review Board, which were perceived as anti-police.

After Lindsay's election, and the joyous celebrations, Susan and I moved to Washington where I joined the staff of New York's respected senior Senator Jacob Javits (Rep), led by the wise Richard Aurelio. After a year or so, I moved to the newly-created Department of Urban Development (HUD), led by its first Secretary Robert Weaver and his deputy Robert Wood, both extraordinary talents appointed by LBJ. After Republican Richard Nixon won the presidency in 1968, I expected to be promptly dismissed. But surprisingly, based on Javits' strong endorsement, I kept my job with new HUD Secretary (former Michigan Governor) George Romney and remained for a year.

We moved back to New York and settled in Carroll Gardens, Brooklyn, an intimate neighborhood where we have happily lived ever since. And my old friend from Senator Javits' office, Dick Aurelio, had by then managed Lindsay's successful re-election in 1969 and was now Deputy Mayor.

Thanks largely to Dick, when a seat on the prestigious City Planning Commission opened in 1970, the Mayor appointed me as the member from Brooklyn. Initial reaction was not promising, with some Brooklyn commentators saying that while my name was Italian, I was obviously just a disguised Ivy Leaguer from Princeton and Yale and had only lived in the borough for three months.

The Commission frequently faced challenging issues, providing an intense learning experience, including the politics of development (this was shortly after the clash in middle class Forest Hills over scatter site housing with low-income units which had been mediated by a young Queens lawyer named Mario Cuomo), and I built strong relations with long-standing Commission Chairman Donald Elliott and Aurelio's successor as Deputy Mayor, Ed Hamilton.

So when Don stepped down as Chairman in 1972 to run for Congress, I was delighted that the Mayor appointed me as the full-time Chairman. While we faced many issues, I focused on two areas in particular.

First, the work of the immensely talented Urban Design Group, an innovation created by Lindsay, with young architects Jaque Robertson, Alex Cooper and Richard Weinstein (who each went on to great careers). Their work guided and enhanced private plans and developments, giving the city government a new role in urban aesthetics based on a skill set that government had never before possessed.

And second, creating a process for community participation in the Commission's planning deliberations and decisions. In my first four months as Chair I went to the evening meetings of all 62 community boards created under the City Charter, but with ill-defined and unclear roles. So we spelled out an orderly way for them to participate, which evolved into the highly effective Uniform Land Use Review Process (ULURP), formalized in the City Charter revisions enacted in 1975 and still in effect today.

Lindsay was interested in this work (especially the Urban Design Group, about which he felt proprietary and whose individual architects he kept in close touch). For me, he was encouraging and supportive and I particularly admired his sense of humor and his ability to laugh at himself in times of difficulty, a refreshing trait for a political leader, which helped enhance the respect of his team and taught us by example how to weather times of tension.■

John Zuccotti served as First Deputy Mayor under Mayor Abraham Beame and is Chairman of Brookfield Financial Properties. To commemorate his work after 9/11, Zuccotti Park in Lower Manhattan was named in his honor.

CHRONOLOGY

PRE-MAYORALTY

1921-1960

November 24, 1921 John Vliet Lindsay (JVL) and twin brother, David, born in New York City. Educated at Buckley School, Manhattan, then St. Paul's, Concord, New Hampshire.

October 29, 1929 Stock market crash begins the Great Depression.

August 26, 1930 Judge Samuel Seabury initially appointed to investigate corruption of police and courts in New York City, then broadens to city government of Mayor "Gentleman Jimmy" Walker, which results in his resignation on January 1, 1932.

March 25, 1931 Nine black teenagers, known as the Scottsboro Boys, arrested in Alabama for allegedly raping two white women. Found guilty in three trials with flimsy evidence, the case dramatized the injustice of all-white juries.

November 8, 1932 New York State Governor Franklin D. Roosevelt (Democrat) defeats incumbent Herbert Hoover (Republican) for president; re-elected in 1936, 1940 and 1944.

January 30, 1933 Adolph Hitler sworn in as Chancellor of Germany.

March 4, 1933 FDR inaugurated as President in the depths of the Depression, stating, "The only thing we have to fear is fear itself.

November 7, 1933 Fiorello La Guardia (Republican) defeats Democratic incumbent John O'Brien to become New York City Mayor; reelected 1937 and 1941.

November 3, 1936 FDR re-elected President in landslide over Kansas Governor Alf Landon, carrying all but two states (Maine and Vermont) with 60.8% of the vote; at inauguration states: "I see one-third of a nation ill-housed, ill-clad, ill-nourished."

November 9, 1938 Kristallnacht, when Nazis terrorize Jewish neighborhoods in Germany and Austria, breaking windows and setting fires.

April 14, 1939 John Steinbeck's "Grapes of Wrath" published, a searing portrait of the Joad family, tenant farmers from Oklahoma ("Okies") forced to flee the drought and Depression-hardship of the Dust Bowl for California. Movie version starring Henry Fonda opens in 1940.

April 30, 1939 1939 World's Fair opens in Flushing Meadows, Queens, with the park newly planned and rebuilt by Robert Moses. Forty-four million attend over two years.

September 1, 1939 Germany invades Poland one week after signing the Molotov-Ribbentrop Non-Aggression Pact with the Soviet Union. Two days later, Great Britain and France declare war on Germany, marking the beginning of World War II.

June 24-28, 1940 Eighteen-year-old JVL and his twin brother David work as pages at the Republican National Convention in Philadelphia, where Wendell L. Willkie secures the party's nomination.

July 10, 1940 The German air force (Luftwaffe) launches the Battle of Britain with more than three months of bombing raids. The Blitz of London kills 40,000

	civilians and destroys one million homes in 57 consecutive days of bombing.
November 5, 1940	FDR re-elected to third term as President over New Yorker Wendell Willkie (Republican); in his State of the Union, FDR describes Four Freedoms that people "everywhere in the world" ought to enjoy: freedom of speech, of worship, from want, from fear.
December 7, 1941	Japanese air forces attack the U.S. Naval installation at Pearl Harbor, Hawaii, called a "date that will live in infamy" by FDR when war is declared the next day. On December 11, Hitler's Germany declares war on the U.S.
June 6, 1943	JVL graduates early from Yale, receives commission in U.S. Navy.
1943-1946	JVL serves as gunnery officer on USS *Swanson* during Allied invasion of Sicily; after *Swanson* is transferred to Pacific, takes part in invasion of Philippines. In March 1946 leaves navy as a lieutenant and *Swanson's* executive officer.
June 6, 1944	D-Day as the Allies launch the Invasion of Normandy, which begins the liberation of Europe from the Nazis.
November 7, 1944	FDR re-elected to fourth term as President over NYS Governor Thomas Dewey (Republican).
January 27, 1945	Soviet troops liberate Auschwitz concentration camp; U.S. troops then liberate Buchenwald (April 11) and Dachau (April 29).
February 4, 1945	FDR, Churchill and Stalin meet at Yalta to discuss the boundaries of Europe after WWII.

April 12, 1945   FDR dies at Warm Springs, GA. Vice President Harry Truman becomes President.

May 7, 1945   Germany signs surrender ending WWII in Europe, eight days after Hitler commits suicide as Russian troops enter Berlin.

May 26, 1945   After guiding Great Britain to victory through the hardships of World War II, Winston Churchill's Conservative Party is thrown out in a surprise election upset.

August 6, 1945   US drops atomic bombs on Hiroshima, Japan, then Nagasaki on August 9. Japan announces surrender on August 15, ending World War II.

November 20, 1945   Nuremberg Trials begin, with U.S. prosecuting senior Nazi officials, including Hermann Goering, Albert Speer, and Rudolf Hess, for crimes against humanity. Creates precedent for international war crimes trials.

March 5, 1946   In a speech at Westminster College in Missouri, Winston Churchill declares that an "iron curtain" has descended across the continent of Europe.

April 15, 1947   Jackie Robinson playing for the Brooklyn Dodgers breaks the color barrier in baseball, spotlighting the issue of race as never before in the modern era.

January 30, 1948   Mahatma Gandhi, leader of the Indian independence movement against Britain is assassinated. (India had become independent in August 1947). Gandhi's non-violent principles are later followed by Martin Luther King and Nelson Mandela.

May 18, 1948   State of Israel declares independence, following 1947 U.N. vote that divides Palestine. David Ben-Gurion becomes first President.

June 20, 1948	JVL graduates from Yale Law School and joins law firm of Webster, Sheffield, Fleischmann, Hitchcock & Chrystie in NYC.
June 26, 1948	U.S. begins Berlin Airlift to overcome Soviet land blockade preventing deliveries by road to West Berlin.
September 14, 1948	Ground is broken for the new United Nations headquarters in New York on the site of a former slaughterhouse on the East River at 42nd Street.
November 2, 1948	President Truman, in stunning upset, defeats NYS Governor Thomas Dewey (Republican).
April 4, 1949	North Atlantic Treaty signed by U.S., Canada and ten European nations, creating NATO.
June 18, 1949	JVL marries Mary Anne Harrison of Greenwich, CT. They rent an apartment in Stuyvesant Town.
December 10, 1949	Chiang Kai-Shek and his government, driven from the Chinese mainland by Communist insurgents led by Mao Zedong, flee to the Island of Taiwan, which the U.S. recognizes as the Republic of China for thirty years until 1979.
June 26, 1950	North Korean troops invade South Korea, provoking a United Nations "police action" primarily carried out by American troops as the Korean War.
August 31, 1950	Under investigation, Mayor O'Dwyer resigns and is appointed ambassador to Mexico by President Truman; succeeded by Vincent Impellitteri as acting Mayor.
November 7, 1950	Mayor Impellitteri is denied the Democratic nomination but wins a special election as an

independent, the first time a Mayor is elected without running on one of the two major party lines. (The only other time is John Lindsay's 1969 re-election.)

1951

JVL becomes active in Republican politics. Visits Paris to urge retired five-star General Dwight D. Eisenhower (Commander of Allied Forces in Europe during WWII, and first Supreme Commander of NATO) to run for president; volunteers in Ike's campaign. With brother David, helps found Youth for Eisenhower.

June 16, 1952

"The Diary of Anne Frank," first published in Holland in 1947 in Dutch, is issued in the U.S. in English; personalizes the devastation of the Holocaust to millions of Americans.

November 4, 1952

Eisenhower elected president (Republican), defeating Democrat Adlai Stevenson; re-elected in 1956.

JVL becomes president of New York Young Republicans.

March 5, 1953

Soviet Union dictator Joseph Stalin dies in Moscow after ruling brutally for 30 years, but persevering through the vast destruction and hardship of the German invasion to victory in WWII.

November 3, 1953

Robert Wagner, Jr. (Democrat) elected Mayor; reelected 1957 and 1961.

March 9, 1954

On CBS's "See It Now," Edward R. Murrow criticizes Wisconsin Senator Joseph R. McCarthy's campaign against alleged Communists in government.

March 16, 1954

Army-McCarthy hearings convened with seven weeks of gavel-to-gavel television coverage, the first demonstration of television's power to impact political events. Contributes to downfall of Senator McCarthy.

May 7, 1954

French forces defeated at Dien Bien Phu, marking the end of French domination of Indochina. A precursor of U.S. military involvement in Vietnam a decade later.

May 17, 1954

Chief Justice Earl Warren delivers unanimous Supreme Court ruling in *Brown v. Board of Education*, outlawing segregation in public schools.

January 14, 1955

Eisenhower's attorney general, Herbert Brownell, appoints JVL his executive assistant; JVL works on immigration issues for Hungarian refugees in 1956, and the 1957 Civil Rights Act.

April 12, 1955

Dr. Jonas Salk announces polio vaccine.

August 28, 1955

Emmett Till, a 14-year old black boy from Chicago visiting family in Mississippi, is murdered for allegedly flirting with a white woman. News photos of Till's open casket profoundly impact public opinion, spurring the civil rights movement.

December 1, 1955

Rosa Parks arrested for refusing to surrender her seat to a white passenger on a Birmingham bus. Provokes the Birmingham Bus Boycott for more than a year, with involvement of Martin Luther King, Jr. Ultimately won when the U.S. Supreme Court overturns laws imposing bus segregation.

June 29, 1956

The Federal Aid Highway Act, advocated by President Eisenhower, is enacted, launching the Interstate Highway System.

March 6, 1957

Ghana becomes the first sub-Saharan African nation to gain independence, with Kwame Nk rumah as first president. An inspiration for U.S. civil rights movement.

September 24, 1957 President Eisenhower dispatches 1,000 101st Airborne troops and federalizes 10,000 Arkansas National Guard to protect nine black students entering Little Rock's Central High School.

September 24, 1957 Brooklyn Dodgers play last game at Ebbets Field before moving to Los Angeles, while New York Giants move to San Francisco. The loss has a profound impact on the psyche of New York, while symbolizing the accelerating growth of the West.

October 4, 1957 Soviet Union launches *Sputnik*, the first space satellite, initiating the Space Race with the United States. Generates a sense of crisis regarding America's scientific and technological capacity and fear of Soviet supremacy in space.

September 2, 1958 In response to *Sputnik* crisis, President Eisenhower signs the National Defense Education Act providing massive funding of technology, science, and languages.

November 4, 1958 JVL elected to Congress as a Republican from 17th ("Silk Stocking") District on Manhattan's East Side; defeats Democrat Tony Akers after winning Republican primary in August over Elliot Goodwin. JVL re-elected three times and serves seven years in the House, defeating Democrat William vanden Heuvel (1960), Democrat Martin Dworkis (1962), and Democrat Eleanor C. French and Conservative Kieran O'Doherty (1964). He works closely with the Democratic Administration on creation of a federal Department of Housing and Urban Development (HUD) and passage of 1964 Civil Rights Act, 1965 Voting Rights Act, and 1965 immigration reform.

Nelson Rockefeller (Republican) defeats incumbent Governor Averell Harriman (Democrat) to become NYS Governor; reelected 1962, 1966, 1970.

February 16, 1959

Fidel Castro becomes Prime Minister of Cuba, after U.S. ally General Fulgencio Batista flees

May 14, 1959

President Eisenhower and John D. Rockefeller III break ground for Lincoln Center for the Performing Arts.

March 21, 1960

The Sharpeville Massacre, where South African police kill 69 blacks protesting the pass book laws of the apartheid system.

July 12, 1960

"To Kill a Mockingbird" published, dramatizing racial inequality. Written by Harper Lee, and winner of the Pulitzer Prize, becomes a movie classic in 1962, starring Gregory Peck as the heroic Atticus Finch.

November 8, 1960

John F. Kennedy (Democrat) elected president over Vice President Richard M. Nixon (Republican).

1961

January 17

President Eisenhower gives farewell address warning of the influence of the military-industrial complex.

January 20

JFK inaugurated, "Ask not what your country can do for you, ask what you can do for your country."

March 1

Peace Corps established by President Kennedy, becoming the symbol of his attracting a generation of young people to public service.

April 17	1400 Cuban exiles, with CIA support, launch disastrous Bay of Pigs invasion of Cuba, poisoning U.S.-Cuban relations for over 50 years.
August 13	Soviets begin construction of Berlin Wall, preventing East Germans from entering West Germany.
September 13	New Yorker Jane Jacobs, opponent of the development policies of Robert Moses, publishes *The Life and Death of Great American Cities*, challenging the "rationalism" of professional city planners.

1962

March	Michael Harrington publishes *The Other America*, estimating that up to 25 percent of the nation is living in poverty. Believed to have inspired President Lyndon Johnson's War on Poverty.
April 16	CBS starts first daily national half-hour news broadcast anchored by Walter Cronkite, who becomes the dominant broadcaster of the era.
July 3	French President Charles de Gaulle declares Algeria independent, ending the eight-year war against French colonial rule.
September 29	"Silent Spring" by Rachel Carson published, a powerful description of the devastating impact of chemical pesticides and the beginning of broad public recognition of environmental concerns.
October 1	James Meredith becomes first black to attend University of Mississippi, which provokes rioting with two deaths. 500 federal marshals deployed by Attorney General Robert Kennedy, plus U.S. Army and federalized National Guard.

October 15

Cuban Missile Crisis begins thirteen days of international tension that seemingly brings the world to the brink of nuclear disaster until Kennedy and Khrushchev reach secret agreement to remove missiles from Cuba.

1963

February 19

Betty Friedan publishes *The Feminine Mystique,* forcefully articulating the rationale for the Women's Movement.

April 16

Martin Luther King, Jr. arrested during the campaign to desegregate Birmingham, AL, issues his "Letter from Birmingham Jail" making the argument for nonviolent resistance to racism.

June 10

Alabama Governor George Wallace stands in the doorway to block black students from entering the University of Alabama, symbolizing his pledge of "segregation now, segregation tomorrow, segregation forever." Steps aside when confronted by U.S. Department of Justice and federalized National Guard.

June 26

President Kennedy speaks in front of the Berlin Wall two years after its construction, declaring "Ich bin ein Berliner" ("I am a Berliner").

August 28

Hundreds of thousands March on Washington to protest racial segregation in the South. Martin Luther King, Jr. delivers "I Have a Dream" speech from Lincoln Memorial.

September 15

16th Street Baptist Church in Birmingham, AL, dynamited, killing four young black girls. No one arrested for over a decade.

October 18

Demolition of New York's Penn Station begins, to be replaced by Madison Square Garden.

Spurs landmark preservation movement.

October 26

Bob Dylan performs "The Times They Are a-Changin'" at Carnegie Hall; released in January 1964 as the title song for his third album, expressing a deep sense of social unrest.

November 22

President Kennedy killed by Lee Harvey Oswald, while riding in an open car in a motorcade in Dallas; Vice President Lyndon Johnson becomes president.

1964

January 8

President Johnson launches "War on Poverty" in his first State of the Union address to the Congress; becomes a central component of LBJ's Great Society.

February 9

The Beatles appear on the *Ed Sullivan Show*.

March 6

After defeating Sonny Liston for the World Heavyweight Championship, Black Muslim Cassius Clay becomes Muhammad Ali.

March 26

Barbra Streisand opens in *Funny Girl* on Broadway (with her signature song "People"), a role she reprised in 1968 movie version.

June 12

Nelson Mandela sentenced to life in prison in South Africa after the Rivonia Trial. He is released after twenty-seven years, mostly served on Robben Island off Cape Town.

June 22

Civil rights workers Andrew Goodman, Michael Schwerner, and James Chaney murdered by the Ku Klux Klan in Philadelphia, MS, during "Freedom Summer" campaign to register black voters. Following national outrage, the FBI launches a massive investigation (called "Mississippi Burning") and finds bodies 44 days later.

June 24   Palestine Liberation Organization (PLO) formed.

July 2   President Lyndon Johnson signs the comprehensive Civil Rights Act of 1964 into law, with its key provision prohibiting discrimination in "public accommodations." JVL plays major role in Congressional enactment.

July 15   Senator Barry Goldwater (AZ), who defeated Governor Nelson Rockefeller in the California Republican primary, accepts nomination in San Francisco and declares "extremism in the defense of liberty is no vice and moderation in the pursuit of justice is no virtue." JVL and a few other moderate Republicans refuse to endorse Goldwater.

July 16   An off-duty New York City white police officer fatally shoots a 15-year-old black youth, setting off four days of riots in Harlem and Bedford-Stuyvesant.

August 7   Gulf of Tonkin Resolution passed by Congress, beginning full-fledged U.S. involvement in Vietnam War.

September 22   *Fiddler on the Roof*—written by Sheldon Harnick and Jerry Bock, produced by Hal Prince, choreographed by Jerome Robbins, and starring Zero Mostel—opens on Broadway at the Imperial Theatre; closes in 1972, the first Broadway show to have more than 3,000 performances.

October 14   Martin Luther King, Jr. receives Nobel Peace Prize.

November 3   President Johnson (Democrat) wins landslide reelection (61 percent of vote) over Republican Senator Barry Goldwater. Robert F. Kennedy elected senator from New York State.

1965

January 25

New York Herald Tribune starts "New York City in Crisis" series documenting the city's ills under three-term Mayor Robert F. Wagner, Jr.

February 21

Malcolm X assassinated in Audubon Ballroom in Washington Heights, Manhattan. Later that year, his autobiography is published, expressing his philosophy of black pride and black nationalism through his dramatic life story.

March 2

"The Sound of Music" film opens, starring Julie Andrews and Christopher Plummer, based on the 1959 Broadway show by Richard Rogers and Oscar Hammerstein.

March 7

"Bloody Sunday" in Selma, AL; State troopers attack 600 peaceful civil rights marchers led by John Lewis as they walk over the Edmund Pettus Bridge; President Johnson proposes a Voting Rights Act before a Joint Session of Congress on March 15, promising that "We shall overcome." On March 21, protected by 2,000 U.S. Army troops and 1,900 federalized Alabama National Guard, the 54-mile march from Selma to Birmingham begins.

April 24

In a speech at Oakland University in Michigan, JVL calls for an international commission to seek an immediate cease-fire in Vietnam. Lindsay is only the third member of Congress to speak in opposition to the war, after Senators Ernest Gruening (D-AK) and Wayne Morse (D-OR).

THE MAYORAL CAMPAIGN

May 13 JVL declares he will run as Republican candidate for Mayor, with endorsements from Republicans Governor Nelson Rockefeller and U.S. Senator Jacob K. Javits. Campaign managed by Bob Price, who managed Lindsay's four congressional campaigns, with David Garth as media advisor. Campaign mounts massive field operation, with 123 storefronts in all neighborhoods, thousands of volunteers, powerful cinema verite TV commercials, and poster of Lindsay in shirtsleeves captioned, "He is fresh and everyone else is tired."

May 21 In his first major campaign speech, JVL calls for the creation of a Civilian Complaint Review Board to examine allegations of police misconduct, which becomes a highly controversial and racially charged issue.

June 6 Rolling Stones release "(I Can't Get No) Satisfaction" written by Mick Jagger and Keith Richards.

June 10 Mayor Wagner announces he will not run for a fourth term.

June 28 Liberal Party endorses JVL, who creates a fusion ticket with Liberal Timothy Costello as candidate for City Council President and Democrat Milton Mollen for Comptroller.

June 29 Five thousand off-duty police officers picket City Hall to protest proposed civilian review board. President Johnson announces the deployment of 50,000 troops to Vietnam, followed the next day by anti-war demonstration at New York's Whitehall Street Army Induction Center, with

	burning of draft cards; and a rally two days later of anti-war demonstrators (and counterdemonstrators) in Times Square.
August 6	President Johnson signs Voting Rights Act. JVL plays major role in Congressional deliberations.
August 11-17	Riots break out in Watts district of Los Angeles, California. Worst race riot since 1943 in Detroit.
October 3	President Johnson signs Immigration Reform Act, opening immigration beyond favored Northern Europeans to Asians, Africans, South Americans, and Southern Europeans.
October 31	Democratic District Leader Edward I. Koch endorses Lindsay, front-page coverage on eve of election.
November 2	JVL elected Mayor on the Republican and Liberal tickets, with 43.3 percent over Democrat Abraham D. Beame (39.5 percent) and Conservative William F. Buckley, Jr. (12.9 percent).
November 22	*Man of La Mancha*, with Richard Kiley singing "To Dream the Impossible Dream," opens at ANTA Washington Square Theatre, and runs until 1971 (2,328 performances).
November 23	JVL's first cabinet appointment: Robert O. Lowery as the city's first black fire commissioner.
December 31	Report of Mayor-elect's Law Enforcement Task Force recommends modernization of police records and systems, court reform and efficiencies, and a Civilian Complaint Review Board.
	U.S. now has 180,000 troops in Vietnam.

THE MAYORAL
YEARS
(1966-1973)

1966

January 1

JVL delivers first inaugural address from steps of City Hall. Transit Workers' Union (TWU) strikes, shutting down subways and buses for two weeks. Massive traffic jams starting at 4 a.m.; millions walk to work. TWU leader Mike Quill, in a gesture of contempt, intentionally garbles Lindsay's name, calling him "Mr. Lindsley."

Simon and Garfunkel's "The Sound of Silence" becomes number one.

January 4

Quill and eight other TWU strike leaders are sent to the Civil Jail for leading an illegal work stoppage by public employees; Quill dies of heart attack on January 28.

January 23

Indira Gandhi becomes third prime minister of India. Lindsay hosts dinner for her at Lincoln Center on March 30, signaling a move from traditional meals in hotel ballrooms to dramatic celebrations at cultural institutions.

February 1

I.S. 201 opens in Harlem and becomes the focal point for the emerging movement for community control of schools.

February 12

JVL proposes state legislation to combine the Triborough Bridge and Tunnel Authority with the Transit Authority so that car tolls could be used to finance the subways, an attack on the long-standing pro-auto, anti-mass transit policy of Robert Moses. It fails but the concept becomes the basis for the MTA enacted in 1968.

JVL agrees to meet monthly with twenty-eight-member board of the Economic Development Council, a new business organization formed to deal with the city's faltering economy.

February 16   JVL appoints Howard Leary from Philadelphia as police commissioner.

February 25   Police Commissioner Leary appoints Lloyd Sealy as assistant chief inspector, the first black officer to attain that senior rank. Rapidly followed by appointment of two other blacks to senior field command positions, Eldridge Waithe and Arthur Hill.

March 2   New York becomes the first city to open a Washington office to lobby and gain federal grants.

March 21   JVL creates NYC Urban Corps, modeled after JFK's Peace Corps, part of Lindsay's broad effort to attract and recruit young people to public service with the City government.

March 26   To stem loss of businesses and jobs, JVL creates Public Development Corporation (PDC) to assist businesses locating in New York. In 1991 PDC made part of Economic Development Corporation (EDC).

May 12   Governor Rockefeller announces plan to create Battery Park City on landfill in the Hudson River.

May 13   In testimony before a U.S. Senate subcommittee, Timothy Leary estimates that one-third of American college students are "experimenting" with LSD.

May 17   Police Commissioner Leary creates a seven-member (four civilians, three police officials) Civilian Complaint Review Board (CCRB).

May 31	JVL issues Executive Order No. 10, creating the Mayor's Film Office and streamlining red tape for movie making, which leads to significant increase in movies shot in NYC. The same procedures remain in effect today, 49 years later.
June 1	JVL launches pilot project on Bowery with the Vera Institute of Justice, with police bringing alcoholics to a Detox Center rather than jail. Becomes Manhattan Bowery Project in 1967. Continues today as Project Renewal.
June 5	JVL and Parks Commissioner Thomas Hoving close Central Park to automobiles on weekends, despite strong opposition from Traffic Commissioner Henry Barnes, taxis and auto advocates. Soon repeated in other parks and remains a fixture today in New York and cities around the world.
June 6	Senator Robert Kennedy delivers "Ripple of Hope" speech at the University of Cape Town, considered by many to be his finest, and an inspiration to the anti-Apartheid movement.
June 19	Student Nonviolent Coordinating Committee (SNCC) leader Stokely Carmichael and others first use the term "Black Power" in Mississippi and suggest that nonviolence is no longer the answer to racism and discrimination; deplored by Martin Luther King, Jr.
June 25	U.S. Government closes Brooklyn Navy Yard: nine thousand jobs lost.
June 30	U.S. Army leaves Governors Island after 150 years, turns it over to the U.S. Coast Guard.
	National Organization for Women (NOW) formed in Washington, D.C. by Betty Friedan, Shirley Chisholm, and others.

July 1

NY State Legislature and Governor Nelson Rockefeller, after much dispute, approve JVL's proposed city income tax (still in effect) and a historic commuter tax, which lasted 33 years until 1999.

July 5

To finance the settlement of the transit strike, subway and bus fares increase from 15 cents to 20 cents (lasts until 1970).

July 7

The Patrolman's Benevolent Association (PBA) and the new Conservative Party deliver 51,000 signatures to the City Clerk to place a referendum challenging the Civilian Complaint Review Board (CCRB) on the November ballot. Their campaign plays on fears of crime and heightens racial tensions.

July 19

Racial tensions between black and white youth erupt in East New York (Brooklyn). JVL visits area, meets with both sides. Lindsay begins regular walks in minority neighborhoods, which creates a visible presence and symbol of government concern and outreach to distressed communities.

July 21

14-year-old black youth Eric Dean is shot in East New York. Police move 1,000 officers into the area, keep the peace, and fire no shots, the first test of Lindsay and Leary's new policy of police restraint.

August 1

JVL appoints Frederick Hayes as budget director. Comes from the federal government with extensive experience in sophisticated budgeting and information systems, beginning a new era of modern municipal management.

August 5

Groundbreaking for the World Trade Center.

August 10	JVL opens first two Little City Halls in Brooklyn's Brownsville and East New York to test his plan to coordinate city services at the local level and monitor community tensions, using city space and private funds. This begins JVL's effort to decentralize city government, replacing the role of the Democratic organization with a non-partisan structure reaching into all communities.
August 13	Chairman Mao Zedong launches Cultural Revolution in China.
August 23	Beatles give concert at Shea Stadium.
September 16	New 3,000-seat Metropolitan Opera House opens at Lincoln Center with performance of Samuel Barber's "Antony and Cleopatra." With a threatened orchestra strike, Met General Manager Rudolph Bing announces settlement before third act. Beloved old Met Opera at 39th Street, opened in 1883, is demolished in 1967.
October 15	Black Panthers founded in Oakland, California.
November 8	Lindsay suffers major electoral defeat as voters reject the controversial CCRB by an overwhelming 63-to-37 percent margin.
	Governor Nelson Rockefeller elected to third term.
November 15	JVL announces his plan to reorganize and streamline the city government, consolidating fifty-three city agencies into 10 superagencies, modeled after the federal cabinet structure.
November 20	*Cabaret* by John Kander and Fred Ebb opens at Broadhurst Theatre, starring Joel Grey and produced and directed by Hal Prince. Becomes a movie in 1972, starring Grey and Liza Minnelli.

November 22	Lindsay appoints Walter Washington as Chair of the NYC Housing Authority. In August 1967, President Johnson appoints Washington as first Mayor-Commissioner of the District of Columbia, who then becomes the first elected Mayor of D.C. in 1975.
November 28	Truman Capote hosts Black and White Ball at Plaza Hotel.
December 14	JVL halts construction of Richmond Expressway route chosen by Robert Moses, which cuts through wooded areas; selects alternative route that preserves the Staten Island Greenbelt, which today includes 2,800 acres of forested hills and wetlands.
December 20	JVL supports Waterside Housing Complex on a platform in the East River at East 23rd Street.
December 31	United States now has 385,000 troops in Vietnam.

1967

January 4	JVL proposes bill to create a network of city-funded Little City Halls to coordinate services in neighborhoods across the city, integral to his plan to decentralize City government. Democrats in City Council refuse to approve.
January 27	Three astronauts die in flash fire of *Apollo* rocket on launch pad.
February 7	Lindsay gets federal government to sell Brooklyn Navy Yard to the City.

Task Force on Urban Design, led by CBS Chair William Paley, releases "The Threatened City" (the Paley Report), which detailed the quality of the city's architecture and design. Results in creation of pioneering Urban Design Group and development offices reporting directly to the Mayor for Midtown, Downtown, Downtown Brooklyn, Staten Island, and Jamaica, Queens.

March 27

In response to president's Crime Commission report, JVL creates nation's first Criminal Justice Coordinating Council, bringing together police, prosecutors, judges, correction officials and business leaders, with agencies sharing data and sponsoring joint programs.

April 15

Rev. Martin Luther King, Jr., Dr. Benjamin Spock, and Harry Belafonte lead 100,000 people in an antiwar march from Central Park to the UN.

April 27

In advance of long hot summer, JVL announces Citizens Summer Committee, led by Andrew Heiskell, chair of Time Inc., and former Parks Commissioner Tom Hoving, which raises private funds for summer youth programs. He establishes the Mayor's Urban Action Task Force under aide Barry Gottehrer to monitor conditions and lead outreach in unstable communities.

April 29

JVL appoints McGeorge Bundy of the Ford Foundation to chair an advisory panel on school decentralization.

May 2

Phoenix House is launched under Dr. Mitchell Rosenthal, which becomes one of the largest drug addiction treatment programs in the nation.

May 13

"Support Our Boys in Vietnam" march down Fifth Avenue draws 70,000.

May 23 Paley Park opens on East 53rd Street as the first privately funded vest pocket park.

June Aretha Franklin's "Respect," reaches the top of record charts, transforming the song originally written and recorded by Otis Redding in 1965 into an anthem for women.

June 5 Six Day War begins with preemptive Israeli attack under General Moshe Dayan against Egypt, Jordan and Syria. Israeli forces achieve major gains, taking control of Gaza Strip and Sinai Peninsula from Egypt, the West Bank and East Jerusalem from Jordan, and the Golan Heights from Syria.

June 17 Barbra Streisand concert in Central Park before 150,000, the largest crowd to attend such an event.

June 24 *La Bohème* becomes the first opera performed for free in Central Park by the Metropolitan Opera.

June 27 Electric Circus opens in the East Village with flashing strobe lights, videos, music—a precursor of the discotheque scene.

July 6 The Ford Foundation grants $135,000 to three school districts to experiment with "community control" in East Harlem, the Lower East Side, and Ocean Hill-Brownsville in Brooklyn.

July 12 City Council approves Lindsay's first superagency, the Human Resources Administration (HRA).

July 12-16 Large-scale riots in Newark with looting and fires; state police and National Guard called in. Indiscriminate shooting (over 13,000 rounds by police and Guardsmen) kills twenty-three people.

July 19	At Lindsay's insistence, the first air-conditioned subway train is put in service on the F line. It takes twenty-five years to convert the entire fleet.
July 22-25	Disturbances begin in East Harlem after a police officer shoots a youth. Brief outbreaks follow the next week in Bedford-Stuyvesant; disorders flare again during early September in Brownsville.
July 23-30	Devastating riots in Detroit, with U.S. Army paratroopers finally called in to support exhausted police and National Guard. Forty-two people killed and 7,000 arrests.
July 27	Facing national wave of urban riots, the worst domestic disorder in 100 years since the Civil War Draft Riots, President Johnson appoints the eleven-member National Advisory Commission on Civil Disorders (the Kerner Commission) to investigate the causes of urban riots. JVL appointed vice chairman.
August 3-5	Ocean Hill-Brownsville holds election for governing board for experimental community-controlled school district.
August 21	In Washington, D.C., a mass anti-Vietnam War march ends at the door of the Pentagon; many New Yorkers take part, with celebrated gesture of protesters putting flowers in soldiers' gun barrels.
September 25	*Bonnie and Clyde* opens, starring Warren Beatty and Faye Dunaway, directed by Arthur Penn.
October 2	President Johnson appoints Thurgood Marshall as the first black justice on the Supreme Court.

October 17	*Hair* opens at Joe Papp's new Public Theater, moves six months later to Broadway at the Biltmore Theatre; inaugurates the rock musical and heralds the "Age of Aquarius," celebrating hippie culture, drugs, nudity and anti-war protests.
December 2	Francis Cardinal Spellman dies after twenty-eight years as archbishop of New York, longest tenure ever, during which he became a major force for political and cultural conservatism; replaced by Terrence Cardinal Cooke.
December 4	During a weeklong anti-war protest at Whitehall Street Army Induction Center, City Hall aides guide protesters from Whitehall to Union Square. Some elected officials criticize City Hall for "interfering" with the police and call for firing of Lindsay aides Barry Gottehrer and Sid Davidoff.
December 7	Lindsay's plan for a Special Theater Zoning District is adopted, with incentives that produce three new theaters, first in 40 years, and 54-story One Astor Place, intended to spur the rebirth of Times Square.
December 13	City Council approves Lindsay's second super-agency, Health Services Administration (HSA).
December 18	Water Commissioner James Marcus indicted by District Attorney Frank Hogan for accepting a $40,000 bribe for a contract to clean the Jerome Park Reservoir.
December 21	*The Graduate*, starring Dustin Hoffman and Anne Bancroft and directed by Mike Nichols, opens in theaters.
December 31	United States now has 485,000 troops in Vietnam.

1968

January 8

JVL signs a bill creating the nation's first Environmental Protection Administration (EPA), his third superagency. Additional superagencies created include Economic Development Administration (EDA), Housing and Development (HDA), Parks, Recreation and Cultural Affairs (PRCA), and Municipal Services Administration (MSA), transforming the structure of city government which, while much modified, remains the basic format of the Mayor's Cabinet today.

January 30

Tet Offensive is launched as surprise attack by North Vietnamese and the Vietcong, shocking the American public by their capacity to mount a major campaign and dashing hopes that the United States can achieve its goals in Vietnam anytime soon.

February 2-10

Sanitationmen go on strike. Governor Nelson Rockefeller resists Lindsay's request that the National Guard be deployed to help collect accumulating garbage, sparking a conflict between the two Republicans that will continue through their careers. Sanitation union leader John DeLury goes to jail for violating the Taylor Law, enacted in 1967 after the transit strike to prevent work stoppages by public employee unions.

February 27

Following a visit to Vietnam, Walter Cronkite reports on CBS that the war is unwinnable and that "the bloody expense of Vietnam is to end in a stalemate." As "the most trusted man in America," Cronkite's pronouncement has major impact on turning public opinion against the war.

February 27

The Kerner Commission report is released condemning excessive police force and calling for police restraint and massive investment in cities. Declares: "our nation is moving towards two societies, one Black and one White—separate and unequal." Lindsay perceived as driving force behind the report, which is still viewed as a landmark description of the history and condition of race in America, and remains the basic blueprint for police-minority relations and restrained use of force in responding to urban disturbances.

March 1 Metropolitan Transportation Authority (MTA) created by the state as a regional transportation agency that combines subway, bus, commuter rail, and bridges, and adopts Lindsay's concept of using road tolls for mass transit. This marks the end of Robert Moses's long dominance of regional transportation with his emphasis on cars and roads instead of rail.

March 8 Fillmore East opens in the East Village, becomes premier rock concert venue on East Coast.

March 12 Senator Eugene McCarthy (MN) wins the New Hampshire Democratic presidential primary over incumbent President Johnson with a startling 42 percent to 29 percent victory.

March 18 Senator Robert F. Kennedy announces his candidacy for the Democratic presidential nomination.

March 19 JVL denounces the Vietnam War in a speech at Queens College.

March 22 Abbie Hoffman's Yip-In in Grand Central Station; 3,000-6,000 Yippies and Hippies converge; the station is cleared by police.

March 31 President Johnson makes surprise announcement that he will not run for reelection.

Democratic contest is now between Senators Kennedy and McCarthy and Vice President Hubert Humphrey.

April 4

Rev. Martin Luther King, Jr. assassinated by James Earl Ray in Memphis, TN, where he had gone to support striking black sanitationmen. Rioting occurs in minority communities across the nation, including Harlem; JVL goes to Harlem where he calms crowds as New York is once again relatively stable. Robert F. Kennedy, in Indiana to campaign for the Democratic primary, addresses grieving crowd.

April 8

First issue of New York magazine published.

April 22

JVL insists that York College be located in Jamaica, Queens, business district to spur development of deteriorated area.

April 23-30

Columbia University students begin protests over construction of gym in nearby Harlem park, expressing racial concerns and opposition to Vietnam War. Thousands of students occupy multiple buildings and disrupt the university. On April 30, 120 students injured when NYPD clears occupied buildings.

April 23-30

JVL and Governor Rockefeller announce memorandum of understanding to allow Battery Park City to be built on landfill.

April 27

Massive anti-war demonstration in Sheep Meadow in Central Park and Loyalty Day Parade supporting the troops on Fifth Avenue; JVL appears at both.

May 6-13

Parisian students begin massive protest, clash with riot police at the Sorbonne; joined by French trade unions in a general strike on May

	13, signaling growing worldwide youth dissatis-faction and protest.
May 8	Ocean Hill-Brownsville governing board dismisses thirteen teachers and six administrators; on May 22, union teachers walk out in sympathy.
May 23	City launches "Give a Damn" campaign created by Y&R advertising agency to promote concern for disadvantaged communities.
June 5	Senator Robert F. Kennedy assassinated in Los Angeles by Sirhan Sirhan moments after declaring victory in the California Democratic primary.
June 21	JVL breaks ground for Westbeth, nation's largest affordable live-work space for artists in reused industrial buildings in Greenwich Village, first project by architect Richard Meier. Opens in 1970.
July 1	NYC introduces the nation's first "911" police emergency number supported by advanced computerized communication center; every officer on patrol to be equipped with miniature walkie-talkie.
July 10	Fifteen hundred youth protest at City Hall for summer jobs; some jump on car of a Queens councilman, who accuses Mayor of ordering police not to act.
August 5	First Jewish Defense League (JDL) demonstration at NYU. JDL leader Meir Kahane becomes a public figure and, eventually, a Lindsay antagonist.
	Republican Convention in Miami Beach nominates former Vice President Richard Nixon. JVL

seconds the nomination of Maryland Governor Spiro Agnew for vice president, and mentions racial unrest, the plight of cities, and growing opposition to the war as critical issues.

August 21

The USSR and four other Warsaw Pact nations invade Czechoslovakia, ending the excitement of the reform "Prague Spring." Three die in Prague after being fired on by Bulgarian tanks.

August 26-29

In Chicago, the Democratic National Convention nominates Vice President Hubert Humphrey, splitting the party over the Vietnam War. Chicago police club and tear gas protestors and demonstrators in Grant Park; "police riot" is nationally televised. Some dissident leaders—the "Chicago Seven"—are later tried and convicted in federal court in a heavily publicized and politicized trial.

September 6

The United Federation of Teachers (UFT) calls a citywide teachers strike, as union president Albert Shanker demands reinstatement of the thirteen Ocean Hill-Brownsville teachers. Strike lasts two days. Three days later, teachers strike again for six days. A third strike begins on October 14, lasting five weeks. Racial tensions heightened, especially between the black and Jewish communities.

September 10

After three months of jockeying between Governor Rockefeller and Mayor Lindsay, Rockefeller appoints upstate Republican Congressman Charles Goodell to fill the Senate seat of the late Robert F. Kennedy.

JVL establishes nation's first Department of Consumer Affairs; appoints former Miss America, Bronx-born Bess Myerson, commissioner on February 2, 1969.

September 26   The Studio Museum opens in a rented loft on 125th Street, Harlem, the first black fine arts museum in America.

September 28   Placido Domingo debuts at Metropolitan Opera in *Adriana Lecouvreur.*

October 15   During the third teachers strike, JVL speaks at the East Midwood Jewish Center (Brooklyn) to urge understanding of school decentralization. He is unable to finish speech over angry crowd and is forced to leave.

October 16   At Olympic Games in Mexico City, two black American runners give the Black Power salute from the medal stand.

October 29   South Street Seaport given landmark protection. In 1972 Lindsay creates special South Street Zoning District to foster targeted development.

November 5   Republican Richard Nixon defeats Vice President Hubert Humphrey with only 43 percent of the vote, as third-party candidate Alabama Governor George Wallace receives 13 percent.

November 28   Luciano Pavarotti makes debut at Metropolitan Opera in *La Bohème.*

December 24   Colonel Frank Borman, Major William Anders, and Captain James A. Lovell fly around the moon.

December 31   U.S. Troops in Vietnam peak at 536,000.

1969

January 6   Black and Puerto Rican Coalition demonstrates at Queens College demanding control over the SEEK program for minority students; college closed next day. Students ransack college offices and college agrees to appoint protesters' choice as director.

January 12

New York Jets, led by quarterback "Broadway Joe" Namath, defeat the heavily favored Baltimore Colts in Super Bowl III, 16-7.

January 18

Harlem on My Mind exhibition opens at Metropolitan Museum of Art, evokes public discussion of the city's long-standing racial divide.

February 1

The city launches pilot Work Release Program for inmates on Rikers Island under new state legislation.

February 2

Six-volume *Plan for New York City* is released, the first Master Plan produced under the 1938 City Charter requirement, the only attempt to compile a comprehensive plan with a detailed inventory, assessment and priorities for each of 62 community boards.

February 3

Yasser Arafat elected head of the Palestinian Liberation Organization (PLO).

February 9

The Great Snowstorm: with an unexpected 15 inches of snow, streets in Queens remain impassable for four days. JVL is confronted by enraged residents when he walks through Queens on February 12.

February 13

Black and Puerto Rican students briefly occupy offices at City College. Vandalism occurs on February 17; the college is closed temporarily.

March 18

JVL announces run for reelection as Mayor on the Republican ticket; endorsed by the Liberal Party on April 16.

U.S. bombing of Cambodia provokes national protests.

March 31   Lindsay wins major victory over police union when state legislature reverses 1911 law and gives police commissioner flexibility to assign police to new Fourth Platoon from 6 p.m. to 2 a.m. the hours of greatest need.

April 24   Lincoln Square Zoning District enacted so that future development complements new Lincoln Center.

April 27   State legislature approves Lindsay plan to create an independent Health and Hospitals Corporation to manage city's hospital system, eliminating city red tape and better able to obtain financing and reimbursement.

April 29   Students protest for preferential minority admissions policies and studies programs at Queens, City, and Brooklyn colleges and Manhattan Community College. Clashes between white and black students at City College shut down school on May 7.

April 30   State legislature passes the School Decentralization Act, which divides the city school system into thirty-one (later thirty-two) districts with elected community boards, ending long-time control by the seemingly remote Board of Education located at 110 Livingston Street, Brooklyn.

May 6   To protect tenants from rapidly rising rents, Lindsay's Rent Stabilization Law enacted by City Council places more than one million apartments under rent regulation, that is still in effect.

May 14   JVL announces agreement with federal government for creation of Gateway, including Jamaica Bay and Rockaway beaches, the first urban

National Park, beginning of major federal investment in New York Harbor's recreational facilities
and nature sites.

May 17   Leonard Bernstein's last concert as conductor
of the New York Philharmonic after a record 939
concerts.

May 25   *Midnight Cowboy* is released, directed by John
Schlesinger and starring Dustin Hoffman and
John Voight, depicting a seedy side of New York
life.

June 17   Mayoral primaries: State Senator John Mar-
chi (113,000 votes) defeats JVL (107,000) for
the Republican nomination; Comptroller Mario
Procaccino (255,000 votes) beats former Mayor
Robert Wagner (224,000), Bronx Borough Presi-
dent Herman Badillo (217,000), author Norman
Mailer (41,000), and Congressman James
Scheuer (39,000) for the Democratic nod.

June 18   Deprived of the Republican nomination, JVL
forms an Independent Party and runs as the
Liberal-Independent candidate, describing New
York's Mayoralty as "the second toughest job in
America." Campaign managed by Dick Aurelio
uses celebrated "Mistakes" TV commercial to
concede errors and show a more humble candidate. Ronnie Eldridge organizes Democrats
for Lindsay and dozens of Democratic electeds
endorse Lindsay's candidacy.

June 27-28   The "Stonewall Riot," where police raid a private
gay club on Christopher Street in early morning
hours, and club patrons fight back, seen as the
beginning of the Gay Liberation Movement.

June 30   Museo del Barrio opens as the city's first Puerto
Rican art museum.

July 9	City University (CUNY) announces open admissions for all city high school graduates beginning September 1970.
July 16	JVL formally ends Robert Moses' plan for the Lower Manhattan Expressway through SoHo
July 20	Neil Armstrong walks on the moon. The three astronauts are later celebrated with a ticker-tape parade up Lower Broadway's "Canyon of Heroes."
July 31	Bella Abzug takes out of a full-page ad in the New York Times for the Taxpayer Campaign for Urban Priorities, calling for an end to the War in Vietnam and supporting Lindsay's candidacy for Mayor. Anti-war rallies held by Women Strike For Peace, led by Abzug, give Lindsay a platform to express his opposition to the war. Abzug later serves two terms in Congress (1973-77).
August 16-19	Woodstock: The "counterculture" music festival is held on a farm in rural New York State.
August 18	The Young Lords protest inadequate sanitation service in East Harlem by dumping and burning garbage, attracting their first press coverage.
September 29 - October 1	A visit by Israeli Prime Minister Golda Meir, American-born and enormously popular, helps JVL's reelection bid with the Jewish community, including a dinner at the Brooklyn Museum, attended by 1,100 guests with a giant sukkah, and a ceremony on the steps of City Hall.
October 15	The Vietnam Moratorium, a nationwide protest against the war in Southeast Asia, is endorsed by JVL and observed throughout New York.
October 16	The "Miracle Mets" win the World Series by beating the Baltimore Orioles at Shea Stadium;

news photos of JVL being doused with champagne in Mets locker room help his reelection bid.

November 4

JVL wins reelection (41.1 percent) over Democrat Mario Procaccino (33.8 percent), Republican John Marchi (22.1 percent) and independent Norman Mailer (3 percent) (running with Jimmy Breslin). Lindsay is the second Mayor since 1898 (along with Vincent Impelleteri in 1950) to be elected without the support of either of the two major parties.

November 10

Sesame Street first broadcast on public television.

November 12

Journalist Seymour Hersh breaks the story of the My Lai massacre of at least 347 South Vietnamese civilians; "My Lai" becomes the symbol of American military abuses in Vietnam.

November 24

Construction begins on 63rd Street Tunnel under East River, a Lindsay and Rockefeller joint project with two subway tracks to Queens (later used by the F train with a station on Roosevelt Island) and two LIRR tracks for future use as East Side Access to Grand Central Station.

December 12

JVL forms The Big Six Mayors of NYS with Albany, Buffalo, Rochester, Syracuse, and Yonkers, who agree for the first time on a joint program for the next Legislative session, including state revenue sharing enacted in 1970.

December 13

Carmine De Sapio, the last Boss of Tammany Hall, convicted of conspiracy; serves two years in federal prison.

December 28

Young Lords occupy First Spanish Methodist Church in East Harlem while demonstrating for free breakfast program

1970

January 1	JVL sworn in and delivers second inaugural address.
	Subway fare increases from 20 cents to 30 cents (lasts two years).
January 5	JVL appoints Robert Morgenthau as Deputy Mayor, after President Nixon forces him out as U.S. Attorney after nine years. Morgenthau later serves as Manhattan District Attorney for 34 years.
	JVL appoints Gordon Chase as health services administrator and directs him to launch attack on lead poisoning. With no medical degree, Chase appointment stirs controversy with health establishment.
January 12	JVL approves start of Third Water Tunnel, the largest construction project in the city's history, needed to allow repair of the first tunnel (1917) and second tunnel (1938). Completion now scheduled for early 2020, after fifty-plus years.
January 14	Leonard Bernstein hosts cocktail party fundraiser for Black Panthers, the symbol of "radical chic."
March 6	Weathermen "bomb lab" on West 11th Street in Greenwich Village blows up, killing three.
March 12	Bombings at the Manhattan corporate offices of IBM, General Telephone and Electronics, and Mobil by an unknown group. Police were tipped by an anonymous call a half hour before; no one hurt.
March 20	Lindsay's plan for the United Nations Development District is enacted.

March 24	Lindsay appoints Eleanor Holmes Norton as Chair of City Human Rights Commission after she sued and beat Lindsay in court on a free speech issue; Commission holds the nation's first hearings on discrimination against women. In 1971, she becomes Executive Assistant to the Mayor. Elected to represent D.C. in Congress in 1991, where she still serves after 24 years.
April 2	JVL speaks at University of California, Berkeley, criticizing Nixon and Agnew for violating basic rights, calling their actions "repression in a business suit."
	Patton starring George C. Scott opens.
April 10	The Beatles break up.
April 11	New York State law legalizing abortions up to the twenty-fourth week of pregnancy, strongly advocated by Lindsay, is signed by Governor Rockefeller, replacing 1830 statute permitting abortions only to save the mother's life.
April 22	The nation's first Earth Day, vigorously supported by Lindsay; thousands committed to the environment converge on Union Square; Lindsay closes Fifth Avenue to vehicular traffic.
April 23	JVL announces creation of a five-member panel, headed by Corporation Counsel J. Lee Rankin, to investigate police corruption in advance of *New York Times* series based on allegations of Detective Frank Serpico that begins on April 25.
April 30	JVL announces $160 million Portman Hotel to spur the revitalization of Times Square. Finally opens fifteen years later, in 1985, as Marriott Marquis.

May 4	Four Kent State students killed by Ohio National Guardsmen during an antiwar protest. More than eighty universities across the country close during May in response to antiwar protests.
May 6-8	"Hard Hat Riot" of construction workers in Lower Manhattan, including those building the World Trade Center, attacking anti-war demonstrators; culminates in May 8 "Bloody Friday" violence against anti-war protesters on Wall Street and at City Hall, where the flag had been lowered to half-staff in honor of the Kent State victims. A worker raises the flag to the cheers of the crowd, which was then lowered again by Mayoral aide Sid Davidoff. Finally, the police restore the flag to full staff to subdue the crowd.
May 8	The New York Knicks win their first championship by defeating the L.A. Lakers at Madison Square Garden, 113-99, following the dramatic entrance of injured Knicks captain Willis Reed.
May 20	Construction workers and others lead pro-Vietnam War and pro-Nixon march of 100,000 from City Hall down Broadway.
May 21	On May 21, 20,000 anti-war demonstrators rally at City Hall. JVL appoints independent five-member commission (the Knapp Commission) to investigate police corruption chaired by P. Whitman Knapp, replacing the Rankin Panel; public hearings begin October 1971.
May 26	Leon Panetta, fired by President Nixon from HEW for vigorously pursuing school integration, hired by JVL to coordinate intergovernmental relations.

June 4	To replace the Little City Hall program which had been blocked by the Democratic City Council, Lindsay creates the Office of Neighborhood Government (ONG) to continue his effort to decentralize city services. Demonstration project launched in eight neighborhoods, each with a Local Service Cabinet with representatives of key city agencies, coordinated by a full-time District Manager. Becomes the model for the decentralization adopted in the 1975 City Charter, with a full-time District Manager and Local Service Cabinet now in every neighborhood of the city.
June 9	A bomb planted by the Weather Underground explodes inside Police Headquarters.
June 25	Federal judge orders McSorley's Old Ale House to admit women, following a suit filed by NOW (National Organization of Women).
June 29	First Gay Pride Parade on the anniversary of the Stonewall Riots.
August 10	JVL signs City Council bill prohibiting discrimination against women; McSorley's opens its doors to women.
August 26	More than ten thousand people, mostly women, march down Fifth Avenue in Women's Strike for Equality, marking the fiftieth anniversary of women obtaining the right to vote under the Nineteenth Amendment.
September 13	First NYC Marathon, led by Fred Lebow, entirely within Central Park. Of the 127 entrants, only 55 men finished (the sole woman entrant dropped out). In 1976, the Marathon moved to the streets of the five boroughs with 2,090 entrants.

October 15   Prison inmates riot and take three hostages in Queens; rioting spreads the next day to the Tombs, where seventeen hostages are taken, then to Brooklyn, three hostages taken (though guards there quickly retake control). On October 4, JVL addresses the inmates at the Tombs by radio, who release their hostages and then meet with the Mayor. The next day, Queens inmates release their three hostages and then meet with JVL.

October 11   Patrick Murphy becomes Police Commissioner after Howard Leary retires. Murphy launches campaign to combat corruption and initiates policy of command accountability.

November 3   Governor Rockefeller elected to fourth term after JVL endorses Democratic challenger Arthur Goldberg, representing full break between the former Republican allies.

1971

January 12   *All in the Family* premiers on CBS, starring Carroll O'Connor as Archie Bunker, a Queens bigot, produced by Norman Lear.

January 14   A six-day police wildcat strike (85 percent walk out) begins over issues of pay and other grievances.

January 22   Lindsay's proposed Taxi and Limousine Commission (TLC) approved by City Council to regulate yellow medallion taxis and black cars; with an emphasis on service, convenience and innovation, it ended the long-time oversight by the Police Department Hack Bureau, which was seen by cabbies as harshly punitive and enforcement-oriented, and by passengers as

insensitive to service. TLC still oversees the
industry today.

January 28

Following Lindsay's 1969 rejection of the Lower
Manhattan Expressway proposed by Robert Moses, zoning is amended to allow certified artists
to live-work in SoHo. In 1973, the SoHo Cast
Iron Historic District is given landmark status.

February 9

Lindsay's plan for the Fifth Avenue Special Zoning District is enacted, with retail uses at street
level and mixed use (commercial and residential) permitted above. Olympic Tower across
from St. Patrick's Cathedral is designed as
nation's first building combining retail, commercial, and residential space.

March 2

After considering a move to New Jersey, Yankees agree to remain in the Bronx and sign
long-term lease with the city. City acquires
Yankee Stadium and begins major reconstruction. Yankees become the most successful and
valuable franchise in American sports.

March 8

Joe Frazier beats Muhammad Ali for the heavyweight title at Madison Square Garden.

March 25

JVL has the city purchase historic Astor Theater
and lease it back to Joseph Papp as the new
home of the Public Theater for an annual rent of
one dollar.

April 8

NYC becomes second jurisdiction in the nation (after Nevada) to authorize off-track betting
(OTB) when state legislature passes Lindsay's
OTB bill with the dual purpose of providing an
alternative to the bookies taking illegal bets on
horse racing and generating public revenue.
Lindsay appoints businessman Howard Samuels as OTB Chair, who launches an aggressive

	program to open 140 OTB parlors in record time, creating jobs and new source of funds for the city.
May 17	JVL endorses City Council bill to eliminate discrimination against homosexuals; bill is defeated on January 27, 1972.
May 21	Marvin Gaye releases album *What's Going On?*
	The Black Liberation Army (BLA) kills two police officers on patrol in the 32nd Precinct in Harlem: Waverly Jones and Joseph Piagentini.
June 6	Conductor James Levine makes his Metropolitan Opera debut with *Tosca.*
June 28	Mobster Joseph Columbo killed at Italian American Unity Day at Columbus Circle.
July 1	Twenty-Sixth Amendment of the U.S. Constitution ratified, giving 18-year-olds the right to vote.
	The U.S. Supreme Court upholds the *Washington Post's* and the *New York Times'* right to publish the Pentagon Papers, the secret report of the United States' military involvement in Southeast Asia, affirming the First Amendment's broad protection against most prior restraints in journalism.
August 2	Governor Nelson Rockefeller, after a public dispute with Lindsay over state aid, appoints Temporary State Commission to Study the City, chaired by Stuart Scott (the Scott Commission), with Stephen Berger as executive director, perceived as an effort to attack city operations and embarrass Lindsay. In response, Lindsay appoints City Commission on State-City Relations, chaired by William vanden Heuvel.

August 11

After long disagreeing with Nixon on the Vietnam War, civil rights enforcement, and civil liberties (including police handling of protests and disorders), JVL switches party enrollment from Republican to Democratic, signaling a probable presidential bid in 1972.

September 9

Riot at Attica state prison by one thousand prisoners, who take thirty-three hostages. After four days, Governor Rockefeller orders state police to retake control with the use of massive gunfire, resulting in thirty-nine deaths (twenty-nine inmates and ten prison employees who had been held as hostages).

October 7

The French Connection premiers, starring Gene Hackman.

November 1

Groundbreaking ceremony for a modern Passenger Ship Terminal to be created through the renovation of four Hudson River piers, aimed at preserving and expanding historic cruise and passenger ship usage, experiencing competitive pressure from growing air travel and other ports.

November 19

The Forest Hills Residents Association, led by Jerry Birbach, pickets the site of proposed city-sponsored high-rise scatter-site housing for low-income residents. Lindsay appoints Queens lawyer Mario Cuomo to negotiate a compromise based on his work earlier in the year in settling a dispute with the city over the location of a high school in Corona that threatened to condemn 69 homes (Cuomo got the city to save 22). In Forest Hills, he reduced three 24-story towers in half to 12 stories each, with 40% for the elderly. Launches Cuomo's public career, later elected as three-term governor.

November 21

JVL initiates massive expansion of city's methadone maintenance program for heroin addicts, which grows to forty clinics treating 8,000 addicts.

December 1

Association for a Better New York (ABNY) formed by business community, led by real estate executive Lewis Rudin, to advocate the city as a location for business and sponsor programs to improve services and amenities.

December 14

Detective Frank Serpico testifies at Knapp Commission hearings, alleging widespread corruption in the Police Department. Serpico was later the subject of a book by Peter Maas and the 1973 movie directed by Sidney Lumet, starring Al Pacino.

December 28

In Miami, JVL announces his candidacy for the Democratic presidential nomination; plans to enter Florida and Wisconsin primaries.

1972

January 1

Subway fare increase from 30 cents to 35 cents (lasts 3 years).

January 27

Members of Black Liberation Army assassinate two police officers on patrol in Ninth Precinct on Lower East Side, Rocco Laurie and Gregory Foster.

January 29

JVL finishes a surprising second in the Democratic caucuses in Arizona, gaining 23.6 percent of the delegates.

January 30

Bloody Sunday in Derry, Northern Ireland as British soldiers attack Catholic protestors, killing thirteen, including seven teenagers.

February 7

JVL issues the first executive order by any government prohibiting discrimination against gays in public sector hiring.

February 21

Nixon arrives in Beijing, China for meetings with Chairman Mao and Zhou Enlai, ending twenty-five years of hostility.

March 7

In the New Hampshire Democratic Primary, anti-war candidate Senator George McGovern (SD), with 37 percent of the vote, comes close to defeating frontrunner Senator Edmund Muskie (ME), with 46 percent. McGovern goes on to become the Democratic nominee.

JVL freezes all city construction ($280 million) in an attempt to force the building trades and construction unions to admit and train more minority members. Freeze ends after six months on September 18, with agreement to some token programs, but no significant progress results.

March 14

JVL finishes fifth, with 7 percent of the vote, in the Florida Democratic primary.

March 15

The Godfather, based on book by Mario Puzo (1969), released as movie, directed by Francis Ford Coppola and starring Marlon Brando and Al Pacino.

April 5

JVL finishes sixth, with 7 percent of the vote, in the Wisconsin Democratic primary; ends his presidential campaign.

Gangster "Crazy" Joe Gallo gunned down at Umberto's Clam House in Little Italy.

April 12

JVL and Chase Bank Chair David Rockefeller announce plan for Manhattan Landing housing development on a platform in the East River south of the Brooklyn Bridge.

April 14

Police officer Phillip Cardillo is fatally shot in Nation of Islam Mosque No. 7 on West 116th Street; intense controversy follows over police handling of the incident.

May 9

President Nixon orders the mining of North Vietnam ports to pressure Hanoi to release prisoners of war and agree to an internationally supervised cease-fire.

May 27

Nixon and Soviet Communist Party chief Leonid Brezhnev sign two agreements limiting the growth of their nations' nuclear arsenals.

June 9

Elvis Presley gives last New York City concert at Madison Square Garden.

June 17

The Watergate break-in occurs at Democratic Party campaign headquarters in Washington, D.C. The White House calls it a "third-rate burglary." *Washington Post* reporters Bob Woodward and Carl Bernstein, relying on an anonymous source known as "Deep Throat," expose funding by the Committee to Re-elect the President and involvement of close aides of the President. In 1974 they publish "All the President's Men," which becomes a 1976 movie starring Robert Redford and Dustin Hoffman.

June 29

The U.S. Supreme Court 5-4 voids 40 state death penalty laws as "cruel and unusual punishment." President Nixon objects to the decision.

August 10

Deputy Mayor Edward Hamilton launches the nation's first government Productivity Program to develop management information systems and upgrade agency performance, forming basis for current Mayor's Management Report.

September 5	At the Munich Olympics, Palestinian terrorists take Israeli Olympic Team members hostage, resulting in the death of all eleven Israeli athletes.
October 20	Federal revenue sharing adopted by Congress; JVL had led the lobbying by a group of seventeen mayors .
October 24	Brooklyn Dodger great Jackie Robinson dies at age 53.
October 27	Lindsay and Rockefeller preside over groundbreaking for the Second Avenue Subway. Construction is twice suspended and eventually restarted in 2007 on phase one from 63rd to 96th Streets.
November 7	President Richard Nixon (Republican) defeats Senator George McGovern (Democrat), winning 60 percent of the vote.
December 27	Knapp Commission issues final report finding widespread police corruption, recommends command accountability and other reforms.

1973

January 3	George Steinbrenner leads group that buys the Yankees from CBS for $10 million.
January 22	U.S. Supreme Court decides *Roe v. Wade*, upholding a woman's right to an abortion.
January 27	The Vietnam Peace Accord is signed in Paris by Henry Kissinger and Le Duc Tho of North Vietnam, both awarded 1973 Nobel Peace Prize. United States has 45,948 combat deaths and 303,000 wounded.

March 7	JVL announces he will not run for a third term as Mayor.
April 4	World Trade Center opens, as the Twin Towers become the two tallest buildings in the world.
May 3-10	JVL visits Moscow and meets with leading Soviet Jewish "Refuseniks" denied the right to emigrate, and interviews key Soviet justice and immigration officials; issues detailed report upon return on the treatment of Soviet Jews seeking to emigrate.
May 10	The Knicks win their second NBA championship by beating the L.A. Lakers, 102-93.
May 17	Senate Watergate Committee hearings begin, led by Chair Sam Ervin (Democrat, NC) and Ranking Minority Member Howard Baker (Republican, TN). Televised live for over 300 hours, seen in 85 percent of U.S. households. Surprise testimony includes White House Counsel Howard Dean ("cancer on the Presidency") and Alexander Butterfield revealing existence of secret White House tapes.
June 9	Secretariat wins the Triple Crown at Belmont.
June 25	JVL opens TKTS discount theater ticket booth in Times Square over opposition by theater owners; expanded operation continues today, more than forty years later, as a major source of Broadway audiences and revenues.
July 11	A key part of Lindsay's plan to expand pedestrian access to midtown streets, the Madison Avenue Mall to be created by closing Madison Avenue to car traffic (bus and taxi only) and widening sidewalks with cafes and pedestrian amenities, defeated by the Board of Estimate in a 12-10 vote.

August 30	Federal Judge John Sirica orders President Nixon to surrender tape recordings of White House conversations as evidence in the Watergate investigation; the president refuses.
September 24	JVL renames Welfare Island as Roosevelt Island in honor of FDR. Long-neglected island to be developed as a new residential community.
October 5	City approves purchase of 197-acre Howland Hook Containership Terminal on Staten Island as part of effort to revive port with modern facilities using new technology there and in Red Hook, Brooklyn.
October 6	Yom Kippur War with surprise attack on Israel lasts three weeks.
October 10	Spiro Agnew resigns the vice-presidency admitting to tax evasion in 1967. Two days later, Representative Gerald Ford (MI) is appointed vice president by President Nixon.
October 13	Arab oil embargo begins in retaliation for West's support of Israel in the Yom Kippur War.
October 16	JVL dedicates modern new police headquarters at One Police Plaza, a priority City construction project.
October 20	Watergate scandal grows with "Saturday Night Massacre" when Attorney General Elliot Richardson and his deputy resign rather than fire Watergate Special Counsel Archibald Cox, who had subpoenaed White House tapes.
November 6	Democratic Party candidate Abraham Beame elected Mayor, defeating Republican John Marchi.

November 15   Board of Estimate approves JVL's plan for greatly expanded, modern Convention Center be built in the Hudson River at 44th Street; state legislature had approved replacing the aging and inadequate Coliseum at Columbus Circle. Project halted during fiscal crisis in 1975; Javits Convention Center opens at 34th Street in 1986.

December 15   Dump truck falls through elevated West Side Highway, which never reopens.

December 18   Governor Rockefeller resigns to head Commission on Critical Choices for Americans. Lieutenant Governor Malcolm Wilson becomes Governor.

December 29   Volume One (of three) of Alexander Solzhenistyn's "Gulag Archipelago" published, based on his imprisonment from 1945-1953 in a Soviet labor camp under Stalin, documenting the history of the Soviet police state.

December 31   JVL's last day as Mayor, after eight years.

POST-MAYORALTY

1974

August 8   After release of White House tapes shows he was deeply involved in Watergate cover-up, Nixon resigns as president, succeeded by Gerald Ford.

November 6   Congressman Hugh Carey (Democrat) defeats incumbent Malcolm Wilson with 58 percent of vote to become governor of New York State; re-elected in 1978.

JVL returns to law firm of Webster, Sheffield.

December 19	Nelson Rockefeller becomes vice president. Only time in history neither the president nor vice president were elected, with both appointed under Twenty-Fifth Amendment procedures.

1975-1979

April 19, 1975	Helicopter evacuation of U.S. troops and diplomats from the Embassy roof in Saigon, Vietnam, as North Vietnam troops prepare to enter Saigon.
June 10, 1975	After New York City is unable to sell bonds in February and runs out of cash in April, creating the Fiscal Crisis, the state legislature acts on Governor Carey's proposal to create the Municipal Assistance Corporation (MAC), which refinances short-term city debt. In November, the state creates the Emergency Financial Control Board to oversee city finances and reforms.
October 30, 1975	"Ford to City: Drop Dead" is front page *Daily News* headline when President Ford refuses federal assistance to help New York City avoid bankruptcy.
September 9, 1976	Mao Zedong dies in China at 82.
November 2, 1976	Georgia Governor Jimmy Carter (Democrat) elected president, defeating incumbent Gerald Ford (Republican).
April 26, 1977	SEC issues report on the NYC fiscal crisis assailing irresponsible practices and finding that "the Mayor [Beame] and the Comptroller misled public investors" regarding billions of dollars of municipal securities.
November 8, 1977	Congressman Ed Koch (Democrat) elected

Mayor, first defeating Mario Cuomo in a Democratic primary run-off (incumbent Mayor Beame had finished third), then Cuomo (running as a Liberal) and Republican Roy Goodman; re-elected in 1981 and 1985.

November 20, 1977   Egyptian President Anwar Sadat becomes the first Arab leader to visit Israel, later participates in the Camp David Accords and then signs Peace Treaty with Israeli Prime Minister Menachem Begin on the White House lawn, hosted by President Carter (1978). Sadat and Begin jointly awarded 1978 Nobel Peace Prize.

August 9, 1978   President Carter signs $1.65 billion federal loan guarantee package for New York on the steps of City Hall.

February 11, 1979   Shah of Iran flees after 37-year reign; Ayatollah Khomeini returns from exile to become Supreme Leader of a theocratic Iranian government. On November 4, Iranian militants seize control of U.S. Embassy in Tehran, with 66 hostages held for 444 days; released during President Reagan's inauguration on January 20, 1981.

1980-2000

September 9, 1980   JVL loses Democratic primary for U.S. Senate, behind Elizabeth Holtzman and Bess Myerson (both former members of his Administration). Al D'Amato defeats incumbent Senator Jacob Javits in Republican primary and goes on to win the general election in November against Javits (Liberal) and Holtzman (Democrat).

November 4, 1980   Ronald Reagan (Republican) elected President defeating incumbent Jimmy Carter (Democrat); re-elected in 1984.

November 2, 1982	Mario Cuomo (Democrat) elected Governor, defeating Mayor Ed Koch in the Democratic Primary, then Republican Lewis Lehrman; re-elected in 1986 and 1990.
September 7, 1985	JVL becomes chairman of the closed Lincoln Center Theater, which reopens in March 1986 with the revival of John Guare's *House of Blue Leaves.*
November 8, 1988	Vice President George H. W. Bush (Republican) elected president (#41) over Massachusetts Governor Michael Dukakis (Democrat).
November 7, 1989	David Dinkins (Democrat) elected city's first black Mayor, defeating incumbent Mayor Koch in Democratic Primary, ending Koch's bid for an unprecedented fourth term, then defeating Republican Rudy Giuliani by 47,000 votes out of almost two million. Lindsay endorses Dinkins, his first mayoral endorsement since leaving City Hall.
November 8, 1989	Berlin Wall falls, allowing East Germans to freely enter West Berlin for the first time since it was erected 28 years earlier (1961).
December 26, 1991	Cold War ends as the Soviet Union is dissolved with the creation of twelve independent Soviet Republics and the resignation of Soviet President Mikhail Gorbachev.
November 3, 1992	Democrat Bill Clinton elected president, defeating incumbent George Bush; re-elected in 1996
November 2, 1993	In a rematch, Republican Rudy Giuliani defeats incumbent Mayor Dinkins by 53,000 votes; re-elected in 1997.
May 10, 1994	Nelson Mandela sworn in as the first black

	president of South Africa, following abolition of the apartheid system by President F.W. de Klerk.
November 8, 1994	George Pataki (Republican) elected governor, defeating incumbent Mario Cuomo's bid for a fourth term; re-elected in 1998 and 2002.
November 1999	John and Mary Lindsay move to Hilton Head, South Carolina.
November 7, 2000	Republican George W. Bush elected president (#43), defeating Vice President Al Gore (Democrat) in controversial Florida recount, ultimately decided by the U.S. Supreme Court; re-elected in 2004.
December 19, 2000	JVL dies of complications of pneumonia and Parkinson's disease.

This chronology is based on the research of Steven H. Jaffe, Warren Wechsler, and others.

25651243R00302

Made in the USA
Middletown, DE
05 November 2015